Big Theories Revisited

**Volume 4 in
Research on Sociocultural Influences on
Motivation and Learning**

BIG THEORIES REVISITED

Edited by

Dennis M. McInerney
and
Shawn Van Etten

INFORMATION AGE
PUBLISHING

80 Mason Street
Greenwich, Connecticut 06830

Library of Congress Cataloging-in-Publication Data

Research on sociocultural influences on motivation and learning
  / edited by Dennis M. McInerney and Shawn Van Etten.
    p. cm.
  Includes bibliographical references and index.
  Contents: v. 1 [without special title] – v. 2. [without
special title] – v. 3. Sociocultural influences and teacher
education programs.
  ISBN 1-930608-63-2 (v. 1) – ISBN 1-930608-62-4 (v. 1 : pbk.)
  ISBN 1-931576-33-5 (v. 2) – ISBN 1-931576-32-7 (v. 2 : pbk.)
  ISBN 1-59311-051-0 (v. 3) – ISBN 1-59311-050-2 (v. 3 : pbk.)
  ISBN 1-59311-053-7 (v. 4) – ISBN 1-59311-052-9 (v. 4 : pbk.)
  1. Motivation in education–Social aspects–Cross-cultural
studies. 2. Multicultural education–Cross-cultural studies.
I. McInerney, D. M. (Dennis M.), 1948-   . II. Van Etten,
Shawn.
LB1065.R45 2001
370.15'4–dc21
                      2002002157

Printed in the United States of America

CONTENTS

List of Contributors   *vii*

1. Big Theories Revisited: The Challenge
    Dennis M. McInerney and Shawn Van Etten   *1*

2. Attribution Theory Revisited: Transforming Cultural
    Plurality into Theoretical Unity
    Bernard Weiner   *13*

3. Self-Determination Theory: A Dialectical Framework for
    Understanding Sociocultural Influences on Student Motivation
    Johnmarshall Reeve, Edward L. Deci, and Richard M. Ryan   *31*

4. Motivation as Personal Investment
    Martin L. Maehr and Dennis M. McInerney   *61*

5. Self-Worth Theory: Goes to College Or Do Our
    Motivation Theories Motivate?
    Martin V. Covington   *91*

6. Self-Efficacy in Education Revisited: Empirical and
    Applied Evidence
    Dale H. Schunk and Frank Pajares   *115*

7. Sociocultural Influence and Students' Development of Academic
    Self-Regulation: A Social-Cognitive Perspective
    Barry J. Zimmerman   *139*

8. Expectancy Value Theory in Cross-Cultural Perspective
    Allan Wigfield, Stephen Tonks, and Jacquelynne S. Eccles   *165*

9. Motivational Messages from Home and School: How Do They
    Influence Young Children's Engagement in Learning?
    Nancy E. Perry and Philip H. Winne   *199*

10. The Influence of Sociocultural Theory on Our Theories of
    Engagement and Motivation
    Daniel T. Hickey and Jeremy B. Granade   *223*

11. Coregulation of Opportunity, Activity, and Identity in Student
    Motivation: Elaborations on Vygotskian Themes
    Mary McCaslin   *249*

12. Metacognitive Theory: Considering the Social-Cognitive Influences
    Douglas J. Hacker and Linda Bol   *275*

13. What We Have Learned About Student Engagement in the Past
    Twenty Years
    Lyn Corno and Ellen B. Mandinach   *299*

14. How Schools Shape Teacher Efficacy and Commitment:
    Another Piece in the Achievement Puzzle
    Helenrose Fives and Patricia A. Alexander   *329*

    Subject Index   *361*

LIST OF CONTRIBUTORS

Patricia A. Alexander	University of Maryland
Linda Bol	Old Dominion University
Lyn Corno	Teachers College, Columbia University
Martin V. Covington	University of California at Berkeley
Edward L. Deci	University of Rochester
Jacquelynne S. Eccles	University of Michigan
Helenrose Fives	University of Maryland
Jeremy B. Granade	University of Georgia
Douglas J. Hacker	University of Utah
Daniel T. Hickey	University of Georgia
Martin L. Maehr	University of Michigan
Ellen B. Mandinach	EDC Center for Children and Technology
Mary McCaslin	University of Arizona
Dennis M. McInerney	University of Western Sydney, Australia
Frank Pajares	Emory University
Nancy E. Perry	University of British Columbia

Johnmarshall Reeve	University of Iowa
Richard M. Ryan	University of Rochester
Dale H. Schunk	University of North Carolina at Greensboro
Stephen Tonks	University of Maryland
Shawn Van Etten	State University of New York College at Cortland
Bernard Weiner	University of California at Los Angeles
Allan Wigfield	University of Maryland
Philip H. Winne	Simon Fraser University
Barry J. Zimmerman	Graduate Center CUNY

CHAPTER 1

BIG THEORIES REVISITED
The Challenge

Dennis M. McInerney and Shawn Van Etten

SETTING THE STAGE

Helping students achieve their best in our classrooms is not an easy task. Students come to class with complex histories, histories that include family, culture, health, physical, social, emotional, and prior learning experiences. These experiences orient the individual in new learning situations - sometimes positively and sometimes negatively. While we cannot expect to understand the full complexity of these forces, we can come to better understand some of the elementary dynamics that are more or less likely to facilitate or impede an individual's interest in classroom learning. Many theories of motivation and learning attempt to help us better understand some of these more elementary dynamics. Even then, the task is not easy, as motivation and learning in classrooms does not stand alone; these processes and dynamics have deep roots traced back into the whole world of the individual. It is reasonable to assume, therefore, that theories of motivation and learning take account of the wider sociocultural environment of the learner. However, many theories of motivation and learning appear to be written in a sociocultural vacuum. As such, this volume seeks to revisit

Big Theories Revisited
Volume 4 in: Research on Sociocultural Influences on Motivation and Learning, pages 1–11.
ISBN: 1-59311-053-7 (hardcover), 1-59311-052-9 (paperback)

major theories of motivation and learning in order to evaluate the relevance of each theory to our complex educational environments. This volume also seeks to investigate whether and how each theory should be revised to reflect the sociocultural forces that might mediate or moderate the effects of such motivational and learning dynamics on achievement outcomes in real-life educational environments.

To this end we approached renowned authors of theories, or authors who have critiqued theories, to write for us chapters that address the mission of this volume. The challenge was for authors to address the issue of whether or not their theoretical perspective was developed in a sociocultural vacuum. In some cases, we approached several people involved in developing specific theories, as they might provide different insights into the sociocultural implications of the theory.

We believe that revisiting "big theories" from this perspective will make a significant contribution to the motivation and learning literature and provide the 'launch pad' for future theory development, research, and integration.

CHAPTER PREVIEW AND AUTHOR FEEDBACK

We have gathered the chapters together in related areas. All chapters deal with the common thread of big motivation and learning theories revisited from a range of social and cultural perspectives. What follows are some of the highlights of each chapter, coupled with the feedback that we provided to help guide author revisions.

Chapter 2

Bernard Weiner raises many questions for the reader and cautions specifically that elements of attribution theory (and by implication, we think, other theories) may be universal but their operationalization in any culture or group must be context sensitive. Weiner raises many of the issues that we think are essential in applying theories to diverse groups and in particular, the need for researchers and educators to avoid applying "content" templates to theories. In other words, researchers/educators need to distinguish between the abstract (perhaps universal) components of a theory and "content exemplars" drawn from one cultural perspective (that the antecedents of success and failure, for example, are defined in the same way for everyone, that success and failure are defined in the same way by everyone, and that the consequences are the same for everyone irrespective of culture). Acknowledging the difference between abstract and content exemplars in theories enriches them for use in a wide variety of cultural and social situations.

We sent Weiner the following puzzle with which to grapple, utilizing his interpersonal and intrapersonal models. In a number of studies with Australian Aboriginal students McInerney and others have found that success and failure have quite different effects for Aboriginal students in contrast to Anglo students. Typically for Anglo students, success is associated with feelings of accomplishment and pleasure, which in general leads to external praise, reward, and support (e.g., from teachers, peers, and parents). Failure is typically associated with feelings of shame or regret (intrapersonal) but is associated with understanding and empathy from others, possibly punishment, but irrespective, the provision of further support (such as tutoring) by parents and teachers to overcome failure in the future (interpersonal). In contrast, success (such as passing a test or getting good grades) for Aboriginal students is not associated with feelings of accomplishment and pleasure, but is often associated with regret and embarrassment, as the success may ostracize them from their peer group by making them appear better than their peers; or they may be considered to have cheated (as being successful is not typical); or success is to be avoided, as it may make them appear to be wanting to be white and hence distances them from their culture. Furthermore, many Aboriginal parents do not appear to know how to support success. To make matters worse, failure is often associated with few negative consequences, as failure is expected by peers (for whom the norm is failure at school), it is expected by parents (for whom failure was the norm when they were at school), and is expected by teachers (who rarely expect Aboriginal students to be successful and have limited experience with successful Aboriginal students). In other words, neither success nor failure experiences are potentially motivational for many Aboriginal students. Indeed, both success and failure can be negative experiences. How would attribution theory interpret this?

Chapter 3

Johnmarshall Reeve, Ed Deci, and Richard Ryan provide many new and valuable insights in their chapter. As we read the first draft, there were many questions that occurred to us, and we threw a few of these back at the authors as they prepared the final manuscript. Consider these as you read through their chapter. What sociocultural forces support autonomy, competence, and relatedness? Do autonomy, competence, and relatedness differ in salience for different social and cultural groups? We could speculate, for example, that personal individual autonomy and its importance is a very Western notion. We could also speculate that there is an inherent tension between autonomy (individualist societies lean more toward autonomy) and relatedness (collectivist societies lean more toward relatedness) that is not entirely resolved in the theory. How are these two components universally compatible in any cultural and social context? Furthermore, we could also assert that the demonstration of competence is culturally/socially determined. For example, it is possible that competence for particular communities is demonstrated by straight A's in academics; for other communities, being top in athletics; and for others, maintaining group allegiance against all the forces opposed to it at school. What is meant by competence in particular cultural settings? What is the nexus between values such as autonomy, competence, and relatedness and cultural/social background and self-determination? Are cultural/social groups that do not support personal individual autonomy and independent thinking, and that promote group allegiance and group identity, and who foster learning through didactic approaches (such as fundamentalist Muslim groups) necessarily less motivated and learn less effectively in classes? This issue is certainly worth addressing "head on." There are many groups served by Western-oriented education that do not like being given choice and options but want be taught directly the "accepted wisdom." Does this mean that self-determination theory does not apply to these groups? Indeed, the notion of individual and personal "self-determination" may be considered anathema to some minority groups (fundamentalist religious groups, gang groups, indigenous groups, and so on). Some teasing questions for self-determination theory (SDT)! Addressing these issues may help broaden SDT to encompass all the possible sociocultural permutations and combinations of autonomy, competence, and relatedness. Read how the authors addressed these issues in their chapter.

Chapter 4

Martin Maehr and Dennis McInerney discuss the development of personal investment theory and use it to challenge the appropriateness of various "Western" models and theories of motivation by examining their relevance for non-Western populations. The case is made that in order for motivation theories and research to be of relevance to societies characterized by diversity they must be sensitive to both etic (universal) and emic (cultural specific) considerations. Personal investment theory is advanced as a model that allows for an examination of both these considerations. An abundance of cross-cultural research is advanced to demonstrate the relevance of personal investment theory. This chapter sets the stage for an examination of the consistency and/or inconsistency of motivational patterns or profiles across cultural groups and in diverse settings (e.g., schools, hospitals, businesses, government organizations). Maehr and McInerney report that there are patterns of predictors across cultural groupings that are both consistent (perhaps universal) and patterns that are variable (emic). This information is of particular relevance to managers of systems (such as teachers, company personnel officers, administrators) as they grapple with the need to organize their systems according to general norms, while allowing for individual and idiosyncratic differences among people. Consider their argument and ask the question "how well have the authors argued their case for a multidimensional model of motivation that is sensitive to sociocultural issues?"

Chapter 5

Martin Covington indicates that fundamentally, self-worth theory argues that all individuals are motivated to establish and maintain a sense of personal worth, approval by others, and acceptance of oneself, a goal that in turn depends on being perceived as competent. In particular, this chapter grapples with the issue of how self-worth theory addresses the matter of an overweening preoccupation among students with grades and various issues of student disengagement and faculty frustration. We posed him the following question: Do the dynamics of self-worth theory apply in a uniform way to groups from a diversity of cultural and social backgrounds? For example, embedded in his description of the theory and the research are notions such as the link established between grades, ability, and worth and because some students fear relatively low grades, they engage in self-protective defenses. In some communities one's worth is not necessarily defined by individual success but rather communal success (whether the family or the cultural subgroup). Hence one works (or avoids work) in order to remain one with the salient community. In this case self-worth is preserved by not competing with others. This profile may characterize groups such as Australian Aboriginals and Navajo Indians. Given this scenario individuals may use defense strategies not so much to avoid being identified as being unable (failures) and therefore less worthy, but to preserve in-group harmony and to protect/foster a feeling of worthiness as determined within one's sociocultural framework. The same speculation could apply to minorities such as gangs, religious minorities, and so on.

Associated with this is the notion of "grade grubbing," which again may be a culturally related phenomenon. Perhaps one of the reasons for the underattendance/performance of minorities within the higher education system may be that they do not engage in grade grubbing, as it is culturally inappropriate. The notion of what makes up effective learning from the self-worth framework (concepts such as self-monitoring, being inquisitive rather than passive learners, etc.) may also be culturally biased, or at least an interpretation of a form of learning that relies heavily again on individualist notions of effective learning—that is, making the learning one's own and possessing it one's self, rather than notions of distributive learning and community ownership of learning.

Is, ultimately, the notion of self-worth a culturally determined phenomenon that can only be effectively understood in context? This is a fruitful area worth investigating. Indeed, self-worth theory lends itself nicely to saying that collectivist groups have it right, and that self-worth theory is seen at its best in indigenous communities who work for the common good, help each other out, and try to avoid individual aggrandizement at the expense of others.

Chapter 6

Dale Schunk and Frank Pajares also provide many new and valuable insights in their chapter. As we read their first draft, we were left with a number of questions and we challenged them with these questions as they prepared their final manuscript. Has the self-efficacy construct been subjected to studies with minorities specifically to test its universality? What social conditions might engender self-efficacy? What social conditions might engender persistent lack of self-efficacy in school settings? Are some groups and communities advantaged over others? Is there such a concept as communal/collective efficacy where the total is greater than the sum of its parts, and how does this interact with personal self-efficacy? These would seem to be important issues to discuss, as lack of self-efficacy might be a key discriminating factor for the relatively poorer school performance of minorities such as Native Americans and African Americans. Indeed, collective efficacy may run counter to personal self-efficacy within some communities. Hence a study of the etiology of self-efficacy and its application within diverse communities could shed further light on social-cognitive theory itself, but perhaps also provide insights to improve the educational experiences of underperforming groups. In other words, can the application of self-efficacy help us understand the school achievement gaps between particular groups?

It's possible that sociocultural factors make the application of the self-efficacy construct more problematic in classrooms than in laboratory settings. Factors such as forming friendships, a desire to avoid trouble, social pressures against working too hard, socioeconomic status (SES), ethnicity, media, technology, and so on may impact on the development of and nature of self-efficacy. How do these dynamics work and how are they resolved within a self-efficacy framework? For example, through their exposure to the Internet and computers, students from many minority and indigenous groups may be exposed to models of self-regulation, self-efficacy, and so on that are not typically culturally or socially relevant. Hence technology may be a very powerful tool for "distributing" a common form of learning and motivation, including SRL and notions of self-efficacy across all groups, which has both positive and negative consequences. Furthermore, students from a wide range of cultural and social backgrounds may be becoming more similar in learning and motivational characteristics through their shared experiences and use of the Internet for learning and hence may be forming an international community of learners for perhaps the first time—particularly when learners can be in instant dialogue with other learners and teachers anywhere at any time. Schunk and Pajares address many of these issues in their chapter.

Chapter 7

The draft chapter by Barry Zimmerman suggested that sociocultural influences and self-regulatory processes become increasingly interdependent as children grew. This proposition left us with a number of questions and issues we asked him to address related to the differential use of strategies by students (e.g., proactive/reactive). We asked: What are the social dynamics that might lead to dependence on some strategies rather than others? Are some groups more proactive/reactive than others? Do the levels of self-regulation, beginning with social levels and shifting to self-levels, apply in the same way in classrooms characterized by ethnic and SES diversity? Are some students, classes, schools, social groups, and so on more or less likely to reflect these levels than others? How may the theory of self-regulation be used to explain the differential school achievement of various minorities such as African Americans, Native Americans, and Hispanics? How may the theory of self-regulation be used to enhance the performance of special needs students? We could even extend the argument to consider a full range of sociocultural influences, including the above but also sexual orientation, religious affiliation, political affiliation, and so on. Clearly these and many other social and cultural influences must be addressed in regard to education if we are to come to a fuller understanding of these dynamics. Finally, we asked Zimmerman what are the major changes and developments to the self-regulation concept over the last 20 years, and have sociocultural issues impacted these? Quite a challenge! Zimmerman addresses many of these issues head on in his chapter.

Chapter 8

Allan Wigfield, Stephen Tonks, and Jacque Eccles critically evaluate elements of Expectancy x Value Theory in terms of cross-cultural issues addressing emics and etics. In general, they review research done in Western cultures on the development of individuals' ability, beliefs, expectancies, and values, and also how they influence choice and performance in different areas, with a focus on academic choice and performance. Possible cultural influences on expectancies and values are then discussed, as well as different research approaches used in cross-cultural research on these constructs. The authors suggest several times throughout that researchers should address a number of key issues such as that children's subjective values may vary more across culture than the factor structure of children's ability beliefs appear to, and we challenged them to give suggestions on the style of research that could examine this and other research issues raised. We also asked the authors to summarize what changes have been made to the theory over the last 20 years, and whether any of these changes were influenced by sociocultural considerations. We further asked them to discuss how they would modify Expectancy x Value Theory on the basis of their review of the literature to make it a more obviously universal theory. Wigfield and colleagues attack these issues directly and provide many new insights into the dynamics of Expectancy x Value Theory in diverse settings.

Chapter 9

Nancy Perry and Phil Winne explore what influences children's attitudes toward, and engagement in, school. What attitudes and actions result in more or less success in learning contexts? How can attitudes be shaped to encourage actions that support learning? In general, this chapter uses an Expectancy x Value Theory of motivation to address how individuals' beliefs, values, and expectations influence their actions. In particular, they report research on the influence of home and classroom environments on young students' (ages 6 and 7) beliefs about learning and their subsequent actions in school. Perry and Winne were asked to clarify the similarities and/or differences of related constructs to provide the readership a more refined understanding and how they fit the data. Stories that are used to represent the constructs were created to differentiate concepts, and sections on home and family influences were given finer detail. This chapter provides many valuable insights!

Chapter 10

Dan Hickey and Jeremy Granade provide a stimulating chapter that challenges current theories of motivation from a sociocultural perspective. Indeed, they critique what they perceive as some of the major limitations of more conventional theories of motivation when they are applied in sociocultural settings. They start by rejecting the prevailing assumption that the goals and values that motivate engagement are acquired "whole cloth" from the participation in sociocultural contexts. Rather, they start with the fundamental sociocultural assumption that participation in knowledgeable activity transforms that knowledge and any associated goals and values. Furthermore, they apply the assumption that all knowledge is socially defined, so that all such participation (with or without actual collaboration) transforms that knowledge and associated values (and therefore contributes to it). Taken in full, the chapter argues that the values and goals that support engagement in learning are defined by and resident in the practices that define knowledgeable communities, rather than the hearts and minds of individuals. The notion of "engaged participation" and "maladaptive nonparticipation" as alternatives to intrinsic and extrinsic motivation are advanced. Hickey and Granade also raise the complex issues of reconciliation between the individual and the social context, contrasting the prevailing "aggregative" approach with a "dialectical" approach that follows from sociocultural perspectives. The chapter concludes by suggesting that this new view of engagement suggests new ways of addressing the seemingly intractable debate over the use of extrinsic rewards to support learning.

Chapter 11

Mary McCaslin's chapter covers a broad sweep of sociocultural theory. A key issue we asked Mary to deal with was the definition of key terms such as tool-mediated, goal-directed action, activity theory, inner speech, social language environment, and motive dispositions in context. We also asked her to explore the social origins of student beliefs about themselves as students, particularly in moderately difficult tasks that appear to provide especially fruitful opportunities. In McCaslin's terms, moderately difficult tasks require and challenge the integration and enhancement of the affective and the intellectual in the mediation of goal-directed action. Moderately difficult tasks are opportunities, therefore, to promote adaptive learning, in part because students impose an expectation of successful solutions on familiar but not automatic tasks. A focus on peers shifts attention from the social origins of emergent identity (with the adults in students' lives) to a notion of continuous coregulation of activity and consciousness—a cultural context that classrooms and their members represent.

We also asked McCaslin to elaborate on her contention that what mainstream American psychology may consider characteristic of individuals, a Vygotskian theorist would consider a continuous negotiation between cultural and self-knowledge, and that the findings that participation in classroom life expands the restrictions of direct individual learning and does not homogenize participants. We believe that these are crucial issues that bear further elaboration.

Chapter 12

Doug Hacker and Linda Bol argue that during the past 40 years research on metacognition has provided lukewarm appraisals of people as metacognizers. Cognitive psychologists have consistently found that at best the accuracy with which people can judge what they know has been 50/50 or slightly better. The authors have found that even over prolonged trials to improve metacognitive accuracy, many students remain inaccurate in their judgments of test performance. Results showing chance to slightly above chance accuracy, argue Hacker and Bol, are due to measurement difficulties and not to people's inabilities to take stock of what they know or what they are currently doing. This chapter concludes with the authors painting a more complete picture of the social and cognitive processes and conditions that may lead to greater metacognitive accuracy, with the hope that future researchers and practitioners will augment their investigations with appropriate social factors.

Chapter 13

Lyn Corno and Ellen Mandinach provide many new and valuable insights. After reading their initial draft we challenged them with the task of discussing the use of computers and the Internet in a sociocultural context. Specifically, we asked them to reflect on the following possibilities: potentially the Internet and computers allow students to rise above limitations imposed by their social and cultural environments; potentially the Internet and computers "equalize" educational opportunities and experiences for diverse (and sometimes impoverished) groups of students internationally; students from a wide range of cultural and social backgrounds may be becoming more similar in learning and motivational characteristics through their shared experiences and use of the Internet for learning and hence may be forming an international community of learners perhaps for the first time—particularly when learners can be in instant dialogue with other learners and teachers anywhere at any time; through their exposure to the Internet and computers students from many minority and indigenous groups may be exposed to models of self-regulation, mastery, performance, and so on that are not typically culturally or socially relevant. Hence technology may be a very powerful tool for "distributing" a common form of learning and motivation including SRL across all groups, which has both positive and negative consequences. It is very interesting to read how Corno and Mandinach addressed these issues and possibilities.

Chapter 14

Helenrose Fives and Patricia Alexander provide a stimulating discussion of how the sociocultural environments of schools shape teacher motivation. They examine how community background and contextual features are influential in determining the type of school settings teachers teach in, which then influences both commitment and teaching efficacy. We challenged them to elaborate on both community background and contextual features by drawing out the more specifically sociocultural elements of these features. In particular, what are the background sociocultural forces operating that make Porter School different from Western School? We also challenged Fives and Alexander to do some theorizing relating various elements of their discussion that could be used for testing in diverse school settings.

THE STAGE IS SET

As we said at the beginning of this chapter, we believe that revisiting "big theories" from a sociocultural perspective will make a significant contribution to motivation and learning literature, and provide the "launch pad" for future theorizing, research, and integration across theories. We hope that after you have read each chapter you will agree with us.

CHAPTER 2

ATTRIBUTION THEORY REVISITED
Transforming Cultural Plurality into Theoretical Unity

Bernard Weiner

INTRODUCTION

Few (if any) psychologists or educators formulate a theory and expressly limit its applicability to a particular culture, ethnicity, or historical period. Perhaps because of cognitive development a theory might not be expected to apply to younger children (e.g., one would not think a theory of prejudice would be pertinent to 1-year-olds). And perhaps one might even specify the theory holds for only one of the genders (e.g., early achievement theory implicitly excluded females, in part because the measurement of achievement needs did not appear valid for them). But for most of the theories with which I am familiar, demographic or sociocultural constraints are ignored, not specified, and/or not anticipated. Even in the recent past

Big Theories Revisited
Volume 4 in: Research on Sociocultural Influences on Motivation and Learning, pages 13–29.
Copyright © 2004 by Information Age Publishing, Inc.
All rights of reproduction in any form reserved.
ISBN: 1-59311-053-7 (hardcover), 1-59311-052-9 (paperback)

when the research subjects were white rats, among the creating motivational psychologists there was little recognition of generality issues. Is this
as it should be? Do theories of human motivation, and particularly of
achievement strivings, and even more specifically the attributional theory
with which I am associated, require basic modification to incorporate
diverse ethnicities and cultures?

For example, suppose I advocate motivation in general (or achievement
motivation as a special case) is determined in part by the expectancy of
goal attainment. Hence, I predict one will not undertake activities for
which the subjective expectancy of success or the likelihood of goal attainment is zero. I might think this principle would not hold for very young
infants, inasmuch as they may lack the cognitive abilities to formulate
means–ends relations and expectations. But I would be unlikely to say my
position holds only for white males, to the exclusion of African Americans,
Asians, females, and others not included in the white male category. Similarly, if I believe learning is maximized with the Socratic method (as did
Socrates), then it is unlikely I would regard this as limited to a particular
race or social class. Neither did Socrates, as he engaged in a Socratic dialogue with Meno's lower-SES Greek slave.

But perhaps life is more complex for an attribution theorist, which I am,
and I have been remiss in not recognizing the diversity of cultures, environments, and personal histories to which I blindly and blithely apply this
conceptual system. In this chapter I confront this issue, conveying those
aspects of the theory I perceive as universal and those features I construe as
culturally bound. This requires me to consider what theoretical modifica-
tions are needed in the face of human variability, whether environmentally
or genetically fostered.

I proceed as follows. First, I outline my formulation of an attribution
theory of motivation (or, I should say, attribution theories, for I have proposed both an intrapersonal and an interpersonal conceptual framework).
Then I present my position regarding whether this conceptual approach is
universal or specific to the dominant white group to which I belong and
not applicable to others, particularly to minority groups in the United
States. I address these issues with illustrations from two very diverse areas of
study: (1) the differential school dropout rates of African American versus
white college students, and (2) disparate reactions to obesity among Hispanics as opposed to Americans (which, it will be seen, has educational
implications).

ATTRIBUTION THEORY

Imagine, for example, a student has just received a poor grade on an exam
and we, as psychologists and educators, want to be able to predict if she will
continue in school or drop out. Among the likely predictors I identify is

the subjective expectancy of future success, as previously mentioned, as well as emotions related to self-esteem, guilt, and shame. These self-directed thoughts and feelings comprise what I label an *intrapersonal* theory of motivation.

Now consider that, following the poor exam performance, significant others including peers, teachers, and parents evaluate or judge this person. They consider her good or bad, responsible or not responsible for the low test score, moral or immoral, and she is the target of emotions including anger and sympathy. These thoughts and emotions, in turn, give rise to help or neglect, positive or negative feedback, and the like. These other-directed thoughts and feelings comprise what I label an *interpersonal* theory of motivation. The boundaries between the intrapersonal and interpersonal motivational systems at times are fuzzy, but nevertheless this distinction is important and, albeit overlapping, the theories are separately presented.

Intrapersonal Motivation from the Attributional Perspective

My approach to intrapersonal motivation is guided by the metaphor that people are scientists, trying to understand themselves and their environment, and then they act on the basis of this knowledge (see Weiner, 1992). This approach begins with a completed event, such as a success or failure at an exam (see Figure 2.1). At the end of this sequence there is a behavioral reaction, which might be dropping out of school. In between is the remainder of the motivational process, guided by attributional inferences and their consequences, which fill the gap between the stimulus (the exam outcome) and the response (dropping out).

In the far left of Figure 2.1 the motivational process begins with the exam outcome. Following this is an affective reaction: one feels happy following goal attainment and unhappy when there is nonattainment of a goal. These general affective reactions are not mediated by a great deal of cognitive work and are labeled "outcome-dependent" emotions. Then individuals ask: "Why did this happen? What caused this outcome?" Because of cognitive limits, search is not undertaken following all events, and is particularly likely when the outcome is negative, unexpected, and/ or important. Thus, if one expects to succeed at something trivial and does, then *why* questions are not likely to follow. In contrast, unexpected failure at an important exam will evoke attributional processes (see Gendolla & Koller, 2001; Weiner, 1986).

The answer to this *why* question, which is a causal attribution, is influenced by many sources of evidence, including past personal history of success and failure and social norms pertaining to the performance of others

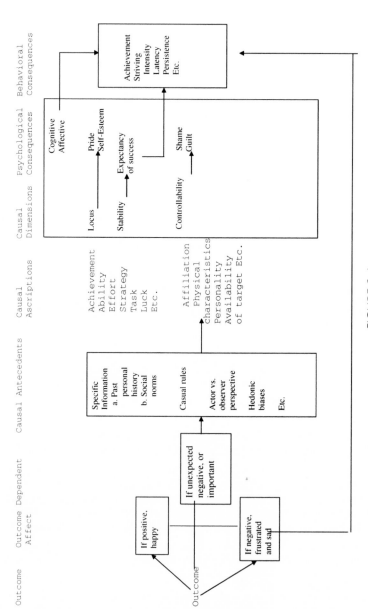

FIGURE 2.1.
An intrapersonal attributional theory of motivation.

(covariation information), rules about the relations between causes (causal schemata), viewer perspective (actor or observer), hedonic biasing, and on and on (see Figure 2.1). More specifically, for example, if the person has always failed in the past, then the current failure is likely to be attributed to the self; if others succeed when that person fails, then again failure is more likely to be attributed to the self (rather than to the task); if one thinks failure requires multiple causality, then even given knowledge of lack of effort, one is nevertheless likely to derogate personal ability and/or also ascribe the failure to some environmental factors; internal factors (dispositional causes) may be more salient to an observer than to an actor (the actor–observer discrepancy); and failure is less likely to be self-attributed than is success (the hedonic bias).

Guided by these sources of information, a cause is selected, such as lack of ability, lack of effort, or bad luck given failure. Similarly, if one is rejected for a date, then again, as shown in Figure 2.1, an array of causes is possible, including unattractive physical characteristics, poor personality, and so forth. Let us assume for purposes of clarity there is only one phenomenological cause, although we all recognize life is not that simple. This sets the stage for the next step in the process, which concerns the underlying characteristics or properties of that cause. These so-called causal dimensions are the very heart and soul of my attributional approach to motivation.

To understand the motivational consequences of causal beliefs, it is necessary the qualitative differences between causes such as effort and ability be altered to quantitative differences, and for this to occur the causes must be comparable on some psychological dimensions. A great deal of research has documented there are three, and indeed only three, underlying causal properties that have cross-situational generality (see Weiner, 1986). These properties are labeled locus, stability, and controllability. Locus refers to the location of a cause, which is either within or outside of the actor. For example, ability and effort are considered internal causes of success, whereas chance and help from others are construed as external causes. Causal stability refers to the duration of a cause. Some causes, such as math aptitude, are perceived as constant, whereas causes such as chance are considered unstable or temporary. Finally, a cause like effort is subject to volitional alteration and is personally controllable, whereas others cannot be willfully changed and are regarded as uncontrollable. Luck and aptitudes have this property.

All causes can be located within this three-dimensional causal space. Although there may be disagreements regarding how a cause is dimensionalized because this depends on "how it seems to me," there also is a great deal of agreement that, for example, aptitude is internal, stable, and uncontrollable, whereas chance, while also uncontrollable, is external to the actor and unstable.

The significance of these causal properties is they map into what are considered by some to be the two main determinants of motivated action: expectancy and value. Expectancy refers to the subjective likelihood of future success, while value in this context is considered the emotional consequences of goal attainment or nonattainment (see Atkinson, 1964). Turning first to expectancy, it has been documented that if a cause is regarded stable then the same outcome will be anticipated following a success or a failure. Hence, if failure is perceived as due to lack of aptitude or to an unfair teacher, then taking another exam from this teacher will be anticipated to result in continued failure. To the contrary, failure perceived due to unstable factors, such as bad luck or lack of preparation because of the flu, is not an indicator there will be further failure (see review in Weiner, 1992).

Locus and controllability relate to feeling states, or to the "value" of achievement outcomes. Note I do not use the concept of locus *of* control, but rather speak of locus *and* control. These are two independent dimensions. A cause may be internal to the person but uncontrollable, such as lack of height as the cause of not being selected for the basketball team.

Locus influences feelings of pride in accomplishment and self-esteem. Pride and increments in self-esteem require internal causality for success. One might be happy following a high grade on an exam (an outcome-dependent feeling), but pride would not be experienced if it were believed the teacher gave only high grades. Controllability, in conjunction with locus, determines whether guilt or shame is experienced following nonattainment of a goal (although in research these two affects tend to be highly correlated, so I have somewhat shaky confidence in the presumptions that follow). Assuming a desire to succeed, attribution of failure to insufficient effort, which is internal and controllable, often elicits guilt. On the other hand, an ascription of failure to lack of aptitude, which is internal but uncontrollable, tends to evoke feelings of shame, embarrassment, and humiliation. The controllability dimension influences other affects as well, including regret, but they are not considered here. Finally, expectancy of success and the emotions of pride, guilt, and shame, are believed to determine subsequent behavior. That is, behavior is a function of thoughts and feelings.

Let me illustrate the logic of this analysis by examining motivation in an affiliative, rather than an achievement, context. Assume Bill is rejected by Mary when asking her for a date. We now want to correctly predict whether Bill will seek further dates or will "hide in his shell" and withdraw. The attributional framework contends that to make this prediction accurately Bill's perceived cause for rejection must be determined (which may or may not be the "real" cause). Assume Bill believes he was rejected because he is too short. This aspect of physical appearance refers to an internal, stable, and uncontrollable cause. Hence, Bill should suffer a decrement in self-esteem (mediated by personal causality); expects to be rejected again (mediated by causal stability); and feel ashamed, humiliated, and embarrassed (mediated by internal causality that is uncontrollable). This analysis leads to the prediction that he will drop out of the social world of seeking dates.

Conversely, assume he thinks he was rejected because the girl already has a date. Inasmuch as this is an external cause, self-esteem is maintained; since this prior engagement presumably is unstable, expectancy of future acceptance is not reduced; and given that having a prior date is uncontrollable by him as well as external, neither shame nor guilt is experienced. Hence, motivation is not dampened and Bill will seek out further dating opportunities.

INTERPERSONAL MOTIVATION FROM
THE ATTRIBUTIONAL PERSPECTIVE

The interpersonal conception of motivation from an attributional perspective is shown in Figure 2.2. For the moment, concentrate on the top row of that figure. It can be seen the motivational sequence again is initiated by an achievement outcome, exam failure. Once more there is causal search (not shown in Figure 2.2), in this case not by the actor but by an involved observer, such as a teacher or parent. And again, based on a variety of factors not included in the figure, a causal explanation is reached. This may or may not be the same inference made by the failing student.

This cause is then placed in the previously described dimensional space, with the dimension of causal controllability of prime importance. That is, thoughts about control versus not control are at the center of the interpersonal theory. As shown in the top row of Figure 2.2, failure is ascribed to a lack of effort, which is subject to volitional change and therefore is regarded a controllable cause. If a cause (and also the linked negative event) "could have been otherwise," then the actor is perceived responsible for the outcome (for greater detail regarding the link between controllability and responsibility, and a discussion of mitigating factors, see Weiner, 1995). Hence, the motivational process is proposed to proceed from a causal decision to an inference about the person. Responsibility for a negative event, in turn, gives rise to anger. One is mad when one's child fails an exam because of not studying, just as one is angry with a roommate for leaving the kitchen dirty following a meal. Anger, in turn, arouses a variety of antisocial responses, including punishment and reprimand.

Now consider the sequence when achievement failure is caused by lack of ability, depicted a few lines lower in Figure 2.2. Ability, conceived here as akin to aptitude, is typically regarded an uncontrollable cause. Because the cause (and the linked exam outcome) cannot be volitionally altered, the failing student is not held personally responsible (able to respond). Lack of responsibility for a negative achievement outcome tends to elicit sympa-

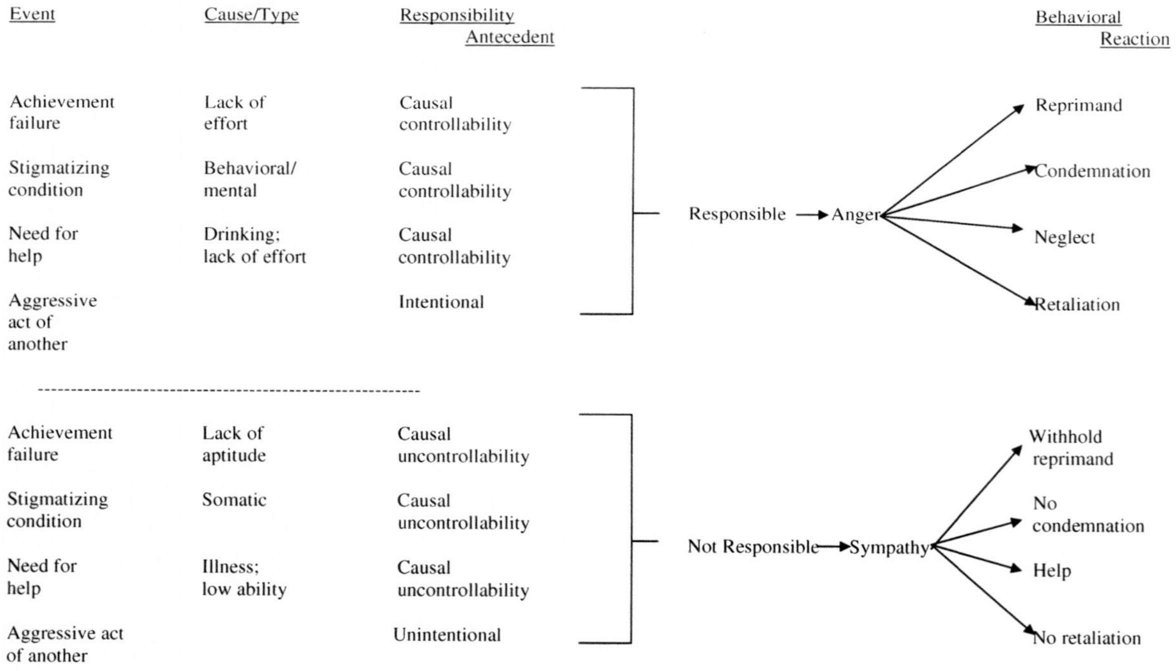

FIGURE 2.2.
An interpersonal attributional theory of motivation.

thy. We feel sorry for the mentally handicapped who cannot perform cognitive tasks and for the physically handicapped who cannot perform motor tasks. Sympathy, in turn, evokes prosocial reactions. Note again, as in intrapersonal theory, a thinking–feeling–acting motivational sequence is posited, although now inferences of responsibility play a major role, whereas the effects of causal locus and causal stability, as well as self-esteem and expectancy of success, are deemphasized.

This interpersonal approach to classroom experience is not confined to an explanation of achievement-related behaviors. A number of other phenomena observed in the classroom can be examined within the same conceptual framework. Figure 2.2 shows, in addition to achievement-related evaluation, reactions to the stigmatized, help giving, and aggression also are subject to a responsibility-mediated analysis. If a person is responsible for being in a stigmatized state, for needing help because of laziness, or for a harmful act such as being aggressive toward someone intentionally, then anger is experienced and the reaction is negative. On the other hand, stigmatization because of noncontrollable causes such as being blind at birth, needing help because of missing school due to illness, and perhaps even aggression against someone by accident (e.g., stepping on toes in a crowded subway) elicit sympathy and prosocial behaviors.

In these situations, an appropriate metaphor to capture the reactions of the involved observer is he or she is a judge presiding in a courtroom. The judge has the right to determine if others are responsible or not for a transgression and then passes a sentence based on these beliefs and other factors, particularly the severity of the transgression. Indeed, life may be considered a courtroom where dramas related to transgressions are played out. The observer is a scientist in making causal decisions, but then acts in a Godlike manner by reaching moral conclusions regarding right and wrong, good and bad.

Interrelations of the Theories

The two motivational systems have been presented as though they are quite separate. In fact, they are closely intertwined and interactive. Consider, for example, a student whom others believe performed poorly because of a lack of aptitude. Inasmuch aptitude is construed as an uncontrollable cause, some involved observers may communicate sympathy and pity to this pupil following failure. These communications provide evidence to the person that he or she "cannot," which then increase the likelihood of personal feelings of shame and humiliation. That is, if sympathy and pity are "accepted," then this is an antecedent for a low-ability self-ascription. On the other hand, if the student is thought by others (e.g., the teacher) to have failed because of lack of effort, then that teacher will communicate anger. Anger is a cue the pupil is responsible for the failure, which need not have taken place. Inasmuch as expressed anger is used to infer causality (see Weiner, 1995), the student may be more likely to ascribe his or her personal failure to lack of effort. This, in turn, increases guilt. In sum, the two motivational theories overlap and are involved in the thoughts, feelings, and actions of both the actor and the observer within the same behavioral episode.

A Concluding Remark

An attributional approach to classroom behavior includes thoughts related to causal beliefs, expectancy of success, inferences of responsibility, and so on. Also incorporated are affects, including happiness and unhappiness (outcome-dependent) and pride, self-esteem, guilt, anger, shame, and sympathy (attribution-dependent). These thoughts and feelings provide the foundation for an understanding of achievement performance, such as trying harder versus dropping out of school (intrapersonal motivation), as well as aiding in the explanation of achievement evaluation, reactions to the stigmatized, help giving, and aggression (interpersonal motivation). And that is not the full range of the conception, but rather captures the theoretical foci. I regard attribution theory as quite rich, integrating thinking, feeling, and doing both for an actor and for the observers of that action. But is it rich enough to incorporate cultural variability, or is it impoverished by not addressing or having the capability of addressing diversity in the classroom?

THE CULTURAL CHALLENGE

My position regarding whether this theory can fit diverse cultures can be summarized as follows. The basic structure of the theory, that is, the concepts and their sequential ordering, are so entrenched in my mind as to make them near inviolable. Thus, postulating that attainment and nonattainment of a goal respectively give rise to happiness and unhappiness; that unexpected, important, and negative outcomes result in attributional search; that there is an attempt to reach a causal explanation; that causes have properties of locus, stability, and control; that these respectively relate to self-esteem, expectancy of success, and the affects of guilt, shame, anger, and sympathy; and that these beliefs and emotions influence action, I regard as (near) universal principles (subject to cognitive limitations). Included among the broader universals are more general beliefs incorporated by these relations, such as thinking gives rise to feelings (the appraisal approach to emotions) and thinking and feeling together determine action.

On the other hand, culture, demographics, personal history, and the like determine, for example, the goals for which one is striving; the definition of a success and a failure; what is unexpected and important; what information is used to determine causality; the causes salient to the person; where a cause is placed in dimensional space; and so on. That is, the antecedents and the determinants of the constructs and their magnitudes may differ between individuals. Attribution theory embraces phenomenology and constructs always have a subjective definition and meaning. For example, in one culture success is defined as a good crop of yams; in another, it is attaining the position of corporate head. Similarly, for one individual a "B" on an exam is defined as a success, whereas for another it is regarded as a failure. And for some the grade of "B" is considered a success by the school, but may be regarded a failure by the student because it results in exclusion from a group. Furthermore, for some a grade of "B" is anticipated and will not result in causal search; for others, the "B" is unexpected and a search is initiated. In some cultures and for some individuals, the search might start with internal causes; for others, the search starts externally; in some instances, the cause of success is thought to be a favor from God; for others, the main perceived cause of success is innate ability. In sum, attributional content is specific. However, the attributional process and structure of the theory are general and transcend specific determinants.

In addition to affecting the antecedents or operationalizations of any particular construct, culture and personal history at times act as moderators between specified associations in the theory. For example, lack of effort is under personal control, so failure due to this factor will result in anger followed by reprimand and punishment. But some cultures (e.g., Japan) regard achievement outcomes more controllable than do other cultures (e.g., the United States), and effort as a key determinant of success. Hence, Japanese teachers may punish lack of effort more than American teachers. That is, individual idiosyncrasies and/or group beliefs are recognized within the theory as functioning as moderators of particular relations. I have been remiss in the past by not sufficiently emphasizing this point because I have been primarily focused on motivational mediators rather than moderators and have paid most attention to the general motivational process.

I now examine two specific content areas to illustrate my beliefs: differences between African American and white students in school dropout rates (to which the intrapersonal theory is applied) and disparities between Hispanics and Americans in reaction to obesity (to which the interpersonal theory is applied). A conceptual analysis of both observations convey how diversity, or individual differences, can be captured within attribution theory.

Ethnic Differences in School Dropout Rates

It is widely recognized that African Americans fare poorly relative to whites on many indicators of academic performance. They have lower grade point averages and drop out of college at a higher rate than white students (see Van Laar, 2000). How might attribution theory address these facts, and specifically differential dropout rates between the races?

Applying the intrapersonal theory to the African American data and mirroring the analysis of affiliative withdrawal presented earlier, attribution theory might suggest the following process. After initial failures in the challenging college environment, African Americans ascribe their poor performance to lack of ability (aptitude). This is because others in class are succeeding, whereas they repeatedly receive low grades (covariation information). Being an internal cause, an ascription to lack of aptitude lowers their self-esteem; since aptitude is perceived as stable, expectancy of success becomes low; and inasmuch as aptitude is perceived uncontrollable, a failing student experiences shame and humiliation. Low self-esteem, low expectancy of success, and feelings of shame and humiliation combine to reduce academic motivation and result in dropping out. This analysis can be depicted as follows:

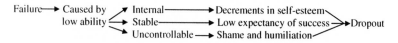

This appears a reasonable conceptual analysis, generating a number of worthy hypotheses that deserve to be true. Indeed, part of it is implicitly behind the movement to raise the self-esteem of students, thereby increasing motivation. But it unfortunately meets with an immediate empirical disconfirmation. African American students do not have lower self-esteem than their white counterparts (see Graham, 1988, 1991; Van Laar, 2000). One might contend this is because self-esteem has many components in addition to achievement performance. However, African American students also score as high as (or higher than) white students in academic self-esteem (see Graham, 1988, 1991; Van Laar, 2000). Does the equivalence in self-esteem between racial groups, which attribution theory posits is in part a function of success and failure and the attributions for these outcomes, point to a theoretical shortcoming?

Van Laar (2000) did not think so, and offered a different attributional interpretation for the high dropout rates of African Americans. This explanation was guided by the insights of Crocker and Major (1989), who noted stigmatized groups typically do not experience deficiencies in self-esteem, even though this is predicted by a number of theories of the self. Crocker and Major contend a variety of mechanisms are activated to protect individuals in the face of negative outcomes and evaluations. One widely used strategy or device is to attribute failure externally to, for example, the prejudice of others. Even a self-perception of low ability (internal causality) can be traced back to inadequate educational opportunities because of discrimination (external causality). External ascriptions maintain self-esteem in the face of failure and prevent self-directed emotions of shame and embarrassment. Thus, here we have a situation where, given the same outcome (failure), members of diverse ethnic groups may differ in their attributions, in part because of disparities between the groups in their perceptions regarding the social system.

However, although the attribution for failure is now external for the African American students, prejudice also is likely to be perceived as stable, so again future success is not anticipated. That is, although the specific attribution has been altered from internal to external, the stability of the cause remains unchanged. Low expectations, Van Laar (2000) suggests, result in dropping out even when self-esteem is high.

In addition, the attribution of prejudice that is the cause of the failure is perceived controllable by others. This activates elements of the interpersonal model, so instead of shame-related emotions, the affective experience of failing minority students is anger. Anger, in turn, evokes antisocial and system-blaming activities. The theoretical analysis pertinent to attributions for failure proposed by Van Laar (2000) can be depicted as follows:

This conceptualization has a number of virtues. First, it enables high academic self-esteem and dropping out to coexist, solving a difficult explanatory barrier. Second, it generates some interesting hypotheses. For example, among African Americans achievement performance should be relatively unrelated to self-esteem, inasmuch as failure does not produce esteem decrements. On the other hand, among white pupils, it might be hypothesized that failure generates a number of internal ascriptions (prejudice is not an available causal explanation), so success and failure will produce disparities in self-esteem. Therefore, among whites' performance in school would be highly related to academic self-esteem. Note finding racial differences in the magnitude of the relation between achievement performance and self-esteem does not invalidate the attributional conception, but rather points out the theory can be used to shed light on between-group differences.

Why, then, do African American and white students not differ more substantially in academic self-esteem (and in a direction opposite to common sense), given that whites are more likely to make internal attributions for failure than African Americans? One speculative answer is that whites have fewer failures than African Americans. The combination of fewer failures—more internal ascriptions (white students) versus more failures—fewer internal ascriptions (African American students) could result in no significant self-esteem differences between these two groups. I doubt I would bet on this explanation, although it logically follows from the discussion. Rather, I use it to show how attributional analyses can be applied to all students, although not in a rigid or static manner

Does, then, attribution theory provide an adequate explanation of the higher dropout rates among African Americans as opposed to whites, with the stability of the perceived cause of failure and its linkage with expectancy of success the crucial factor? I do not think so. The theory offered by Van Laar (2000) does implicate low expectancy of success as causing achievement motivation and performance differences between the ethnic groups. Yet even in the face of poor performance, expectancy of success remains high among African Americans in college, and again is as high as or higher than that of whites (see Graham, 1988, 1991; Van Laar, 2000). The theory therefore again falls short. It apparently does not have the conceptual tools to handle ethnic differences in dropout rates inasmuch as neither self-esteem nor expectancy of success differentiates between the African American students and their white counterparts.

Are other attributional interpretations available that might be more useful? I question this also. One might speculate, for example, African Americans do not perceive low grades in school as a failure inasmuch as high grades are not a goal for them. Hence, the attributional process is not even activated by poor grades. Or, perhaps African American students have a lower grade threshold when defining failure, so again attributional search is more limited. But these so-called explanations do not address the basic issues of why achievement is not a goal or why there are lower standards for success for the African American students. I suspect answers to these questions are important for the dropout issue and they are not attributional issues.

In sum, it seems likely that dropout differences between the two racial groups are not mediated by (or are only weakly related to) causal beliefs. As intimated above, this leaves many other concepts available to explain racial differences in school performance, ranging from innate intelligence to learned values, from the influence of peer groups to familial socialization, and from the perception of group belonging to teacher warmth and school climate. It is not my goal here to understand achievement differences between racial groups, or to point out some of the important disparities in achievement performance that seem to fall beyond the range of attribution theory. Rather, I hope I have illustrated how to apply attribution theory to classroom diversity issues. The theory has remained intact, even though differentially utilized for white and African American students.

The prior analysis is not the only road for attribution theorists to take when addressing diversity. I now turn to a totally different phenomenon to expand my position: the differential reactions to obesity exhibited by Hispanics versus Americans. This is not as strange a jump as it initially must appear to the readers.

Ethnic Differences in Reactions to Obesity

I now shift from primarily the intrapersonal theory to the interpersonal theory and from achievement performance to reactions to the stigmatized. The observation I examine concerns reactions to obesity. It has been documented that Hispanics react less negatively to obesity in females than do Americans (Crandall & Martinez, 1996). Why, one might ask, should this be of importance to educators? The reason is that Crandall (1995) also reports Americans with a conservative ideology use withholding money for college tuition as a form of punishment of their obese daughters. Hence, there is an important connection between reactions to obesity and educational opportunities. For some, being overweight results in being denied access to educational institutions.

Guided by Figure 2.2, the following motivational analysis seems to fit these data. For Americans, obesity is perceived to be caused by overeating and/or exercising too little. These are controllable causes, so the outcome of obesity "could have been otherwise." Perceptions of controllability elicit the inference that the overweight (daughter) is responsible for her "failed" condition. This, in turn, evokes anger. Anger, along with responsibility as either a direct or an indirect influence, results in an antisocial response such as some form of punishment (withholding college tuition).

But Hispanics do not react as negatively to obesity. According to attribution theory, why might this be the case (more generally, how does attribution theory handle cultural diversity and differences in responses between ethnic groups)? Here are some possible answers to that question (although not necessarily agreed with by Crandall (1995):

1. Hispanics do not regard obesity as a "failure." That is, thinness does not represent a goal for which they strive and/or the definition of obesity starts at a higher weight than for Americans. Therefore, among Hispanics the attribution process is not activated by a "heavy" daughter and negative emotions and their linked behaviors do not follow.

2. Hispanics regard obesity as a personal "failure" but the causes are external and/or uncontrollable rather than internal and controllable. For example, the perceived causes may be poverty, which results in the ingestion of fatty and less nutritional food; lack of education regarding the adverse consequences of being overweight; lack of

time to engage in exercise and other healthy activities; and on and on.

3. Even given the same perceived causes as Americans (eating too much and exercising too little), these nonetheless are regarded less controllable by Hispanics than Americans (see above).

4. Controllable causes among Hispanics are less likely to give rise to anger and other negative emotions than among Americans. That is, even given the identical causal analysis, their emotional reactions are more muted.

5. Given the presence of anger, Hispanics are less likely than Americans to react with punitive responses that impede education. Perhaps their anger is more directly physical or verbal, or takes any of a number of other forms.

In sum, culture not only alters the operational definition of the constructs in the theory, but also acts as a moderator between some of the linkages specified in the theory. The overall conception does not vary across the ethnic groups: There are outcomes, causal antecedents, selected causes, dimensional placement, affective and further cognitive reactions, and behavioral responses among both ethnic groups. But nonetheless diversity can be captured within the theoretical framework.

CONCLUSION

I started this chapter by exclaiming few theorists limit the applicability of their theories to a particular culture, or time, or place in history, or gender. I certainly am among those who might be faulted for this rigidity. Skinner derided theorists for their tendency to force data into their prevailing theories even when the fit was less than clear. I also would have been one of his targets (assuming he was aware of attribution theory, which is probably an unreasonable assumption).

I have contended in this chapter that attribution theory as a theory, that is, as a set of interrelated constructs, is not in need of alteration. But one must be very careful in the assumptions being made when contrasting ethnic groups, cultures, genders, and so on. Success for one may be failure for another; causal information for one may be perceived as useless for another; causes salient to one group may be in the far background for the other; and so on. That is, content must be distinguished from process inasmuch as content is culturally specific, whereas process is culturally general. This means the theorist must be alert for differences between individuals. However, at the same time one must be equally alert to convert phenotypic disparities into genotypic similarities. What appears to be a qualitative difference between cultures may be subject to a similar conceptual analysis.

That is, the unique is nonetheless included within more general laws. That is the theoretical goal guiding my thinking.

REFERENCES

Atkinson, J. W. (1964). *An introduction to motivation.* Princeton, NJ: Van Nostrand.

Crandall, C. S. (1995). Do parents discriminate against their own heavyweight daughters? *Personality and Social Psychology Bulletin, 21,* 724–735.

Crandall, C. S., & Martinez, R. (1996). Culture, ideology, and anti-fat attitudes. *Personality and Social Psychology Bulletin, 22,* 1165–1176.

Crocker, J., & Major, B. (1989). Social stigma and self-esteem: The self- protective properties of stigmas. *Psychological Review, 96,* 608–630.

Gendolla, G. H. E., & Koller, M. (2001). Surprise and causal search: How are they affected by outcome valence and importance? *Motivation and Emotion, 25,* 237–250.

Graham, S. (1988). Can attribution theory tell us something about motivation in blacks? *Educational Psychologist, 23,* 3–21.

Graham, S. (1991). A review of attribution theory in achievement contexts. *Educational Psychology Review, 3,* 5–39.

Van Laar, C. (2000). The paradox of low academic achievement but high self-esteem in African-American students: An attributional account. *Educational Psychology Review, 12,* 33–61.

Weiner, B. (1986). *An attributional theory of motivation and emotion.* New York: Springer-Verlag.

Weiner, B. (1992). *Human motivation: Metaphors, theories, and research.* Newbury Park, CA: Sage.

Weiner, B. (1995). *Judgments of responsibility: A foundation for a theory of social conduct.* New York: Guilford Press.

CHAPTER 3

SELF-DETERMINATION THEORY
A Dialectical Framework for Understanding Sociocultural Influences on Student Motivation

Johnmarshall Reeve, Edward L. Deci, and Richard M. Ryan

INTRODUCTION

On a beautiful summer day, I (J.R.) spent the afternoon at the local park hitting some golf balls at a practice range. A few moments into the effort, a dozen eager 7- and 8-year-old summer campers swarmed over to the adjacent putting green. They were led by a no-nonsense-looking pro who was going to teach them how to play golf, or at least how to chip and putt.

As I was enjoying the sunshine, my ears could not help absorbing an endless barrage of two-word sentences ("Do this," "Listen here," "Stop that," "Look look"). In less than 10 minutes, the golf pro succeeded in

Big Theories Revisited
Volume 4 in: Research on Sociocultural Influences on Motivation and Learning, pages 31–60.
Copyright © 2004 by Information Age Publishing, Inc.
All rights of reproduction in any form reserved.
ISBN: 1-59311-053-7 (hardcover), 1-59311-052-9 (paperback)

using every controlling motivational strategy in the book—directives, orders, bribes, surveillance, deadlines, imposed goals, imposed priorities, and interpersonal competition (e.g., "First one to make a putt gets 5 cents"). Literally no coordination existed between what the children wanted to do and what the pro wanted them to do. The sociocultural clash was fierce. Fifteen minutes later, the lesson was over and the would-be golfers scattered off to do something else. The children did not seem to learn much. Nor did they internalize any new values. I did not see much in the way of skill development or the piquing of interest either. I did see that they liked getting a pocketful of nickels though.

My eavesdropping left me with two things: a knot in my stomach and a question of what the pro could have done differently. What could he have done to enrich the children's interest, learning, and sense of valuing?

This scene symbolically represents much of the research agenda for self-determination theory's first 20 years. In the 1970s and 1980s, researchers learned a lot about the sociocultural conditions that undermine people's intrinsic motivation and autonomous self-regulation (for a comprehensive review, see Deci & Ryan, 1987). More recently, however, a greater focus on people's psychological needs, social development, and psychological well-being has expanded research activity to focus on factors that promote intrinsic motivation and the internalization of extrinsic motivation (for a comprehensive review, see Ryan & Deci, 2000b). Because of these advances, we can now work with cultural representatives (like the golf pro) to find ways to promote students' intrinsic motivation, sense of valuing, and achievement. This chapter summarizes the theory's recent advances and its capacity to offer practical recommendations on how to support students' autonomous motivation.

When students walk into classrooms, they bring with them an energizing set of needs, interests, and values. The classrooms into which they walk offer a number of interesting things to do, teachers to relate to, and an instructional agenda to guide their classroom activity. When these interactions go well, the educational environment functions as a support system for students to satisfy needs, explore interests, refine skills, internalize values, and develop socially. Under these supportive conditions, students' classroom behavior reflects their needs, interests, and values, and they show strong motivation (interest, excitement, confidence), active engagement, and meaningful learning (Deci, Vallerand, Pelletier, & Ryan, 1991; Reeve, 2002; Ryan & Deci, 2000b). When these interactions go poorly, the educational environment asks students to put aside their personal preferences and instead follow a classroom prescription that tells them what they have to do. Under these controlling conditions, students' classroom behavior reflects socially engineered motivation engendered by incentives and threats that is associated with lackluster engagement, superficial learning, challenge avoidance, and a proneness to negative emotionality.

Self-determination theory (SDT) is a macrotheory of motivation that provides an approach to understanding and enhancing student motivation. The theory assumes that all students, no matter how unskilled or how impoverished their backgrounds, possess inherent growth tendencies and innate psychological needs that provide a motivational foundation for their autonomous motivation and healthy psychological development (Deci & Ryan, 1985b, 1991, 2000; Ryan, 1995; Ryan & Deci, 2000b, 2002). The three psychological needs are autonomy, competence, and relatedness. From an educator's point of view, finding ways to support students' active nature is the means to facilitate students' optimal functioning, academic engagement, constructive social development, and personal well-being (Deci et al., 1991; Ryan & Deci, 2000b). The theory acknowledges, however, that students sometimes reject opportunities for growth, lack self-motivation, and act irresponsibly. To resolve this seeming paradox, SDT research focuses on sociocultural influences to identify those conditions that support versus undermine students' inner motivational resources (Deci & Ryan, 1985b; Ryan & La Guardia, 1999).

In the present chapter, we pursue three goals. First, we provide an overview of self-determination theory. This macrotheory exists as a collection of four interrelated mini-theories, including basic needs theory, cognitive evaluation theory, organismic integration theory, and causality orientations theory. Second, we present a SDT analysis of how sociocultural variables sometimes contribute to but other times interfere with students' active nature and optimal functioning. For this discussion, we present a dialectical framework in which the student engages in and affects the educational environment and the educational environment, in turn, affects the student. Third, we apply both SDT and the dialectical framework to the design of classrooms capable of optimizing students' engagement, performance, development, and well-being. This discussion centers on the provision of autonomy-supportive classroom environments.

SELF-DETERMINATION THEORY

Self-determination theory (SDT) is an approach to human motivation that highlights people's inner motivational resources in explaining healthy personality development and autonomous self-regulation. It addresses how people's inherent growth tendencies and psychological needs interact with sociocultural conditions that nurture versus hinder these inner resources, resulting in varying levels of effective functioning and well-being.

In the empirical study of these motivational processes, research typically investigates specific sets of motivational phenomena, and the four mini-theories formulated as different sets of phenomena emerged. *Basic needs theory* focuses on the fundamental psychological needs for autonomy, competence, and relatedness as the basis of students' intrinsic motivation and autonomous self-regulation. *Cognitive evaluation theory* explains how external events (e.g., rewards, feedback) sometimes support but other times interfere with students' intrinsic motivation. *Organismic integration theory* focuses on extrinsic motivational processes and on the development of internalized motivations. And *causality orientations theory* concerns the contribution of enduring personality orientations to the quality of students' autonomous motivation and classroom functioning.

Basic Needs Theory

Basic needs theory addresses people's essential nature by specifying the requisite nutriments for intrinsic motivation, autonomous motivation, and healthy development. Three psychological needs are posited to underlie students' inherent tendency to seek out novelty and optimal challenge, to exercise and extend their capacities, to explore, and to learn. These psychological needs are for the experiences of autonomy, competence, and relatedness. When environmental conditions acknowledge and support these needs, students experience need satisfaction and show active engagement, positive emotionality, and psychological growth. When conditions neglect or frustrate these needs, students' experiences are displaced from their inherent needs, and some type of negative psychological consequence is predicted. Through basic needs theory, SDT explains not only the origins of students' active nature but also why students often and paradoxically show only passivity and alienation (viz., because social conditions thwart their basic needs).

Autonomy is the psychological need to experience one's behavior as emanating from or endorsed by the self rather than being initiated by forces or events that feel alien or with which they do not identify (Deci & Ryan, 1985b). Hence, behavior is autonomous or self-determined when students' inner resources (e.g., interests, values) guide and remain closely aligned with their behavior. When autonomous, students perceive an internal locus of causality, feel high freedom and low pressure, and perceive a sense of choice or value about whether or not to engage in a given course of action. Thus, the behavior is accompanied by an internal locus, volition, and perceived choice (Reeve, Nix, & Hamm, 2003).

Competence is the need to be effective in interactions with the environment, and it reflects the inherent desire to exercise one's capacities and, in doing so, seek out and master optimal challenges (Deci, 1975). Hence, behavior emanates from the need for competence when students seek out and persist in developmentally appropriate challenges and also when they welcome and show interest in activities that test, inform, develop, stretch, extend, and help them diagnose their developing capacities, skills, and talents.

Relatedness is the need to establish close bonds and secure attachments with others, and it reflects the desire to be emotionally connected to and interpersonally involved in warm, caring relationships (Baumeister & Leary, 1995; Deci & Ryan, 1991; Ryan & Powelson, 1991). It is the need for relatedness that supplies students with the inherent motivation to relate the self authentically to others. In doing so, students gravitate toward those whom they perceive to care about and respect them, and it is these people to whom the self becomes related. Relatedness also contributes positively to students' willingness to internalize the values and regulations endorsed by those others.

Basic needs theory contributes to the overarching SDT framework in three ways. First, basic needs theory places the origins of students' active nature in the three psychological needs. Second, basic needs theory explains why students show active versus passive engagement during learning activities, as social conditions sometimes involve and nurture these needs but other times neglect and thwart them. Specifically, research based on the theory shows that satisfaction of these three psychological needs promotes well-being and positive functioning whereas thwarting of the needs results in poorer functioning, and ill-being (Deci & Ryan, 2000; T. Kasser & Ryan, 1993, 1996; V. Kasser & Ryan, 1999; Reis, Sheldon, Gable, Roscoe, & Ryan, 2000; Ryan & Deci, 2001; Sheldon, Ryan, & Reis, 1996). Third, the three needs provide the basis for predicting a priori which aspects of the environment will be supportive versus antagonistic to the individual's inherent nature. Those likely to be need satisfying are predicted to be supportive and those likely to be need thwarting are predicted to be antagonistic.

Cognitive Evaluation Theory

Cognitive evaluation theory explains how external events (e.g., rewards, praise, surveillance) affect intrinsic motivation. Intrinsically motivated behaviors are those initiated and sustained by the spontaneous sense of satisfaction students experience while engaged in an activity (i.e., feeling self-determined, feeling competent). Being rooted in people's proactive nature, intrinsic motivation emerges spontaneously to motivate growth-promoting behavior when environmental and social conditions permit. But when conditions are antagonistic to autonomy or competence, they undermine intrinsic motivation. In short, external events that affect students' perceptions of autonomy or competence will necessarily affect their intrinsic motivation.

According to the theory, external events have two functional aspects that affect students' intrinsic motivation: a controlling aspect and an informational aspect (Deci & Ryan, 1980, 1985b). Cognitive evaluation theory proposes that it is the relative salience of the controlling and informational aspects of an event (such as a grade or a communication) that determines the effect of the event on intrinsic motivation. Controlling aspects pressure students toward a specific outcome or a specific way of behaving. How controlling an event is perceived to be affects intrinsic motivation because it affects satisfaction of the students' need for autonomy. When experienced as highly controlling, the external event promotes an external perceived locus of causality (deCharms, 1968) and decreases students' perceived self-determination, resulting in diminished intrinsic motivation. When perceived as noncontrolling, in contrast, the external event preserves perceived self-determination and maintains intrinsic motivation. Informational aspects of an event are those that communicate effectance feedback in a noncontrolling way. When perceived as competence-affirming information (positive feedback), the external event increases students' perceived competence and, consequently, their intrinsic motivation. When perceived as communicating incompetence (negative feedback), the external event decreases perceived competence and thus intrinsic motivation. In many cases, negative feedback also decreases extrinsic motivation by conveying that students cannot attain desired outcomes.

Cognitive evaluation theory has been used to explain the motivational effects of a wide range of classroom events, but the most widely studied external event has been extrinsic rewards (Deci, Koestner, & Ryan, 1999). When students are engaged in an interesting activity and educators begin to provide students with an extrinsic reward for doing so, cognitive evaluation theory explains how that reward will affect the students' subsequent intrinsic motivation. If the reward is offered to pressure students into behaving in a particular teacher-determined way, then the student will tend to experience it as controlling and will lose intrinsic motivation (in proportion to changes in the student's perceived autonomy). If the same reward is offered in a noncontrolling way, then the student will not experience it as controlling and intrinsic motivation will remain high. Rewards also feature an informational aspect. If the reward communicates a message of a job well done, then the student may experience it as positive feedback that will increase intrinsic motivation (in proportion to changes in the student's perceived competence).

Much of the research in cognitive evaluation theory has detailed how specific external events can interfere with perceived autonomy and hence intrinsic motivation, including surveillance (Lepper & Greene, 1975), threats of punishment (Deci & Cascio, 1972), deadlines (Amabile, DeJong, & Lepper, 1976), limits (Koestner, Ryan, Bernieri, & Holt, 1984), imposed goals (Mossholder, 1980), competition (Deci, Betley, Kahle, Abrams, & Porac, 1981), and evaluation (Ryan, 1982). Other research has detailed how external events can increase intrinsic motivation by preserving self-determination and enhancing perceived competence. Such events include choice (Zuckerman, Porac, Lathin, Smith, & Deci, 1978), opportunities for self-direction (Reeve et al., 2003), rationales (Reeve, Jang, Hardre, & Omura, 2002), acknowledgment of feelings (Koestner et al., 1984), and positive feedback (Fisher, 1978; Ryan, 1982; Vallerand & Reid, 1984). Overall, studies have found that the interpersonal climate in which the external event is administered—that is, whether the climate is primarily controlling versus informational—further predicts variance in intrinsic motivation. This has been shown in relation to praise (Ryan, 1982), tangible rewards (Ryan, Mims, & Koestner, 1983), rules/limits (Koestner et al., 1984), and competition (Reeve & Deci, 1996).

Cognitive evaluation theory complements basic needs theory within the larger SDT framework. Basic needs theory articulates the source of students' inherent willingness to engage their environment (i.e., psychological needs), and cognitive evaluation theory specifies how sociocultural conditions can foster or impair students' intrinsic motivational processes.

Organismic Integration Theory

Organismic integration theory proposes that external regulations can be internalized and become internal regulations, and thus that extrinsic motivation can become self-determined motivation. To illustrate how extrinsic motivation can become self-determined, organismic integration theory proposes that different types of extrinsic motivation exist and fall along a continuum of self-determination between amotivation and intrinsic motivation. Unlike amotivation, extrinsic motivation involves intentional activity, but different processes can regulate this activity. The least autonomous type of extrinsic motivation is external regulation, followed by introjected regulation, which is slightly autonomous; identified regulation, which is mostly autonomous; and integrated regulation, which is fully autonomous. Integrated regulation approximates intrinsic motivation in its degree of self-determination, but the two differ in that integrated regulation is based on the importance of the activity for the person's internalized values and goals, whereas intrinsic motivation is based on people's interest in the activity itself. Hence, extrinsic motivation is a differentiated construct, as different types of extrinsic motivation differ in their degree of self-determination. The study of types of extrinsic motivation is important because how self-determined a student's extrinsic motivation is during a learning activity forecasts the quality of his or her functioning, as relatively self-determined students, even when extrinsically motivated, experience positive educational outcomes (Deci et al., 1991; Ryan & Deci, 2000b; Reeve, 2002; Reeve et al., 2002).

The self-determination continuum of motivation appears in Figure 3.1. The continuum is organized by types of motivation, ranging from amotivation, through four types of extrinsic motivation, to intrinsic motivation. These types of motivation appear in the figure from left to right to show the extent to which each type of motivation emanates from one's sense of self. These motivations are described fully elsewhere (see Deci & Ryan, 1985b; Ryan & Connell, 1989; Ryan & Deci, 2000b, 2002), so we just define them here.

Amotivation is the state in which the student lacks an intention to act. Amotivated students passively "go through the motions" of classroom work, but they experience neither extrinsic nor intrinsic motivation. Amotivation may be present either because the student cannot do the work or because he or she sees no reason, either intrinsic or extrinsic, for doing it. *External regulation*, the least self-determined type of extrinsic motivation, is the type of regulation central to operant theory (e.g., Skinner, 1953). External regulation exists as a contingency-based, "in order to" type of extrinsic motivation in which the student engages in classroom activities in order to obtain a reward or avoid a punishment. *Introjected regulation* involves acting from an internalized, but not personally endorsed, regulation (i.e., doing what people think they should do because it is generally expected of them). With introjected regulation, students are internally controlled to do what they have to do to maintain self-esteem (e.g., to affirm their self-worth) or to silence a self-esteem threat (e.g., to avoid feeling guilty). *Identified regulation* is a self-determined type of extrinsic motivation in which students see value in the external regulation and willingly transform it into a personally endorsed internalized regulation. They identify with the value of the regulation and embrace it as their own. *Integrated regulation* is the most self-determined type of extrinsic motivation. It occurs as people evaluate and bring an identification into coherence with other aspects of the self. Without integration, the identification could remain separate and somewhat isolated from people's other values, goals, and needs. *Intrinsic motivation* is the innate motivation that emerges spontaneously from psychological needs, and is manifest as being interested in the activity itself.

Organismic integration theory investigates how students acquire, internalize, and integrate extrinsic motivational processes. The theory proposes that students are naturally inclined to internalize aspects of their social surroundings and, eventually, to integrate these values and ways of behaving into the self-system. When the sociocultural context provides autonomy-supportive (or need-satisfying) conditions, people are able and willing to internalize and integrate external regulations into their sense of self (Deci, Eghrari, Patrick, & Leone, 1994; Grolnick & Ryan, 1989; Reeve et al., 2002; Williams & Deci, 1996). To the extent that students internalize and integrate healthy external regulations (i.e., achieve organismic integration), they experience greater autonomy in the relevant domains and

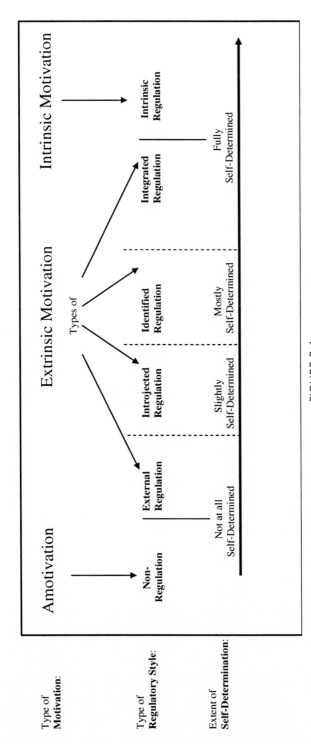

FIGURE 3.1.
Self-determination continuum of types of motivation.

show enhanced functioning and well-being. This has been shown for students' internalizations in schools (Ryan & Connell, 1989) as well as in domains such as the home (Grolnick & Ryan, 1989), exercising (Mullan & Markland, 1997), marriage (Blais, Sabourin, Boucher, & Vallerand, 1990), health care (Williams, Rodin, Ryan, Grolnick, & Deci, 1998), weight loss (Williams, Grow, Freedman, Ryan, & Deci, 1996), political participation (Koestner, Losier, Vallerand, & Carducci, 1996), religion (Ryan, Rigby, & King, 1993), and environmental conservation (Green-Demers, Pelletier, & Menard, 1997).

Like cognitive evaluation theory, organismic integration theory complements basic needs theory. Whereas cognitive evaluation theory specifies how need satisfaction relates to intrinsic motivation, organismic integration theory articulates how need satisfaction relates to extrinsic motivation and healthy development. As such, the theory clarifies how students become increasingly able to generate self-determined, extrinsically motivated actions.

Causality Orientations Theory

Causality orientations theory describes individual differences in people's orientations toward motivational forces that cause their behavior. In the classroom, some students adopt a general orientation that allows their behaviors to be initiated and maintained over time by self-determined guides. To the extent that students regulate themselves in accord with their needs, interests, and values, they embrace an autonomous causality orientation. Other students adopt a general orientation involving their behaviors being initiated and maintained by environmental incentives, social guides, and internal controls such as contingent self-esteem. To the extent that students rely on controlling forces to guide their plans and behaviors, they embrace a *controlled* causality orientation.[1]

Causality orientations reflect the extent of self-determination in the personality. Highly autonomy-oriented individuals are motivated primarily by intrinsic motivation and autonomous types of extrinsic motivation, relying heavily on psychological needs, personal interests, and integrated values in regulating their behavior. The autonomy causality orientation reflects a personal history of having developmental and sociocultural supports for one's perceived autonomy and competence. Highly control-oriented individuals are motivated primarily by external and introjected regulations, relying principally on environmental rewards and constraints, social directives, and beliefs and values that have been introjected but not personally endorsed. The autonomy orientation has been associated with more positive functioning, such as more advanced ego development and successful long-term behavioral change, whereas the controlled orientation has been associated with proneness to conformity, public self-consciousness, and less maintenance of positive change (Deci & Ryan, 1985a; Williams et al., 1996). Causality orientations theory, which adds the personality perspective to SDT, completes the overall framework.

THE DIALECTICAL FRAMEWORK

According to the self-determination theory framework, students possess inherent needs and growth propensities to constructively engage their sociocultural surroundings. These surroundings, in turn, feature conditions that tend either to support or thwart students' motivation. To the extent that students are able to express themselves and master classroom challenges, the dialectical outcome will be synthesis, resulting in greater autonomy and well-being. But to the extent that the controlling and amotivating forces in classrooms overpower students' proactive (autonomous) engagement, synthesis will be impaired and less optimal outcomes will result (e.g., control and amotivation rather than autonomy; less rather than more conceptual understanding).

This dialectic framework appears in Figure 3.2. It is within the context of this figure that the theory conceptualizes and investigates sociocultural influences on students' motivations. The upper arrow communicates that students proactively engage in classroom challenges as an expression of their inner motivational resources. The quality of this engagement can be characterized by the student's causality orientations and types of regulation. The lower arrow communicates that sociocultural influences sometimes nurture students' self-determined motivation but other times neglect, disrupt, and fragment these same inner resources, thus strengthening or weakening the autonomous motivational propensities.

Students' Inner Motivational Resources

Some inner resources are inherent, including psychological needs and developmental tendencies (see left side of "Individual" box in Figure 3.2). Other motivational resources are internalized, including certain preferences, values, and regulations (see right side of "Individual" box in Figure 3.2). Collectively, these inner resources motivate students to engage the classroom environment as an expression of themselves and out of the desires to interact effectively and to differentiate the self into a greater complexity.

Psychological needs and developmental tendencies. In SDT, the self is viewed as action and development from within that forever aims toward a unity

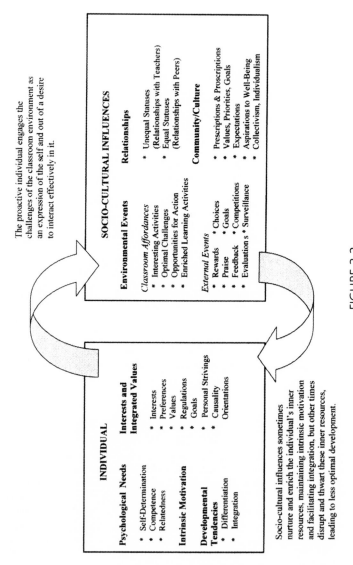

FIGURE 3.2.

Dialectical framework for the study of personality growth and development.

and sense of coherence in experience. That is, it serves a synthetic function that is at the center of the dialectic (Deci & Ryan, 1991). By exercising and developing its innate resources, the self has the developmental means to advance from heteronomy (a dependence on controlling forces) toward autonomy (a reliance on the self). Intrinsic motivation, for instance, spontaneously energizes important growth-fostering behaviors, such as seeking out challenges, exercising skills, and pursuing interests. The three psychological needs energize and direct behavior too, as outlined by basic needs theory. The two inherent developmental processes of differentiation and integration guide ongoing action from within (Ryan, 1993). Differentiation is a growth tendency to expand and elaborate the self into an ever-increasing complexity. As the self engages its surroundings, it expands and elaborates by developing increasingly sophisticated interests, preferences, skills, talents, and relationships. Integration synthesizes the self's emerging complexity into a coherent whole, thereby preserving a unified sense of self—what SDT refers to as the "integrated self" (Deci & Ryan, 1991).

Interests and integrated values. As students come to associate classroom activities with psychological need satisfaction, they develop interests in those activities (Deci, 1992). As these interests develop, students express preferences for engaging in those activities when they are free to do what they choose. Through environmental transactions, students also become aware of the culture's values, priorities, ideals, goals, aspirations, expectations, regulations, requirements, prescriptions ("do this"), and proscriptions ("don't do that"). Some of these ways of thinking and behaving become valued and, hence, are internalized and personally endorsed by the student (Ryan & Connell, 1989; Ryan et al., 1993). Students internalize external regulations partly to become increasingly competent in interacting with the social world and partly to relate the self more closely to others, as integrated values promote a greater unity between self and community.

Sociocultural Influences

Classroom environments have the potential to either buttress or impede students' active nature and self-determined strivings. Some influences are specific objects or contingencies in the environment, such as affordances (interesting activities) and external events (rewards, surveillance). Other influences are interpersonal relationships, including those with individuals (parents, teachers, peers) and those with groups, communities, organizations, or the nation in general. Collectively, these sociocultural influences provide opportunities, hindrances, and an overall climate in which the self develops (Ryan & La Guardia, 1999).

Affordances and external events. Affordances are objects or opportunities in the environment that provide students with access or hindrance to exercising and developing their interests, preferences, and skills. Affordances that support students' self-determined strivings include interesting activities, developmentally appropriate challenges, opportunities for action in a valued domain (e.g., music program, extracurricular activities), and enriched learning activities (e.g., field trips, service learning). Hindrances include restrictions and barriers, such as a lack of resources. External events are classroom contingencies offered to motivate students to engage in a particular course of action. While some external events generally nurture students' inner resources (e.g., action choices) and others generally thwart these same resources (e.g., deadlines), any external event (e.g., reward, evaluation, praise, feedback) can be administered in a way that supports or interferes with students' self-determined strivings, as explained by cognitive evaluation theory.

Relationships and communities. Many relationships have implications for students' motivation, but self-determination theory focuses mostly on those in which a person of high status or expertise attempts to motivate or socialize another who is of a relatively lower status or expertise, as with parents and children (Grolnick, 2002), teachers and students (Reeve, Bolt, & Cai, 1999), school administrators and students (Vallerand, Fortier, & Guay, 1997), or coaches and athletes (Ryan, Vallerand, & Deci, 1984). In the language of Figure 3.2, an unequal relationship implies that, to a significant degree, it is the responsibility of teachers to affect students' motivation, as represented by the lower arrow; whereas it is not the students' responsibility to affect teachers, even though students' behavior does, of course, affect teachers' motivation and behavior, as represented by the upper arrow (Pelletier, Seguin-Levesque, & Legault, 2002). Communities and cultures also present motivating styles or climates (e.g., home schooling; Cai, Reeve, & Robinson, 2002), as they offer a sociocultural context in which to express, develop, differentiate, and integrate the self. For example, high-stakes testing policies are having a dramatic effect on teacher strategies and thus on students' motivation (Ryan & La Guardia, 1999). Nations too offer climates, as self-determination theory has been studied in the United States, Bulgaria (Deci et al., 2001), Russia (Chirkov & Ryan, 2001), Japan (Hayamizu, 1997), and South Korea (Sheldon, Elliot, Kim, & Kasser, 2001).

Does Everyone Need Autonomy?

Self-determination theory is rooted in the assumption that autonomy, competence, and relatedness are cross-culturally universal needs. When satisfied, they promote well-being and optimal functioning in all global classrooms, even in those embedded in collectivistic (Sheldon et al., 2001) and dogmatically traditional (Cai et al., 2002) cultures. For instance, when college-age students from individualistic (United States) and collectivistic (South Korea) cultures both ranked the motivational importance of 10 different needs, autonomy, competence, and relatedness emerged at the top of both lists (Sheldon et al., 2001). Furthermore, in both cultures, the satisfaction of these three needs explained unique variance in students' emotional well-being. The appearance of autonomy near the top of the list for the South Korean students was particularly important because this finding supports SDT's claim that autonomy is a universal psychological need (Deci & Ryan, 2000).

Some question this universality claim (Bond, 1988; Carver & Scheier, 2000; Markus, Kitayama, & Heiman, 1996). Self-determination theory research in non-Western cultures supports the universality claim, though it also identifies three findings that point to some cultural specificity. First, though members of all cultures find an autonomy experience to be both satisfying and positive-affect producing, members of collectivistic cultures generally find a relatedness experience to be even more satisfying (Sheldon et al., 2001). Second, though members of all cultures show positive functioning in autonomy-supportive environments, members of collectivistic cultures generally find a controlling climate to be relatively less disruptive to their psychological needs (Deci et al., 2001). Third, though members of all cultures show greater intrinsic motivation and performance when offered choice rather than when told what to do by an experimenter, members of collectivistic cultures generally experience a lesser magnitude of these benefits (Iyengar & Lepper, 1999).

We highlight this universality issue because critics repeatedly and inaccurately portray SDT's concept of autonomy as being equal to individualism and independence (Kashima et al., 1995) or even selfishness (Carver & Scheier, 2000). In SDT, autonomy means the self-endorsement of one's actions and expressed beliefs (Reeve et al., 2003; Ryan, 1993). This does not imply individualism, independence, separateness, or selfishness (Ryan, 1993; Ryan & Deci, 2000a). Rather, in SDT, it is fully consistent for individuals to be both related to their culture and autonomous in their actions. Everyone needs autonomy, though members of collectivistic cultures particularly value relatedness and members of individualistic cultures particularly value autonomy.

Interpersonal Motivating Styles

Teachers cannot give students an experience of autonomy, they can only encourage it. Even when teachers provide students with choices and options, students often do not experience autonomy (Reeve et al., 2003). Instead, what teachers can do is provide classroom supports for students' perceived autonomy, competence, and relatedness, create opportunities for students to align their classroom activity with their innate and developing inner resources, and patiently support the students to become engaged.

Some relationships encourage students to develop a sense of congruence between their inner resources and classroom behaviors, although other relationships ask students to put aside their inner resources and, instead, act in ways that conform to some outside agenda. To dissociate students' classroom activity from their inner resources, educators offer extrinsic motivators, such as gold stars, stickers, privileges, awards, honor rolls, the promise of an A, no-nonsense language, pressuring deadlines, standards, imposed goals, external evaluations, token economies, and other such instruments common to behavior modification programs; Kohn, 1993; Ryan & La Guardia, 1999). It is a relatively easy undertaking to recognize and implement a controlling environment. After all, it took me (J.R.) only about 30 seconds to recognize the golf pro's controlling motivating style. But recognizing and implementing an autonomy-supportive environment requires a more subtle involvement and a more complex set of skills. These issues are discussed in the next section.

AUTONOMY SUPPORT IN THE CLASSROOM

Autonomy-supportive environments are those that involve and nurture (rather than neglect and frustrate) students' psychological needs, personal interests, and integrated values. A teacher's effort to find ways to nurture students' inner resources is worthwhile because students in autonomy-supportive classrooms, compared to those in controlling classrooms, experience not only greater autonomy, competence, and relatedness (Gurland & Grolnick, 2003; Hardre & Reeve, 2003; Vallerand et al., 1997) but also an impressive range of positive educational outcomes (Deci & Ryan, 1985b, 1987; Deci et al., 1991; Reeve, 2002; Ryan & Grolnick, 1986), including greater creativity (Koestner et al., 1984), enhanced well-being (Black & Deci, 2000), and better academic performance (Boggiano, Flink, Shields, Seelbach, & Barrett, 1993).

The empirical study of autonomy-supportive environments focuses on (1) specific sociocultural influences that serve as conduits of a teacher's autonomy support and (2) the quality of teachers' motivating styles during instruction. As to the first focus, cognitive evaluation theory and organismic integration theory explain how sociocultural conditions act as environmental supports for students' psychological needs. For instance, environmental supports for an experience of autonomy include opportunities for self-direction (Reeve et al., 2003) and the provision of rationales (Reeve et al., 2002). Environmental supports for an experience of competence include optimal challenges (Shapira, 1976) and positive feedback (Vallerand & Reid, 1984). Environmental supports for an experience of relatedness include teacher involvement (Skinner & Belmont, 1993) and rapport (Gurland & Grolnick, 2003). In the present section, we focus attention not on these individual environmental supports but, instead, more generally on teachers' interpersonal motivating styles. The discussion below illuminates the motivating style of teachers, but the same conclusions also generalize to the motivating styles of parents (Grolnick, 2002), workplace supervisors (Deci, Connell, & Ryan, 1989), athletic coaches (Ryan et al., 1984), and physicians (Williams, 2002).

A teacher's motivating style toward students can be understood along a continuum that ranges from highly controlling to highly autonomy supportive (Deci, Schwartz, Sheinman, & Ryan, 1981). In general, autonomy-supportive teachers facilitate, whereas relatively controlling teachers interfere with, students' congruence between their self-determined inner guides and their day-to-day classroom activity. Autonomy-supportive teachers facilitate congruence by identifying and nurturing students' needs, interests, and preferences and by creating classroom opportunities for students to have these internal states guide their behavior. In contrast, relatively controlling teachers interfere with students' self-determination because they tend to establish and ask students to adhere to a teacher-constructed instructional agenda that defines what students should do. Controlling teachers then offer extrinsic incentives and pressuring language to shape students toward that agenda.

Autonomy-Supportive Motivating Style

What autonomy-supportive teachers do to support students' perceived self-determination and active engagement (Deci et al., 1991, 1994; Reeve, 1996; Reeve et al., 2003; Ryan & La Guardia, 1998) can be summarized under four topics: (1) nurturing of inner motivational resources; (2) relying on informational, noncontrolling language; (3) communicating value in uninteresting activities and rationales for requested behaviors; and (4) acknowledging and accepting students' expressions of negative affect.

Nurture inner motivational resources. When teachers nurture students' inner motivational resources they find ways to build instructional activities around students' interests, preferences, sense of challenge and fun, competencies, or choice making, rather than relying on external regulators such as incentives, consequences, directives, deadlines, assignments, or compliance requests. This first aspect of an autonomy-supportive style represents teachers' efforts to nurture students' intrinsic motivation and self-determined extrinsic motivation during learning activities rather than trying to socially engineer non-self-determined types of extrinsic motivation.

Rely on informational, noncontrolling language. When teachers rely on informational, noncontrolling language they communicate classroom opportunities and requirements through messages that are informational and flexible rather than controlling, rigid, pressuring, and coercive. This second aspect of an autonomy-supportive style shows that teachers use communications to help coordinate students' inner resources with their moment-to-moment activity (while controlling teachers use communications to push students into compliance with the teacher's agenda).

Communicate value in uninteresting activities and rationales for requested behaviors. When teachers promote valuing for their requests, they go out of their way to identify and explain the use, value, personal benefit, or importance of the requested activity, lesson, behavior, procedure, or requirement. Controlling teachers generally neglect to communicate this otherwise hidden personal utility that justifies an investment of effort. This third aspect of an autonomy-supportive style acknowledges that teachers frequently ask students to invest their effort in undertakings that are not intrinsically interesting and are, in fact, often unappealing things to do (e.g., complete a worksheet, wear protective gear during a laboratory exercise). But autonomy-supportive teachers help students generate self-determined motivation by articulating why the undertaking is truly a useful thing to do. When autonomy-supportive teachers provide students who face an uninteresting lesson with a rationale, students are more likely to have an "identification experience" that facilitates both internalization and subsequent effort (Reeve et al., 2002).

Acknowledge and accept students' expressions of negative affect. Because classrooms have rules, requests, and instructional agendas that are sometimes at odds with students' preferences, students often complain and express resistance. When teachers acknowledge and accept such feelings, they are communicating an understanding of the students' perspectives and accepting the negative affect as a valid reaction to the demands, structures, and uninteresting activities. Controlling teachers, in contrast, react to students' expressions of negative affect by trying to counter it. They communicate that such an "attitude" is unacceptable, something that needs to be changed, fixed, or reversed into an attitude more acceptable to the teacher. This fourth aspect of an autonomy-supportive style acknowledges the inevitable conflict between what teachers want students to do and what students may initially want to do (or not do). It further presumes that students' expression of negative affect can be important and helpful information for teachers as they think about how they can more effectively communicate their classroom requests and activities away from "things not worth doing" into "things worth doing" (from the student's perspective).

Specific, moment-to-moment autonomy-supportive behaviors. At a more concrete level, researchers have identified what autonomy-supportive teachers

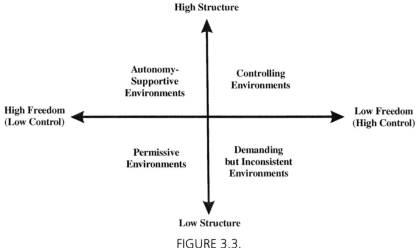

FIGURE 3.3.
A 2 x 2 framework to distinguish environmental
dimensions of structure and control.

encounter the structures to be internalized and integrated as a basis of more effective regulation during activities they do not find interesting. Finally, classrooms with low structure and low freedom are less common than the other types because they do not really represent a motivational approach; rather, they constitute a poor instantiation of a controlling approach. That is, just as the permissive environment is a misrepresentation of an autonomy-supportive environment, a demanding but inconsistent environment is a misrepresentation of a controlling environment. Specifically, classrooms have low freedom and low structure to the extent that they are demanding, with contingencies of reward and punishment, but the demands and sanctions are inconsistently administered. Thus, students experience them as chaotic because the students have been subjected to demands, incentives, and threats, but they cannot rely on the teacher to follow through and they cannot trust that they will receive the outcomes they deserve.

Studies on specific elements of teacher-provided structure illuminate why students benefit from highly structured autonomy-supportive environments. When teachers impose rules or limits on students (Koestner et al., 1984), offer praise (Ryan et al., 1983), provide rationales (Reeve et al., 2002), impose learning goals (Jang & Reeve, 2003), or communicate an instructional set (Grolnick & Ryan, 1987), teachers provide students with an intention to act. A fundamental contribution of self-determination theory to the study of motivation is its emphasis that not all intentions are equal: self-determined intentions promote optimal functioning, whereas non-self-determined intentions forecast poor functioning (Deci & Ryan,

1987). Hence, autonomy support and structure work well together because structure facilitates in students an intention to act, while autonomy support allows those formulated intentions to be self-determined and coordinated with one's inner resources.

DEVELOPMENTAL COSTS OF CONTROL: DEVELOPMENTAL GAINS FROM AUTONOMY-SUPPORT

Following the 1978 publication of the *Hidden costs of rewards* (Lepper & Greene, 1978), psychologists and educators alike realized that extrinsic motivators frequently fall short in their role as optimal motivators. The hidden costs of rewards are that they often undermine intrinsic motivation, learning, creativity, and prosocial behavior (Ryan & Deci, 2000c). These costs notwithstanding, some educators continue to view the strategic management of extrinsic motivators as an effective approach to motivating students (Cameron, 2001). But even when extrinsic motivators promote compliance, they ask recipients to put aside inner resources and instead allow their activity to be externally regulated. Self-concordance, however, is an important developmental event, as self-concordance explains people's enduring and self-generated willingness to invest effort in the pursuit of their goals (Sheldon, 2002; Sheldon & Elliot, 1999; Sheldon & Houser-Marko, 2001).

How controlling environments undermine students' long-term capacity for autonomous self-regulation is well illustrated in the field of special education with respect to mental retardation and learning disabilities (Wehmeyer, Agran, & Hughes, 1998). While many special education practitioners find utility in administering a steady stream of extrinsic motivators to externally regulate the behavior of people with disabilities, others favor exerting the effort necessary to promote people's long-term capacity for autonomous self-regulation (Algozzine, Browder, Karvonen, Test, & Wood, 2001). Instead of reacting to the incentives and consequences offered by others, the emphasis is on promoting self-determination in people's lives. For instance, individuals with disabilities are taught skills like self-advocacy and choice making. The idea is to empower people with disabilities to first voice their interests and preferences and then exercise choices that express those preferences. After individuals with disabilities learned self-advocacy and choice-making skills, researchers observed their activity in naturalistic settings such as restaurants in which participants acted on their preferences for beverages (Belfiore, Browder, & Mace, 1994) and foods (Cooper & Browder, 1998). Empowered with self-determination in their lives, these individuals showed more positive functioning and enhanced well-being.

Self-determination theory explains human motivation and, in doing so, presents a program of research capable of promoting the well-being of individuals, including students in classrooms (Ryan & Deci, 2000b). When students walk into classrooms, they take with them a set of inherent and developing inner motivational resources. The classrooms into which they walk sometimes offer learning environments that support and nurture these resources but other times neglect and frustrate these resources. Three decades of empirical research confirms the validity of the SDT framework and also the benefit to students' functioning and well-being when sociocultural conditions are responsive to students' inner resources. This research also points the way to educators' attempts to create class-room communities capable of supporting students' active nature and opti-mal functioning.

CONCLUSION

In conclusion, we return to the golf pro and the question of what he could do to nurture the would-be golfers' autonomy and, hence, their interest, engagement, valuing, learning, and well-being. After all, the most fre-quently asked question a motivational psychologist hears in the schools is, "How can I motivate my students?" Once asked, teachers await recommen-dations on what actions they can enact to energize disaffected students. Asking the question this way, however, is unfortunate because it primes the ears for a reply that reflects a controlling and unilateral style, as in doing or offering something so students will respond in kind (e.g., reward them, grade them, push them, offer an incentive). This same question, however, can be asked in a different way, namely: "How can I create the conditions under which students will be able to motivate themselves?" Asked in this way, the question readies the ears for a reply that reflects an autonomy-sup-portive and dialectical style, as it acknowledges that students harbor inner resources and seek to internalize healthy external regulations that can sup-port their adjustment and development.

Such recommendations can be quite specific and apply to one particu-lar learning activity, or they can be more general and speak to one's inter-personal motivating style. Specifically, teachers support students' autonomy when they listen carefully, create opportunities for students to talk and to work in their own way, arrange learning materials and seating arrangements so to encourage activity rather than passivity, encourage effort when it occurs, give progress-enhancing hints and praise progress, reply wholeheartedly to student-generated questions, and acknowledge students' perspectives. More generally, teachers support autonomy when they nurture students' inner motivational resources, rely on informational and noncontrolling language, communicate value in uninteresting activi-ties and rationales for requests, and acknowledge and accept students' expressions of negative affect.

NOTE

1.   When students fail to rely on either organismic, autonomy-syupportive guides, or external controls to regulate their behavior, they adopt an *impersonal* causality orientation, which is associated with amotivation.

REFERENCES

Algozzine, B., Browder, D., Karvonen, M., Test, D. W., & Wood, W. M. (2001). Effects of interventions to promote self-determination for individuals with disabilities. *Review of Educational Research, 71*, 219–277.

Amabile, T. M., DeJong, W., & Lepper, M. (1976). Effects of externally imposed deadlines on subsequent intrinsic motivation. *Journal of Personality and Social Psychology, 34*, 92–98.

Baumeister, R., & Leary, M. R. (1995). The need to belong: Desire for interpersonal attachments as a fundamental human motivation. *Psychological Bulletin, 117*, 497–529.

Belfiore, P. J., Browder, D. M., & Mace, C. (1994). Assessing choice making and preference in adults with profound mental retardation across community and center-based settings. *Journal of Behavioral Education, 4*, 217–225.

Black, A. E., & Deci, E. L. (2000). The effects of instructors' autonomy support and students' autonomous motivation on learning organic chemistry: A self-determination theory perspective. *Science Education, 84*, 740–756.

Blais, M. R., Sabourin, S., Boucher, C., & Vallerand, R. J. (1990). Toward a motivational model of couple happiness. *Journal of Personality and Social Psychology, 59*, 1021–1031.

Boggiano, A. K., Flink, C., Shields, A., Seelbach, A., & Barrett, M. (1993). Use of techniques promoting students' self-determination: Effects on students' analytic problem-solving skills. *Motivation and Emotion, 17*, 319–336.

Bond, M. H. (Ed.). (1988). *The cross-cultural challenge to social psychology.* Newbury Park, CA: Sage.

Brophy, J. (1986). Teacher influences of student achievement. *American Psychologist, 41*, 1069–1077.

Cai, Y., Reeve, J., & Robinson, D. T. (2002). Home schooling and teaching style: Comparing the motivating styles of home school and public school teachers. *Journal of Educational Psychology, 94*, 372–380.

Cameron, J. (2001). Negative effects of rewards on intrinsic motivation—A limited phenomenon: Comments on Deci, Koestner, and Ryan (2001). *Review of Educational Research, 71*, 29–42.

Carver, C. S., & Scheier, M. F. (2000). Autonomy and self-regulation. *Psychological Inquiry, 11*, 284–290.

Chirkov, V. I., & Ryan, R. M. (2001). Parent and teacher autonomy support in Russian and U. S. adolescents. *Journal of Cross-Cultural Psychology, 32*, 618–635.

Connell, J. P., & Welborn, J. G. (1991). Competence, autonomy, and relatedness: A motivational analysis of self-system processes. In M. R. Gunnar & L. A. Sroufe

(Eds.), *Self processes in development: Minnesota Symposium on Child Psychology* (Vol. 23, pp. 167–216). Chicago: University of Chicago Press.

Cooper, K. J., & Browder, D. M. (1998). Enhancing choice and participation for adults with severe disabilities in community-based instruction. *Journal of the Association for Persons with Severe Handicaps, 23,* 252–260.

deCharms, R. (1968). *Personal causation.* New York: Academic Press.

deCharms, R. (1976). *Enhancing motivation: Change in the classroom.* New York: Irvington.

Deci, E. L. (1975). *Intrinsic motivation.* New York: Plenum Press.

Deci, E. L. (1992). The relation of interest to the motivation of behavior: A self-determination theory perspective. In K. A. Renninger, S. Hidi, & A. Krapp (Eds.), *The role of interest in learning and development* (pp. 43–70). Hillsdale, NJ: Erlbaum.

Deci, E. L., Betley, G., Kahle, J., Abrams, L, & Porac, J. (1981). When trying to win: Competition and intrinsic motivation. *Personality and Social Psychology Bulletin, 7,* 79–83.

Deci, E. L., & Cascio, W. F. (1972, April). *Changes in intrinsic motivation as a function of negative feedback and threats.* Paper presented at the Eastern Psychological Association, Boston.

Deci, E. L., Connell, J. P., & Ryan, R. M. (1989). Self-determination in a work organization. *Journal of Applied Psychology, 74,* 580–590.

Deci, E. L., Eghrari, H., Patrick, B. C., & Leone, D. R. (1994). Facilitating internalization: The self-determination theory perspective. *Journal of Personality, 62,* 119–142.

Deci, E. L., Koestner, R., & Ryan, R. M. (1999). A meta-analytic review of experiments examining the effects of extrinsic rewards on intrinsic motivation. *Psychological Bulletin, 125,* 627–668.

Deci, E. L., & Ryan, R. M. (1980). The empirical exploration of intrinsic motivational processes. In L. Berkowitz (Ed.), *Advances in experimental social psychology* (Vol. 13, pp. 39–80). New York: Academic Press.

Deci, E. L., & Ryan, R. M. (1985a). The General Causality Orientations Scale: Self-determination in personality. *Journal of Research in Personality, 19,* 109–134.

Deci, E. L., & Ryan, R. M. (1985b). *Intrinsic motivation and self-determination in human behavior.* New York: Plenum Press.

Deci, E. L., & Ryan, R. M. (1987). The support of autonomy and the control of behavior. *Journal of Personality and Social Psychology, 53,* 1024–1037.

Deci, E. L., & Ryan, R. M. (1991). A motivational approach to self: Integration in personality. In R. Dienstbier (Ed.), *Nebraska Symposium on Motivation: Perspectives on motivation* (Vol. 38, pp. 237–288). Lincoln: University of Nebraska Press.

Deci, E. L., & Ryan, R. M. (2000). The "what" and "why" of goal pursuits: Human needs and the self-determination of behavior. *Psychological Inquiry, 11,* 227–268.

Deci, E. L., Ryan, R. M., Gagne, M., Leone, D. R., Usunov, J., & Kornazheva, B. P. (2001). Need satisfaction, motivation, and well-being in the work organizations of a former Eastern Bloc country. *Personality and Social Psychology Bulletin, 27,* 930–942.

Deci, E. L., Schwartz, A., Sheinman, L., & Ryan, R. M. (1981). An instrument to assess adult's orientations toward control versus autonomy in children: Reflections on intrinsic motivation and perceived competence. *Journal of Educational Psychology, 73*, 642–650.

Deci, E. L., Spiegel, N. H., Ryan, R. M., Koestner, R., & Kauffman, M. (1982). Effects of performance standards on teaching styles: Behavior of controlling teachers. *Journal of Educational Psychology, 74*, 852–859.

Deci, E. L., Vallerand, R. J., Pelletier, L. G., & Ryan, R. M. (1991). Motivation and education: The self-determination perspective. *Educational Psychologist, 26*, 325–346.

Fisher, C. D. (1978). The effects of personal control, competence, and extrinsic reward systems on intrinsic motivation. *Organizational Behavior and Human Performance, 21*, 273–288.

Flink, C., Boggiano, A. K., & Barrett, M. (1990). Controlling teaching strategies: Undermining children's self-determination and performance. *Journal of Personality and Social Psychology, 59*, 916–924.

Green-Demers, I., Pelletier, L. G., & Menard, S. (1997). The impact of behavioral difficulty on the saliency of the association between self-determined motivation and environmental behaviors. *Canadian Journal of Behavioural Sciences, 29*, 157–166.

Grolnick, W. S. (2002). *The psychology of parental control: How well-meant parenting backfires*. Hillsdale, NJ: Erlbaum.

Grolnick, W. S., & Ryan, R. M. (1987). Autonomy in children's learning: An experimental and individual differences investigation. *Journal of Personality and Social Psychology, 52*, 890–898.

Grolnick, W. S., & Ryan, R. M. (1989). Parent styles associated with children's self-regulation and competence in school. *Journal of Educational Psychology, 81*, 143–154.

Gurland, S. T., & Grolnick, W. S. (2003). Children's expectancies and perceptions of adults: Effects on rapport. *Child Development, 74*, 1212–1224.

Hardre, P. L., & Reeve, J. (2003). A motivational model of rural students' intentions to persist in, versus drop out of, high school. *Journal of Educational Psychology, 95*, 347–356.

Hayamizu, T. (1997). Between intrinsic and extrinsic motivation: Examination of reasons for academic study based on the theory of internalization. *Japanese Psychological Research, 39*, 98–108.

Iyengar, S. S., & Lepper, M. R. (1999). Rethinking the value of choice: A cultural perspective on intrinsic motivation. *Journal of Personality and Social Psychology, 76*, 349–366.

Jang, H., & Reeve, J. (2003). *Preserving and enhancing students' autonomy by delivering directed instruction in an autonomy-supportive way*. Unpublished manuscript, University of Iowa.

Kashima, Y., Yamaguchi, S., Kim, U. Choi, S., Gelfand, M., & Yuki, M. (1995). Culture, gender, and self: A perspective from individualism–collectivism research. *Journal of Personality and Social Psychology, 69*, 925–937.

Kasser, T., & Ryan, R. M. (1993). A dark side of the American dream: Correlates of financial success as a central life aspiration. *Journal of Personality and Social Psychology, 65*, 410–422.

Kasser, T., & Ryan, R. M. (1996). Further examining the American dream: Differential correlates of intrinsic and extrinsic goals. *Personality and Social Psychology Bulletin, 22*, 80–87.

Kasser, V., & Ryan, R. M. (1999). The relation of psychological needs for autonomy and relatedness to vitality, well-being, and mortality in a nursing home. *Journal of Applied Social Psychology, 29*, 935–954.

Koestner, R., Losier, G. F., Vallerand, R. J., & Carducci, D. (1996). Identified and introjected forms of political internalization: Extending self-determination theory. *Journal of Personality and Social Psychology, 70*, 1025–1036.

Koestner, R., Ryan, R. M., Bernieri, F., & Holt, K. (1984). Setting limits on children's behavior: The differential effects of controlling versus informational styles on intrinsic motivation and creativity. *Journal of Personality, 52*, 233–248.

Kohn, A. (1993). *Punished by rewards: The trouble with gold stars, incentive plans, A's, praise, and other bribes.* Boston: Houghton Mifflin.

Lepper, M. R., & Greene, D. (1975). Turning play into work: Effects of adult surveillance and extrinsic rewards on children's intrinsic motivation. *Journal of Personality and Social Psychology, 31*, 479–486.

Lepper, M. R., & Greene, D. (Eds.) (1978). *The hidden costs of reward.* Hillsdale, NJ: Erlbaum.

Markus, H. R., Kitayama, S., & Heiman, R. J. (1996). Culture and "basic" psychological principles. In E. T. Higgins & A. W. Kruglanski (Eds.), *Social psychology: Handbook of basic principles* (pp. 857–913). New York: Guilford Press.

Mossholder, K. W. (1980). Effects of externally mediated goal setting on intrinsic motivation: A laboratory experiment. *Journal of Applied Psychology, 65*, 202–210.

Mullan, E., & Markland, D. (1997). Variations in self-determination across the stages of change for exercise in adults. *Motivation and Emotion, 21*, 349–363.

Pelletier, L. G., Seguin-Levesque, C., & Legault, L. (2002). Pressure from above and pressure from below as determinants of teachers' motivation and teaching behavior. *Journal of Educational Psychology, 94*, 186–196.

Reeve, J. (1996). *Motivating others: Nurturing inner motivational resources.* Boston: Allyn and Bacon.

Reeve, J. (1998). Autonomy support as an interpersonal motivating style: Is it teachable? *Contemporary Educational Psychology, 23*, 312–330.

Reeve, J. (2002). Self-determination theory applied to educational settings. In E. L. Deci & R. M. Ryan's (Eds.), *Handbook of self-determination theory* (pp. 183–203). Rochester, NY: University of Rochester.

Reeve, J., Bolt, E., & Cai, Y. (1999). Autonomy-supportive teachers: How they teach and motivate students. *Journal of Educational Psychology, 91*, 537–548.

Reeve, J., & Deci, E. L. (1996). Elements of the competitive situation that affect intrinsic motivation. *Personality and Social Psychology Bulletin, 22*, 24–33.

Reeve, J., & Jang, H. (2003). *What autonomy-supportive teachers say and do during instruction.* Unpublished manuscript, University of Iowa.

Reeve, J., Jang, H., Carrell, D., Barch, J., & Jeon, S. (2003). *Enhancing high school students' engagement by increasing teachers' autonomy-supportive instructional strategies.* Unpublished manuscript, University of Iowa.

Reeve, J., Jang, H., Hardre, P., & Omura, M. (2002). Providing a rationale in an autonomy-supportive way as a strategy to motivate others during an uninteresting activity. *Motivation and Emotion, 26*, 183–207.

Reeve, J., Nix, G., & Hamm, D. (2003). Testing models of the experience of self-determination in intrinsic motivation and the conundrum of choice. *Journal of Educational Psychology, 95*, 375-392.

Reis, H. T., Sheldon, K. M., Gable, S. L., Roscoe, J., & Ryan, R. M. (2000). Daily well-being: The role of autonomy, competence, and relatedness. *Personality and Social Psychology Bulletin, 26*, 419–435.

Rogers, C. R. (1969). *Freedom to learn.* Columbus, OH: Charles E. Merrill.

Ryan, R. M. (1982). Control and information in the intrapersonal sphere: An extension of cognitive evaluation theory. *Journal of Personality and Social Psychology, 43*, 450–461.

Ryan, R. M. (1993). Agency and organization: Intrinsic motivation, autonomy and the self in psychological development. In J. Jacobs (Ed.), *Nebraska Symposium on Motivation: Developmental perspectives on motivation* (Vol. 40, pp. 1–56). Lincoln: University of Nebraska Press.

Ryan, R. M. (1995). Psychological needs and the facilitation of integrative processes. *Journal of Personality, 63*, 397–427.

Ryan, R. M., & Connell, J. P. (1989). Perceived locus of causality and internalization: Examining reasons for acting in two domains. *Journal of Personality and Social Psychology, 57*, 749–761.

Ryan, R. M., & Deci, E. L. (2000a). The darker and brighter sides of human existence: Basic psychological needs as a unifying concept. *Psychological Inquiry, 11*, 319–338.

Ryan, R. M., & Deci, E. L. (2000b). Self-determination theory and the facilitation of intrinsic motivation, social development, and well-being. *American Psychologist, 55*, 68–78.

Ryan, R. M., & Deci, E. L. (2000c). When rewards compete with nature: The undermining of intrinsic motivation and self-regulation. In C. Sansone & J. M. Harackiewicz (Eds.), *Intrinsic and extrinsic motivation: The search for optimal motivation and performance* (pp. 13–54). San Diego, CA: Academic Press.

Ryan, R. M., & Deci, E. L. (2001). To be happy or to be self-fulfilled: A review of research and eudaimonic well-being. In S. Fiske (Ed.), *Annual Review of Psychology* (Vol. 52, pp. 141–166). Palo Alto, CA: Annual Reviews, Inc.

Ryan, R. M., & Deci, E. L. (2002). An overview of self-determination theory: An organismic-dialectical perspective. In E. L. Deci & R. M. Ryan (Eds.), *Handbook of self-determination research* (pp. 3–33). Rochester, NY: University of Rochester Press.

Ryan, R. M., & Grolnick, W. S. (1986). Origins and pawns in the classroom: Self-report and projective assessments of individual differences in children's perceptions. *Journal of Personality and Social Psychology, 50*, 550–558.

Ryan, R. M., & La Guardia, J. G. (1999). Achievement motivation within a pressured society: Intrinsic and extrinsic motivations to learn and the politics of school reform. In T. Urdan (Ed.), *Advances in motivation and achievement: Vol. 11* (pp. 45–85). Greenwich, CT: JAI Press.

Ryan, R. M., Mims, V., & Koestner, R. (1983). Relation of reward contingency and interpersonal context to intrinsic motivation: A review and test using cognitive evaluation theory. *Journal of Personality and Social Psychology, 45*, 736–750.

Ryan, R. M., & Powelson, C. (1991). Autonomy and relatedness as fundamental to motivation and education. *Journal of Experimental Education, 60*, 49–66.

Ryan, R. M., Rigby, S., & King, K. (1993). Two types of religious internalization and their relations to religious orientations and mental health. *Journal of Personality and Social Psychology, 65*, 586–596.

Ryan, R. M., & Stiller, J. (1991). The social contexts of internalization: Parent and teacher influences on autonomy, motivation and learning. In P. R. Pintrich & M. L. Maehr (Eds.), *Advances in motivation and achievement: Vol. 7. Goals and self-regulatory processes* (pp. 115–149). Greenwhich, CT: JAI Press.

Ryan, R. M., Vallerand, R. J., & Deci, E. L. (1984). Intrinsic motivation in sport: A cognitive evaluation theory interpretation. In W. F. Straub & J. M. Williams (Eds.), *Cognitive sport psychology* (pp. 231–241). Lansing, NY: Sport Science Associates.

Shapira, Z. (1976). Expectancy determinants of intrinsically motivated behavior. *Journal of Personality and Social Psychology, 34,* 1235–1244.

Sheldon, K. M. (2002). The self-concordance model of healthy goal striving: When personal goals correctly represent the person. In E. L. Deci & R. M. Ryan (Eds.), *Handbook of self-determination research* (pp. 65–86). Rochester, NY: University of Rochester Press.

Sheldon, K. M., & Elliot, A. J. (1999). Goal striving, need-satisfaction, and longitudinal well-being: The self-concordance model. *Journal of Personality and Social Psychology, 76,* 482–497.

Sheldon, K. M., Elliot, A. J., Kim, Y., & Kasser, T. (2001). What is satisfying about satisfying events? Testing 10 candidate psychological needs. *Journal of Personality and Social Psychology, 80,* 325–339.

Sheldon, K. M., & Houser-Marko, L. (2001). Self-concordance, goal attainment, and the pursuit of happiness: Can there be an upward spiral? *Journal of Personality and Social Psychology, 80,* 152–165.

Sheldon, K. M., Ryan, R. M., & Reis, H. T. (1996). What makes for a good day? Competence and autonomy in the day and in the person. *Personality and Social Psychology Bulletin, 22,* 1270–1279.

Skinner, B. F. (1953). *Science and human behavior.* New York: Macmillan.

Skinner, E. A. (1995). *Perceived control, motivation, and coping.* Newbury Park, CA: Sage.

Skinner, E. A., & Belmont, M. J. (1993). Motivation in the classroom: Reciprocal effects of teacher behavior and student engagement across the school year. *Journal of Educational Psychology, 85,* 571–581.

Vallerand, R. J., Fortier, M. S., & Guay, F. (1997). Self-determination and persistence in a real-life setting: Toward a motivational model of high school dropout. *Journal of Personality and Social Psychology, 72,* 1161–1176.

Vallerand, R. J., & Reid, G. (1984). On the causal effects of perceived competence on intrinsic motivation: A test of cognitive evaluation theory. *Journal of Sport Psychology, 6,* 94–102.

Wehmeyer, M. L., Agran, M., & Hughes, C. A. (1998). *Teaching self-determination to students with disabilities: Basic skills for successful transition.* Baltimore: Brookes.

Williams, G. C. (2002). Improving patients' health through supporting the autonomy of patients and providers. In E. L. Deci & R. M. Ryan (Eds.), *Handbook of self-determination research* (pp. 233–254). Rochester, NY: University of Rochester Press.

Williams, G. C., & Deci, E. L. (1996). Internalization of biopsychosocial values by medical students: A test of self-determination theory. *Journal of Personality and Social Psychology, 70,* 115–126.

Williams, G. C., Grow, V. M., Freedman, Z. R., Ryan, R. M., & Deci, E. L. (1996). Motivational predictors of weight loss and weight-loss maintenance. *Journal of Personality and Social Psychology, 70,* 115–126.

Williams, G. C., Rodin, G. C., Ryan, R. M., Grolnick, W. S., & Deci, E. L. (1998). Autonomous regulation and long-term medication adherence in adult outpatients. *Health Psychology, 17,* 269–276.

Zuckerman, M., Porac, J., Lathin, D., Smith, R., & Deci, E. L. (1978). On the importance of self-determination for intrinsically-motivated behavior. *Personality and Social Psychology Bulletin, 4,* 443–446.

CHAPTER 4

MOTIVATION AS PERSONAL INVESTMENT

Martin L. Maehr and Dennis M. McInerney

INTRODUCTION

Awareness of something like "achievement motivation" may not be "as old as dirt," but probably is nearly "as old as sin." And, interestingly enough, it was a concern with religion and its effects that figured significantly in the emergence of the contemporary scientific approach to the study of achievement motivation. In 1904 (see also 1992) renowned German sociologist Max Weber published two articles, later republished in English as a book, *The Protestant Ethic and the Spirit of Capitalism.* Weber hardly spelled out a psychological theory of motivation, but he did provide a framework and a stimulus for the later work of David McClelland.

The study of achievement motivation owes much to the work of McClelland and his associates (Atkinson, 1958, 1964; Atkinson & Feather, 1966; Atkinson & Raynor, 1974; McClelland, 1961; McClelland, Atkinson, Clark, & Lowell, 1953; McClelland, Baldwin, Bronfenbrenner, & Strodbeck, 1958). They suggested that achievement motivation was a personality trait that developed in some people more than others as a result of early socialization experiences, and the emotional concomitants of these experiences.

Big Theories Revisited
Volume 4 in: Research on Sociocultural Influences on Motivation and Learning, pages 61–90.
ISBN: 1-59311-053-7 (hardcover), 1-59311-052-9 (paperback)

As socialization practices were presumed to vary across cultures, McClelland's conceptualization provided a "ready-made" theoretical basis for the examination of achievement motivation in a range of groups, societies, and cultures. As a result, McClelland's work gave impetus to many research programs investigating a range of issues related to achievement motivation in cross-cultural settings.

Specifically, early cross-cultural studies inspired by McClelland typically examined the antecedent–consequent variables associated with the development of achievement motivation among diverse social and cultural groups. Some of these studies were particularly concerned with relationships between achievement motivation and such variables as racial and cultural identity, self-esteem, and academic achievement. Other studies were concerned with the sociocultural antecedents of achievement motivation, including independence training, social class, and acculturative stress. McClelland suggested that achievement behavior was comprised of four distinct but related elements. These were competition with a standard of excellence, affective concern for goal attainment, an evaluation of performance, and some standard for the attainment of a long-term goal. These elements were typically identified in the projective responses to selected TAT cards. In general, this approach categorized individuals as high or low in achievement motivation, and determined those situations that would maximize their performance. McClelland's work, culminating in a massive cross-cultural study on the nature, origins, as well as economic and societal importance of achievement motivation, has framed many of the basic questions of importance even today.

THE INTRODUCTION OF DECISION THEORY

Building on McClelland's description of the highly achievement-motivated person as an entrepreneur, a "moderate" risk-taker, J. W. Atkinson (1964) adapted features of then-current decision theory to model achievement behavior. This work was important for many reasons. First of all, it introduced, or reintroduced, cognitive constructs as major motivational causes. Probability or expectancy of success (Ps) and failure (Pf) came close to making sense of self a major causal construct, a formulation that was later reformulated in terms of causal attributions (Weiner, 1986a, 1986b), furthering the change of focus to social cognitions as a cause of achievement behavior. The examination of the role of attributions not only implicated the self, but as attributional patterns varied for women, minorities, and cultural groups (e.g., Maehr & Nicholls, 1980; Nicholls, 1978, 1980), there emerged questions about the different definitions that individuals might have vis-à-vis situations that might first change how their attributions would lead to task investment—or the role that self, especially sense of competence, might play. Specifically, individuals defined situations differently in ways that made their feelings about self more or less important. Atkinson's work was developed further by Wigfield, Tonks, and Eccles as expectancy value theory (see Chapter 8, this volume). Today, as "goal theory" has emerged as perhaps the dominant conception of achievement, perhaps human motivation more broadly (cf. Pintrich & Schunk, 2002), the interplay of self and purpose have been focal in motivation research.

Within its cultural context, McClelland and Atkinson's conceptualization was (and, to some extent, still is) quite an adequate interpretation of what constitutes achievement motivation. However, few early studies based on McClelland and Atkinson's conceptualization questioned the basic premises of this conceptualization in terms of its cross-cultural validity. In contrast, most studies assumed that the conceptualization, its premises, and its associated methodologies were essentially culturally transferable. Thus, when measures of differences between cultural groups on achievement and achievement motivation constructs were apparent, it was assumed that these reflected significant differences between groups *on the constructs themselves*, rather than reflecting the *applicability* (appropriateness and salience) of the constructs across cultural groups. The non-Western cultural groups examined often performed poorly with respect to the given constructs. The conclusion drawn from such research was that "poor" performance either reflected:

- a deficiency in the group being examined (genetic inferiority, inadequate socialization for achievement), or
- an incongruence and incompatibility between the values and norms held by the dominant cultural group and the assumptions, norms, values, and behaviors of the minority or culturally different group.

Perhaps more importantly, however, such studies often had the effect of "elevating" the goals, perceptions, and behaviors of Western cultural groups to the status of universal norms.

It seems that such an approach, by focusing extensively, almost exclusively, on motivation as a personal "need" that is acquired and established through early socialization processes, provided a limited perspective on the very practical issue of how one motivates others on the job, in school, or in sports activities. Moreover, it also likely, as suggested above, lead to misreadings of motivation (or lack of same) in cross-cultural contexts. Early on, for example, Maehr (1974) pointed out that a "developmental" perspective such as is reflected in McClelland's work, was likely to view the apparent lack of investment in school tasks on the part of cultural minorities, as "deprivation" of a basic potential instead of a difference in orientation that was situationally based. Observations of poor African American children on the basketball courts and street corners of Chicago would hardly suggest a lack of motivation, even a lack of achievement motivation as defined and characterized by McClelland and colleagues. Moderate risk-taking, challenge seeking, and concern with winning or succeeding at challenging tasks was indeed very much present on the playground and in a variety of neighborhood venues—just not as often in schools. Others also pointed out that the apparently lower achievement motivation of women found in some early studies may not have been a function of a lack of motivation, per se, but a realization of the differential role expectations extant for men and women in most societies. Indeed, how well we know that today!

Since this early research a significant amount of evidence has accumulated that indicates sociocultural sources, and modes of expression, of achievement and achievement motivation are not culturally invariant, but related to, and embedded in, cultural contexts as illustrated by Moeller and Kramer (1995), Salili and Hoosain (2002), and Villani (1999). In particular, the emphasis placed on *individual* achievement and success in McClelland's theory is now extensively questioned. In contrast, it is now argued that achievement must be analyzed in its total cultural context, including the various roles, both economic and noneconomic, through which achievement motivation may be directed. A wide range of studies in many different cultural settings supports this view. A common theme identified in these studies is that socialization patterns identified as important to developing achievement motivation in Western contexts (e.g., independence and self-reliance) are clearly not manifest (or, at least, not manifest in the same ways or for the same reasons) in other non-Western cultural contexts. From this research researchers were able to extract both common and differentiating features and then compare cultures on the basis of these features.

The overriding insight, however, might be that it is well to look first at achievement behavior, where it occurs, when, and how. Behavior, like choices made, persistence in these choices: where, when and how do individuals *invest* their personal resources of time, talent, and effort? The framework above acted (and still acts) as a useful starting point for investigating achievement and achievement motivation across cultures. However, this framework needed to be supported by more detailed conceptualizations of achievement and motivation. In response to this need, many theoretical models, which attempted to define such conceptualizations more explicitly, emerged.

Attributional and Cognitive Style Models

Attributional and cognitive style models of achievement motivation stimulated considerable interest into the workings of motivation in educational settings as well as much cross-cultural and cross-ethnic research directed at comparing attributional styles among varying ethnic groups. Some studies were content with transporting the unmodified theoretical constructs to foreign parts in an attempt to assess the attributional style of non-Western groups over a range of concerns such as responsibility, morality and achievement—other research sought to establish the cross-cultural generalizability of theoretical principles through comparative research.

Attribution theory, in general, hypothesizes that achievement motivation is influenced by causal attributions, that is, that attributions play a central role as cognitive mediators of achievement behavior (see Weiner, Chapter 2, this volume). According to early attribution theory (Weiner, 1972), the individual is more or less likely to engage in or withdraw from particular behavior, depending on the attributions the individual makes for success or failure. Each attribution has a concomitant affective reaction that influences the probability of further achievement behavior. According to attribution theory, it is important that individuals attribute the success or failure of previous performance to causes that will positively motivate future performance, and not to ones that will discourage further involvement. It was found through a number of early research programs with American groups (Dweck & Repucci, 1973; Kukla, 1972: Weiner, 1972; Weiner & Kukla, 1970) that people high in achievement motivation generally attribute their successes to ability and effort (internal causes) and failure to lack of effort or external factors, while those low in achievement motivation generally attribute their successes to external causes and exclude effort and ability attributions, and hence experience less pride for their successful performance. These people also attribute their failures to lack of ability rather than to external factors or lack of effort (Bar-Tal, 1978). Weiner (1972) suggested that the major differences between individuals high and low in achievement needs are that individuals in the high motive group are more likely to *initiate* achievement activities, work with greater *intensity, persist* longer in the face of failure, and *choose* more tasks of intermediate difficulty, than persons low in achievement needs (Weiner, 1972). Among factors that were found to influence achievement motivation and attributions are sex differences, ethnic differences, achievement needs, self-esteem, emotional state, reinforcement schedules, and internal–external control perceptions (Bar-Tal, 1978).

For attributional research to derive valid cross-cultural conclusions, two issues needed to be considered. First, there was a need to understand the concepts of success and failure and achievement from differing cultural perspectives, and second, there was a need to investigate the kinds of causal explanations or cognitive systems that members from different cultural backgrounds employ in their attributions of success, failure and achievement. While a large number of studies suggested the cross-cultural relevance of attributional and cognitive style models of research (Faustman & Mathews, 1980; Fry & Ghosh, 1980; Munro, 1979; Nicholls, 1978), many of these studies made the assumption that the instruments used (e.g., "Man in a Frame" box and TAT materials) in fact measure social motives that are relevant culturally to the groups studied. Concepts such as internality–externality and field dependence and independence may have been quite appropriate to guide research within a given cultural context, but little work took place to assess the universal relevance of the dimensions. Without this consideration, research was simply showing that groups differ on the degree to which they reflect specific research constructs. Much early attributional work was also based on the assumption that dimensions such as internality and field independence are more culturally adaptive than externality and field dependence (Rupp & Nowicki, 1978). The belief, for example, that internal–external orientation is a universal continuum linked to academic performance had to be tested in a range of cultures radically different from the achievement-oriented Americans and Europeans. The relatively well-established link between locus-of-control orientation and academic achievement in Western cultures may not stand up under close enquiry in a range of other societies.

Early work by Duda (1980) looked closely at the attributional theory of achievement motivation from a cross-cultural perspective. Her conclusions questioned the cross-cultural generalizability of Weiner's position. Duda suggested that the bipolar nature of the causal dimensions used in attributional theory may be inappropriate with groups such as the Navajo and believed that a continuous rather than a dichotomous dimension would better capture such an orientation. Attribution theory was also founded on several epistemological assumptions about the way people think and perceive their world that Duda challenged. She presented some compelling evidence against the cross-cultural generalizability of these assumptions by considering Navajo beliefs that relate to the attributional concepts of time and causality, orientation to space, linearity of cause and effect, and reality orientation of the world, demonstrating that modes of thinking and perspectives of causality are culturally determined.

Maehr and Nicholls (1980) addressed the problem of developing an attributional model that might form a more adequate basis for future cross-cultural research into achievement motivation. These authors presented two models for consideration. The first model sets out to analyze achievement motivation in terms of the *subjective meaning* of behavior and achievement for a group or the persons who compose that group, that is, it is concerned with the phenomenology of achievement. This phenomenological approach to defining achievement behavior cross-culturally required that the researcher elicit definitions of achievement behavior from people of different cultures rather than imposing inappropriate definitions on their behavior. It also required an analysis of the attributions for achievement. In Western society, research indicated that achievement and success and failure are best thought of as psychological reactions to outcomes, not as objective outcomes, and that the attributions, which produce greatest feelings of pleasure or regret, are ability and effort (Weiner, 1972).

More generally, attributions that enable a person to demonstrate to self or others that one possesses desirable qualities are considered important motivators. Research concerned with examining the antecedents of success and failure across cultures (Duda, 1980; Osgood, Miron, & May, 1975; Salili, Maehr, & Gillmore, 1975; Triandis, 1973) suggested that ability and effort attributions are not necessarily salient to all groups. Maehr and Nicholls (1980) suggested that attribution theory, in its emphasis on ability and effort as the most important causes of perceived success and failure, may be a culture-specific theory. However, it would appear that the general principle of finding out the attributions salient to each group in eliciting feelings of success or failure are important for the cross-cultural researcher. Unfortunately, Maehr and Nicholls did not give any suggestions how this approach, which might be termed emic, may be carried out.

In a second model for research, Maehr and Nicholls refined the attributional model to make it more cross-culturally applicable and attempted to develop a model that would enable the researcher to seek similar behavior in diverse cultures even if such behavior may vary in frequency and in importance across cultures. These authors presented three theoretical definitions of achievement motivation, which emphasized the importance of goals and definitions of self in relationship to such goals, and which were essentially etic in nature while allowing for cross-cultural comparison. The actual content for each dimension was assumed to be emic and is elicited separately from each specific group using culturally relevant techniques. These three positions were:

1. *Ability-oriented motivation.* Characterized by striving to maintain a favorable perception of one's ability to demonstrate competence. That is, the goal is to maximize the subjective probability of attributing high ability to oneself in culturally relevant areas. This approach focused on the goal or function of behavior for the person rather than on the inevitably ambiguous external form of behavior.

2. *Task-oriented motivation.* Behavior where the primary goal is to produce an adequate product or to solve a problem for its own sake rather than to demonstrate ability. Maehr and Nicholls (1980) suggested that there was a class of achievement behavior where people either assume they have the necessary ability to do the task or where the question of their competence is for some reason not salient. In this case the immediate goal is simply to accomplish the task to demonstrate mastery. The goal of maintaining as high a perception of ability as possible may be behind this behavior, but it is not focal in the sense that people are not, during task performance or on completion, attributing outcomes to ability or seeking to demonstrate ability. The completion of the task itself is its own reward, the development of mastery is intrinsically satisfying.

3. *Social approval-oriented motivation.* Behavior where the goal is to maximize the probability of attributing high effort to oneself and minimizing the probability of attributing low effort to oneself in conformity with social approval. This theoretical position is based on the assumption that effort (unlike ability) is seen as voluntary and something that anyone can display. It can, therefore, indicate conformity to norms or virtuous intent rather than superior talent. Conversely, lack of effort may indicate lack of virtuous intent rather than inferior ability.

Essentially, Maehr and Nicholls developed a cognitive view of achievement motivation wherein thought processes about the nature of achievement, the purposes in performing a given act, and the individual's attributions regarding the causes of outcomes mediate achievement behavior. The attributional approach suggested here opened up new possibilities for the cross-cultural study of achievement motivation.

Etic–Emic Model

An important theoretical development, which had significant implications for methodological improvements in cross-cultural research on achievement motivation, was presented by Davidson, Jaccard, Triandis, Morales, and Diaz-Guerrero (1976). These authors suggested an etic–emic model where an individual's behavior is considered a function of his or her intention to perform that behavior and the "habits" of the individual to perform that behavior, that is, the frequency with which the individual has performed the act in the past. An individual's behavioral intention in turn is a function of his or her affect toward performing the act (Aact), his or her beliefs about the consequences of performing that behavior and the evaluation of those consequences (PC)(VC), and the perceived appropriateness of a particular behavior for the subject's specific reference groups (NB) and persons holding similar positions to those held by the subject in the social structure (RB). These last two elements refer to the norms and roles appropriate to a particular group. The subject's personal normative beliefs about what he or she should or ought to do with regard to the behavior of interest (personal norms, PNB) also affect the behavioral intention. The relative importance of Aact, PCVC, NB + RB, and PNB as determinants of behavioral intentions is expected to vary as a function of the type of behavior under consideration and the individual differences (including cultural differences) of the respondents. According to this framework, cultural differences are operationalized not as mean level differences between cultural groups on some dependent measure, but as differences in the within-culture relationship of two or more variables to some dependent variable. That is, cultural differences are implied from different patterns of correlation (Davidson et al., 1976).

According to Malpass (1977), application of this model in different cultural settings requires the following steps:

1. obtaining evaluative (semantic differential) ratings of the particular act under investigation (Aact);
2. eliciting from subjects and other sources the referent persons or groups whose normative influence might be relevant to the performance of this behavior;
3. asking subjects for judgment of the degree to which the respective sources of normative influence believe that the subjects should perform the particular behavior, and the subject's motivation to comply with the wishes of these referents;
4. asking the subjects for a judgment of the degree to which they believe they should perform the particular behavior.

The Aact term is investigated by developing a list of consequences associated with the performance of the particular behavior and asking subjects for their evaluation of each consequence along with their subjective judgment of the probability of each consequence given performance of the act. The sum of the products of the evaluations and probabilities for each consequence defines Aact. The components of this model are assumed to be universal (etic), while the operationalization of these must be culturally specific (emic), that is, the data must be gathered using techniques appropriate to the cultural group, for example, the sum of PCVC presents the calculus for combining subjective probabilities and values, but it does not provide any content in terms of which consequences should be studied.

The major test of this model concerns the degree to which Aact, PCVC, NB + RB, and PNB predict intention to engage in particular behaviors. Davidson and colleagues' 1976 study of fertility-relevant behaviors of a sample of U.S. and Mexican women provides support for this model of behavioral intentions. This model provided a valuable framework for examining achievement and other behavior in cross-cultural contexts. The crucial step was the development of explicit procedures for developing local contents that could be applied in different cultural settings with comparable theoretical meaning (cf. Malpass, 1977).

Davidson (1979) refered to such an approach as the cultural similarities approach, where the researcher looks past content differences in beliefs in an attempt to identify cross-cultural similarities in either *belief and attitude structure, or in the processes whereby beliefs combine to form attitudes*. He stated that this approach has important advantages in that first, only the functional equivalence of measures is required, and second, cultural differences can often be meaningfully interpreted because they tend to appear as a differences in one relationship in the presence of cultural similarities in other relationships. As Davidson states (quoting Malpass, 1977):

> The development of measures that are functionally equivalent is always difficult. However, the difficulty decreases as the strength of the theory or model tested increases. If the terms of the theory are at a high level of abstraction (i.e., not content or method bound) then culturally relevant measures of the theoretical constructs can be constructed.... The construct validity of these measures can, in turn, be investigated within each culture to determine, psychometrically their functional equivalence.... Here again, a strong theoretical framework is a help because it indicates how the newly constructed measure should relate to other variables in the framework. (Davidson, 1979, p. 143)

Two other advantages cited for this approach to research are that it alleviated the problems of culture sampling, and it allowed the selection of groups that would provide the most stringent test of the generalizability of the theory.

Ecological Model

At about the same time as personal investment theory was being developed, Berry (1979, 1980) attempted to redress the balance in cross-cultural research between laboratory-based programs and research set in naturalistic environments by proposing an ecological model for cross-cultural studies. This model (or, at least, its general approach; see, e.g., Bronfenbrenner, 1986a, 1986b) continues to be relevant for contemporary cross-cultural studies as represented by Johnson (1994), Neuman and Celano (2001), and Strohschneider and Guss (1998). Berry suggested that research that is largely based on experiment, with little consideration of the wide range of variables operating in natural environments, holds little value. In order to make the task of effective naturalistic research easier, Berry proposed a multilevel model. This model describes research that moves from a naturalistic–holistic level to a controlled–reductionist level through (a) four environmental contexts—ecological, experiential, performance, and experimental, and (b) four effects—achievements, behaviors, responses, and scores.

The ecological context (also referred to as the natural–cultural habitat) refers to all the relatively permanent characteristics that provide a context for human action. The experiential context is the pattern of recurrent experiences that provide a basis for learning. The performance context is the limited set of environmental circumstances immediate in space and time that may be observed to account for particular behaviors. The experimental context represents those environmental characteristics that are designed by the psychologist to elicit a particular response or test score. The experiential and performance contexts are always nested within the ecological context, while the experimental context may, or may not, be contained within the first three contexts. Berry suggests that the degree to which the experimental context is nested within the other three contexts represents the ecological validity of the experimental task.

Four effects parallel the four contexts described above: achievements, behaviors, responses, and scores. Achievements refer to the complex, long-standing behavior patterns that develop as an adaptive response to the ecological context, and include established and shared patterns of behavior that can be found either in an individual or distributed in a cultural group. Behaviors are those acts that have been learned over time in the experiential context, and include the skills, traits, and attitudes that have been acquired in particular roles, or fostered by specific training or education. Responses, on the other hand, are those "fleeting" performances that occur in response to immediate stimulation or experience. Finally, scores comprise those behaviors that are observed, measured, and recorded during a psychological experiment or testing. Berry (1979, 1980) argues that between each of the four environmental contexts and effects exists a relationship that should be considered in any effective cross-cultural research.

Some attempt was made by Berry (Berry & Annis, 1974) to use this model to examine acculturative stress in three American Indian groups in relationship to ecology, culture, and differentiation. The full scope of the model is not illustrated in this study, although the authors do demonstrate an integration between the ecological and experimental levels.

Dasen (1977) presented a study designed to verify Berry's ecological model within a Piagetian framework. In a cross-cultural study of three cultural groups (Central Eskimos, Australian Aborigines, and Ebrie Africans), Dasen found support for the model, stating that "(n)ot only do these data support the model, they also indicate that relationship between ecology and culture is positive at both ends of the ecological scale, in different areas of operational development." While Berry's model is a very thorough attempt to set up a framework that will maximize the data coming to researchers in the cross-cultural arena, the scope of the dimensions he refers to are more than likely to deter even the keenest of researchers, with the likely result that studies would encompass at least two of the dimensions considered important by Berry, but few that would generate data across the four contexts cited. The complexity of the model therefore limited its usefulness to researchers.

While the complexity of Berry's model may have limited its usefulness to some researchers, the general ecological approach has proved very useful in recent research by Conner (1998), Johnson (1994), and Ogbu and Simons (1998) investigating motivation, achievement, and related constructs. Specifically, such research has arguably produced data with acceptable ecological validity, and has specified a range of experiential, performance, and experimental variables that are associated with motivation and achievement across a range of "natural" habitats.

Goal Theory

Goal theory developed by Ames, Dweck, Nicholls, Pintrich, and Midgley provides a model that enables researchers to identify similar motives in diverse cultures, even if such behavior may vary in frequency and in importance across cultures. Goal theory emphasizes the importance of goals, and definitions of self in relationship to such goals. Goal theory differs from attribution theory in that attribution theory explores perceived reasons for success or failure while trying to succeed, whereas goal theory explores perceived reasons for trying to succeed in the first place. These reasons for trying to succeed are labeled "goals" in the context of goal theory. Some important goals (or goal "orientations") postulated by goal theory are:

- *Ability-oriented (performance) motivation.* Characterized by striving to maintain a favorable perception of one's ability to demonstrate competence.
- *Task-oriented (mastery) motivation.* Characterized by behavior where the focus is on producing a product or solving a problem rather than demonstrating one's competence.
- *Socially-oriented (social) motivation.* Characterized by behavior where the goal is to maximize the probability of attributing high effort to oneself (and minimizing the probability of attributing low effort to oneself) in conformity with perceptions of the probability of gaining social approval, respect, or recognition. This orientation (really a class of orientations) is based on the assumption that effort (unlike ability) is voluntary, and something that anyone can display. It can, therefore indicate conformity to social norms or virtuous intent, which in turn can lead to social approval, respect, or recognition. Conversely, lack of effort in conforming to social norms or virtues may result in a reduced approval, respect, or recognition and is, hence, to be avoided.

Goal theory has provided, and continues to provide, a cogent and coherent platform for investigating cross-cultural issues in achievement and achievement motivation, especially where the purposes for achievement are the focus of investigation. This is because it allows for a range of possible intents (purposes, reasons) for achievement, and for the possibility that the range and salience of possible intents may vary considerably from group to group. As a result, significant cultural differences in goal orientations, and their impact on motivation and achievement, have been noted in a range of studies such as Kaplan and Maehr (1999) and Niles (1998). However, there is also contrary evidence from studies by McInerney and others that suggests that the goals that people espouse, and the effects these goals have on motivation and achievement, may be relatively stable across cultures, for example McInerney, Yeung, and McInerney (2001) and Watkins, McInerney, Lee, Akande, and Regmi (2002).

While these and a number of other theoretical perspectives influenced research on achievement motivation during the 1970s and 1980s, our major focus in this chapter is on personal investment theory. We now wish to briefly describe the theory and then present past and recent research that demonstrates its value as a means of understanding motivation in cross-cultural and socioculturally diverse settings.

A Brief Overview of Personal Investment Theory

Maehr and Braskamp's (1986) original Personal Investment model of achievement motivation built upon and integrated various dimensions from earlier conceptualizations of the nature of motivation described above. Personal investment (PI) theory, as its name implies, stressed that the study of motivation must begin and end with the study of behavior, specifying very carefully the behavior that gave rise to motivational inferences. Personal investment theory is, therefore, concerned with how persons *choose* to invest their energy, talent, and time in particular activities. PI theory is particularly relevant in investigations into how individuals of varying social and cultural backgrounds relate to differing achievement situations. This is because it does not assume that people from a given culture or group will invest effort in the same achievement situations or, if they do, for the same reasons, as those from other cultures and groups. PI theory also emphasizes the role played by social and cultural contexts in determining motivational patterns in performing achievement tasks. Moreover, it is phenomenologically based, and emphasizes the subjective meaning of situations in light of individuals' culturally determined belief systems such as beliefs about self, perceptions of appropriate goals, and perceived alternatives available for pursuing these goals.

PI theory is a social-cognitive theory, as it assumes that the primary antecedents of choice, persistence, and variations in activity levels are thoughts, perceptions, and beliefs that are embedded in cultural and social beliefs about self and situation. Specifically, PI theory designates three basic components of meaning as critical to determining personal investment in specific situations:

- Beliefs about self, referring to the more or less organized collections of perceptions, beliefs, and feelings related to who one is.
- Perceived goals of behavior in given situations, referring to the motivational focus of activity, importantly what the person defines as "success" and "failure" in this situation. Among these goals are task, ego, social solidarity, and extrinsic rewards.
- Perceived alternatives for pursuing these goals, referring to the behavioral alternatives that a person perceives to be available and appropriate (in terms of sociocultural norms and opportunities that exist for the individual) in a given situation.

Each of these components of PI theory may be influenced differentially by the structure of tasks and situations, personal experience and access to information and, importantly, the sociocultural context in which tasks, situations, and persons are embedded. As a model, PI alleviates many of the problems inherent in monocultural research models. In particular, it conceptualizes achievement motivation in terms that recognize the possibility of diverse modes of achievement behavior across cultures and groups. PI theory also strikes a balance between the interaction of personality and situations, while incorporating dimensions (such as locus of control) that have been found useful in analyzing levels of achievement motivation.

PI theory predated goal theory but incorporates within its framework three elements that were to become increasingly the major focus of motivational research in educational settings, namely, mastery (task) goals, ego (performance) goals, and social goals. However, while much goal theory research over the last 20 years has concentrated on comparing and contrasting the effects on behavior of mastery and performance with a much more recent and somewhat belated attempt to broaden goals to include social goals, PI was not only a multiple, goal-oriented theory from its inception, but also included sense of self and action possibility dimensions that made it, potentially, a far richer and more sensitive source of information on the motivational determinants of behavior. This was particularly the case in socioculturally diverse settings. Effectively, PI is far more complex than goal theory, but life and motivated behavior is complex and should not be reduced to simple dimensions.

The essential elements of the personal investment theory perspective were spelled out in an early cross-cultural study of achievement motivation (Fyans, Salili, Maehr, & Desai, 1983). The research reported emerged out of the work on meaning systems and subjective culture conducted by Charles Osgood and his research group (cf. Osgood et al., 1975). Indeed, it was specifically based on a massive amount of cross-cultural data gathered with the "semantic differential" method developed and extensively employed by Osgood and his colleagues. A secondary analysis of these data was conducted to address two basic issues. The first issue was whether one could identify a meaning system, a "factor," that reflected "achievement motivation" similarly across the varied cultural groupings contained in the Osgood and colleagues data set. Such a factor, or "meaning system," was indeed identified. Fyans and colleagues (1983) found support for a cross-cultural factor of achievement very similar to the concept of achievement developed by McClelland. The achievement motivation factor appeared to be relevant regardless of culture. The cross-cultural factor of achievement that was isolated could be described as decidedly masculine in orientation, with the concepts of father and masculinity loading high on the vector. Notably, the factor was associated with concepts that at least in the United States connote an achievement orientation, concepts such as worker, work, and freedom. The concept of knowledge and courage also figured strongly in this cross-cultural factor, and it was found that achievement was conceptually linked to pragmatic end products such as success and power. The authors suggested that an arguably valid cross-cultural standard of achievement meaning was determined, and cultures scoring high and low in this regard could be identified.

A second phase of the research examined the issue of how groups rated high or low on this cross-cultural factor compared on a series of criterial concepts related to this factor; in other words, to determine how the meaning of achievement was differentially constructed within the highest and lowest groups. Among the significant findings were that high-scoring cultures on the cross-cultural achievement factor tend to see success associated with self, initiative, freedom, education, work, and masculinity, while the low-scoring cultures associate success with femininity, devotion, and the past. There was an emphasis on *the future* in high-scoring cultures and an emphasis *on the past* in low-scoring cultures.

Overall, low-scoring cultures tended to view education as a means of confirming old ways rather than ushering in new, with concepts such as competition and champion tied negatively in such cultures. In high-scoring cultures concepts such as competition and champion were connected with achievement. With regard to the criterial concept of self as cause, Fyans and colleagues (1983) found that whereas in high-scoring cultures self seems to be tied to achievement, in low-scoring cultures it is tied to family, cooperation, and love. Fyans and colleagues went on to say that "high-scoring cultures appear to stress achievement, and low-scoring cultures affiliation, a point quite in accord with McClelland's (1961) suggestion in The Achieving Society" (p. 1008). These authors suggested that although a universal factor seemed to be identified, this factor did not seem to have equal relevance for all cultural groups, and that striving for success was likely to take different forms in different cultures. While those who scored high on the cross-cultural factor appeared to view success in terms of demonstrating independent competence, it was found that those who scored low appeared to stress retaining social ties and enhancing interpersonal relationships as the means to success.

The findings of the Fyans and colleagues (1983) study were, then, interesting in a number of respects. The study was initially conducted to consider the cross-cultural variability of motivation. Importantly, however, the results reflected not only variability but also similarity in the construction of achievement and possibly achievement motivation across widely diverse cultural groups. A thorough examination of cross-cultural interpretations of the meaning of achievement indicated in these data suggested a near-universal and widely shared view of achievement and possibly a substantially universal view of achievement motivation. However, instead of attributing this to one specific "need," the results in this study suggested that they may be best attributable to three sociocognitive systems: the self, first of all, some incentive or possibly purposive system and perhaps also a too-seldom-ignored presence of what might be called "normative options" for choosing, acting, thinking, and feeling.

Arguably, these earlier data can be interpreted in accord with current social-cognitive perspectives on motivation, on the one hand. On the other hand, they may also be considered as suggesting that instead of limiting the study of motivation to purpose and self, we need also to consider the perceived "choice options" that individuals acquire and act in terms of as members of a cultural community.

CURRENT CROSS-CULTURAL RESEARCH

While this early work established an empirical as well as conceptual basis for personal investment theory, current efforts have been particularly useful not only in expanding the samples studied but therewith also enhancing the empirical and conceptual basis for the theory. A number of research groups have figured prominently in current work.

Extending the Empirical Base: Enriching the Theory

Probably the largest program of research utilizing the full PI model has been conducted by McInerney and his colleagues, who have not only tested the full model utilizing the Inventory of School Motivation (ISM) and the Facilitating Conditions Questionnaire (FCQ) but, in particular, extended the application of personal investment theory to a variety of cultural groups. The results and conclusions of these studies are multifaceted. First, and foremost, considerable empirical evidence has been amassed to support the dimensions of the Personal Investment model (see, e.g., McInerney, 1990, 1991, 2000; McInerney, Hinkley, Dowson, & Van Etten, 1998; McInerney, Roche, McInerney, & Marsh, 1997; McInerney & Sinclair, 1991;

McInerney, Yeung, & McInerney, 2001; Watkins, McInerney, & Boholst, 2003; Watkins et al., 2002; Watkins, McInerney, & Lee, 2002), which suggests that the range of goal orientations (task, performance, social, and extrinsic), sense of self values (sense of purpose for the future, self-esteem, and self-reliance), and facilitating conditions for action, appear broadly valid and reliable across very diverse sociocultural and cultural groups. The scales based on PI seem to have equivalent statistical validity and reliability across many diverse groups, reveal very few significant differences between groups, and predict in similar ways achievement outcomes across groups. For example, rather than the expected polarities between Anglo, European, Asian, Aboriginal, Middle Eastern, African, and Native American groups on key dimensions such as competition, affiliation, social concern, power, and extrinsic rewards, all groups are very similar in means and standard deviations across the range of scales analyzed across multiple studies. Even where there are significant differences, these are a matter of degree rather than kind, of little practical significance, and often run counter to cultural stereotypes. For example, much of the data indicates that while all groups are relatively low on competitiveness and social power, Anglo groups are relatively lower than others such as Navajo Indians and Australian Aboriginals who are stereotypically presumed to be less competitive and social power seeking than Anglos (see, e.g., McInerney, 2003; McInerney et al., 1997).

The research indicates that, by and large, diverse groups endorse the same educational goals and values as each other. So, for example, mastery goals such as task and effort are strongly endorsed irrespective of the group, while performance goals such as competition and social power are not endorsed. Extrinsic rewards such as token and praise are moderately endorsed. Sense of purpose and self-reliance are also strongly endorsed across all groups.

In multiple regression analyses using scales from the ISM and FCQ, equivalent levels of variance in achievement outcomes such as academic marks and school attendance are explained across widely diverse groups, and key predictors are consistent across all groups. Furthermore, goals and values that are stereotypically used to distinguish between Western and other cultural groups (such as competition, affiliation, social concern, and social power) do not appear to be salient in the school contexts studied. In other words, they don't, in general, predict academic outcomes, and this finding is generalizable across groups. Factors that have been considered important by many as key determinants of indigenous minority student's poor achievement and dropping out of school, such as the supposed mismatch between the school's goals and values and the student's goals and values are, in general, not supported by findings from a range of studies. What clearly emerge as important predictors of student academic achievement across all groups are:

- their values, beliefs, and goals relating to a positive sense of self, in particular the students' positive self-esteem at school (feeling good about themselves as students), sense of purpose (having a goal of doing well at school and getting ahead in life), and sense of reliance (I can do this work);
- their level of mastery motivation, in particular task and effort orientation.

Also emerging from the psychometric analyses are the clear findings that:

- perceived parental support is a major determinant of student academic achievement across all groups
- the degree to which students value education for its instrumental purpose is strongly related to academic achievement (McInerney, 1991, 1994, 1995; McInerney et al., 1997; McInerney & Swisher, 1995).

While there is considerable consistency indicated above in motivational patterns across groups, there were also significant variations. The relative importance of motivational predictors varied within groups and across groups, which provides culturally specific (emic) information with which to explore the motivational characteristics of particular groups. For example, in the McInerney (2003) study, social power is a strong predictor of further education, affect, and valuing education for the Asian group but not for the Aboriginal group. Token is a strong negative predictor of further education for Australian, European, Aboriginal, and Asian groups but not for the European, Navajo, and Middle Eastern groups. Social concern varies in its salience across the three outcomes and six groups in the study. Competition appears to be salient for all groups (except Middle Eastern) for valuing education, but not for affect toward school or desire for further education. Affiliation and praise appear to be relatively unimportant as predictors in the school setting across all outcomes and all groups.

Accompanying the psychometric research is a series of large-scale qualitative interviews also based on PI (McInerney, McInerney, Ardington, & De Rachewiltz, 1997; McInerney, McInerney, Bazeley, & Ardington, 1998). These interviews reveal the complex forces that operate in molding school motivation and in particular focus on the perceived options available to students and how these options moderate motivation in school settings. In particular, the interviews reveal the dilemmas and shifting value orientations that occur as children from a variety of cultural groups attempt, on the one hand, to preserve cultural traditions, while on the other seek to modernize through education in which alternative and sometimes competing values are seen to have a place. Clearly emerging from the qualitative interviews is the importance of mastery goals and social concern, and to a lesser extent, affiliation, recognition, and praise, across all groups. In contrast, emerging from the interviews is the relative unimportance (and negative valuing) of competition, social power, rewards, and tokens, again across *all* groups. Parental and community support for education and learning is consistently mentioned as important, as are the norms and role beliefs held by the students. Students argue that in order to feel motivated it is important for them to believe that it is "appropriate" for them to be successful at school; that they like and value school; and that they have access to models of successful schooling (either students, parents, or community members who do well at school and influence the student) (McInerney et al., 1997, 1998). According to the students themselves, students who espouse these norms and role beliefs, and have access to successful models, are more likely to be successful at school.

The Inventory of School Motivation (ISM) dimensions utilized in the quantitative studies discussed earlier were also critically evaluated by the interviewees for cultural relevance and perceived importance in predicting school motivation and success. All dimensions of the ISM were considered culturally relevant. Dimensions that were considered most important to determining students' level of motivation were task (intrinsic motivation) and sense of purpose. These qualitative results support the results of the psychometric studies.

Personal Investment and Learning Strategies

A recent review of classroom and laboratory studies (Covington, 2000) concluded that there was adequate empirical support for the theoretical propositions that mastery goals are associated with deeper, meaning-oriented learning strategies, whereas performance goals tend to be associated with superficial, rote-level processing. Covington (2000) warned, however, that the bulk of the research he reviewed is based on mainstream American students and there is little evidence that the theory and these findings can be generalized to other cultural groups. In an extension of the McInerney research, Watkins and colleagues (Watkins, McInerney, & Lee, 2002; Watkins et al., 2002) not only tested using factor analysis the validity of the Inventory of School Motivation (based on translation for a Chinese sample), but also set out to examine the construct validity of the dimensions by finding out if they correlated as predicted with independent measures of Intellectual Self-Esteem and Surface, Deep, and Achieving Learning Strategies (Biggs, 1987; Entwistle & Ramsden, 1983). In particular, they tested the hypotheses that Intellectual Self-Esteem (10 items measuring the intellectual self from the Chinese Adolescent Self-Esteem Scale; Cheng & Watkins, 2000) would correlate highly with the ISM Self-Reliance and Self-Esteem scales; that the mastery oriented scales would correlate significantly and positively with the Leaning Process Questionnaire Deep and Achieving Strategy scales, but negatively, if anything, with the Surface Strategy scale; and that performance-oriented scales, including Extrinsic Motivation, would be the only ISM scales to correlate significantly positively with the Surface Strategy scale.

Deep Learning Strategies are concerned with the intention to understand by means of interrelating ideas, reading widely, and thinking independently and critically. Surface Learning Strategies, on the other hand, tend to be associated with fear of failure and an external locus of control, and a context characterized by boredom or fear, and assessment methods such as multiple-choice items, perceived as rewarding low-quality learning. The third commonly found strategy is Achieving, where students tend to work hard and be well organized and use whatever specific strategy they feel will maximize their chances of high marks, be it gaining mastery of what is to be learned or, in extreme cases, cheating. Adoption of this strategy is thought to be dependent on both the students' need for success and their perception of the assessment task.

As expected, the mastery-oriented scales correlated most highly with the Deep and Achieving Strategy scales, although performance- and social-oriented scales also correlated positively with the Deep and Achieving scales, but not so strongly. The mastery-oriented scales also correlated negatively and significantly with the Surface Strategy scale. Only the extrinsic motivation scale correlated positively ($p < .01$) with the Surface Strategy scale, indicating that those engaging in surface strategies were more likely to say they value extrinsic rewards for their study. All other significant correlations with Surface Strategy were negative, although it is interesting to note that, in general, performance-oriented scales were unrelated to Surface Strategies. The three Sense of Self scales (Self-Reliance, Self-Esteem, and Sense of Purpose) all correlated as predicted, quite highly and positively with the Deep and Achieving Strategy scales. Self-Reliance and Self-Esteem were also negatively and significantly correlated with the Surface Strategy scale.

The mastery-oriented scales were most strongly positively related to Intellectual Self, although the performance- and social-oriented scales were also positively related to Intellectual Self. However, the two strongest correlations were, as expected, with Self-Reliance and Self-Esteem. Sense of Purpose was also positively related to Intellectual Self.

In summary, this study demonstrated the usefulness of the Inventory of School Motivation and the Personal Investment model on which it is based for drawing a motivational profile on Chinese-speaking students in Hong Kong, and for examining the relationship of this profile to learning strategies. It provided some limited support for the contention that mastery but not performance goals would be related to Deep Learning Strategies, as mastery-oriented goals were most strongly correlated with Deep Strategies. While the mastery-oriented scales were clearly negatively related to Surface

Strategies, which supports the researchers' hypothesis, there was, rather than a positive relationship, no relationship between the performance-oriented scales and Surface Strategies (except for Extrinsic Motivation, discussed above).

This study was further extended to a range of other cultural groups including students from Malawi, Nepal, South Africa (black and white samples), and Zambia, as well as Hong Kong (Watkins et al., 2002). Initial factor-analytic studies with these groups supported the validity of the Inventory of School Motivation for use with these very diverse groups. The reliability estimates on each scale were also very similar across the groups, and in general quite high, although there was some variability across groups, with the Nepalese group recording lower reliabilities across most scales including the Learning Process Questionnaire scales. While initially this might suggest that either there was a language difficulty (the ISM was administered in Nepalese) or that the ISM was less valid than for the other groups, the overall evidence is that on 12 of the 17 scales utilized in the study the reliability estimates for the Nepalese were very similar to the other groups. It is interesting to note that the scales that seemed to be least reliable for the Nepalese group were those dealing with more collectivist values such as affiliation and social concern. The reliability for Self-Reliance was also low for this group. The reasons for these low reliabilities need to be further investigated.

In order to examine the relationship of the ISM scales to Deep, Surface, and Achieving Learning Strategies, a series of multiple regressions were conducted with the scales of the LPQ as dependent variables and the scales of the ISM as predictor variables. Across all samples the combination of ISM scales were able to predict Deep, Achieving, and Surface Strategies quite well, although least well for the Surface Strategy scale. Mastery-oriented scales, Sense of Purpose, and Self-Reliance were consistently strong predictors for Deep and Achieving Strategies across most samples. Indeed, most of the other scales contributed little to the variance explained. The results for the Surface Strategy are not as clear cut, with performance-oriented motivation, extrinsic motivation, Self-Reliance, and Self-Esteem providing the highest beta weights across most samples.

While the authors had expected that a Deep approach to learning might be triggered by motivation impetus based not only on mastery but also on a mix of intense personal ambition, family face, peer support, and/or material reward for various groups in the study, the scales significantly related to Deep, Achieving, and Surface strategies were remarkably similar across groups. Considering the diversity of the samples utilized in the study, it does seem that motivational variables relate in similar ways to the learning strategies students adopt in a range of cultures. The results of this study are consistent with previous Western research showing that Mastery goals tend to be associated with deeper, better-organized learning strategies. While there is some evidence that performance-oriented goals are associated with Surface Learning, the evidence is not as strong. Given the fact that the Surface Strategy scale had a lower reliability than either the Deep or Achieving Strategies across all groups, the lack of definitive results regarding the relationship of the motivational scales to Surface Learning might reflect the inadequacy of the Surface Strategy scale as an outcome measure.

"ORGANIZATIONAL CULTURE" AND PERSONAL INVESTMENT

While McInerney and his colleagues took the lead in the continued development of PI theory in the examination of cultures across various societal groups, Maehr and others (e.g., Maehr & Braskamp, 1986; Maehr & Midgley, 1991, 1996) pursued a different tack: the study of "organizational culture." Arguably, the formulation proved useful in this enterprise as well.

Conceptualizing Organizational Culture

Following a trend of the time, the concept of "culture" was applied to organizations: places of work as well as schools (e.g., Maehr & Braskamp, 1986). Not surprisingly, the general Personal Investment framework was increasingly applied to the study of "organizational culture" in general and school culture in particular (e.g., Maehr & Midgley, 1991, 1996) during this period. Especially important in this regard was that this eventuated in a serious and systematic consideration of whether there was an "optimum culture" for personal development. Most, if not all, of this concern with an "optimal culture" for personal development focused on schools and there the specific issue was whether a school that stressed Mastery goals was preferable to a school or classroom that stressed Performance goals so far as the degree and quality of personal investment was concerned.

Especially of interest in this context is the issue of goals and certain presumed "culturally different" and possibly therewith "disadvantaged" groups. Much of the argument in this regard revolved around the question of how Task/Mastery and Performance goals were more or less facilitative in meeting the goals of learning. The underlying argument in this regard related to how cultures or learning environments that stressed Performance goals were likely to make one's self salient. Related to the literature on self-awareness there was some basis for arguing that self-awareness was a "two-edged sword." While "self-awareness" might not be debilitating, even be facilitative, if one felt positively about oneself vis-à-vis performance of the achievement task at hand, it could be—was likely to be—problematic if the individual was ambivalent about her abilities or acceptance within the group. Several lines of research seemed to underline this potential. First, there was an established literature on self-awareness that indicated the varying role that such awareness might play in behavior. Related to this was a literature on social stigma, including especially the work of Steele (e.g., Steele & Aronson, 1995), particularly as it dealt with members of an ethnic or cultural minority for which there existed harsh stereotypes vis-à-vis achievement in a given domain, such as education.

Arguably, the research prompted in part by PI theory may be of relevance yet today. Particularly so, as the focus of much of the work on "goal theory" has tended to follow an individual difference paradigm and paid only small and occasional attention to the social and interpersonal context of achievement. But it might be most especially relevant as it refers very specifically to the fact that one of the critical facets of motivation is the perceived options from which the individual must choose in acting. Motivation theory today focuses exclusively on Purpose and Self, important antecedents of motivation, to be sure. But there is also the fact that individuals always act in terms of viable and culturally allowable options. This was emphasized in the work of Triandis (e.g., 1973, 1977, 1980a, 1980b, 1995, 2001) and embodied in his theory of "subjective culture." It may also be viewed as embedded in the work of Markus and Kitayama (e.g., 1991a, 1991b, 1994). Arguably, however, it is no more salient than when expressed as a major factor in a choice and decision theory of motivation: When a person acts, invests in a particular activity, decides to do "this" rather than "that" with more or less enthusiasm and involvement—the basis of the decision is the set of options perceived and deemed acceptable. Indeed, such perceptions of options may well be at the heart of cross-cultural differences in motivation and achievement—just as much at the heart as self and purpose.

A COMPLEX PERSPECTIVE:
IS IT JUSTIFIED, USEFUL, AND PRACTICAL?

In general, social-cognitive theories of motivation (in particular, personal investment theory) have alerted researchers to the ways in which motivation and achievement may be differentially constructed across cultural (and other) contexts. However, a significant remaining question from this perspective is: Is there a single motivational environment that can be constructed in most applied settings (e.g., schools, hospitals, businesses, government organizations), especially when these settings are typically diverse in many ways with respect to individuals' age, sex, cultural backgrounds, and social economic status? This is an important question because a range of different motivational environments cannot be easily generated in most applied settings. Theory and research, including much cited above, has gone a considerable distance in demonstrating that mastery goals are preferable to ability performance goals. This is because mastery goals focus an individual's attention on the task(s) to be completed, rather than on the individual's perceived ability (or otherwise) to complete the task(s). Psychologically, this appears to "free" individuals to perform at optimal levels, even in the face of difficulties. Indeed, it might also be that performance goals are dysfunctional in many applied settings, although not in all cases (cf. Pintrich & Schunk, 2002). More recently, social goals have also been shown to have adaptive effects on an individual's engagement in a variety of achievement and social situations (e.g., Dowson & McInerney, 1997, 2001; Urdan & Maehr, 1995; Wentzel, 1991a, 1991b). These social goals may be particularly relevant in non-Western cultural settings where the social dimensions of motivation and achievement may be more salient than in Western settings.

Finally, two questions can be asked about personal investment and the research it has generated. First, does a multiple goal, sense of self, and facilitating conditions perspective add anything to our understanding of student motivation and achievement, and second, does cultural background make a difference? Clearly, a complex model such as Personal Investment does add considerable depth to our understanding of student motivation in school settings. Using such an approach enables us to see the relative importance of a complex set of motivational goals to students, and how they interact with sense of self and the action possibilities available to students in their real-life settings. All of the variables considered in the research reported in this chapter help explain, to varying degrees, variance in academic outcomes. It is more than likely that in noneducational settings, such as sporting, social, and familial settings, the relative salience of the variables may vary, and this is worth studying.

The consistency in the salience of mastery-oriented motivation and sense-of-self variables, as well as the importance of future perspective and parents to students' engagement in schooling across widely divergent cultural groups, provides evidence that these factors may be universal (etic) in their salience. On the other hand, the different patterning of significant predictors across cultural groupings provides culturally specific (emic) information with which to explore the unique motivational characteristics of particular groups.

These patterns of predictors across cultural groupings in which there is both consistency (perhaps universality) and variability give the researcher much rich information with which to explore the emics and etics of student motivation in school settings. This would not be possible unless a complex perspective was taken. In other words, the nature of the outcome measured is differentially related to the range of variables considered and this varies across cultures. While evidence suggests few mean differences between groups on many of the dimensions, it appears that culture does matter when these dimensions are used to predict outcomes. The possibilities for understanding motivation uncovered in these analyses would not have been possible if only mastery and performance goals, for example, had been considered.

A REAFFIRMATION OF
PERSONAL INVESTMENT THEORY

And so we close with the suggestion that we may have lost something very important by limiting our focus in the study of motivation to the self. It is of course well that we study this as well as purpose—if we are to understand personal investment in our culture or in any other culture. Personal investment theory and research made a start here. It is well that motivation researchers endeavor to redeem that start and make "perceived options" as well as self and purpose focal elements of their work on culture and motivation.

REFERENCES

Atkinson, J. W. (Ed.). (1958). *Motives in fantasy, action and society*. Princeton, NJ: Van Nostrand.

Atkinson, J. W. (1964). *An introduction to motivation*. Princeton, NJ: Van Nostrand.

Atkinson, J. W., & Feather, N. T. (Eds) (1966). *A theory of achievement motivation*. London: Wiley.

Atkinson, J. W., & Raynor, J. O. (1974). *Motivation and achievement*. Washington, DC: C. H. Winston.

Bar-Tal, D. (1978). Attributional analysis of achievement-related behavior. *Review of Educational Research, 48*, 259–271.

Berry, J. W. (1979). Research in multicultural societies. Implications of cross-cultural methods. *Journal of Cross-Cultural Psychology, 10*, 415–434.

Berry, J. W. (1980). Ecological analysis for cross-cultural psychology. In N. Warren (Ed.), *Studies in cross-cultural psychology* (Vol. 2). London: Academic Press.

Berry, J. W., & Annis, R. C. (1974). Acculturative stress. The role of ecology, culture, differentiation. *Journal of Cross-Cultural Psychology, 5*, 382–405.

Biggs, J. B. (1987). *Student approaches to learning and studying: A research monograph*. Melbourne: Australian Council for Educational Research.

Bronfenbrenner, U. (1986a). Ecology of the family as a context for human development: Research perspectives. *Developmental Psychology, 22*, 723-742.

Bronfenbrenner, U. (1986b). Alienation and the four worlds of childhood. *Phi Delta Kappan, 67*, 430, 432-436.

Cheng, C., & Watkins, D. (2000). Age and gender invariance of self-concept factor structure: An investigation of a newly developed Chinese self-concept instrument. *International Journal of Psychology, 35*, 186–193.

Conner, R. F. (1998). Toward a social ecological view of evaluation use. *American Journal of Evaluation, 19*, 237–241.

Covington, M. V. (2000). Goal theory, motivation, and school achievement: An integrative review. *Annual Review of Psychology, 51*, 171–200.

Dasen, P. R. (1977). Are cognitive processes universal? A contribution to cross-cultural Piagetian psychology. In N. Warren (Ed.), *Studies in cross-cultural psychology*. London: Academic Press.

Davidson, A. R. (1979). Culture and attitude change. In A. J. Marsella, R. G. Tharp, & T. J. Ciborowski (Eds.), *Perspectives on cross-cultural psychology*. New York: Academic Press.

Davidson, A. R., Jaccard, J. J., Triandis, H. C., Morales, M. L., & Diaz-Guerrero, R. (1976). Cross cultural model testing: toward a solution of the etic-emic dilemma. *International Journal of Psychology, 11*, 1–3.

Dowson, M., & McInerney, D. M. (1997, March). *Psychological parameters of students' social and academic goals: A qualitative investigation*. Paper presented at the annual meeting of the American Educational Research Association, Chicago.

Dowson, M., & McInerney, D. M. (2001) Psychological parameters of students' social and work avoidance goals: A qualitative investigation. *Journal of Educational Psychology, 93*, 35–42.

Duda, J. L. (1980). Achievement motivation among Navajo Indians. *Ethos, 8*, 316–331.

Dweck, C. S., & Repucci, N. D. (1973). Learned helplessness and reinforcement in children. *Journal of Personality and Social Psychology, 25*, 109–116.

Entwistle, N. J., & Ramsden, P. (1983). *Understanding student learning*. London: Croom Helm.

Faustman, W. O., & Mathews, W. M. (1980). Perception of personal control and academic achievement in Sri Lanka: Cross cultural generality of American research. *Journal of Cross-Cultural Psychology, 11*, 245–252.

Fry, P. S., & Ghosh, R. (1980). Attributions of success and failure: Comparison of cultural differences between Asian and Caucasian children. *Journal of Cross-Cultural Psychology, 11*, 343–363.

Fyans, L. G., Salili, F., Maehr, M. L., & Desai, K. A. (1983). A cross-cultural exploration into the meaning of achievement. *Journal of Personality and Social Psychology, 44*, 1000–1013.

Johnson, G. M. (1994). An ecological framework for conceptualizing educational risk. *Urban Education, 29*, 34–49.

Kaplan, A., & Maehr, M. L. (1999). Achievement goals and student well-being. *Contemporary Education Psychology, 24*, 330-358.

Kukla, A. (1972). Attribution determinants of achievement-related behavior. *Journal of Personality and Social Psychology, 21*, 166–174.

Maehr, M. L. (1974). Culture and achievement motivation. *American Psychologist, 29*, 887–896.

Maehr, M. L., & Braskamp, L. A. (1986). *The motivation factor: A theory of personal investment*. Lexington, MA: Lexington.

Maehr, M. L., & Midgley, C. (1991). Enhancing student motivation: A school-wide approach. *Educational Psychologist, 26*, 399–427.

Maehr, M. L., & Midgley, C. (1996). *Transforming school cultures*. Boulder, CO: Westview Press.

Maehr, M. L., & Nicholls, J. C. (1980). Culture and achievement motivation. A second look. In N. Warren (Ed.), *Studies in cross-cultural psychology* (Vol. 2). London: Academic Press.

Malpass, R. S. (1977). Theory and method in cross-cultural psychology. *American Psychologist, 2,* 1069–1079.

Markus, H. R., & Kitayama, S. (1991a). The cultural construction of self and emotion: Implications for cognition, emotion, and motivation. *Psychological Review, 98,* 224–253.

Markus, H. R., & Kitayama, S. (1991b). Cultural variation in the self-concept. In J. Strauss & G. R. Goethals (Eds.), *The self: Interdisciplinary approaches.* New York: Springer-Verlag.

Markus, H. R., & Kitayama, S. (1994). The cultural constuction of self and emotion: Implications for social behavior. In S. Kitayama & H. R. Markus (Eds.), *Emotions and culture: Empirical studies of mutual influences.* Washington, DC: American Psychological Association.

McClelland, D. C. (1961). *The achieving society.* Princeton, NJ: Van Nostrand.

McClelland, D. C., Atkinson, J. W., Clark, R. A., & Lowell, E. L. (1953). *The achievement motive.* New York: Appleton-Century-Crofts.

McClelland, D. C., Baldwin, A. L., Bronfenbrenner, U., & Strodbeck, F. L. (1958). *Talent and society. New perspectives in the identification of talent.* Princeton, NJ: Van Nostrand.

McInerney, D. M. (1990). The determinants of motivation for urban Aboriginal students in school settings: A cross-cultural analysis. *Journal of Cross-Cultural Psychology, 21,* 474–495.

McInerney, D. M. (1991). Key determinants of motivation of urban and rural non-traditional Aboriginal students in school settings: Recommendations for educational change. *Australian Journal of Education, 35,* 154–174.

McInerney, D. M. (1994). Psychometric perspectives on school motivation and culture. In E. Thomas (Ed.), *International perspectives on culture and schooling.* London: Institute of Education, London University.

McInerney, D. M. (1995). Goal theory and indigenous minority school motivation: Relevance and application. In M. L. Maehr & P. R. Pintrich (Eds.), *Advances in motivation and achievement: Culture, motivation, and achievement* (Vol. 9). Greenwich CT: JAI Press.

McInerney, D. M. (2000, July). *Relationships between motivational goals, sense of self, self-concept and academic achievement for aboriginal students.* Paper presented at the Aboriginal Studies Association Annual Conference, Sydney.

McInerney, D. M. (2003). *School motivation in cultural context: A multiple goal analysis.* Paper presented at the EARLI conference, Padua, Italy.

McInerney, D. M., Hinkley, J., Dowson, M., & Van Etten, S. (1998). Aboriginal, Anglo, and immigrant Australian students' motivational beliefs about personal academic success: Are there cultural differences? *Journal of Educational Psychology, 90*(4), 621–629.

McInerney, D. M., McInerney, V., Ardington, A., & De Rachewiltz, C. (1997, March). *School success in cultural context: Conversations at Window Rock. Preliminary Report.* Paper presented at the annual meeting of the American Educational Research Association, Chicago.

McInerney, D. M., McInerney, V., Bazeley, P., & Ardington, A. (1998, April). *Parents, peers, cultural values and school processes: What has most influence on motivating indigenous minority students' school achievement? A qualitative study.* Paper presented at the annual meeting of the American Educational Research Association, San Diego, CA.

McInerney, D. M., Roche, L. A., McInerney, V., & Marsh, H. W. (1997). Cultural perspectives on school motivation: The relevance and application of goal theory. *American Educational Research Journal, 34,* 207–236.

McInerney, D. M., & Sinclair, K. E. (1991). Cross-cultural model testing: Inventory of school motivation. *Educational and Psychological Measurement, 51,* 123–133.

McInerney, D. M., & Sinclair, K. E. (1992). Dimensions of school motivation: A cross-cultural validation study. *Journal of Cross-Cultural Psychology, 23,* 389–406.

McInerney, D. M., & Swisher, K. G. (1995). Exploring Navajo motivation in school settings. *Journal of American Indian Education, 34*(3), 28–51.

McInerney, D. M., Yeung, S. Y., & McInerney, V. (2001) Cross-cultural validation of the Inventory of School Motivation (ISM). *Journal of Applied Measurement, 2,* 134–152.

Moeller, A., & Kramer, E. (1995). The teaching of culture and language in the second language classroom: Focus on the learner. *International Journal of Educational Research, 23,* 571–652.

Munro, D. (1979). Locus-of-control attribution. Factors among blacks and whites in Africa. *Journal of Cross-Cultural Psychology, 10,* 157–172.

Neuman, S. B., & Celano, D. (2001). Access to print in low-income and middle-income communities: An ecological study of four neighborhoods. *Reading Research Quarterly, 36(1),* 8–26.

Nicholls, J. B. (1978). The development of causal attributions and evaluative responses to success and failure in Maori and Pakeha children. *Developmental Psychology, 14,* 687–688.

Nicholls, J. B. (1980). A re-examination of boy's and girl's causal attributions for success and failure based on New Zealand data. In L. J. Fyans (Ed.), *Achievement motivation: Recent trends in theory and research.* New York: Plenum Press.

Niles, S. (1998). Achievement goals and means: A cultural comparison. *Journal of Cross-Cultural Psychology, 29,* 656–667.

Ogbu, J. U., & Simons, H. D. (1998). Voluntary and involuntary minorities: A cultural-ecological theory of school performance with some implications for education. *Anthropology and Education Quarterly, 29,* 55–88.

Osgood, C. E. Miron, M., & May, W. (1975). *Cross-cultural universals of affective meaning.* Urbana: University of Illinois press.

Pintrich, P. R., & Schunk, D. H. (2002). *Motivation in education: Theory, research, and applications* (2nd ed.). Upper Saddle River, NJ: Merrill Prentice Hall

Rupp, M., & Nowicki, S. (1978). Locus of control among Hungarian children. Sex, age, school achievement, and teachers' ratings of developmental congruence. *Journal of Cross-Cultural Psychology, 9,* 359–365.

Salili, F., & Hoosain, R. (2002). Cross-cultural differences in affective meaning of achievement: A semantic differential study. In D. M. McInerney & S. Van Etten (Eds.), *Research on sociocultural influences on motivation and learning* (Vol. 2). Greenwich, CT: Information Age.

Salili, F., Maehr, M. L., & Gillmore, G. (1976). Achievement and morality: a cross-cultural analysis of causal attribution and evaluation. *Journal of Personality and Social Psychology, 33,* 327–337.

Steele, C., & Aaronson, J. (1995). Stereotype threat and the intellectual test performance of African Americans. *Journal of Personality and Social Psychology, 69*, 797–811.

Strohschneider, S., & Guss, D. (1998). Planning and problem solving: Differences between Brazilian and German students. *Journal of Cross-Cultural Psychology, 29*, 695–716.

Triandis, H. (1995). Motivation and achievement in collectivist and individualist cultures. *Advances in motivation and achievement* (Vol. 9). Greenwich, CT: JAI Press.

Triandis, H. C. (1973) Subjective Culture and economic development. *International Journal of Psychology, 8*, 163–180.

Triandis, H. C. (1977). *Interpersonal behavior.* Monterey, CA: Brooks/Cole.

Triandis, H.C. (1980a). Introduction to handbook of cross-cultural psychology. In H. C. Triandis and W. W. Lambert (Eds.), *Handbook of cross-cultural psychology* (Vol. 1). Boston: Allyn & Bacon.

Triandis, H. C. (1980b). Value, attitudes and interpersonal behavior. In M. M. Page (Ed.), *Nebraska Symposium on Motivation: Vol. 1. Beliefs, attitudes and values.* Boston: Allyn & Bacon.

Triandis, H. C. (2001). Modern education needs cross-cultural psychology. In D. M. McInerney & S. Van Etten (Eds.), *Research on Sociocultural influences on motivation and learning* (Vol. 1). Greenwich, CT: Information Age.

Urdan, T. C., & Maehr, M. L. (1995). Beyond a two-goal theory of motivation and achievement: A case for social goals. *Review of Educational Research, 65*, 213–243.

Villani, C. J. (1999). Community culture and school climate. *School Community Journal, 9*, 103–05.

Watkins, D., McInerney, D., & Boholst, F. (2003). The reliability and validity of the Inventory of School Motivation: A Filipino investigation. *Asian-Pacific Education Researcher, 12*, 87-100.

Watkins, D., McInerney, D., & Lee, C. (2002). Assessing the school motivation of Hong Kong students. *Psychologia, 45*, 144–154.

Watkins, D., McInerney, D. M., Lee, C., Akande, A., & Regmi, M. (2002). Motivation and learning strategies. A cross-cultural perspective. In D. M. McInerney & S. Van Etten (Eds.), *Research on sociocultural influences on motivation and learning* (Vol. 2). Greenwich, CT: Information Age.

Weber, M. (1904). Die protestantische Ethik und der Geist des Kapitalismus [The Protestant ethic and the spirit of Capitalism, 1930]. In T. T. Parsons (Ed.), *Archiv fur Sozial Wissenschatt und Sozial Politik; 1904, 1905* (Vol. 20, pp. 1–54; Vol. 21, pp. 1–110). New York: Scribner.

Weber, M. (1992). *The Protestant ethic and the spirit of capitalism* (T. T. Parsons, Trans.). London: Routledge.

Weiner, B. (1972). Attribution theory, achievement motivation and the educational process. *Review of Educational Research, 42*, 203–215.

Weiner, B., (1986a). An attributional theory of achievement motivation and emotion. *Psychological Review, 92*, 548–573.

Weiner, B. (1986b). An attributional theory of motivation and emotion. New York: Springer-Verlag.

Weiner, B., & Kukla, A. (1970). An attributional analysis of achievement motivation. *Journal of Personality and Social Psychology, 15*, 1–20.

Wentzel, K. R. (1991a). Social and academic goals at school: Motivation and achievement in context. In M. L. Maehr & P. R. Pintrich (Eds.), *Advances in motivation and achievement. A research annual* (Vol. 7). Greenwich, CT: JAI Press.
Wentzel, K. R. (1991b). Social competence at school: Relation between social responsibility and academic achievement. *Review of Educational Research, 61*, 1–24.

CHAPTER 5

SELF-WORTH THEORY GOES TO COLLEGE
Or Do Our Motivation Theories Motivate?

Martin V. Covington

Our biggest problem here is that students are just not motivated. They just don't seem to care, they are not interested in learning. I can't teach students like this.
—*Faculty member (Pintrich, 1991)*

Well, to me, it is up to the professor to motivate me. I mean, I want to learn and all, but sometimes the material is so boring and the professor just loves it and they go on and on about meaningless things
—*College student (Pintrich, 1991)*

Big Theories Revisited
Volume 4 in: Research on Sociocultural Influences on Motivation and Learning, pages 91–114.
Copyright © 2004 by Information Age Publishing, Inc.
All rights of reproduction in any form reserved.
ISBN: 1-59311-053-7 (hardcover), 1-59311-052-9 (paperback)

INTRODUCTION

The concern that animates this volume is that our motivational theories do not always take full account of the social, cultural, and individual contexts in which these theories are intended to apply. In short, our theories often remain abstractions, aloof from the demands of application. This concern is well founded. Many of our research efforts are limited to the testing of propositions flowing from our theories in laboratory contexts far from the needs of teachers and students. Indeed, part of the problem is that researchers have all too often invited themselves into classrooms, not as supplicants or even as guests, but to use classrooms as laboratories to pursue answers to questions that teachers may see as arcane, distant, and often quite divorced from the practical realities of schooling.

The dictum famously advanced by Kurt Lewin in the early 20th century, that "there is nothing so practical as a good theory," reminds us anew of our larger responsibilities as theoreticians. If good practice depends on the application of sound theoretical principles—and it certainly does—then our theories need be tested in the crucible of real-life situations, which means *contextualizing* our efforts to gauge the relevance of theory to complex educational environments.

Arguably, the most important step in the process of contextualizing our theory building is to take heed of the voices of those clients whom we ultimately serve: students and teachers. There is good reason to wonder if students understand the rationale behind those theories of motivation and learning intended to guide their education, and whether our theories, when made manifest, pass the common-sense tests of appearing reasonable to students, of being fair, and most important, perhaps even being perceived as personally meaningful. Putting this latter point differently, we may ask if sharing our notions about human motivation can actually lead to changes in the ways students view and value the processes of learning as well as think about their roles as students in more inspired ways. The good reason for sharing our theories and their rationale with our clients rests squarely on the fact that for schooling to be most effective, the "rules of the learning game" (including our motivational assumptions) need be as transparent as possible to all the players. By being transparent, I mean the emission of light—the end result of a process of disclosure in which instructors and students together enter into a frank, wide-ranging dialogue regarding the realities of the learning game, including a consideration of the obstacles to learning and teaching that face each stakeholder.

This shared information can take many forms, but for simplicity's sake is characterized here by three descending layered levels; each more complex, veiled, and remote from common discourse than the last. The typical college course syllabus exemplifies the first level of specificity. Here the conditions of an implied learning contract are presented—setting out schedules, deadlines, elaborating grading policies, and the like. This transaction fulfills a basic housekeeping function and represents the simplest, albeit essential, level of disclosure. A second, deeper level of revelation provides for conversations regarding the nature of the subject matter under study: what makes the topic difficult to master, how best to approach the topic, what are the benefits of such mastery, and what standards of competency are desirable or demanded. This level concerns the processes of specific subject-matter mastery. And, at a third deeper level still are potential conversations about the fundamental nature of the teaching/learning process irrespective of subject-matter discipline: what pressures turn instructors and students into adversaries, and how to create alliances and communities of learning in the face of student fears about potential failure.

It is at this last level that the true potential of transparency occurs—an open and intimate discussion of the hopes and fears, goals and expectations of all the players. It is here that motivation theory takes its rightful place as a subject of paramount importance. Indeed, it is at this juncture that motivational considerations become woven into the very fabric of the teaching/learning act—contextualized, or as Webster defines it, "assembling parts into a connected structure."

The purpose of this chapter is to report on the results of our efforts to enter into a dialogue with students at this third, most intimate level of transparency—basically sharing with students the motivational rationale around which their course was created. The course was a large-enrollment introductory psychology class that I teach each year at Berkeley. The theory in question was self-worth theory (Beery, 1975; Covington, 1992, 1998; Covington & Beery, 1976). Basically, this project was undertaken in an effort to test the power of motivation theory to encourage students to higher achievement, to stimulate their caring about their learning, and, especially to diffuse the cross-complaints of students and faculty so vividly portrayed in the pair of oppositional quotes with which this chapter began. As we shall see, this cross-complaint is, in essence, a motivational crisis resulting from a mismatch of perspectives about the roles and responsibilities of faculty and students, respectively.

This study became a possibility by my appointment as the Berkeley Presidential Chair in Undergraduate Education in 2001, an award based on an open competition among all ladder-rank faculty on campus. The 6-year mission of the chairholder is to propose and then to implement ways to enhance the quality of undergraduate teaching and learning across the campus, irrespective of discipline or department. My proposal seeks to sensitize Berkeley faculty, graduate student instructors, and teaching staff to ways that the concept of motivation, especially intrinsic motivation, can be taken into account in the improvement of already-existing courses and in the development of new offerings. An emphasis was placed on working with the teaching staff in large-enrollment, lower-division classes because of our previously gathered data from Berkeley undergraduates indicating that once our freshmen enter the university, they experience a substantial decline in their commitment to learning for its own sake, far below the levels of intrinsic engagement enjoyed in high school (Covington & Dray, 2001). Moreover, while forsaking learning for its own value, students simultaneously become more grade-driven, not to say, "grade grubbing." Indeed, we have found that our students rate achieving the highest grade possible as the main reason for undertaking assignments, with such intrinsic reasons as overcoming a personal challenge rated as far less important (Covington & Wiedenhaupt, 1997).

This project has proceeded in close collaboration with Dr. Linda von Hoene, Director of the Graduate Student Instructor (GSI) Teaching and Resource Center, and her staff. The mission of the Center is in part to assist faculty in mentoring the GSIs with whom they teach, and to rethink their courses as sites in which staff collaborate as teams to form a community of teachers as learners.

SELF-WORTH THEORY

Now then, briefly stated, what is self-worth theory and how does it address the matter of an overweening preoccupation among students with grades and various issues of student disengagement and faculty frustration? Basically, self-worth theory argues that fundamentally all individuals are motivated to establish and maintain a sense of personal worth, approval by others, and acceptance of oneself, a goal that in turn depends on being perceived as competent. In schools (at least as many are presently constituted) this dynamic is represented in its simplest form as Grades (G) = Ability (A) = Worth (W), that is, top grades imply competence, and conversely, poor grades imply incompetence. It is these self-perceptions of competence or incompetence that, in their turn, determine one's feelings of worthiness or worthlessness, respectively. Thus, by this analysis individuals strive for success not only to benefit from the social and personal rewards of high accomplishment, but also to aggrandize their reputation for high ability, hence worthiness. And, if success becomes unlikely, as is typically the case when rewards (grades) are distributed on a competitive basis—with the greatest number of rewards going to those who perform best or fastest—then the first priority becomes the avoidance of failure, or at least the implications of failure, that one is incompetent.

Over the years researchers have investigated a number of defensive ploys that students use in attempts to avoid the onerous implications of inability, that they are unworthy (e.g., Birney, Burdick, & Teevan, 1969). As a group, such tactics are intended to shift the presumed causes of failure from internal (ability) factors to external causes beyond the individual's control or responsibility. In effect, they work by obscuring the causes of failure, which calls to mind Nietzsche's celebrated remark that "Those who know they are profound strive for clarity. Those who would like to seem profound to the crowd strive for obscurity."

One group of such ploys that has received considerable attention has been described collectively as "self-handicapping" strategies (Thompson, 1993, 1994)—self-handicapping because, ironically, in the process of establishing excuses, individuals set up the very failures that they are attempting to avoid, but at least they are "failures with honor," that is, readily explained failures, if not always excused. The most frequently mentioned self-handicapping strategy is procrastination (e.g., McGown & Johnson, 1991). By postponing study for a test until it is virtually too late or by starting work on a term paper only at the last minute, individuals can argue that any subsequent failures are not reflective of what they could really have achieved had they not run out of time. In short, one's ability is never put to the test. These procrastinators attempt to sever, psychologically speaking, the presumed $G = A$ linkage, arguing that one's poor showing is not indicative of one's ability. Students have also been known to take on so many tasks that they cannot give sufficient time to any one of them. This self-handicapping ploy not only allows students to score big points for being energetic. Being busy also makes one feel important despite the mediocre performances that are certain to result, but mediocrity that can be attributed to being too busy, not to incompetence.

A second group of failure-avoiding tactics, unlike self-handicapping, seemingly accents the positive by which some students attempt to guarantee success through an almost slavish devotion to study and a deep commitment to a work ethic. But here success is sought not so much for the sake of resulting pride in accomplishment or for the intrinsic satisfaction of personal inquiry, but out of an essentially defensive strategy as a way to avoid failure by succeeding. These "overstrivers," as they have been called (Covington, 1992, 1998), reflect a desire simultaneously to approach success largely for its high ability status and to avoid failure given its implications that the failing person is not worthy of perfection. This hybrid quality of hope and fear as motivators can drive individuals to extraordinary accomplishments. But despite their successes, these students nonetheless remain self-doubting because of the essentially defensive nature of this achievement strategy.

Cognitive, attribution models of motivation have stressed those aspects of worthiness associated with hard work (Weiner, 1974), whereas self-worth theory stresses those aspects of worth associated with feelings of competency. But are these two sources of worth necessarily incompatible? Cannot students achieve via hard work and in the process also increase their sense of competency? Yes, possibly, but it is an unlikely proposition—at least when rewards for learning are distributed on a competitive basis, where the fear of falling short is common, even among those students whose records of accomplishment are adequate. Thus, in competitive circumstances, effort itself may become a threat to one's worth because if a student tries hard and fails anyway, then explanations go to low ability. But teachers reward effort, and students are expected to comply with this work ethic (Covington & Omelich, 1984). Therein lies the self-worth dilemma for students: To try hard and to do poorly leads to feelings of shame driven by self-perceptions of low ability; but not trying leads to feelings of guilt and teacher punishment for not trying. Little wonder, then, that the most adaptive, self-protective tactics—those that minimize both guilt and shame for students—are those that involve trying, or at least appear to try, but not too energetically and with excuses always available! It is difficult to imagine a strategy better calculated to sabotage the pursuit of personal excellence.

It was this broad outline of self-worth principles that we shared with students in ways that will be described in some detail shortly.

CROSS-COMPLAINTS

Now how can self-worth theory help clarify the faculty/student cross-complaints in which faculty, on the one hand, lament the forsaking of learning by students in their head-long pursuit of grades and the retort of students, on the other hand, accusing faculty of providing little information of relevance to their lives and in boring and uninspired ways?

Student Dynamics

First, consider the alleged "grade grubbing" by students. To the extent that students equate their worth with competitive achievement, grades can take on a disproportional, distorted meaning and become pursued with an unnatural urgency. When this intensity is combined with the fear of failure—essentially the fear that one may be judged incompetent, hence unworthy, then the pursuit of grades becomes an ordeal and the virtually assured result is defensiveness and excuse making. These excuse-making strategies, whatever their specific form or character, all contribute to a timid, fearful countenance that adds to the picture painted by faculty of students as listless, indifferent, and essentially passive learners. Obviously, however, according to self-worth theory, passivity can mask a highly motivated state, but being motivated for the wrong reasons—as a means to avoid the threatening implications of expending effort in a potentially failing enterprise. Naturally, there is more to this story of student indifference than being immobilized by fear. Beginning college students also often come to adopt a passive attitude toward learning simply because it has worked in the past. Teachers across the grade levels have traditionally assumed that the transmission of knowledge is largely a one-way street in which authority figures convey information in a predigested form and students are expected to assimilate it in a relatively unaltered form. Indeed, when we asked Berkeley undergraduates to describe their roles as learners, they responded in essentially passive ways—for example, to absorb material presented by the instructor—and likewise, indicated their responsibilities in equally passive terms—for example, to follow directions, to keep up with the readings, and to attend class faithfully. While these resolutions are clearly admirable, and speak well of a commitment to learning, this absorption of information is often practiced by students in mindless rituals of memorizing without understanding, akin, metaphorically, to acting like thirsty sponges that are squeezed dry at test time. Such passive acquiescence, which bestows neither the benefits of critical judgment nor the buoyancy of creativity, is now understandable in self-worth terms. Fear drives many students desperately at times to simplify and curtail the demands of learning, reducing the task of learning to its simplest denominator and narrowest, most manageable scope. In this mindset, students expect instructors to be the active agents in the teaching/learning partnership, supplying the reasons that they should learn and by making the subject matter relevant, if not enjoyable and fun.

Faculty Dynamics

Faculty for their part often unwittingly reinforce this climate of passivity by expecting students to be active, self-monitoring, inquisitive learners, yet without guidance as to the kinds of skills needed for independent inquiry. Moreover, faculty often test student knowledge in mechanical, uncreative ways that supports and justifies uninspired study strategies on the part of students. As part of this dynamic faculty also often assume naively that students will automatically adopt course objectives simply because they are part of the syllabus. What, for example, does it mean (if anything) to passively-oriented students when instructors include in their course syllabi such animating goals as subject-matter appreciation and the search for personal meaning in what is being learned? We investigated this question by including in the syllabus of a previously offered introductory psychology course various goals concerned with the encouragement of learning for its own sake, gaining an appreciation of knowledge for its elegance and explanatory value, and an invitation for students to role-play the intellectual processes by which knowledge is created. Attention was drawn to these objectives during the first day of class, several examples given, and their importance stressed. Several weeks later, students were polled by means of brief essays as to whether or not such intrinsically-oriented goals were appropriate to college courses; what concrete actions each student had already taken in this course, or might take, subsequently, to engage themselves in achieving such goals; and finally, to describe the instructor's role in encouraging these goals. The results were as instructive as they were sobering. First, the good news: students generally concurred that these goals were appropriate as well as valuable enough to pursue, even if they were not made explicit by an instructor. Yet on the negative side of the ledger, student perceptions of their personal responsibility for realizing these aims traced a decidedly passive theme that related fundamentally to the basic housekeeping functions already noted (e.g., keeping up with the readings, taking good notes). The other most frequently mentioned personal strategy for pursuing these noble objectives was to "keep an open mind," but as can be deduced from the foregoing observations, only a mind ready to be filled by someone else, namely the instructor. Only a decided minority of students suggested personally active tactics such as "looking beyond what at first glance might seem boring," or "relating what is being learned in one course with that in another course." Intrinsic engagement was equated in the minds of most students with the transfer of enthusiasm from instructors to themselves via entertaining lectures.

Directions for Solutions

The vision of schooling conjured up by self-worth theory is that of a battleground set in motion largely by a limited supply of achievement rewards with the result that the rules of engagement favor deception, sabotage, and lackluster effort. This confection of discouragement and defeat is made more harsh and unforgiving still by the presence of a mutual misunderstanding of the respective roles and responsibilities of teachers and students.

How might these dynamics be set straight? Basically, the answer involves altering the relationship between students and instructors, recasting their respective roles and reapportioning their responsibilities in ways that are mutually supportive. This process first requires that the initial reasons for a battleground mentality and feelings of siege be made transparent to both parties. This is where motivational perspectives, like self-worth theory, come into their own as contextualized explanations for otherwise inexplicable behaviors in which, for example, students set up the very failures they are hoping to avoid or appear passive and indifferent in situations that demand vast effort and diligence. Understanding the root causes of these puzzles and frustrations not only clarifies the directions in which solutions might be sought, but also as a consequence of having this knowledge, students and teachers alike can more fully appreciate the rationale by which instructional changes are made. Such appreciation is a vital part of the process of creating transparency.

Returning to the question of solutions, from a self-worth perspective, the answer involves negotiating a better-informed learning contract among the stakeholders, one that favors active participation among students, not passive acquiescence, and features direct efforts by teachers to make intellectual risk-taking safer as well as more rewarding for students. As we will see, much of the heavy lifting in this process depends on teachers adopting grading policies that allow all students to strive for success rather than forcing many of them to struggle to avoid failure, a struggle that inevitably occurs when rewards are competitively distributed.

But students, too, must also assume responsibility in this drama—in effect, inviting students to approach success does not ensure that they will always accept the invitation, especially those students who are threatened by failure or sufficiently demoralized already. What, then, is the task of students? Basically, students must come to grips with the implications of the $G = A = W$ formulation. They must gauge the extent to which this dynamic controls their achievement behavior in school, and even beyond. And, if found complicit, they need be encouraged to reconsider the kinds of yardsticks that define their worth, potentially moving from a narrow emphasis on those questionable, ephemeral, and fleeting payoffs associated with winning over others to those self-defining rewards associated with learning and becoming the best one can be. As Pinder the Elder put it metaphorically 20 centuries ago, "become who you are," which, in effect, means to grow into ones' talents and abilities that may otherwise be hidden from view unless or until discovered and exercised.

Obviously, such a transformation involves an exceedingly complex, demanding process—far reaching, enduring, and somewhat paradoxical—paradoxical because while grades need to be minimized as a test of one's worth, at the same time, students must not disregard the importance of grades in the short term as gatekeepers of prestigious future occupations. In effect, grades *are* important. There can be no denying of this fact, but their importance is, in fact, sharply limited. For example, my students are always surprised to learn that GPA is virtually worthless as a predictor of lifetime income compared to predictions based on simply tallying the number of years one spends in school!

One perspective on the best ways to juggle grade goals and learning goals for the individual's sense of sustained "well-being" as well as their "well-doing" is for students to view grades as a by-product of learning, but learning for the right reasons—for the sake of self-improvement, to help others, and for the satisfaction of curiosity—*best*, because far from dismissing grades, the elevation of learning goals to prominence and the redirection of the causal linkage in which grades follow learning, not eclipse learning, increases the likelihood of attaining even better grades than otherwise would be the case in a renewed atmosphere of reduced anxiety and fear; *best*, because grades can now assume their rightful, more constructive role as feedback for how students can improve their future performance, not standing solely as a test of worth; and *best*, because the rewards of learning are not a scarce commodity, limited by competitive rules, but open to all. By contrast, in the process of winning over others the defining reward involves power. But only a few can be very powerful, and only one can be the most powerful. On the other hand, when the learning game is transformed, as implied by the dictates of self-worth theory, the prevailing value becomes strength—strength of will, of persuasion, and of endurance; qualities that can be attributed to anyone. It is messages such as these that formed the vanguard of our experimental presentation to students.

Now consider the kinds of instructional and pedagogical strategies that teachers can adopt that will support the struggle of students to establish and maintain learning goals as a priority. Three fundamental strategies follow from self-worth interpretations of achievement motivation.

Positive goals and safety. First, grading policies need to be adopted that emphasize learning goals, not competitive grade goals. Basically, this involves favoring a merit-based approach to assessment in which students are rewarded individually for attaining or surpassing known standards of excellence. Here the focus is on encouraging the processes by which individuals become competent, not rewarding students to outperform others driven by a fear of losing out. Typically, merit-based or absolute grading systems operate by providing students at the beginning their work with specific, clearly defined requirements so that any number of students can achieve a given grade as long as they satisfy the quality of workmanship demanded by the instructor. One version of the merit-based concept is a grade-choice arrangement (Covington, 1992). Under this system students are encouraged to work for any grade they choose by amassing grade credits (e.g., so many points for A, B, etc.) with the understanding that the higher the grade to which they aspire, the better they must perform or the more they must accomplish (or both). Students must still enter a contest of sorts—not, however, competing against one another for a limited number of rewards, irrespective of their final levels of competency, but rather working to measure up individually to the absolute standards that the teacher requires of all students.

Our research has identified several motivational advantages of this arrangement, all of which provide some degree of psychological safety—a buffer, in effect, against those negative dynamics that occur when students tie their sense of worth to the results of a competitive contest (Covington, 1992; Covington & Omelich, 1984). For example, in the event of falling short gradewise, the presence of well-defined standards of performance tends to motivate students to try harder the next time. In contrast, when the instructor's evaluation focuses only on the performance itself without reference to internal, absolute standards, then doing poorly tends to lower motivation. In effect, in the presence of absolute standards, failure implies falling short of a goal; without such standards failure seems to imply falling short as a person.

By focusing attention on creating a sense of safety, we can anticipate that the fear that creates mindlessness among students and dampens academic risk-taking will be forestalled. Ultimately, however, our goal for students should not be merely psychological survival, but rather thriving. Where is the self-monitoring, inquisitive student prized by faculty, and where is passion? Other steps also need to be taken. One step involves providing curricula that mobilizes student interest, curiosity, and intrigue. Another involves providing opportunities for students to practice the skills that support active intellectual inquiry as well as rewarding their use by students. Neither of these proposals is new, but relocating them in a larger motivational context may allow us to appreciate their individual and collective potential anew. Consider each in turn.

Interest and intrigue. When educators consider how best to maximize student engagement, one possibility immediately springs to mind: organizing learning around student interests or around issues that arouse an intrinsic curiosity. Given the widespread popularity of this motivational strategy at all educational levels and the general dearth of hard evidence as to its actual effectiveness, we undertook a study of interest-based learning among Berkeley undergraduates, especially its potential role in offsetting the negative consequences of grading pressures (Covington & Wiedenhaupt, 1997). The results were gratifying. Interest appears to provide a positive motivational impetus. For example, degree of subject-matter interest proved to be a powerful predictor for many of the behaviors associated with intrinsic task engagement. As personal interest in an assignment increased, so, too, did the frequency of self-reports describing students as being caught up in the act of learning, of experiencing feelings of wonder and joy at their discoveries, and of even having serendipitous experiences—that is, discovering unexpectedly something of heretofore hidden value. But what about the impact of topical interest on the realities of being graded and on the role of grades as a motivational device? Our findings can be summarized in two parts, depending on whether student interest is high or low. First, when interest is high, the importance of grades as a goal to perform is substantially diminished since other reasons for learning, largely intrinsic in nature, emerge to sustain student involvement such as feelings of having done well and of achieving mastery. And, even when these same task-interested students acknowledged that they would be graded—nothing obscures this fact of academic life for long—they believe that the presence of grades actually inspires them to do their best. This uplifting sentiment stands in stark contrast to the reactions of those students who showed little task interest. Rather than believing themselves maximally challenged by the presence of grades, this latter group perceived grades as a way only to ensure a minimum amount of effort! In effect, when task interest is low, grades become the most prominent justification or imperative for undertaking a task. It is these perceptions that lead students to worry about grades as they work, of not feeling smart enough (or worthy) to do well, of perceiving the chances of success as remote, and even complaining that they did not get enough grade credit given the amount of work involved. Clearly, the encouragement of student interest benefits our larger motivational objectives.

PAYING FOR ENGAGEMENT

Now what would happen if intriguing assignments were combined with the opportunity for students to receive grade credit for exploring the *processes* by which they created insightful solutions and discoveries? To pursue this inquiry, in a previous offering of the introductory psychology course, we gave students a small extra-credit percentage of the total points they could earn toward their final grade for seeking personal relevance in their assignments. This involved, for example, encouraging students to modify otherwise uninteresting tasks in order to increase their attractiveness for challenge and exploration; to seek out deeper connections that might link assignments within the course or even across courses; and to reflect on their own thought processes as they worked on protracted tasks, remaining alert to serendipity, chance, and the opportunity for expanded exploration. In this latter instance, students were encouraged to maintain personal, process-oriented journals in which they recorded their thoughts, reservations, plans of action, and those emotions associated with intellectual discovery, including wonder, awe, suspense, and even self-doubt.

Paying people to engage in behaviors associated with intrinsic motivation is an interesting gamble. Over the past several decades an impressive volume of research has been marshaled in support of the proposition that the offering of tangible rewards—such as gold stars, praise, and grades—in an effort to motivate learning may inhibit creativity and interest-driven discovery on the theory that such rewards distract the learner, and draw attention away from the inherent benefits of learning so that when these rewards are no longer available, the willingness of students to learn will decrease (for a review, see Covington, 2002). We have recently argued that these conclusions are misplaced because the reasons for diminishing task engagement has less to do with the tangible nature of rewards per se than with the defensive, self-worth motives aroused by a scarcity of rewards and the resulting fear of failure (Covington, 1999; Covington & Müeller, 2001). It is this fear that is the root cause of the threat to intrinsic valuing. By this reasoning, extrinsic payoffs such as social recognition, money, or grades stand as independent factors, so to speak—neutral in their motivating effect, until associated with either approach or avoidant goals. In effect, extrinsic payoffs can either advance a love of learning, if they serve to reinforce positive, task-focused reasons for learning as when the purpose is to satisfy one's curiosity; or conversely, interfere with caring about learning when such rewards are sought after in conditions of scarcity for self-aggrandizing reasons or are threatened to be withheld as a means of controlling students.

In any event, the results of our classroom research suggest that the presumed negative consequences to intrinsic engagement of paying students to be thoughtful and creative are overstated. Students were uniformly positive about this extra-credit feature of the course, not simply because it presented a foolproof way to enhance their grade, but more importantly, because the process-related thoughts and personal insights experienced by students were precisely the kinds of intangible benefits of academic inquiry that students feel are typically disregarded when instructors calculate grades. These personal satisfactions take on a disproportional importance, far beyond their modest contribution to the final grade tally, by elevating intrinsic task engagement to a favored instructional priority. Regarding the controversy over the effects of employing tangible rewards in the service of intrinsic goals, our informants conceded that without this tangible payoff, they would have given little if any attention to the rich personal satisfactions associated with their learning. Yet once engaged, the fact of their having been paid initially was generally discounted by students as being a distraction.

The Experiment

Now what would happen if we designed a new offering of the introductory course around the motivational strategies just described in the hope of dispelling fear-based learning and creating a mutually advantageous alliance between teaching staff and students? At the core of such a course, according to our self-worth analysis, would be a grading policy committed to clarity and fairness and that would also provide an opportunity for any number of students to pursue individual grade goals to exacting levels of excellence. Such a course would also feature thought-provoking tasks as part of the teacher's responsibility to infuse relevance and excitement into his/her relationship with students as well as to reward the processes by which students exercise independent thought, judgment, and imagination in the form of direct grade-goal incentives.

But would our students seize spontaneously on the opportunities afforded by a combination of safety and freedom to create their own personal relevance, thus cementing an alliance in which the goals of teacher and student become synonymous? Herein lies the essence of our basic inquiry: Is it necessary that our theories of motivation be made explicit for students to become motivated in positive ways, that is, prompted to create an enriched personal and academic perspective on their roles and responsibilities as learners? Given the evidence cited earlier regarding the incredibly entrenched intellectual passivity exhibited by many of our students, the prospects appeared dim for any automatic self-engagement. We therefore judged that in order to be effective in challenging students, our theory of motivation and its rationale and, indeed, our more fundamental expectation that students examine critically their own personal reasons for learning, all needed to be made "transparent." But how could we best engage students in a dialogue about self-worth dynamics, about the risks and benefits of choosing learning goals over grade goals as a measure of one's worth, and about the dangers inherent in a breakdown of mutual expectations among teachers and students—issues that permeated all the major decisions around which the course would be constructed?

The vehicle we chose to convey this multiheaded message consisted of two lectures delivered by me at the beginning of the course. The lecture format was considerably enlivened by an unusual form of presentation, if we are to judge by the incredulous looks, yet highly focused attention of a large audience for 2 hours. I lectured not to the students but to another professor—counseling him, actually. This imaginary guest had come seeking advice from our "teaching clinic," which had just swollen in size to include 450 newly minted, young psychologists. Professor X was both angry and frightened over the prospects of having to teach the same introductory college course (in an unnamed discipline at an unspecified university) that he had taught the year before. Things had ended disastrously despite his well-intentioned efforts. The reader can quickly grasp the essence of his complaints (and, in turn, those of his students) by recalling the two adversarial quotes with which this chapter began.

The role-playing, counseling session began by sharing with Professor X (and the audience too, of course) the results of an actual questionnaire administered by me several semesters earlier asking students to list their goals for their taking the class and any potential obstacles to these goals. Professor X expressed some surprise that so many goals were stated in negative terms—in effect, things to be avoided, like not making mistakes or not procrastinating, as well as the fearful, self-doubting quality of the potential obstacles: feeling insecure, having to do things one is not good at doing, and being overwhelmed with anxiety.

The causes behind this "hidden agenda," as I coined the phrase, were best understood through the $G = A = W$ formulation. The motivational implications of this proposition were quickly apparent to Professor X (and to my students as well, judging from the forest of waving hands in the audience). These insights included the fact that (1) many students were motivated, but for the wrong reasons—reasons that could actually lead to extraordinary accomplishments, but with persistent feelings of self-doubt, nonetheless; (2) grade pressures can lead students into defensive, self-defeating behaviors that can create the very failures they are attempting to avoid; (3) paradoxically, student effort (and help-seeking) is a potential threat to worth when rewards are in short supply; and (4) instructors and students are sometimes at cross-purposes regarding their goals with frustrating consequences.

The second, follow-up lecture focused on various instructional strategies that Professor X could adopt to avoid a disastrous repeat of his earlier teaching experience, strategies that by this time were clearly understood by my students to be the underpinnings of the current course.

Findings

Data were collected in two waves. The first, initial wave of data gathering took place shortly after the two Professor X lectures were delivered during the first of the weekly section meetings. Students completed, anonymously, a series of brief essays to solicit their immediate reactions to the lectures. The second wave of data collection occurred at the end of the course some 3 months later. These latter essay questions were designed to provide a retrospective view of the impact, if any, of the introduction of self-worth theory both for making the course curriculum decisions understandable and for its potential as a catalyst for self-reflection. It is important to note that no particular reference was made to these lectures for the remainder of the course once the initial lecture presentations were made. Thus, student reactions comprised a record of freely occurring thoughts, feelings, and insights that, once set in motion, reverberated spontaneously through time with no further prompting by the teaching staff.

Initial reactions. Our interest in assessing the impact of disclosing self-worth principles went beyond judging the ability of students merely to reproduce the theory accurately from memory. We also hoped the lectures would trigger broader self-referent insights by means of such nonspecific essay prompts as, "What was the single most important thing you learned [from lectures] and why?" or "What points raised might help you become the best student you can be not only in this course, but in all your courses?"

Not surprising, the overwhelming majority of essays embraced self-worth theory as the broad framework within which answers were couched. Consider sample reactions in a stepwise fashion, moving from basic factual restatements of the theory to more personal interpretations. First, as noted, some students were content simply to summarize the lectures and in the process reiterate the essential elements of the theory in a more or less abstract, disembodied yet accurate form. By contrast, many other students personalized the theory to the extent that they recognized the operation of the $G = A = W$ model in the behavior of friends and acquaintances (e.g., "I have a roommate who really beats up on herself over poor grades"). Other students rejected the implied equivalency of $G =$

W, or as one informant put it, "The [grades] don't in fact measure my worth as a person, though it would be nice to be gratified by doing well." The G = A linkage was also widely disputed, again based typically on personal experience or on that of friends (e.g., "Grades are an inaccurate measure of my ability since grades depend on so many things"). Finally, some essays far from questioned the reality of these linkages, actually recognized their own misguided actions and in a personal revelation of sorts, concluded that they had been in the thrall of these dynamics, unwittingly, and sometimes for years (e.g., "The idea about reframing the meaning of grades is significant to me because I was able to recognize my self-sabotage strategies and hidden agendas and hope to better cope with my stress from now on."). Other observations, while far less autobiographical, still followed the main points of the lecture. They often came in the form of dire warnings or admonitions about the dangers of linking a sense of worth exclusively to grades. Here students frequently counseled against procrastination—but, importantly, with a more sophisticated appreciation of the dynamics involved; no longer simply being dismissed as a matter of someone being "lazy," but of their being driven to procrastinate by threats to one's sense of worth.

Now, what was the impact of the self-worth message on students' initial perceptions of the course itself and of the teaching staff on hearing a frank, theory-driven presentation about issues of vital concern to them? Students reacted warmly to the presentation and repeatedly expressed appreciation for the emotional support implied by the willingness of the teaching staff to confront and then defuse their fears and anxieties. These positive feelings often translated into a commitment by students to do their best, to strive to make learning their primary goal for the course, and occasionally, cited self-worth insights as central to making these aspirations come true. These noble sentiments were frequently mixed with feelings of relief which, by student admission, came from anxiety reduction (e.g., "Relieving tension, the lecture made a positive difference in my approach to the class because I felt that I could take this class for a learning experience rather than for just a requirement"; "After the Professor X lecture, my anxiety, fear, and stress toward college life experienced a substantial reduction").

Clearly, as an emotion, relief is insufficient to sustain long-term academic commitments, but at least it is a starting point, potentially so, for the lifting of otherwise debilitating anxiety. At the same time, however, when relief permutes into feelings of comfort, it can lead to a misreading of situations. This is likely what happened in those several cases where students concluded, erroneously as they came to discover, that the course would be easy, gradewise!

In summary, it was clear that on initial exposure to self-worth principles, students readily understood the concepts involved, gave the theory high marks for providing insights into the intrapsychic pressures that sometimes bedeviled other students, if not always themselves, and in many instances, responded with personal insights and relevant anecdotes stimulated by the theory. Moreover, students almost universally valued this process of disclosure for its capacity to put them at ease, to convey a sense of caring and support by the instructional staff, and for establishing a sense of academic community, especially where fellow students could be viewed as advocates for learning, not adversaries.

Retrospective reactions. Now what were the longer-term results of disclosing a motivational rationale underlying the course? The overall reaction of students via this retrospective evaluation was generally positive regarding the sustaining value of self-worth theory for promoting serviceable insights that endured throughout the course. Yet, beyond this general trend, it was the diversity of ways in which students appropriated the motivational messages and in many cases the depth of emotional reactions expressed that was most intriguing. Of equal interest was the fact that students seized on different aspects of the theory—sometimes focusing on mere fragments of the message, but always in ways meaningful to them, and without doing violence to the overall theory. Students also drew reassurances from the Professor X lectures for a variety of highly personalized reasons, ranging from the comfort derived from knowing they were not alone in their struggles (e.g., "Because it helped me understand that I was not the only one who struggled with grades") to feeling that a vote of confidence had been cast in their favor, implying that they were worthwhile enough to be part of the process of sharing (e.g., "Professor X lectures worked best in making me feel that the teaching staff was on my side and led me to trust them more readily…simply knowing that they are aware of those issues and their wish to help gave me confidence and assurance.").

The most salient theme that reverberated for students throughout the semester both by reason of the frequency with which it was mentioned and the depth of accompanying emotions expressed was a struggle about how best to define one's worth. We had clearly aroused a debate in students' minds regarding the wisdom of linking one's self-definition exclusively to performance goals and grades.

This struggle manifested itself in several ways, neatly reflected in the pattern of numerical, Likert-type ratings that were sometimes solicited along with the open-ended responses. Not surprisingly, students rated the theory most valuable when it stimulated a personal dialogue of self-searching, despite the occasional sharp discomfort of resulting uncertainty and doubts. At the same time, other seemingly more self-assured students gave relatively lower ratings when they felt the issue of defining personal worth had already been securely settled for them, invariably in favor of valuing learning goals. In none of these latter instances, however, did students reject the theory as irrelevant to their lives, but rather accepted it as confirmatory of what they already firmly believed. For other, perhaps less self-assured students, the fact of ruminating about the theory for a time led to a dawning recognition that actually learning *was* the truest goal of schooling (e.g., "At first I was shocked. I became very intrigued with the fact of going to classes for its enjoyment rather than anything else!"). For other students, the theory led to insights retrospectively regarding the destructive nature of their past reasons for learning and the negative consequences for effective coping. A few notable quotes make the point:

> It [the theory] helped me realize the self-defeating nature of defining my self by arbitrarily assigned letter grades.

> It [the theory] made me realize how engulfed [I was]…, feeling worthy only in times of success.

> The information is important because I realize that sometimes I am driven by fear.

Other students reported taking action for positive change based on their reactions to the Professor X lectures:

> I try to achieve these [learning] goals instead of blindly working to avoid failure.

> The theory has taught me which behaviors and actions trigger the feelings of unworthiness, and as a result I try my best to steer clear of those behaviors and actions.

> Unlike my previous reaction to adversity and challenge, I now look at 'failure' in terms of grades as acceptable as long as I enjoy what I am learning and try my best as a student.

> I felt worthless without the ability to attain exceptional grades. However, this entire concept…was not conscious until the 'Professor X' lectures provided a jolting slap into reality…losing my fear over classes and grades allowed me to focus on course material itself.

> The idea about reframing the meaning of grades is significant to me because I was able to recognize my self-sabotage strategies and hidden agendas and better cope with my stress.

Now, consider student evaluations regarding the role of a supportive environment, or as one informant called it, "a culture of caring," in efforts to empower learning goals. Some sources of support and reassurance were seen as stemming directly from the presence of a merit-based grading system (e.g., "By not having a curve, you create an environment where a grade is truly reflective of the time and effort you put into it, which makes learning more intrinsically valuable." 12"It was a relief to know that at least in this class, I could feel free of competition and I was going to be able to see my classmates as friends, not as enemies."). Other students cited efforts to diffuse the mismatch of faculty and student roles as the source of motivational significance (e.g., "Simply saying that they [the staff] recognize students' fears of failing helps relieve those fears, as it creates a sense of trust between the students and the staff." "Matching student and faculty roles is one idea that best increased my confidence, trust. If teachers and students can see each other in the same light, then it provides a better learning environment for everyone."). Others stressed the presence of a community of cooperation (e.g., "I felt as though I was part of a community where I could seek and get help without feeling self-conscious and scared.").

Naturally, not all student evaluations were fully positive. A minority of students provided crucial insights regarding the limits of our intervention. For example, several students expressed frustration over our implied idealism in advancing learning as the primary educational goal, indicating for them at least such considerations would always be trumped by grading pressures (e.g., "There is a lot of pressure and fear for the students to do well because a disappointing grade is a lethal blow to the student's self-esteem." E "I feel the pressure of grades and the idea of not making learning a chore is impossible to overcome.") In this connection, what was thought to be the ultimate irony was touched on, in good humor, by a skeptic who pointed out that despite our efforts to minimize the importance of grades, the faculty were still required to give grades! Actually, this is less an irony than a misreading of our intentions. Grades *are* important and to suggest otherwise is neither helpful nor credible—or as one of my graduate student colleagues put it, "We would be singing to deaf ears." Several less subtly disposed students expressed undisguised outrage at any thought of dismissing grades (e.g., "I personally violently disagree with the statement that grades are unimportant"). These perceptions were also a misreading of our message. Our intention was to challenge students to relocate the meaning of grades—to "decatastrophize" grades and place them in a constructive alignment with learning goals, not to dismiss grades. Perhaps, after all, this message is too subtle for some students to appreciate—hard enough to get one's arms around in the easiest of times, let alone in the face of the reality that many in our audience not only live by grades, but owe their very presence at a prestigious university to an unbroken string of highly visible academic successes, often defined by competitive excellence. Our question to students, of course, is what happens if the string gets broken, or try as one might, what if a student's days of outperforming others as a test of worth are numbered? An additional point is that students may not fully appreciate how much of a dead end the treadmill of chasing grades can be: endless, unforgiving—one failure can be devastating, and always demanding of more and increasingly extraordinary accomplishments.

Moreover, thinking about transforming the G = A = W formula is difficult enough in an achievement setting of relative safety that has been deliberately designed to encourage this process of self-examination. Although some of our students clearly embarked on this journey, what about the viability of sustaining change when they must go outside this target course to less forgiving environments, where, for example, as a matter of teaching philosophy some instructors may deliberately encourage competition? Or, alternatively, perhaps other instructors are forced by circumstances to tolerate competitive selection, reluctantly so, in the role as "gatekeepers" to prestigious occupations, like medicine, where the number of aspirants exceeds the openings? The success of our ability to project our motivational message beyond the limits of a particular place or time may well be taken as the ultimate criterion by which one answers the question of whether or not our theories of motivation can actually motivate students to higher purpose and achievement. Some of our students appear to be on their way to making this generalized transformation (e.g., "The [theory]...made me think differently about professors...I have actually gained the courage to approach my professors to clarify a point or to ask about other courses they teach. It has improved my interest in my classes."). But many other students did not feel themselves successful in this regard, and sometimes expressed frustration with what they considered an expectation by the staff that they could have succeeded in this transformation. Obviously, the issue of the generalizability of motivational insights is of great concern and will be closely addressed in our future work.

CONCLUSIONS

We began with an interest in exploring the implications for educational practice of contextualizing motivational theories, an inquiry organized around the broad question, "Can our motivation theories motivate?," and its subtext: (1) Can students understand the rationale behind the theories of motivation intended to guide their education?; (2) Do these propositions make sense?; and finally, (3) Are motivation theories perceived as being of personal use and value to learners? Based on our present data, we can answer in the affirmative on all these counts—but a qualified affirmative for several reasons, some of which have already been addressed and for at least three additional reasons.

First, we are concerned about the representativeness of self-worth theory. In effect, would students respond in similar circumstances to other contemporary motivation theories in essentially the same ways, or perhaps quite differently? It would seem important to identify those shared as well as distinct attributes of all our collective theories that are most likely to affect student self-perceptions as learners. Although this question was not the object of our inquiry, certain characteristics of self-worth theory may offer some clues. Basically, when put into practice as we attempted here, self-worth theory becomes more than an explanation for various puzzling achievement behaviors. It also implies a broad educational philosophy complete with a hierarchy of desired goals. It also provides for a relatively transparent instructional rationale for promoting both student self-examination and the means that can be employed by instructors to improve student learning, satisfaction, and performance. I suspect that the presence of these elements in any theory will prove to be the active ingredients for success. Moreover, I believe it is the open, frank disclosure and discussion of these issues that ultimately carries the motivational freight for any theory, a point to which I will return shortly.

Second, the population chosen for study here is clearly different from the vast majority of students who pass through the American educational system, thereby limiting the generalizability of our observations. Obviously, any temptation to ascribe college dynamics wholesale to other groups must be avoided. In this cautionary spirit, we may only regard these findings largely as a means to raise and illustrate motivational issues that may have broader implications across the grade levels and for a variety of students.

Having said this, it may be useful to comment briefly on some of these broader implications, especially regarding sociocultural and ethnic differences among our students. For example, one might ask if self-worth motivational principles apply uniformly across groups from a diversity of social and ethnic backgrounds. Unfortunately, because of the anonymity with which the present data were collected, we are unable to address this question directly here. However, several other data sets gathered previously and representing all major ethnic groups among Berkeley undergraduates provide some guidance. Some ethnic differences in self-worth-linked variables were observed, especially regarding the extent to which students defined their sense of worth in terms of grades, with Chinese American students being most dependent on this index and Hispanic and African Americans least so. However, whenever such ethnic variations occurred, the magnitude of these differences was invariably quite modest compared to variations in self-worth dynamics associated with personality factors, including openness to experience, tendencies toward depression, consciousness, and trait-like feelings of well-being. Indeed, such personality-type variables cluster reliably enough to differentiate students into distinct achievement types that are largely independent of ethnicity. This is not to suggest that ethnic membership plays little role in determining the quality and expression of achievement motivation. This is simply the wrong place to assess the true nature of these dynamics given the highly selected nature of these Berkeley subsamples where the range of ethnically related variations are far more restricted than is likely the case in the general population.

A third qualification reflects questions about the nature of the causal factors at work in this demonstration. We may wonder if it was the exposition of self-worth theory per se or the presence of the instructional strategies that follow from the theory, or a combination, that led to the present results. Obviously, we cannot resolve this question with the data at hand, but one thing seems clear. An awareness and understanding of motivational principles acted on students in important ways, but perhaps not because of the specifics of the given theory but simply because of the presence of a reasonable organizing rationale that gives meaning, direction, and purpose to one's work.

This brings us to what I believe is the broader import of the present inquiry. It comes in two parts.

The first point of significance concerns identifying those dimensions of our theories that arouse action, encourage meaning-making, and inspire students to their best efforts. Effective motivation theories not only explain events and account for purposeful as well as contrary behaviors, but they also imply what those positive purposes should be—goals, by another name. It strikes me that engaging student's best efforts depends largely on helping them discover the purpose and true meaning of their labors. At their best this is what motivation theories should be about. The present data demonstrates this point. Recall the struggle of students to reconcile what many of them considered the nobler, self-defining values of learning for its own sake with those less attractive, often overwhelmingly intense distracters in the form of grade-goal motives associated with competitiveness and self-aggrandizement. This struggle is an exercise in the forging of personal values and of meaning-making, the ultimate of all human motivators.

Second, beyond the motivating potential of sense-making is the motivating value inherent in the mere act of sharing our theories with students, as was demonstrated in the present case. And, again, it may matter little the particular form or content of the theory. The very act of confiding implies that teachers care about their students, not just as passive recipients of information, but, once again, as meaning-making, willful, and active participants in the educational drama. These disclosures activate feelings of trust, support, and a sense of security that was so evident from the reactions of our students. One student put it best: 22 "Finally, the Professor X series reassured me that [the teaching staff] that had hundreds of other students and a million other responsibilities and worries was and is concerned about me, individually, not only for my grade, but for my sanity as a student and as an individual." So it is likely that in the act of sharing our theories of learning and motivation with students—deliberately, candidly, and transparently, and in ways that convey a sense of safety, we will mobilize students to seek out their highest potential.

These observations bring us full circle to the mission of the Berkeley Presidential Chair in Undergraduate Education, which prompted this entire line of inquiry. My experience in working with Berkeley faculty as a "motivational consultant" has convinced me of the value they accord to students being intrinsically invested in their learning. Yet, in practice, these values are often honored more in the breach than in the observance. There are several reasons for this. First, concepts like motivation are viewed by many instructors as mysterious and elusive, hence unlikely to contribute significantly to tangible performance goals. Second, it is sometimes argued that because of the highly selected nature of Berkeley students, everyone is already motivated to perform, and if not, they will soon be replaced by an eager set of new recruits who *are* motivated. Third, there is also the belief that personal engagement is itself a by-product of doing well academically, and therefore makes no direct contribution to the pursuit of academic goals. Fourth, some instructors feel it is beyond their expertise, and even beyond their responsibility, to encourage these motivational goals.

These concerns are legitimate, but largely misguided. Yet they illustrate the very real obstacles to be overcome. Major outreach efforts are needed to allay these concerns and encourage a more accurate and constructive vision of the motivational basis of the learning process. This message should include the following points: (1) that the instructional principles that control the motivational climate of classrooms are lawful, well documented, and accessible to all teachers; (2) that students are, indeed, motivated, but often motivated, even overmotivated, for fear-driven reasons that undercut both the acquisition and retention of knowledge as well as its appreciation; and (3) that being intrinsically engaged contributes directly to academic goals.

Finally, it is obvious that the particular vehicle we chose for raising issues of classroom motivation with students—a direct, extensive treatment via faculty role-playing—is not suitable in all teaching situations, nor is it compatible with all faculty teaching styles. For this reason, we continue to explore various methods and means by which these messages can be introduced comfortably and effectively by faculty across a wide spectrum of subject-matter disciplines and teaching contexts. These and other ongoing efforts associated with the mission of the Presidential Chair in Undergraduate Education represent part of the larger responsibility of educational researchers to "contextualize" our theories of motivation whenever possible.

REFERENCES

Beery, R. G. (1975). Fear of failure in the student experience. *Personnel and Guidance Journal, 54*, 190–203.

Birney, R. C., Burdick, H., & Teevan, R. C. (1969). *Fear of failure.* New York: Van Nostrand.

Covington, M. V. (1992). *Making the grade: A self-worth perspective on motivation and school reform.* New York: Cambridge University Press.

Covington, M. V. (1998). *The will to learn.* New York: Cambridge University Press.

Covington, M. V. (1999). Caring about learning: The nature and nurturing of subject-matter appreciation. *Educational Psychologist, 34,* 127–136.

Covington, M. V. (2002). Rewards and intrinsic motivation: A needs-based developmental perspective. In T. Urdan & F. Pajares (Eds.), *Motivation of adolescents* (pp. 169–192). New York: Academic Press.

Covington, M. V., & Beery, R. G. (1976). *Self-worth and school learning.* New York: Holt, Rinehart & Winston.

Covington, M. V., & Dray, E. (2002). The developmental course of achievement motivation: A need-based approach. In A. Wigfield & J. S. Eccles (Eds.), *Development of achievement motivation* (pp. 33–56). New York: Academic Press.

Covington, M. V., & Müeller, K. J. (2001). Intrinsic versus extrinsic motivation: An approach/avoidance reformulation. In M. V. Covington & A. J. Elliott (Eds.), *Educational Psychology Review* (pp. 111–130). New York: Plenum Press.

Covington, M. V., & Omelich, C. L. (1984). Task-oriented vs. competitive learning structures: Motivational and performance consequences. *Journal of Educational Psychology, 76,* 1038–1050.

Covington, M. V., & Weidenhaupt, S. (1997). Turning work into play: The nature and nurturing of intrinsic task engagement. In R. Perry & J.C. Smart (Eds.), *Effective teaching in higher education: Research and practice* (p. 101–114). New York: Agathon Press.

McCown, W., & Johnson, J. (1991). Personality and chronic procrastination by university students during an academic examination period. *Personality and Individual Differences, 12,* 413–415.

Pintrich, P. (1991). Student motivation in the college classroom. In K. W. Prichard & R. M. Sawyer (Eds.), *Handbook of college teaching: Theories and applications* (pp. 23–43). London: Greenwood Press.

Thompson, T. (1993). Characteristics of self-worth protection in achievement behavior. *British Journal of Educational Psychology, 63,* 469–488.

Thompson, T. (1994). Self-worth protection: Implications for the classroom. *Educational Review, 46,* 259–274.

Weiner, B. (1974). *Achievement motivation and attribution theory.* Morristown, NJ: General Learning Press.

CHAPTER 6

SELF-EFFICACY IN EDUCATION REVISITED
Empirical and Applied Evidence

Dale H. Schunk and Frank Pajares

INTRODUCTION

> Psychological procedures, whatever their form, alter expectations of personal efficacy. . . . An efficacy expectation is the conviction that one can successfully execute the behavior required to produce the outcomes. . . . Efficacy expectations determine how much effort people will expend, and how long they will persist in the face of obstacles and aversive experiences. The stronger the efficacy or mastery expectations, the more active the efforts. (Bandura, 1977b, pp.79–80)

When Albert Bandura (1977a, 1977b) introduced self-efficacy to the psychological literature, he may not have thought that more than 25 years later self-efficacy would be one of the most heavily researched and viable psychological constructs in different areas of human functioning. Since 1977 researchers have explored the operation of self-efficacy in different individuals (e.g., children, adolescents, adults), within various develop-

Big Theories Revisited
Volume 4 in: Research on Sociocultural Influences on Motivation and Learning, pages 115–138.
Copyright © 2004 by Information Age Publishing, Inc.
ISBN: 1-59311-053-7 (hardcover), 1-59311-052-9 (paperback)

mental levels (e.g., normal learners, gifted students, students with learning difficulties), in differing contexts (e.g., athletics, business, education, health, careers), and in diverse cultures (e.g., North American, European, Asian). Self-efficacy also has been prominently incorporated into numerous theories, including those of career choice (Lent, Brown, & Hackett, 1994), motivation (Schunk & Pajares, 2002), and self-regulation (Bandura, 1997; Zimmerman, 2000).

In this chapter we revisit Bandura's original writings on self-efficacy in light of events of the past quarter century. Our focus is on the operation of self-efficacy in educational settings, although the points we raise also may be pertinent to other contexts. Two conclusions are inescapable. First, self-efficacy is a remarkably potent construct whose applicability to human functioning has been conclusively demonstrated (for reviews or meta-analyse, see Bandura, 1997; Multon, Brown, & Lent, 1991; Pajares, 1997; Schunk, 1991; Stajkovic & Luthans, 1998). Second, the complexities of educational contexts have led researchers to identify points of clarification required of the original formulation (Pajares, 1996a, 1997; Schunk, 1989, 1991).

Initially we provide background information on self-efficacy to include its causes, consequences, role in the larger framework of social-cognitive theory, and distinction from other similar constructs. We then discuss self-efficacy in educational settings. We mention methodological differences between early self-efficacy research and research in education, and we discuss five areas in which research findings have clarified and enhanced the original self-efficacy theoretical formulation. For each of these we provide the empirical and applied evidence that forms the basis for these clarifications. We conclude these discussions with suggestions for future self-efficacy research.

The complexities of educational contexts referred to earlier involve a combination of social and cultural factors; for example, peer friendships, students' desire to avoid trouble, social pressures against working too hard or appearing overly intelligent, students' socioeconomic status and ethnicity, and teachers' feedback to students. These factors are not unique to school settings; they occur in varying degrees in any social context. But school settings present special challenges because sociocultural factors can work at cross-purposes; for example, schools stress achievement but students want to be socially accepted by peers. These conflicting sociocultural pressures make direct application of self-efficacy theory problematic.

BACKGROUND

Conceptual Framework

Self-efficacy refers to "people's judgments of their capabilities to organize and execute courses of action required to attain designated types of performances" (Bandura, 1986, p. 391). Self-efficacy is hypothesized to affect choice of activities, effort, persistence, and achievement. Compared with students who doubt their capabilities, those with high self-efficacy for accomplishing a task are hypothesized to participate more readily, work harder, persist longer, and achieve at higher levels (Bandura, 1997).

People can acquire information to gauge their self-efficacy from their actual performances, vicarious (e.g., modeled) experiences, forms of social persuasion, and physiological indexes. Actual performances provide the most reliable information for assessing self-efficacy, because they are tangible indicators of people's capabilities. Successes should raise self-efficacy and failures lower it, although an occasional failure/success after many successes/failures should not have much impact.

Individuals can acquire much information about their capabilities through knowledge of how others perform. Similarity to others is a key cue for gauging one's self-efficacy (Schunk, 1987). Observing similar others succeed can raise observers' self-efficacy and motivate them to try the task because they are apt to believe that if others can succeed they can as well. But a vicarious increase in self-efficacy can be negated by subsequent performance failures. Persons who observe peers fail may believe they lack the competence to succeed, which can dissuade them from attempting the task.

People often receive persuasive information that they possess the capability to perform well ("You can do it!"). Although positive feedback can raise self-efficacy, the increase will not endure if they subsequently perform poorly. Individuals also acquire some self-efficacy information from physiological indicators, such as sweating and heart rate. When emotional indicators are interpreted to mean that one lacks competence—such as when one feels tense about speaking in front of a large group or when one's mind goes blank during an exam—they can lower self-efficacy. Conversely, when people notice that they are reacting in less-agitated fashion to situations, they may feel more self-efficacious.

Bandura (1977a, 1977b, 1982) made it clear that information acquired from these sources does not influence self-efficacy automatically but rather is cognitively appraised. Self-efficacy appraisal is an inferential process in which persons weigh and combine the contributions of personal, environmental, and behavior factors. In forming and modifying self-efficacy perceptions people might consider factors such as perceptions of their ability, effort expended, task difficulty, assistance from others, and number and pattern of successes.

The self-efficacy appraisal process has itself been the subject of research (Cervone & Peake, 1986; Pajares & Miller, 1997). Cervone and Peake (1986), for example, found that self-efficacy judgments were affected by anchoring. College and high school students judged self-efficacy for solving problems. Before judging self-efficacy they were exposed to either a high or low anchor value of performance. Students shown a high anchor value (representing a higher number of problems solved correctly) judged self-efficacy higher and subsequently persisted longer than did students exposed to the low anchor value.

Self-efficacy is not an isolated construct but rather an integral component of social-cognitive theory. A hallmark of this theory is its view that human functioning involves reciprocal interactions between behaviors, environmental events, and cognitions and other personal factors (Bandura, 1986).

This system of *triadic reciprocality* can be illustrated with self-efficacy—a personal factor. Much research shows that self-efficacy can influence such actions as effort, persistence, and achievement (Schunk, 1995). Conversely, actions can affect self-efficacy beliefs. Personal accomplishments are an important source of self-efficacy information. Persons who perform a task well are apt to feel more efficacious about continuing to perform well, whereas those who have difficulty may feel less self-efficacious.

The interaction between self-efficacy and environmental events is evident in classrooms. The types of questions that teachers ask students, how teachers group students for instruction, and the feedback that teachers give to students about their performances are environmental variables that can affect students' self-efficacy (Schunk, 1995). Students are apt to feel more self-efficacious when they believe that teachers are asking them harder questions, are grouping them with smarter classmates, and are giving them feedback stressing their high competence. In contrast, students' self-efficacy may decrease when they perceive that teachers are asking them easier questions, grouping them with less-intelligent peers, and giving them feedback linking their successes on easy tasks to high effort.

In return, teachers' perceptions of students' self-efficacy can affect how teachers interact with them. Thus, teachers may believe that students with learning difficulties have low self-efficacy and treat them accordingly regardless of how self-efficacious the students feel.

The reciprocal influence between students' behaviors and their environments can be seen in the domain of academic studying (Zimmerman & Paulsen, 1995). Self-efficacious students create learning environments that are conducive for studying by setting up study routines and eliminating distractions. When environmental problems arise, they take steps to overcome them. Students with lower self-efficacy do not exert as much environmental self-regulation and their behaviors often are easily affected by environmental events (e.g., they talk on the phone to friends who call while they are studying rather than telling their friends they will call back later).

Distinctions with Other Constructs

Self-efficacy is a belief about what one is capable of doing; it is not the same as knowing what to do. In gauging self-efficacy, individuals assess their skills and capabilities to translate those skills into actions. Possessing skill positively affects self-efficacy, which in turn influences subsequent skill attainment; however, skill and self-efficacy are not synonymous in meaning. Self-efficacy is a key to promoting a sense of *agency* that people can influence their lives (Bandura, 1997, 2001).

Self-efficacy also depends partly on students' abilities. High-ability students generally feel more self-efficacious about performing well than do low-ability students, but self-efficacy is not the same as ability. This was demonstrated in a study by Collins (1982) in which high-, average-, and low-ability students in mathematics were identified. Within each level she determined which students had high and low self-efficacy. Students were given problems to solve and told they could rework those they missed. Ability was positively related to achievement, but regardless of ability level students with high self-efficacy solved more problems correctly and chose to rework more problems they missed than did those with low self-efficacy.

Self-efficacy also is differentiated from outcome expectations. Self-efficacy refers to perceptions of one's capabilities to produce actions; *outcome expectations* are beliefs about the anticipated results of those actions. Students may believe that a positive result will follow from certain actions but also believe that they lack the competence to produce those actions. It is not uncommon for students to believe that diligent studying will produce high test scores while doubting their capability to study diligently.

Although self-efficacy and outcome expectations are conceptually distinct, they often are related. Students who typically perform well have confidence in their learning capabilities and expect (and usually receive) positive outcomes for their efforts. At the same time, there is no necessary relation between self-efficacy and outcome expectations. Even students with high self-efficacy for performing well may expect a low grade if they believe that the teacher does not like them.

Self-efficacy can be applied across a vast range of tasks, activities, and situations at differing levels of specificity. However, depending on what is being managed, the events over which personal influence is exercised may entail regulation of one's own motivation, thought processes, affective states and actions, or changing environmental conditions. Self-efficacy beliefs are sensitive to these contextual factors. As such, they differ from other expectancy beliefs in that self-efficacy judgments are both more task- and situation-specific and individuals make use of these judgments in reference to some type of goal (Pajares, 1997; Pintrich & Schunk, 2002). Consequently, self-efficacy generally is assessed at a more micro-analytic level than are other expectancy constructs, which, although they are typically domain-specific, form more global and general self-perceptions.

It is meaningful to speak of self-efficacy for comprehending a scientific text, balancing chemical equations, solving algebraic equations, running a track event in certain times, and so forth. An expectancy construct such as *self-concept*, on the other hand, consists of one's collective self-perceptions formed through experiences with and interpretations of the environment and that depends heavily on reinforcements and evaluations by significant others (Pajares & Schunk, 2002; Shavelson & Bolus, 1982). Self-concept is one's general self-perception that includes self-efficacy in specific areas. For its part, self-efficacy is assessed at the optimal level of specificity that corresponds to the criterion task being assessed and the domain of functioning being analyzed.

It also merits pointing out that self-efficacy differs from the colloquial and catchword term "confidence" in important ways. For one, as has general self-concept, the construct of confidence typically has been used by researchers to describe a general, trait-like self-belief of capability that fails to specify the object of that belief. For another, the self-efficacy construct is situated carefully within a social-cognitive theory of human behavior that embeds cognitive development within a sociostructural network of influences. Finally, as Bandura (1997) has stated, people can be highly confident that they will fail at a particular task or activity. Self-efficacy is a positive, agentic self-belief of one's perceived capability to produce given levels of attainment in diverse contexts. For this reason, self-efficacy assessments include both judgments of capability and the perceived strength of those judgments.

SELF-EFFICACY IN EDUCATIONAL SETTINGS

In this section we illuminate areas where educational research and practice have clarified the operation of self-efficacy in achievement contexts. Before proceeding, however, it is important to bear in mind that self-efficacy originally was discussed by Bandura (1977a, 1977b) in the context of therapeutic behavior change. The limited therapeutic context in which the construct was initially elucidated and the complexity of environments to which it subsequently has been applied have brought to light points that require clarification.

Early self-efficacy studies dealt with persons with snake phobias (e.g., Bandura & Adams, 1977). The behaviors (e.g., touch a snake) were ones that participants knew how to perform, so self-efficacy reflected the perceived capability to perform feared actions. Treatments, which were administered in small groups or individually in a participant modeling, guided mastery approach, involved development of coping skills; learning of motor, cognitive, or social skills was not required. Participants were adults who could accurately judge their self-efficacy for performing tasks, which yielded high correspondence between self-efficacy and actual performance.

These conditions present quite a contrast to those found in educational settings in which the participants often are children who may not be able to appraise their capabilities accurately. Although some time is spent on review, most of students' time is spent learning new skills. The context is not a controlled laboratory but rather a classroom with multiple environmental distractions. There also are socio-cultural factors at work in educational settings—such as pressure to form friendships and desire to avoid trouble—that are not present in laboratories. Individual difference variables (e.g., gender, ethnicity, socioeconomic status, academic ability) may affect how teachers interact with students. For self-efficacy to affect performance there must be requisite effort and persistence, but these qualities may be socially devalued by students in favor of high ability.

Thus, even when skills are reasonably established, many factors other than self-efficacy can affect students' thoughts and actions. One could argue that students engage in many academic activities in part because they feel self-efficacious about succeeding but also because the teacher keeps them on task, because they anticipate social rewards or positive outcomes, because they do not want to appear incompetent, and so forth.

Research and practice have shown that this complexity necessitates clarification of the operation of self-efficacy in educational settings. We now discuss five areas of interest: effects of self-efficacy, self-efficacy for learning, calibration between self-efficacy and achievement, environmental conditions, and generalized self-efficacy.

Effects of Self-Efficacy

Bandura (1977a, 1977b) hypothesized that self-efficacy affects choice of activities, effort, and persistence. Research has shown that these effects are reliably obtained when participants possess the skills required (Pajares, 1996a); however, there are occasions when even persons who are skillful do not work up to the level of their capabilities because of factors such as inadequate motivation or excessive fear. For example, students who have acquired the skills required to complete a review activity and who feel self-efficacious about successfully completing it may work halfheartedly because they are unmotivated to finish. Should the teacher announce that once they finish the activity they can have free time, their motivation to complete it may improve and they are likely to display heightened effort and persistence. Snake phobics who know how to touch a snake but do not do so because of excessive fear are apt to demonstrate greater effort and persistence as their self-efficacy increases.

The relation of self-efficacy to effort and persistence can become problematic in educational contexts in which students are acquiring skills. Initially, students will not possess the skills and likely will have low self-efficacy for performing them. As they begin to acquire skills, their self-efficacy will increase with the resulting greater effort, persistence, and skill acquisition.

Once skills become reasonably well established, self-efficacy for achieving should be high; however, compared with the early stages of learning, students should have to expend less effort and persist for a shorter period of time to demonstrate successful performance. In other words, as self-efficacy and skills develop, effort and persistence may decrease, which means that self-efficacy will have a negative (rather than a positive) relation to effort and persistence.

In support of this contention, Salomon (1984) assessed sixth-graders' perceptions of self-efficacy for learning from television and print materials. They then either watched a program on television or read the comparable text, after which they were administered tests of achievement and mental effort. The latter asked students to judge how difficult the material was to understand (print or television) and how much mental effort they expended to understand it.

Students initially judged themselves significantly more self-efficacious in learning from TV than from print. Students also judged mental effort significantly greater for print compared with that of TV. Interestingly, students in the print group scored significantly higher on the achievement test than did students in the TV group. Correlations showed that the print group's self-efficacy was significantly and positively related to mental effort and achievement, which is consistent with Bandura's original predictions. In the TV group, however, self-efficacy correlated significantly and negatively with mental effort and with overall achievement. Thus, when students perceive learning to be easy they judge self-efficacy high and invest less mental effort, and thereby run the risk of achieving at a lower level.

With respect to persistence, Schunk (1995) reports analyses from various studies in which students were pretested on self-efficacy and achievement. The self-efficacy test asked students to judge their certainty for solving given types of mathematical problems. Students were shown examples of problems for brief periods of time and judged their self-efficacy for solving each type correctly. After the self-efficacy test they were given comparable problems to solve. Since pretest skills of students typically were low, their achievement scores ranged from zero to a few correct. In these studies pretest self-efficacy was not strongly related to subsequent performance, largely because of the restricted range of variability. Persistence scores also were computed for each type of problem the student attempted to solve. Among students with low self-efficacy, many give up readily but some persist for a long time attempting to solve a problem.

An entirely different picture emerged on the posttest given following a multisession instructional unit. Students with developed skills typically judged self-efficacy for solving problems high, whereas those with less-developed skills judged self-efficacy lower. Thus, the predicted positive correlation between self-efficacy and achievement was obtained. Results for persistence were inconsistent. Students with higher skills and self-efficacy typically spent less time solving problems than did students with lower skills and self-efficacy. The negative correlation between posttest self-efficacy and persistence is intuitively reasonable: As students build skills and self-efficacy they should not have to persist as long to succeed.

Thus, it seems that the relation of self-efficacy to effort and persistence is complex. In school situations, we might expect the strongest relation when skills are developed to some extent and students hold a moderate sense of self-efficacy for succeeding. Complicating the relation is the fact that teachers expect students to work on tasks regardless of the level of students' self-efficacy. Students who waste time are apt to be disciplined!

We recommend that researchers explore in depth how self-efficacy changes as skills develop at a task. In particular, it would be valuable to determine how the relation of self-efficacy to effort and persistence changes with skill acquisition. Such research would clarify the conditions under which the theoretical effects of self-efficacy manifest themselves most strongly.

This research also could address the potential influence of sociocultural factors on the link between self-efficacy and achievement outcomes. While students' self-efficacy typically increases with skill acquisition, this increase does not guarantee enhanced achievement. Research might examine whether peer school cultures moderate the link. If the culture is such that students do not want to appear too intelligent, increased self-efficacy may yield negligible gains in achievement outcomes.

Given the research findings on the predictive power of self-efficacy in academic contexts, how and to what degree does self-efficacy help explain achievement differences? There is much interest in this topic today because educators seek explanations for the *achievement gap*—the difference in achievement by different groups of students (e.g., between nonminority and minority students). More importantly, educators are searching for ways to lessen or eradicate the gap. If self-efficacy is a contributing factor—and it may well be but more research is needed—then educational interventions should include features that help raise minority students' self-efficacy for learning and performing well in school.

Clearly, differences in students' academic achievement is too complex a matter to permit the contention that differences in achievement are due to differences in perceived competence (Schunk, 1984). Self-efficacy is neither the major determinant of achievement nor the magic elixir that can make all learners work to their full potential. Students perform differently in school for myriad reasons, including differences in aptitude, general mental ability, interest, perceived value, effort, perseverance, use of self-regulatory strategies, teaching and instruction, and availability of materials (Gustafson & Undheim, 1996; Keogh & MacMillan, 1996; Snow, Corno, & Jackson, 1996). Social and familial variables such as peer influence, family income, and parental expectations also play a hand in the academic outcomes that students will attain (Steinberg, 1998; Steinberg, Brown, & Dornbusch, 1996).

There is, nonetheless, good reason to believe that many differences in achievement can be better explained by the beliefs that students come to develop about their academic capabilities than by constructs often thought to be the key determinants of achievement. The Collins (1982) study, discussed earlier, illustrated this point. Other researchers have found that self-efficacy determines academic achievement independent of ability and skills (Pajares & Kranzler, 1995). Researchers have also reported that students with high self-efficacy engage in more effective self-regulatory strategies at each level of ability (Bouffard-Bouchard, Parent, & Larivèe, 1991; Zimmerman, 2000) and engage the academic persistence necessary to maintain high academic achievement (Lent, Brown, & Larkin, 1984, 1986; Schunk, 1984).

In a meta-analysis of studies conducted between 1977 and 1988, Multon and colleagues (1991) reported that efficacy beliefs were related to performance (r_u = .38) and accounted for approximately 14% of the variance in academic performance. However, effect sizes depended on specific characteristics of the studies, notably on the types of efficacy and performance measures used. Stronger effects were obtained by researchers who compared specific efficacy judgments with basic cognitive skills measures of performance, developed highly concordant self-efficacy/performance indices, and administered them at the same time. In another meta-analysis, Stajkovic and Luthans (1998) found that the average weighted correlation between self-efficacy and work-related performance was (G)r = .38, which transforms to an impressive 28% gain in task performance.

It is clear that academic achievement requires both the skills and the confidence to optimally use these skills. There is also little doubt that students' difficulties in basic academic skills are often directly related to their beliefs that they cannot read, write, handle numbers, or think that they cannot learn, even when such things are not objectively true. That is to say, many students have difficulty in school not because they are incapable of performing successfully but because they are incapable of believing that they can perform successfully. They have learned to see themselves as incapable of handling academic work or to see the work as irrelevant to their life. Consequently, taking into account students' self-efficacy beliefs is critical to the success of academic strategies and instructional interventions.

Self-Efficacy for Learning

Subsequent to Bandura's (1977a, 1977b) original writings researchers in various domains realized the potential widespread applicability of self-efficacy as an explanatory construct for behavioral change. As self-efficacy was applied outside of the limited therapeutic context, it became evident that the original definition did not adequately capture the scope of its influence.

To explain this point we first describe the context of the early clinical studies. Bandura, Adams, and Beyer (1977) administered adult snake phobics a self-efficacy and a behavioral pretest consisting of progressively more threatening encounters with a snake. For the self-efficacy assessment, participants rated magnitude of self-efficacy by designating which tasks they judged they could perform; tasks were ordered from easy to difficult. They then rated strength of self-efficacy by judging how sure they were that they could perform the tasks they had judged they could perform. To measure generality of self-efficacy, participants made magnitude and strength ratings for the same tasks but with a type of snake different from the type used on the pretest.

There were three experimental conditions. In the participant modeling condition, participants initially observed therapists model encounters with a snake. Performance aids were introduced so that participants could perform the activities. These aids included decomposing complex tasks into basic components, performing activities jointly with participants, gradually increasing the duration of performance, and using protective devices. As treatment progressed the aids were gradually withdrawn. After participants completed all tasks on the hierarchy, a short period of self-directed mastery was given during which they performed tasks unaided.

In the modeling condition, participants observed therapists model all of the feared activities but did not perform the activities themselves. Control participants were given only the pre- and postassessments, separated by time intervals comparable to those of participant modeling participants. Following training, all participants received a posttest that was comparable to the pretest except that self-efficacy was assessed before and after the behavioral test and the test included both the pretest snake and a generalization snake comparable in fear arousal.

In these and similar clinical studies (e.g., Bandura & Adams, 1977), participants possessed the skills required to perform the behaviors; for example, they knew how to touch a snake and allow it to sit in their laps. They did not perform skills, however, because of feared consequences. The situation is much different in educational settings because most of the time students are engaged in learning. Especially on pretests or at the outset of instructional units, students have little or no self-efficacy for performing skills they have not acquired.

A better predictor of subsequent motivation and performance is *self-efficacy for learning*. We should expect that students who judge themselves self-efficacious for learning skills (as opposed to already performing them) would be more likely to choose to engage in the learning, expend effort, and persist at the task. These motivational effects should result in greater learning and higher achievement.

These predictions were supported in early research by Schunk and Hanson (1985). Following a pretest on subtraction self-efficacy and skill, children who lacked subtraction skills observed videotaped peer models demonstrate either rapid (mastery model) or gradual (coping model) acquisition of subtraction skills, observed teacher models demonstrate subtraction operations, or did not observe models. Children then judged their self-efficacy for learning to solve different types of subtraction problems, after which they received subtraction instruction and practice over sessions. Posttest assessments included self-efficacy and skill.

Although Schunk and Hanson (1985) were interested in differential effects due to type of model, for our purposes the key findings involve self-efficacy for learning. Across all conditions this measure proved to be an accurate predictor of instructional session performance (a measure of motivation), and posttest self-efficacy and skill. Additionally, self-efficacy for learning related negatively to posttest persistence, which supports our earlier point that as skills develop, less persistence may be needed to achieve.

Different learning situations call forth different self-efficacy beliefs. When students are familiar with task demands, they call on the self-efficacy beliefs that closely correspond to that task. In these cases, students can interpret their prior attainments and identify the skills on which to formulate their *self-efficacy for performance*. At this level, specificity of self-belief and correspondence with a task works with familiarity to maximize prediction of performance.

When task demands are unfamiliar, however, students must generalize from prior attainments perceived as similar to the required task and gauge their self-efficacy with judgments they believe correspond to the novel requirements. Such judgments cannot be based on perceived skills related to the tasks, for students are not clear which skills will be required. If the task is completely novel, the student may have no task skills to assess. At this level, self-efficacy either is lacking or must be inferred from past attainments in situations perceived as similar to the new one. In these cases, self-efficacy for performance is predictive to the degree that self-regulatory skills and strategies have generalized to the novel task.

Consequently, self-efficacy for learning should be an excellent predictor of motivation and achievement in any setting in which knowledge and skills must be acquired to perform the tasks (Schunk, Hanson, & Cox, 1987). If the learning is complex and involves several substeps, then the self-efficacy assessment can reflect this by asking students to judge their self-efficacy for learning these substeps. Self-efficacy for learning also is useful for instruction. Self-efficacy for learning judgments inform teachers which activities students perceive as the most difficult, and teachers can tailor their instruction and practice accordingly.

An important area for future research deals with self-efficacy for learning from various forms of technology. Technology has opened the door to new means of learning including distance education, e-learning, blended instruction (part face to face and part distance), chatrooms, e-mail, and the like. Some students who feel confident about learning in traditional formats may feel less efficacious about learning from technology. Research is required to explain and clarify how self-efficacy for learning changes as students gain experience with information technology and whether self-efficacy for learning via technology accurately predicts motivation and learning.

Such research could address sociocultural issues bearing on the access that various groups have to technology. Thus, computers and the Internet expose students from minority groups to social models of self-efficacy and self-regulation who differ from their own cultural models. Technology may be a powerful tool for disseminating a common model of learning and self-regulation, which might have the effect of making learners from different cultural and ethnic groups more similar in their learning, motivation, and achievement beliefs.

While such an international community of learners would have instructional advantages, this will depend on access to technology. Students in areas highly impacted by poverty may have limited access, with the result that they will fall farther behind in educational achievement and opportunities. Such students might become demoralized even if they feel efficacious about learning if they believe they have inadequate opportunities to learn in their present environments.

Calibration between Self-Efficacy and Performance

Calibration refers to how well self-efficacy judgments relate to actual performance on the accompanying tasks (Pajares & Kranzler, 1995). Bandura (1977a) recommended a microanalytic strategy to study calibration. For the domain under study a hierarchy of tasks is developed, ranging from easy to difficult. Individuals judge self-efficacy for each task, after which they are given the same or similar tasks to perform.

When people judge themselves capable of performing a task and then perform it, or when they judge themselves incapable of performing it and cannot perform it, they are said to be well calibrated because, in essence, their self-efficacy and performance correspond as regards accuracy of judgment. Alternatively, when students judge themselves efficacious but cannot perform a task or judge themselves inefficacious but are indeed able to perform the task, they are said to possess poor calibration because their judgment of capability and their subsequent performance fail to correspond.

In the early clinical studies (Bandura & Adams, 1977; Bandura et al., 1977) the percentage of calibration between self-efficacy and performance was typically very high; it was not unusual to obtain 90% or higher calibration. This situation changes when we move to cognitive skill acquisition. Educational studies typically have obtained lower percentages (Schunk, 1995). For example, using children in mathematical division Schunk (1981) obtained percentages ranging from approximately 30–85%. Moreover, researchers typically report that students at various academic levels often display poor calibration, particularly a bias toward overconfidence (Hackett & Betz, 1989; Pajares & Kranzler, 1995; Pajares & Miller, 1994, 1997; Schraw, Potenza, & Nebelsick-Gullet, 1995).

There are several possible reasons for the discrepancies between the early self-efficacy studies and recent findings. The early clinical studies used adults; most educational studies use children. Children may not fully understand the range of skills required to successfully solve a math problem, answer a comprehension question, write a coherent paragraph, and so forth. Cognitive skills are hard to judge; it is difficult to know when one is becoming more skillful (e.g., becoming a better writer or problem-solver). Sometimes cognitive skill tasks may seem deceptively easy. Thus, many children unskilled at subtraction judge a problem such as 111 – 57 = __ as relatively easy because they erroneously believe that solving it requires subtracting the smaller number from the larger one in each column (which leads to the answer of 146, a number larger than the one with which they began).

In school, sociocultural factors may also come into play. Most learning at the elementary level is geared toward basic skills, and the expectation is that children will master them. Teachers provide much encouragement. Presenting children with a self-efficacy assessment may seem unrealistic to them, and they may be tempted to answer positively due to the constant encouragement they receive about being able to learn. Children may be reluctant to report that they feel incapable of performing a task.

The issue of calibration is educationally important. Children who overestimate their capabilities may try many tasks and fail, which can decrease motivation. Those who underestimate what they can do will be averse to trying tasks and thereby preclude skill development. Instructional procedures that provide information about skills required actually may increase calibration. Schunk (1981) found that a powerful treatment combining modeling of division operations and effort attributional feedback (i.e., linking children's outcomes with effort expended) led to significantly higher calibration between self-efficacy and performance than did modeling alone, a didactic instructional strategy, and the didactic strategy plus attributional feedback. The implication is that the modeling plus attributions treatment conveyed the clearest information to children about competencies required for task success.

Bandura (1986, 1997) argued that successful functioning is best served by reasonably accurate self-efficacy appraisals, although the most functional judgments are those that slightly exceed what one actually can accomplish because this overestimation increases persistence. But how much self-efficacy is too much self-efficacy, when can overconfidence be characterized as excessive and maladaptive in an academic enterprise, what factors help create inaccurate self-perceptions, and what are the likely effects of such inaccuracy? Bandura contends that the stronger their self-efficacy, the more likely are students to select challenging tasks, persist at them, and perform them successfully. Researchers will have to determine to what degree high self-efficacy demonstrated in the face of incongruent performance attainments ultimately results in these benefits. Efforts to lower students' self-efficacy percepts or interventions designed to raise already overconfident beliefs should be discouraged, but improving students' calibration—the accuracy of their self-perceptions—will require helping them to better understand what they know and do not know so that they may more effectively deploy appropriate cognitive strategies as they perform a task.

Issues of accuracy, however, should not be divorced from issues such as well-being, optimism, and will—all of which can be affected by sociocultural factors. As people evaluate their lives, they are more likely to regret the challenge not confronted, the contest not entered, the risk unrisked, and the road not taken as a result of self-doubt rather than the action taken as a result of optimism (Bandura, 1997). The challenge to educators on this account will be to make students more familiar with their own internal mental structures without lowering their self-efficacy, optimism, and drive.

Greater awareness of educators of potentially damaging sociocultural influences is important, because students who lack confidence in skills they possess are less likely to engage in tasks in which those skills are required and may quickly give up in the face of difficulty. For example, some researchers have found that girls perform as capably as do boys in varied academic tasks but often report lower self-efficacy, particularly at higher academic levels (Pajares & Miller, 1994, 1997). In one study, gifted girls were actually biased toward underconfidence (Pajares, 1996b).

Additional studies are required to discover the extent of these phenomena across academic areas and levels, and how differing beliefs are created and maintained in the face of similar ability and performance. Investigations are particularly needed at lower academic levels, especially those in which these sorts of self-beliefs begin to be created. Exploring the nature of the relationship between efficacy judgments, calibration, performance attainments, and the hypothesized effects of self-efficacy among diverse groups continues to be a promising avenue of inquiry to establish the universality of the components of self-efficacy and their application.

Future research might explore how sociocultural influences in classrooms affect calibration. If calibration between self-efficacy judgment and related performance requires understanding task demands and assessing one's competencies, then treatments that convey information about these should increase calibration. Potential ways to increase calibration might be to have students observe models who explain and demonstrate what they are doing, provide students with specific feedback about which steps they are and are not accomplishing properly, and allowing students to periodically self-assess their skills and areas in which they need further work.

Researchers might explore how the achievement culture of the school affects calibration. Thus, we might compare school cultures that stress high achievement where students are expected to attend the best universities with cultures in which a smaller percentage of students attend college because the community places greater value on work after high school rather than college. Would the high expectations in the former lead to lower calibration? Might students in the latter underestimate their self-efficacy relative to their actual skills? Such research will shed light on a potentially moderating influence of self-efficacy on achievement.

Environmental Conditions

In a perfect world, students with higher self-efficacy would choose to engage in academic tasks, expend effort to succeed, persist to overcome obstacles, learn knowledge and skills, and achieve at a high level. But we know that school environments do not offer a perfect world. Indeed, sociocultural factors associated with schools can make the effects of self-efficacy problematic. As Bandura (1986) discussed:

> There are a number of school practices that, for the less talented or ill prepared, tend to convert instructional experiences into education in inefficacy. These include lock-step sequences of instruction, which lose many children along the way; ability groupings which further diminish the self-efficacy appraisal of those cast into subordinate ranks; and competitive practices where many are doomed to failure for the success of a relative few. (p. 417)

These factors can lower self-efficacy with the predicted effects, but there also are factors that will not necessarily lower self-efficacy but can produce diminished motivation, learning, and achievement. One of these is *feedback*. There are many types of feedback; our interest here is in feedback that conveys information to students about what the feedback provider thinks of his or her capabilities. We use attributional feedback as an illustration.

Attributional feedback links performance with one or more attributions (perceived causes). Much research has explored the effects on achievement outcomes of effort (e.g., "That's correct. You are working hard.") and ability (e.g., "That's correct. You are good at this.") attributional feedback. Although both types of feedback can strengthen students' self-efficacy, the key is feedback credibility (Schunk, 1995). Effort feedback is credible when students believe they are working hard, and ability feedback when they believe they are performing well with less effort. When a mismatch occurs it can send the wrong message. Thus, when students who believe they are improving and are not having to work so hard to succeed receive effort feedback, they may believe that the teacher doubts they can perform well. Although these students may maintain high self-efficacy, they may become less motivated to achieve in class.

Attribution researchers have shown how students' perceptions of attributions change with development (Covington, 1992; Harari & Covington, 1981). In young children effort and ability are not differentiated. As students become older these causes become distinguished and effort often is devalued in favor of ability: Students would rather be seen as intelligent than as hard workers. Nonetheless, teachers tend to stress effort to students as the cause of their academic outcomes. If there are social pressures against working too hard, students, despite their self-efficacy beliefs, may not work as diligently as they could and performance may suffer.

Bandura (1997) explained how grouping can influence self-efficacy. We wish to underscore the potential effects of grouping practices that do not allow students to change groups. Within any group students' skills will progress at different rates. Those who show greater improvement are apt to feel self-efficacious and simultaneously demoralized because they cannot move to the next group, which is not a desirable situation for motivation.

In short, schools are complex environments in which a multitude of sociocultural factors operate that can affect students' performances independently of their self-efficacy. Thus, highly efficacious and skillful students who desire friendships with less-talented peers may purposely perform at a lower level to compare more favorably with their peers and not appear superior in ability. Students low in self-efficacy may nevertheless work diligently to avoid being criticized by their teachers and thereby lose privileges. Students who believe that their teachers perceive them as lacking skills may work only as hard as they must to meet the teachers' standards, regardless of how self-efficacious the students feel. The latter situation could occur among students with limited English proficiency who despite their abilities and self-efficacy for learning may be viewed by teachers as less capable than nonminority peers.

Schools are a far cry from controlled laboratory settings, which makes the operation of self-efficacy more variable and its mediational and predictive power more complex. We suggest that researchers continue to examine how social and cultural variables affect students' learning and motivation, as well as the conditions that undermine the effects of self-efficacy. This focus seems especially germane given the increasing diversity found in schools, which brings together more sociocultural factors that potentially can affect achievement outcomes.

For example, the influx of Asian and Hispanic American students in schools has resulted in often-rapid shifts in school cultures. From a self-efficacy perspective, we might investigate how well these changing demographics have been taken into account in instructional planning. Do teachers keep teaching the same as before even though the background experiences of their students have changed? Do teachers who attempt to integrate these experiences into their lessons build students' self-efficacy for learning better than teachers who do not? These types of research questions also will yield information highly useful for teacher preparation programs.

General Versus Specific Self-Efficacy

We noted earlier that self-efficacy is a belief about what one can do. It is reasonable to speak of a sense of self-efficacy for tasks such as reading and comprehending the main ideas in a Steinbeck novel, using a graphing calculator to graph linear equations, solving time–rate–distance problems in science, and writing a descriptive paragraph in French. Self-efficacy is contrasted with general or global self-beliefs such as self-concept and self-esteem (Pajares & Schunk, 2002).

Despite this definitional emphasis on specificity, some investigators have examined whether self-efficacy has predictive generality. We might expect that self-efficacy developed in one context in which people learn adaptive skills should generalize to other situations to the degree that individuals believe those same skills will help them in the new situations.

Smith (1989) tested this idea with text-anxious college students. Participants were taught skills for coping with anxiety (e.g., cognitive restructuring, self-instructional statements, relaxation training). Self-efficacy was assessed both specifically (i.e., relative to the behaviors taught in the coping skills program) and generally (i.e., being able to perform behaviors that facilitate control of their lives outside of the training setting). Relative to a control condition, coping-skills students demonstrated an increase in both specific and general self-efficacy. Thus, exposure to the coping skills program increased students' general perceptions of their behavioral effectiveness.

We also know that self-efficacy beliefs generalize across the self-system and can inform the execution of novel tasks. In fact, most experimental tests of self-efficacy's causality employ novel tasks. Bouffard-Bouchard (1990), for example, experimentally induced high or low self-efficacy in college students by providing positive or negative feedback and found that students whose self-efficacy had been raised used more efficient problem-solving strategies on a novel task and outperformed students whose self-efficacy had been lowered.

In addition to the theoretical rationale for why self-efficacy perceptions might generalize, there also is a practical issue. School curricula are based on the expectation of transfer; for example, skills used in algebra 1 should transfer to algebra 2, writing and vocabulary skills taught in grade 7 are expected to transfer to grade 8, and so forth. Many states have mandated end-of-grade/course tests designed to ensure that students have mastered the basic curriculum objectives. The idea of building students' self-efficacy for specific skills is useful to the extent that this self-efficacy generalizes beyond the specific content to cover other material in the course or grade level.

We are well familiar with the conditions under which judgments of competence can generalize across activities; that is, the extent to which they relate to, or transfer across, different performance tasks or domains (Bandura, 1986; Schunk, 1991). When differing tasks require similar subskills, self-efficacy to demonstrate the requisite subskills should predict the differing outcomes. Generality also can take place when the skills required to accomplish dissimilar activities are jointly acquired. Students' mathematics and verbal self-efficacy may generalize if the skills for each subject are adequately taught and developed by a competent teacher. Subskills required to organize a course of action are themselves governed by broader self-regulatory skills such as knowing how to diagnose task demands or constructing and evaluating alternative strategies. Possessing these self-regulatory skills permits students to improve their performances across varied academic activities (Zimmerman, 1989).

Generalized coping skills work in similar fashion by reducing stress and promoting effective functioning across varied domains. Self-efficacy also should generalize when commonalities are cognitively structured across activities. For instance, if students realize that increased effort and persistence result in academic progress and greater understanding in mathematics, it is likely that similar connections may be made to other subjects. Finally, there are "transforming experiences" that come about as the result of powerful performance attainments and strengthen beliefs in diverse areas of one's life—areas often greatly unrelated.

The hypothesized conditions under which judgments of competence should generalize across varied activities and domains provide rich opportunity for empirical investigation that would help trace the genesis of self-beliefs as well as their possible interconnections. Such insights also might shed light on findings demonstrating that students often have great difficulty transferring strategies and various types of knowledge across academic domains (Pressley et al., 1990). It is possible that, although the use of strategies or knowledge functions may not so easily transfer, the beliefs that accompany these cognitive processes may more easily travel. That is, cognitive, knowledge-based components required to accomplish a task may make the voyage from one task to another greater in difficulty than the belief components that provide the effort and persistence necessary to succeed at the novel task. It should prove beneficial to discover the degree to which the process of transferring beliefs resembles or differs from the process of transferring other cognitive processes.

One of the reasons for exploring the generality of self-efficacy is to increase its practical utility. Results from such studies would inform theoretical contentions about the influence of self-efficacy on academic performances and about the relationship between self-efficacy and other motivation constructs. However, Bandura (1997) cautioned that empirical results verifying that efficacy beliefs generalize across domains should not result in the "pursuit of a psychological Grail of generality" (p. 24) that would seek to find root cause for varying self-beliefs. Similar cognitive subskills or strong self-regulatory efficacy should aid performance in varied domains, but specific pursuits will usually differ in the specialized competencies they require. With these cautions in mind, understanding the conditions and contexts under which self-beliefs will generalize to differing academic activities offers valuable possibilities for intervention and instructional strategies that may help students build both competence and the necessary accompanying self-perceptions of competence.

Research especially is needed on how curricula can be structured to facilitate self-efficacy generalizing beyond the specific context in which it is developed. We might expect that teachers could foster generalization by pointing out to students how the skills they previously learned are needed with the new material, showing how new material is similar to previous material, and including periodic review activities intermixed with new learning.

Generalization also may be fostered when teachers work in interdisciplinary teams so they can stress the same skills in their respective classes. As with other ideas we have presented in this chapter, sociocultural factors can affect generalization of self-efficacy. Although teams are common in middle schools, they function with varied effectiveness, and in some schools "teaming" means little more than students taking classes from different teachers. To foster self-efficacy may require shifting the school culture to one where teachers work in teams to ensure integration of content and use of skills and strategies across contexts. Research should address how the effectiveness of teacher teams affects students' self-efficacy.

CONCLUSION

A theory is a scientifically acceptable set of principles offered to explain a phenomenon. Self-efficacy is a central construct in social-cognitive theory, which seeks to explain a broad range of phenomena by taking into account the reciprocal influences among persons, their actions, and their environments.

Social-cognitive theorists do not contend that self-efficacy is the only, or even the most important, factor in learning and behavioral change. Researchers sometimes forget this fact, such as when they explore the effects of self-efficacy on other variables and find that its influence is not as strong as they had anticipated. Rather, social-cognitive theorists readily acknowledge that self-efficacy will have little or no effect on behavior when requisite skills are lacking. Moreover, the effects of self-efficacy can be outweighed by many other factors—motivational and behavioral—including outcome expectations, values, goals, environmental contingencies, and myriad social demands and pressures.

We believe that the years since 1977 have shown that self-efficacy is a robust construct that plays an influential role in much learning, motivation, self-regulation, and other forms of human functioning. We also believe that, like many other theoretical constructs, the original specifications of the causes, operation, and consequences of self-efficacy require ongoing clarification and modification in light of empirical and practical evidence.

These conclusions are especially pertinent to educational settings. Researchers have shown that self-efficacy is highly applicable to educational contexts: It exerts a significant influence on students' and teachers' thoughts and actions. At the same time, educational settings complicate the relation of self-efficacy to outcomes. Multiple factors influence students' learning, motivation, and achievement, one of which is self-efficacy. As Bandura (1977a, 1977b) hypothesized, self-efficacy exerts its greatest effects when skills are at least reasonably established and there are no powerful external forces at work to affect students' actions. With respect to schooling, self-efficacy for learning and refining one's skills is often a better predictor of motivation and achievement than is self-efficacy for what one can do at present.

We have suggested clarifications and some directions for future self-efficacy research in education. It is encouraging to see so much interest by researchers and practitioners in self-efficacy. This suggests that we will continue to learn about the role of self-efficacy in education and that practitioners will increasingly attend to how their instructional practices affect students' learning and self-efficacy. If self-efficacy's second 25 years show as much activity as its first 25, the field of education will benefit immensely.

REFERENCES

Bandura, A. (1977a). Self-efficacy: Toward a unifying theory of behavioral change. *Psychological Review, 84*, 191–215.

Bandura, A. (1977b). *Social learning theory.* Englewood Cliffs, NJ: Prentice Hall.

Bandura, A. (1982). Self-efficacy mechanism in human agency. *American Psychologist, 37,* 122–147.

Bandura, A. (1986). *Social foundations of thought and action: A social cognitive theory.* Englewood Cliffs, NJ: Prentice Hall.

Bandura, A. (1997). *Self-efficacy: The exercise of control.* New York: Freeman.

Bandura, A. (2001). Social cognitive theory: An agentic perspective. *Annual Review of Psychology, 52,* 1–26.

Bandura, A., & Adams, N. E. (1977). Analysis of self-efficacy theory of behavioral change. *Cognitive Therapy and Research, 1,* 287–308.

Bandura, A., Adams, N. E., & Beyer, J. (1977). Cognitive processes mediating behavioral change. *Journal of Personality and Social Psychology, 35,* 125–139.

Bouffard-Bouchard, T. (1990) Influence of self-efficacy on performance in a cognitive task. *Journal of Social Psychology, 130,* 353–363.

Bouffard-Bouchard, T., Parent, S., & Larivèe, S. (1991). Influence of self-efficacy on self-regulation and performance among junior and senior high-school aged students. *International Journal of Behavioral Development, 14,* 153–164.

Cervone, D., & Peake, P. K. (1986). Anchoring, efficacy, and action: The influence of judgmental heuristics on self-efficacy judgments and behavior. *Journal of Personality and Social Psychology, 50,* 492–501.

Collins, J. L. (1982, March). *Self-efficacy and ability in achievement behavior.* Paper presented at the annual meeting of the American Educational Research Association, New York.

Covington, M. V. (1992). *Making the grade: A self-worth perspective on motivation and school reform.* Cambridge, UK: Cambridge University Press.

Gustafson, J., & Undheim, J. O. (1996). Individual differences in cognitive functions. In R. C. Calfee & D. C. Berliner (Eds.), *Handbook of educational psychology* (pp. 186–242). New York: Macmillan.

Hackett, G., & Betz, N. E. (1989). An exploration of the mathematics self-efficacy/ mathematics performance correspondence. *Journal for Research in Mathematics Education, 20,* 261–273.

Harari, O., & Covington, M. V. (1981). Reactions to achievement behavior from a teacher and student perspective: A developmental analysis. *American Educational Research Journal, 18,* 15–28.

Keogh, B. K., & MacMillan, D. J. (1996). Exceptionality. In R. C. Calfee & D. C. Berliner (Eds.), *Handbook of educational psychology* (pp. 311–330). New York: Macmillan.

Lent, R. W., Brown, S. D., & Hackett, G. (1994). Toward a unifying social cognitive theory of career and academic interest, choice, and performance. *Journal of Vocational Behavior, 45,* 79–122.

Lent, R. W., Brown, S. D., & Larkin, K. C. (1984). Relation of self-efficacy expectations to academic achievement and persistence. *Journal of Counseling Psychology, 31,* 356–362.

Lent, R. W., Brown, S. D., & Larkin, K. C. (1986). Self-efficacy in the prediction of academic performance and perceived career options. *Journal of Counseling Psychology, 33,* 265–269.

Multon, K. D., Brown, S. D., & Lent, R. W. (1991). Relation of self-efficacy beliefs to academic outcomes: A meta-analytic investigation. *Journal of Counseling Psychology, 38,* 30–38.

Pajares, F. (1996a). Self-efficacy beliefs in academic settings. *Review of Educational Research, 66*, 543–578.

Pajares, F. (1996b). Self-efficacy beliefs and mathematical problem solving of gifted students. *Contemporary Educational Psychology, 21*, 325–344.

Pajares, F. (1997). Current directions in self-efficacy research. In M. Maehr & P. R. Pintrich (Eds.), *Advances in motivation and achievement* (Vol. 10, pp. 1–49). Greenwich, CT: JAI Press.

Pajares, F., & Kranzler, J. (1995). Self-efficacy beliefs and general mental ability in mathematical problem-solving. *Contemporary Educational Psychology, 29*, 426–443.

Pajares, F., & Miller, M. D. (1994). The role of self-efficacy and self-concept beliefs in mathematical problem-solving: A path analysis. *Journal of Educational Psychology, 86*, 193–203.

Pajares, F., & Miller, M. D. (1997). Mathematics self-efficacy and mathematical problem-solving: Implications of using different forms of assessment. *Journal of Experimental Education, 65*, 213–228.

Pajares, F., & Schunk, D. H. (2002). Self and self-belief in psychology and education: A historical perspective. In J. Aronson (Ed.), *Improving academic achievement: Impact of psychological factors on education* (pp. 3–21). San Diego, CA: Academic Press.

Pintrich, P. R., & Schunk, D. H. (2002). *Motivation in education: Theory, research, and applications* (2nd ed.). Upper Saddle River, NJ: Merrill/Prentice Hall.

Pressley, M., Woloshyn, V., Lysynchuk, I. M., Martin, V., Wood, E., & Willoughby, T. (1990). A primer of research on cognitive strategy instruction: The important issues and how to address them. *Educational Psychology Review, 2*, 1–58.

Salomon, G. (1984). Television is "easy" and print is "tough": The differential investment of mental effort in learning as a function of perceptions and attributions. *Journal of Educational Psychology, 76*, 647–658.

Schraw, G., Potenza, M. T., & Nebelsick-Gullet, L. (1995). Constraints on the calibration of performance. *Contemporary Educational Psychology, 18*, 445–463.

Schunk, D. H. (1981). Modeling and attributional effects on children's achievement: A self-efficacy analysis. *Journal of Educational Psychology, 73*, 93–105.

Schunk, D. H. (1984). Self-efficacy perspective on achievement behavior. *Educational Psychologist, 19*, 48–58.

Schunk, D. H. (1987). Peer models and children's behavioral change. *Review of Educational Research, 57*, 149–174.

Schunk, D. H. (1989). Self-efficacy and achievement behaviors. *Educational Psychology Review, 1*, 173–208.

Schunk, D. H. (1991). Self-efficacy and academic motivation. *Educational Psychologist, 26*, 207–231.

Schunk, D. H. (1995). Self-efficacy and education and instruction. In J. E. Maddux (Ed.), *Self-efficacy, adaptation, and adjustment: Theory, research, and applications* (pp. 281–303). New York: Plenum Press.

Schunk, D. H., & Hanson, A. R. (1985). Peer models: Influence on children's self-efficacy and achievement. *Journal of Educational Psychology, 77*, 313–322.

Schunk, D. H., Hanson, A. R., & Cox, P. D. (1987). Peer-model attributes and children's achievement behaviors. *Journal of Educational Psychology, 79*, 54–61.

Schunk, D. H., & Pajares, F. (2002). The development of academic self-efficacy. In A. Wigfield & J. S. Eccles (Eds.), *Development of achievement motivation* (pp. 15–31). San Diego, CA: Academic Press.

Shavelson, R. J, & Bolus, R. (1982). Self-concept: The interplay of theory and methods. *Journal of Educational Psychology, 74,* 3–17.

Smith, R. E. (1989). Effects of coping skills training on generalized self-efficacy and locus of control. *Journal of Personality and Social Psychology, 56,* 228–233.

Snow, R. E., Corno, L., & Jackson, D. III. (1996). Individual differences in affective and conative functions. In R. C. Calfee & D. C. Berliner (Eds.), *Handbook of educational psychology* (pp. 243–310). New York: Macmillan.

Stajkovic, A. D., & Luthans, F. (1998). Self-efficacy and work-related performance: A meta-analysis. *Psychological Bulletin, 124,* 240–261.

Steinberg, L. (1998). Standards outside the classroom. In D. Ravitch (Ed.), *Brookings papers on educational policy* (pp. 319–358). Washington, DC: Brookings Institute.

Steinberg, L., Brown, B. B., & Dornbusch, S. M. (1996). *Beyond the classroom: Why schools are failing and what parents need to do.* New York: Simon & Schuster.

Zimmerman, B. J. (1989). A social cognitive view of self-regulated academic learning. *Journal of Educational Psychology, 81,* 329–339.

Zimmerman, B. J. (2000). Attaining self-regulation: A social cognitive perspective. In M. Boekaerts, P. R. Pintrich, & M. Zeidner (Eds.), *Handbook of self-regulation* (pp. 13–39). San Diego, CA: Academic Press.

Zimmerman, B. J., & Paulsen, A. S. (1995). Self-monitoring during collegiate studying: An invaluable tool for academic self-regulation. In P. R. Pintrich (Ed.), *New directions in college teaching and learning: Understanding self-regulated learning* (pp. 13–27). San Francisco: Jossey-Bass.

CHAPTER 7

SOCIOCULTURAL INFLUENCE AND STUDENTS' DEVELOPMENT OF ACADEMIC SELF-REGULATION
A Social-Cognitive Perspective

Barry J. Zimmerman

INTRODUCTION

On the first day of kindergarten, children begin the daunting task of adapting to the social and physical environment of a school system that assumes they will develop key self-regulatory processes and self-beliefs. *Academic self-regulation* has been defined as self-generated thoughts, feelings, and actions for attaining educational goals (Schunk & Zimmerman, 1994),

Big Theories Revisited
Volume 4 in: Research on Sociocultural Influences on Motivation and Learning, pages 139–164.
Copyright © 2004 by Information Age Publishing, Inc.
All rights of reproduction in any form reserved.
ISBN: 1-59311-053-7 (hardcover), 1-59311-052-9 (paperback)

and it includes such processes as planning and managing time; attending to and concentrating on instruction; organizing, rehearsing, and coding information; establishing a productive work environment; and using social resources effectively (Corno, 1993; Pintrich & De Groot, 1991; Pressley et al., 1990; Weinstein & Mayer, 1986; Zimmerman, 1989). Because self-regulation is self-initiated, it also involves important motivational beliefs, such as self-efficacy, outcome expectations, task interest or valuing, a learning goal orientation, and self-satisfaction with one's learning and performance (Zimmerman, 2000).

Schools are organized to provide greater instructional assistance to students in the early grades, and then teachers progressively reduce that support as students enter middle school, high school, and college. For example, during the primary school grades, teachers regulate students' learning by setting explicit guidelines for classroom functioning and by requiring few student-regulated learning experiences outside the classroom, such as studying. However, as students enter subsequent levels of schooling (i.e., middle school, high school, and college), they encounter more fluid classroom environments and higher expectations for personal responsibility. For example, in middle school, students are often taught academic subjects, such as mathematics or English, by different teachers and are expected to manage multiple homework assignments on their own (De Corte, Verschaffel, & Op'T Eynde, 2000). To succeed in these more demanding academic settings, students need greater personal initiative and self-regulation, but how do they become self-regulated as learners? Although many students develop the requisite underlying skills and motivational beliefs, some do not (Zimmerman & Martinez-Pons, 1986). What are the sources of these individual differences?

Although students' development of academic self-regulation is affected by many factors, sociocultural forces figure prominently. Although these forces include national, local, and familial sociocultural groups, this chapter focuses on familial influences. Children learn to manage their personal and academic responsibilities within a rich social milieu that involves such significant others as parents, siblings, teachers, and peers. Social-cognitive researchers have studied how children acquire self-regulatory processes from these socializing agents and how these self-regulatory processes, in turn, enhance children's adaptation, resourcefulness, and creativity (Bandura, 1986; Beimiller, Shany, Inglis, & Meichenbaum, 1998; Pajares, 1996; Schunk, 1989, 2001; Zimmerman, 1989, 2000). Self-regulatory processes not only enable children to manage their personal and academic activities more effectively, they also prepare children to manage social resources as well, such as help-seeking or working with a study partner (Newman, 1994; Zimmerman & Martinez-Pons, 1986). During the course of students' academic development, sociocultural influences and self-regulatory processes become increasingly interdependent. Although students are initially very dependent on teachers and parents to initiate and structure their learning, they become increasingly able to utilize these sociocultural agents on a self-initiated and self-regulated basis during development. For example, academic experts, such as professional writers, will seek out respected colleagues to provide feedback in selected areas when they run into difficulties. The increasing interdependence of sociocultlural influences and self-regulatory processes will be discussed in detail later in this chapter.

In this chapter, I describe children's development of academic self-regulatory skill from a social-cognitive perspective. First, students' academic self-regulation is discussed in terms of key underlying processes and motivational beliefs that are linked in a series of phases. Second, sociocultural influences on children's personal and academic self-regulation are considered with special attention to the role of parents. Third, research on basic socialization processes, such as modeling, social feedback, and social collaboration, are discussed in terms of students' academic self-regulation. And finally, I discuss students' development of self-regulatory competence in a series of qualitatively distinct levels along with research demonstrating the sequential validity of these levels.

ACADEMIC SELF-REGULATION: A CYCLICAL PROCESS ANALYSIS

According to a social-cognitive perspective, students' academic effectiveness depends on their use of key self-regulatory processes and their beliefs about the effectiveness of those processes. These motivational beliefs and learning processes are self-regulated in three cyclical phases: forethought, performance, and self-reflection (Zimmerman, 2000). Forethought phase processes and beliefs prepare students for learning, whereas performance phase processes are designed to improve the quality of students' mental and physical activities. Finally, self-reflection phase processes and beliefs occur after performance and influence students' reactions to those efforts. Self-reflection processes also influence forethought planning for subsequent efforts to learn in cyclical fashion.

Although all learners attempt to self-regulate in some fashion (Winne, 1997), proactive learners self-regulate more effectively because they engage in high-quality forethought, which in turn improves their self-regulatory functioning during subsequent phases. In contrast, *reactive* learners self-regulate less effectively because they rely mainly on self-reflective phase processes (see Figure 7.1). Later I consider how social learning experiences, such as modeling, can enhance specific forethought processes that underlie proactive self-regulation.

FIGURE 7.1.
Cyclical phases of academic self-regulation.

Forethought Phase

There are two major forms of forethought: task analysis and self-motiva-tional beliefs. Task analysis refers to breaking an academic task into com-ponents and setting goals and planning strategies for their attainment. *Goal setting* refers to specifying the intended outcomes for learning or per-formance (Lock & Latham, 1990), such as deciding on a topic for a term paper in an English class. Proactive learners set goals that are specific, proximal, and challenging, whereas reactive learners rely on unspecified or vague goals, such as "to do better." The superior effectiveness of the former goal properties is well established (Bandura & Schunk, 1981; Locke & Latham, 1990). With complex tasks, proactive learners often organize their goals hierarchically, with key goals (e.g., writing an essay) divided into subordinate goals (e.g., writing the introductory paragraph of the essay). A hierarchal system of goals enables proactive learners to direct their learning over lengthy time intervals because learners can shift to the next goal in a hierarchy as each subordinate goal is accomplished.

Strategic planning refers to the choice or creation of strategies designed to enhance learning (Weinstein & Mayer, 1986). Strategies are succinct, powerful, and transferable cognitive methods for enhancing learning and performance, such as using the spelling strategy "*i* before *e* except after *c.*" This self-instruction strategy involves verbal rhyming, but mental imagery strategies are also used widely, such as visualizing one's home to remember the Spanish word *casa*. Both imagistic or self-instruction strategies have proven very effective in enhancing memory (Bandura & Jeffery, 1973; Pressley, 1977). When proactive learners encounter difficult tasks, they adopt or create specific strategies to assist them, whereas reactive learners can express only vague intentions, such as "to do better." This proactivity is not viewed as a personal trait that some sociocultural groups have in greater abundance but rather as task-specific capability to function in a self-initiated and self-regulated way. The skills and self-beliefs that underlie proactivity can be acquired from sociocultural models that are perceived as similar (Brown & Inouye, 1978).

Proactive learners are also distinguished from reactive learners by their favorable self-motivational beliefs, such as self-efficacy, outcome expectations, task interest or valuing, and learning goal orientation. *Self-efficacy* beliefs refer to students' capability to learn or perform effectively, such as their self-beliefs about earning a passing grade in an anatomy course. Self-efficacy beliefs have been found to predict a wide range of motivational and achievement outcomes among students (Bandura, 1997). *Outcome expectancies* refer to beliefs about the ultimate benefits or liabilities of performance, such as an anatomy student's beliefs about becoming a physician. Outcome expectancies are also significant predictors of academic motivation and achievement (Zimmerman & Schunk, in press). *Task interest* involves valuing a task, activity, or skill for its intrinsic properties rather than for its ultimate external ends (Deci, 1975; Lepper & Hodell, 1989), and there is evidence that task interest is a significant predictor of student motivation and achievement (Zimmerman & Kitsantas, 1999). A learner's *goal orientation* refers to their rationale for learning and studying. The most advantageous goal orientation for initiating and sustaining academic study has been described as a learning, mastery, or task goal orientation, which all refer to students' valuing of the process of learning. By contrast, the most disadvantageous belief has been labeled a performance or ego goal orientation (e.g., Ames, 1992; Boekaerts & Niemivirta, 2000; Dweck, 1988; Nicholls, 1984), which both refer to valuing or fearing the outcomes of learning. For example, a student who learns to read poetry orally for personal enjoyment will be more highly motivated than a student who learns to read poetry to overcome a fear about reading aloud in class. There is extensive evidence that learning goals are associated with positive academic outcomes (Harackiewicz, Barron, Pintrich, Elliot, & Thrash, 2002).

Self-motivational beliefs are closely related to task analysis processes during forethought. For example, students' self-efficacy beliefs influence their goal setting because the more capable they believe themselves to be, the higher the goals they set for themselves and the more firmly committed they are to those goals (Bandura, 1991; Locke & Latham, 1990). Similarly, when students have an intrinsic interest in doing a task well, they are more likely to plan and implement learning strategies during studying (Zimmerman & Kitsantas, 1997). Finally, students with a learning goal orientation use cognitive strategies, such as elaboration and comprehension monitoring, more frequently than students with a performance goal orientation (Pintrich & DeGroot, 1990).

Performance Phase

Learners use two classes of self-regulatory processes to enhance their performance: self-control and self-observation. Self-control processes involve specific methods or strategies, such as *self-instructions, imagery, attention focusing,* and *task strategies,* to enhance performance. I have already discussed students' use of self-instruction and imagery processes. Task strategies, which grow out of task analyses, focus on improving one's performance of task subcomponents, such as breaking a math story problem into parts and using specific strategies for solving each part, such as division or multiplication. Attention-focusing strategies are designed to protect one's concentration from distractions (Corno, 1993; Hidi, 1995), such as using earplugs to block out noise while studying. Proactive learners' strategic planning during the forethought phase prepares them to implement their planned strategies during the performance phase. By contrast, reactive learners are unplanned and intuitive, and they must rely on discovery during the performance phase.

Self-observation processes involve metacognitive self-monitoring and self-recording. Metacognitive self-monitoring refers to mentally tracking one's performance, whereas self-recording refers to keeping a physical record of one's performance, such as a graph for the completion of homework assignments. Self-recording enables students to capture personal information as it occurs, preserve its accuracy, and provide a longer database for discerning change. Both forms of self-observation can enhance students' performance (Zimmerman & Kitsantas, 1997, 1999). Because of their strategic planning during the forethought phase, proactive learners can implement their self-control strategies systematically. By contrast, reactive self-regulators engage in learning without a detailed plan and instead rely on subjective impressions or trial and error to learn. In terms of their self-observations, proactive self-regulators display greater metacognitive self-monitoring of their performance as well as more frequent self-record-ing when learning is especially difficult. Because of their superior metacog-nitive monitoring and self-recording, proactive self-regulators have more accurate knowledge of their academic progress. Reactive learners seldom spontaneously engage in either form of self-observation, and are usually "in the dark" about issues of task difficulty and their learning progress.

Self-Reflection Phase

There are two major classes of self-reflection processes: self-judgment and self-reactions. *Self-evaluation* judgments involve comparing self-monitored information with a standard or goal, such as when an aspiring historian compares her daily efforts to recall the names of the Presidents of the United States, (a) to her best previous practice effort (i.e., a self-improve-ment criterion), (b) to the recall of her classmates (i.e., a social compari-son criterion), or (c) to the entire list of Presidents in an encyclopedia (e.g., a mastery criterion). Because learners often select their own self-eval-uative criteria, they often differ in the way they interpret the same perfor-mance. The learning process goals of proactive self-regulators lead them to self-evaluate using a self-improvement or mastery criterion because these criteria provide feedback regarding the effectiveness of their learning pro-cesses. Self-improvement criteria as well as mastery criteria are advanta-geous motivationally because both self-evaluative criteria are sensitive to improvement with practice. In contrast, reactive self-regulators' lack of forethought and preoccupation with performance outcomes prompts them to rely on a social comparative criterion to self-evaluate (Zimmerman & Kitsantas, 1997, 1999). A social comparative criterion is insensitive to improvement because one's competitors may start ahead or progress faster.

   Causal attribution self-judgments refer to ascriptions of personal out-comes to controllable or uncontrollable causes. Attributions of poor out-comes to uncontrollable sources, such as fixed ability, lead to negative self-reactions and discourage further efforts to improve (Weiner, 1979), whereas attributions of outcomes to personally controllable sources, such as strategies for test preparation, sustain learners' motivation during peri-ods of deficient performance (Zimmerman & Kitsantas, 1997, 1999). Attri-butions vary from person to person depending on preceding self-regulatory processes and beliefs, such as task analysis, goal setting, and perceptions of self-efficacy (Bandura, 1991). Because reactive self-regula-tors lack process goals and process methods (i.e., strategies) of learning, they are prone to attributing causation of errors to uncontrollable sources, such as ability, task difficulty, or luck (Cleary & Zimmerman, 2000; Kitsantas & Zimmerman, 2002). By contrast, proactive self-regulators tend to attribute negative outcomes to ineffective strategy use because of their process goals and use of strategies. Strategy attributions have the advantage of sustaining motivation to adapt the strategies further.

Two key forms of self-reactions are self-satisfaction and adaptive/defensive inferences. Students' perceptions of *self-satisfaction* or dissatisfaction with their prior academic performance influence their future courses of action (Bandura, 1991). *Adaptive inferences* refer to self-reactions by students regarding the effectiveness of their self-regulatory strategy during previous efforts to learn or perform, such as the decision to retain or adapt a rehearsal strategy for remembering math facts. Adaptive reactions are prompted by feelings of satisfaction, and they enhance flexibility and sustain persistence—even in the face of obstacles. By contrast, *defensive inferences* refer to self-reactions to prior performance that protect a person from dissatisfaction and aversive affect. These inferences are prompted by feelings of dissatisfaction, and they lead to procrastination, task avoidance, cognitive disengagement, and apathy (Garcia & Pintrich, 1994).

Proactive learners experience greater self-satisfaction than reactive learners because the former learners attribute their errors to strategic processes, which are personally controllable. Proactive learners' high level of satisfaction can sustain their strategy adjustments until they develop an effective approach (Cleary & Zimmerman, 2000). By contrast, reactive self-regulators experience greater dissatisfaction because they attribute their errors to uncontrollable factors, such as a lack of underlying ability, and this undermines further adaptive efforts. Reactive learners' preoccupation with outcomes leads them to avoid future learning opportunities or to disclaim personal responsibility for adverse outcomes defensively. Thus, the strategic process goals set by proactive self-regulators during forethought lead to greater self-satisfaction and more effective forms of adaptation. These self-reactions in turn influence forethought self-motivational beliefs, goals, and strategy choices regarding further efforts to learn (Cleary & Zimmerman, 2000; Kitsantas & Zimmerman, 2002).

SOCIOCULTURAL INFLUENCES ON STUDENTS' PERSONAL AND ACADEMIC SELF-REGULATION

There is evidence that social and cultural variables play an important role in students' academic self-regulation. Zimmerman and Martinez-Pons (1986, 1988) developed a structured interview methodology to assess middle-class American high school students' use of 14 self-regulatory strategies with hypothetical academic problems, such as studying for tests, homework completion, or motivating oneself. Students' strategies were designed to optimize specific self-regulatory processes, such as goal setting or self-evaluation, and were found to be highly predictive of the students' achievement track in school and standardized test performance. High achievers not only reported greater use of personal self-regulatory strategies, such as rehearsing and memorizing, but also social assistance strategies, such as help-seeking. In addition, American elementary, middle school, and high school students attending schools for the gifted were found to use self-regulatory strategies more frequently than students attending regular schools (Zimmerman & Martinez-Pons, 1990). This methodology has also been used to study the impact of parental and cultural variables on children's academic self-regulation in other countries.

Using a variant of Zimmerman and Martinez-Pons's methodology, Purdie, Hattie, and Douglas (1996) compared Australian and Japanese high school students' conceptions of learning and use of self-regulated learning strategies. Regarding their use of self-regulated strategies, Japanese students displayed significantly more information seeking, rehearsing and memorizing, reviewing tests, and reviewing textbooks than Australian students. However, Australian students reported significantly more of the following strategies: goal setting or planning, keeping records, using self-consequences, seeking teacher assistance, seeking adult assistance, and reviewing notes. Overall, the Australian students reported significantly greater use of all strategies than Japanese students. Unexpectedly, none of the individual learning strategies was linked to any of nine conceptions of learning that were studied. There was, however, evidence that both Australian and Japanese students who conceptualized learning as a source of understanding did report greater use of self-regulatory strategies than students who viewed it as rote learning.

In a second study, Purdie and Hattie (1996) compared Japanese and Australian students to a group of Japanese students who attended high schools in Australia. Although the students in the three groups employed a similar range of strategies, their pattern of strategy use did vary in this study. Japanese students used memorizing and reviewing textbook strategies significantly more often than Australian students did. Compared to Japanese students, the Australian students used the following strategies more frequently: goal setting and planning, keeping records, using self-consequences, seeking teacher assistance, reviewing notes, and reviewing tests. Although Japanese students who studied in Australia resembled their Australian classmates more than their Japanese countrymen in their use of self-regulatory strategies, they differed in three areas: They displayed significantly less environmental structuring and seeking teacher assistance than Australian students, but they displayed significantly more memorizing. Compared to Japanese students, Japanese students studying in Australia reported significant greater use of the following strategies: keeping records, reviewing notes, reviewing tests, and reviewing textbooks. For the Australian students, high achievers were less inclined to use the strategy of seeking adult assistance. For Japanese students, high achievers had lower scores in seeking teacher assistance. When considering students of the combined ethnic groups, the high achievers surpassed medium and low achievers in using most of the self-regulated learning strategies. Thus, although foreign students displayed cultural differences in their patterns of self-regulated strategy use, they used these strategies extensively, and their strategy use was predictive of their academic achievement.

Rao and Sachs (1999) studied self-regulation of learning by Chinese students attending a high school in Hong Kong using the Motivated Strategies for Learning Questionnaire (MSLQ)—Chinese version (Pintrich, Smith, Garcia, & McKeachie, 1991). This research revealed that Chinese students relied heavily on memorization and rehearsal strategies, which Rao and Sachs attributed to the students' Confucian learning heritage. This Chinese tradition draws a distinction between rote memorization and a higher form that emphasizes internalizing or understanding the material.

These studies revealed that, although there are cultural differences in students' conceptions of learning, there is considerable commonality in students' use of self-regulatory strategies in disparate geographical locations around the world. Nevertheless, these findings raise questions about the origins of these cultural variations in preference for self-regulation strategies. What is the role of parents in their children's acquisition of self-regulatory strategies?

Grolnik and Ryan (1989) studied the styles of childrearing of Caucasian American parents' and their children's self-regulation and competence in school during grades 3 through 6x. Three *styles of parenting* were assessed: autonomy support, involvement, and provision of structure. The parenting style of autonomy support refers to parents' encouragement of their children's independent problem solving, choice, and decision making; the parenting style of involvement refers to parents' interest in, knowledge about, and active participation in their children's life; the parental style of structure refers to parents' provision of clear and consistent guidelines, expectations, and rules for their children's behavior. The children rated their reasons for self-regulating, which ranged from external factors (e.g., avoiding negative consequences or following externally imposed rules) to internal factors (e.g., pursuing self-valued goals or intrinsically interesting activities). The researchers found that the autonomy support by the parents was positively related to (a) their children's reports of autonomous self-regulation, (b) competence ratings of the children by their teachers, and (c) the children's behavioral adjustment. Although maternal involvement was related to the children's achievement, competence, and behavioral adjustment, paternal involvement was unrelated to these measures.

Evidence of causality between parental processes, students' self-regulation, and their academic achievement was reported by Martinez-Pons

(1996). He measured parents' activities that could influence children's development of academic self-regulation—namely, modeling, encouraging, facilitating, and rewarding of their children's self-regulatory efforts. A factor analysis revealed that all four parental activities loaded on a common factor, which was labeled *parental inducement of self-regulation*. Parents' inducement of self-regulation was significantly correlated with their children's level of self-regulation, which in turn was correlated with the children's achievement on a standardized test. Furthermore, path analyses revealed that parents' inducement of self-regulation predicted their children's achievement via their children's academic self-regulation. This evidence of causality indicates that parents can have a significant direct effect on their children's academic self-regulation and a significant indirect effect on their children's academic achievement.

There is other evidence that children's acquisition of self-regulatory competence mediates parental influences on the children's academic and personal outcomes. Brody and Flor (1997, 1998) studied the self-regulation by children raised in single-parent families of African American descent from a rural area of the southern United States. Self-regulation was assessed using the Children's Self-Control Scale (Humphrey, 1982), which was completed by both the parents and the teachers. The scale contains items such as (a) thinks ahead of time about the consequences of his or her actions, (b) plans ahead before acting, (c) pays attention while working toward goals, and (d) persists on difficult tasks. These youngsters varied in age from 6 to 9 years, and the families had few financial resources. Three types of *parental processes* were studied: "no-nonsense" parenting, mother–child relationship quality, and maternal involvement in the child's school activities. "No-nonsense" parenting refers to firm but warm discipline. Three types of child outcome measures were employed: cognitive competence, social competence, and internalizing problems (i.e., symptoms of depression). Path analyses revealed that each of the three maternal measures was highly predictive of their children's level of self-regulatory functioning. This self-regulatory measure was in turn highly predictive of three student outcomes: cognitive competence, social competence, and depression or emotional functioning. Thus, the influence of these single mothers on their children's acquisition of diverse competencies was mediated through their children's degree of self-regulation.

These studies indicated that various measures of parenting, such as styles of parenting, parental self-regulation inducement, and parenting processes, play an important role in children's development of self-regulatory skill. We now turn to the issue of what types of specific social learning processes might be used by not only parents but also by teachers and peers to increase students' level of academic self-regulation.

SOCIALIZATION PROCESSES AND
STUDENTS' ACADEMIC LEARNING

Three types of socialization processes have been studied as methods for transmitting self-regulatory strategies and skills: social modeling, social guidance and feedback, and social collaboration.

Social Modeling

There is extensive evidence that self-regulatory beliefs and skills are acquired readily through observation of a proficient model (Bandura, 1986; Schunk, 1987; Zimmerman & Rosenthal, 1974). This research has revealed that observational learning involves four key subprocesses: (a) attending to a model, (b) encoding the information for retention, (c) enacting the demonstrated responses motorically, and (d) motivating one-self to perform the modeled behaviors (Bandura, 1986). If students experience a deficiency in one or more of these processes, they would not display learning from a model.

In support of this analysis, there is a high correlation between students' attention to a model and students' observational learning (Yussen, 1974). Furthermore, students are more likely to attend to a model who is perceived as similar to them (Brown & Inouye, 1978) because the appropriateness of a model's behavior to a student often depends on the model's age, gender, culture, or status. In general, the greater the similarity of observers to models in these factors, the greater the probability that emulative actions by observers will be socially appropriate and successful (Bandura, 1986; Bussey & Bandura, 1984). The model similarity criterion is especially important when observers have little information about the functional value of a model's behavior. However, when this information is available, such as by witnessing vicarious outcomes, students will emulate the most effective models even when these models are unlike them in many attributes (Zimmerman & Koussa, 1975, 1979). For example, an aspiring young pianist who is admittedly lax about practicing might choose to study with an elderly but very successful teacher with a reputation for disciplined practice.

Students are more able to encode modeled information if *cognitive modeling* is displayed, which refers to models' verbalizations of their thoughts and reasons for performing (Meichenbaum, 1977; Zimmerman & Rosenthal, 1972). For example, Schunk (1981) provided elementary schoolchildren who experienced difficulty in mathematical division with either cognitive modeling or didactic instruction. During cognitive modeling, children observed an adult model verbalize a long-division strategy when solving the math problems, whereas during the didactic treatment, children reviewed a written instruction that conveyed the same strategy for solving the math problems. Although both cognitive modeling and didactic instruction led to significant increases in self-efficacy, skill learning, and persistence, cognitive modeling resulted in significantly greater acquisition of division skill. Graham, Harris, and colleagues (Graham & Harris, 1989a, 1989b; Sawyer, Graham, & Harris, 1992) also used a cognitive modeling procedure to teach an essay-writing strategy to students with learning disabilities. These researchers found that cognitive modeling not only improved the students' self-efficacy and writing performance, these gains were generalized to other settings and academic content. Clearly, cognitive modeling can help the students to strategically encode the modeling sequence more effectively.

Even when students attend to a model and cognitively encode a model's academic performance, they may be unable to emulate the model motorically. To assist learners with motoric deficits, *participant modeling* has been used (Bandura, 1986). During this form of social learning, a model demonstrates selected aspects of the strategy and then physically guides an observer's efforts to emulate. As an observer acquires motoric skill, the model diminishes the level of support, such as when an elementary schoolteacher guides the hand of a second grader who is having trouble emulating a model's cursive writing of the letter *W*.

Finally, students who are otherwise capable of emulating a model may fail to do so because of motivational reasons. These learners can be greatly assisted by *coping models,* who initially struggle to overcome their errors, but they persist and eventually succeed. There is evidence that coping models are more effective than mastery models (who perform flawlessly) in motivating self-doubting observers to persist and ultimately succeed in their learning (Kitsantas, Zimmerman, & Cleary, 2000; Schunk & Hanson, 1985). The students not only displayed increases in self-efficacy beliefs about learning but also in their academic learning. Coping models also convey the message that they value the task in question so highly that they persist in learning it. Vicarious expressions of the value of a task can influence observers' valuing of that task (Zimmerman & Koussa, 1975, 1979).

Social Feedback

As was discussed with regard to participant modeling, observers often have difficulty in emulating a model accurately. The reasons for this deficiency can range from a lack of motoric skill to an inability to self-monitor or self-evaluate one's performance. Social feedback can play an invaluable role in assisting learners to self-monitor, self-evaluate, and self-adjust their performance efforts. For example, Schunk and Swartz (1993) provided social feedback to elementary schoolchildren as they learned to write descriptive, narrative, or informative paragraphs. After the children observed an adult model demonstrate a five-step writing strategy, they were given an opportunity to practice it. Children in a progress-feedback condition periodically received verbal feedback from the adult model that linked their use of the strategy with improved writing performance (e.g., "You're doing well because you followed the steps in order."). Eventually the instructor's social guidance and feedback was discontinued, and students practiced independently on their own. Students were also given either strategy process or product outcome goals to guide their learning. Schunk and Swartz discovered that the combination of setting a strategic process goal plus receiving verbal feedback was the most effective in improving the use of strategies and the quality of the paragraph writing. In addition to the immediate posttest gains, these students maintained their gains after 6 weeks and generalized to new paragraphs.

Kitsantas and Zimmerman (2002) found that social feedback designed to help college students acquire a writing revision strategy significantly increased their self-efficacy beliefs, satisfaction with their performance, and writing quality. This feedback was helpful whether the student had learned from a high-quality coping model or from personal discovery.

Social Collaboration

This form of learning refers to joint efforts to improve students' academic self-regulation, such as when teachers, tutors, or peers help students overcome misconceptions about learning and construct self-regulatory plans that are likely to succeed. These change agents have been called self-regulation coaches (Cleary & Zimmerman, 2003), transactional strategy instructors (Pressley, El-Dinary, Wharton-McDonald, & Brown, 1998), and strategic content learning instructors (Butler, 1998), among other titles. A collaborative approach is more interactive than a traditional modeling approach in that learners and change agents jointly define the academic problem, formulate strategies, and evaluate performance. Social collaboration focuses the participants' discussion on the unique properties of an academic problem, and the change agent's questions and comments are designed to guide students' strategic decision making and performance. Students' proactive role during the development of a personalized academic plan is expected to increase their sense of ownership and commitment to carrying it out. There is extensive evidence of the effectiveness of social collaboration approaches (Butler, 1998; Cleary & Zimmerman, 2003; Graham & Harris, 1989a, 1989b; Pressley et al., 1998).

Problem-based (PB) learning is another form of social collaboration that focuses on students' self-regulatory development (Evenson & Hmelo,

2000). Medical educators developed PB learning as an alternative to the traditional lecture instructional format. Although there are many variations in PB learning, most versions involve the formation of small groups who are given specific medical problems to study, such as the diagnosis of a patient. Often a faculty member serves as an adviser to the group to assist them when needed, but he or she plays a relatively passive role in the proceedings. Instead of relying on an expert's lecture to learn, PB learners analyze a topic as a group, and they assign the subtasks to group members. The group members must then locate the necessary information from diverse sources such as library books, journals, expert consultants, the Internet, and many others. In the PB approach, students share information with the other group members and cognitively model medical procedures for solving their part of the problem. Recently, the effectiveness of PB curricula have been evaluated, and they show promise in preparing physicians to pass not only medical examinations but to self-regulate their effectiveness better in naturalistic settings (Blumberg, 2000; Domans & Schmidt, 2000; Evenson, 2000; Hmelo & Lin; 2000).

Three classes of self-regulatory processes have been involved in PB learning programs in medical schools: identifying learning objects, pursuing learning issues, and self-evaluating learning outcomes (Zimmerman & Lebeau, 2000). It is important to note that PB learning differs from discovery learning because it relies on many social resources, such as peers, academic advisers, and resource persons in the field. Much of PB learning is planned and interpreted as a shared experience, and this methodology encourages students to adopt modeling, coaching, and cooperating roles at various times. Although the evaluation of this research is largely qualitative to date, there is evidence that PB learners make increasingly focused use of clinical and basic science texts (Hmelo & Lin, 2000). There is also evidence that PB learners are more likely to develop their own libraries (Bloomberg, 2000), are more focused on underlying meaning of studied material, and are less oriented toward memorizing (Evenson, 2000).

STUDENTS' DEVELOPMENT OF
SELF-REGULATORY COMPETENCE

From a social-cognitive perspective, learners develop academic competence in a series of self-regulatory levels (Zimmerman, 2000), beginning with social levels and shifting to self levels (see Table 7.1). This multilevel formulation is predicated on considerable research indicating that novice learners readily acquire self-regulatory strategies and motivational beliefs through social learning processes such as modeling, tuition, social feedback, and encouragement (Rosenthal & Zimmerman, 1978; Schunk & Zimmerman, 1997; Zimmerman & Rosenthal, 1974).

TABLE 1.
Multi-Level Features of Self-Regulation.

	Features of Regulation			
Levels of Regulation	Sources of Regulation	Sources of Motivation	Task Conditions	Performance Indices
1. Observation	Modeling	Vicarious reinforcement	Presence of models	Discrimination
2. Emulation	Performance and social feedback	Direct/social reinforcement	Correspond to model's	Stylistic duplication
3. Self-control	Representation of process standards	Self-reinforcement	Structured	Automaticity
4. Self-regulation	Performance outcomes	Self-efficacy beliefs	Dynamic	Adaptation

An observational level of academic skill is attained when learners induce the major features of skill from watching others perform, such as when an aspiring public speaker discerns a difference between a seasoned speaker's speech on civic responsibility and a novice speaker's (see Table 7.1, first row). To achieve a high level of skill, learners usually need repeated observations of models, especially across variations in task (Rosenthal & Zimmerman, 1976), such as seeing speeches on a variety of topics by skilled orators. A novice's motivation to learn from a model is enhanced greatly by positive vicarious consequences to the model, such as awards given to a public speaker. Observers not only learn task skills from a model, they typically acquire self-regulatory processes, such as adherence to performance standards, motivational orientations, and task values (Zimmerman & Ringle, 1981). For example, a public-speaking model may react to his or her audience's signs of difficulty in hearing by slowing their speech and projecting their voice more effectively, and this adjustment in speech can convey vicariously to observers the need to monitor their own audiences and to adjust their voice appropriately.

When an observer's motoric performance approximates the general form of one or more models, an *emulative level* of self-regulatory competence is attained (see Table 7.1, second row). Emulation does not involve copying the exact actions of the model but rather the general pattern or style of functioning, such as when a learner emulates the type of question a model asks but not the precise wording (Rosenthal, Zimmerman, & Durning, 1970). The scientific distinction between an observational level and an emulative level of skill can be traced to early social-cognitive research that distinguished cognitive acquisition from motoric performance (Bandura, 1965). In recent research on writing, Zimmerman and Kitsantas (2002) showed that the quality of students' observational learning is highly predictive of the quality of their emulative performance in writing revision. In addition, social feedback given during efforts to emulate was found to enhance not only writing skill acquisition but also self-motivational beliefs, such as self-efficacy. Interestingly, students' reception of social feedback did not compensate for the absence of observational learning experiences in this research. Virtually identical findings were reported in research with an athletic task (Kitsantas et al., 2000). These results confirmed the sequentiality of the first two levels of the multilevel model of self-regulatory development: observational and emulative learning. The source of self-regulatory skill for the first two levels of competence is primarily social (i.e., modeling and social feedback). During the third and fourth level of a social-cognitive approach, the task control shifts to self sources.

When learners can perform a skill in structured settings outside the presence of models, they have attained a *self-controlled level* of self-regulatory skill. For example, aspiring public speakers could practice modulating their voice when reading from published speeches (see row three in Table 7.1). Learning is enhanced at this level when students rely on self-evaluative standards that had been induced from the performance of proficient models (Bandura & Jeffery, 1973). These student performers will be motivated by their personal success in matching these covert standards during practice—a phenomenon that is called self-reinforcement. Bandura (1986) has noted, "By making self-satisfaction conditional on a selected level of performance, individuals create their own incentives to persist in their efforts until their performances match internal standards" (p. 467). In research on speech acquisition, students who self-evaluated their phoneme pronunciation on an audiotape using a covert standard were highly motivated by close approximations (Ellis & Zimmerman, 2001).

Students can enhance the quality of their self-control by engaging in self-instructions, such as self-praise or self-critical statements (Bandura, Grusec, & Menlove, 1967). These verbalizations enable students to encode and utilize strategies more effectively (Meichenbaum & Beimiller, 1990). For example, elementary school students who were poor listeners were trained to verbalize a listening strategy for choosing a pictorial referent to a story (Schunk & Rice, 1984). Students who verbalized the strategy displayed greater self-efficacy and listening accuracy than did students who did not verbalize it. Strategy verbalization also enhanced students' perceptions of efficacy and their academic performance (Schunk & Rice, 1984) in research on reading comprehension as well.

Self-controlled learners who focus on fundamental processes or technique rather than on task outcomes during practice are more successful in achieving automaticity, which is the ultimate criterion for level-three functioning (Zimmerman & Kitsantas, 1997, 1999). By focusing their practice goals on the strategic processes of proven models initially, level-three learners can circumvent the frustrations of trial-and-error learning and can instead reinforce themselves for motoric correspondence to a modeled standard. By contrast, learners who focus on outcomes before fundamental techniques are acquired are expected to display lower levels of learning because novices make poor strategy process adjustments until they acquire self-evaluative expertise (Ellis & Zimmerman, 2000). Thus, although a skill becomes internally self-controlled at level three, it remains dependent on a covert representation of a social model's standard.

To achieve the fourth or *self-regulated level* of task skill, learners should practice the skill in unstructured settings involving dynamic personal and contextual conditions and must learn to make adjustments in their skill based on the outcomes of practice (see row four in Table 7.1). For example, public speakers could learn to modify their eye contact with their audience on the basis of the audiences' attentiveness. Unlike level-three learners, level-four speakers' adaptations stem primarily from self-monitored audience outcomes rather than covert modeled standards. Learners' motivation to learn at level four depends on their perceptions of self-efficacy in making these adaptations. At level four, learners can practice the skill in question with minimal process monitoring, and they can shift their attention to performance outcomes without detrimental consequences. When learners can adapt their performance to changing personal conditions and outcomes, a self-regulated level of skill has been attained.

Level-four learners are distinctive because their cognitive processing has become automatized (i.e., when level three is attained), and this achievement frees them to focus on their response outcomes (LaBerge, 1981; Neves & Anderson, 1981). Self-regulated learners are distinguished behaviorally by their development of their own distinctive styles of performing. In support of the sequentiality of the third and fourth level of the multilevel model, Zimmerman and Kitsantas (1999) found that students who initially practiced a writing task by focusing on strategic process goals and then shifted to outcome goals at the point of automaticity learned significantly better than students who learned using fixed process or outcome goals. The students in the shifting goal group also displayed significantly higher levels of self-efficacy than students in either fixed goal group.

Thus, students' acquisition of self-regulatory competence begins with the most extensive social guidance at the first level, but this social regulation is systematically reduced as students acquire the models' underlying self-regulatory skill. However, these students do not become increasing asocial as they acquire self-regulatory skill but rather become increasingly resourceful socially (Newman, 1994; Zimmerman & Martinez-Pons, 1986). For example, veteran public speakers routinely seek advice from highly proficient colleagues to refine their skill. Every skill constantly needs to be adapted because variations in performance conditions can uncover limitations in existing skills and require additional social learning experiences.

According to this social-cognitive formulation, learners do not advance through the four levels in an invariant sequence and do not adhere rigidly to the highest level once it is attained (as developmental stage models assume). Instead, the multilevel model assumes that students who master each skill level in sequence will learn more easily and effectively. However, level-four learners will experience periods of adverse performance, such as when basketball players go into a shooting "slump," and may seek advice or even training from a coach. Furthermore, level-four learners may not engage in physically demanding forms of self-regulation, such as self-recording, if they feel tired, disinterested, or uncommitted.

SOCIOCULTURAL DIMENSIONS OF A MULTILEVEL MODEL OF SELF-REGULATORY DEVELOPMENT

This multilevel formulation focuses on students' development of task-specific regulatory skills, and it assumes that students will vary in their level of self-regulation depending on the task in question, such as solving math problems versus writing essays. This task specificity means that students' opportunities to learn to self-regulate their performance will vary depending on social learning opportunities. For example, in some sociocultural settings, successful social models may be less available or less valued, and this may diminish students' rate of progress or even may compel them to skip the first two levels. For example, an aspiring forensic speaker from a poor inner-city high school comprised of mainly minority students would be at a considerable competitive disadvantage in state tournaments if he or she did not have access to highly successful peer models. The student in question would lack the opportunity to learn at observational and emulative levels before relying on learning from personal self-regulatory outcomes. Very different results have occurred when compelling inner-city teachers have developed winning school traditions in forensics or math teams, and thereby creating favorable sociocultural environments wherein successful upperclassmen can serve as exemplary models for aspiring underclassmen.

In addition to influences associated with students' race and socioeconomic community, other sociocultural influences, such as students' political preferences, religious affiliations, and gender, could also be barriers or resources for learning. For example, students from Christian fundamentalist families are often discouraged from reading books on evolution, and this could significantly reduce their success in a biology course. By contrast, Mormon students would have an advantage in studying genealogy in school due to their religion's interest in and database for tracing ancestors. Because a multilevel formulation posits that observational learning forms the basis for students' subsequent development of self-regulatory expertise, it can readily explain sociocultural variations in academic functioning, including variations in motivation, achievement, and dropout rate by minorities, such as African Americans, Native Americans, and Hispanics.

In addition to students' politics, religion, and gender, their intellectual characteristics are linked to their level of self-regulation. For example, there is evidence that gifted students display greater use of self-regulatory strategies than regular students (Zimmerman & Martinez-Pons, 1990). Because the development of a high level of skill requires considerable self-directed studying and practicing (whether in academics, sports, or the arts), gifted students need high levels of self-regulatory skill to attain their potential. There is also evidence that learning-disabled students display significant deficits in self-regulation (Borkowski & Thorpe, 1994). For example, these students typically lack specific strategies to learn, fail to self-monitor their progress and to self-reflect on their learning efforts. Teaching learning-disabled students specific self-regulatory skills has proven very effective (Butler, 1998; Graham, Harris, & Troia, 1998).

CONCLUSION

In this chapter, children's development of academic self-regulatory skill is considered from a social-cognitive perspective. Academic self-regulation involves specific underlying processes and motivational beliefs that are linked in three cyclical phases, and differences in these beliefs and processes between proactive and reactive learners are crucial to their academic success. Reactive students' failure to engage in effective forms of forethought, such as goal setting or strategic choice, greatly limits the quality of subsequent phase processes and beliefs, and ultimately, students' academic success. Research also reveals that despite significant cultural differences in students' conceptions of learning throughout the world, there is much commonality in their use of self-regulatory strategies. Parents are key sociocultural influences on children's self-regulatory functioning and achievement. Children's development of personal and academic self-regulation is linked in path analyses to a variety of parenting processes, including social modeling and feedback.

Research on social modeling has found four key subprocesses: attention, retention, motoric processes, and motivation. Deficiencies in one or more of these subprocesses can be overcome by adaptive forms of modeling, such as cognitive, participatory, and coping variations, and by social feedback during student efforts to emulate the model. Social collaborative forms of learning enable students to work with a study partner, classmates, or change agent (e.g., teachers, coaches, or tutors) to develop a number of highly effective forms of academic self-regulation, such as self-regulation coaching, transactional strategy learning, strategic content learning, and problem-based learning. Finally, social-cognitive researchers have demonstrated that students can develop high levels of academic competence in four qualitatively distinctive levels—beginning with observation of proficient models and ending with self-regulation of personal outcomes in dynamic contexts. From this rich sociocultural milieu, students develop self-regulatory processes and motivational beliefs that are essential for not only their passage through the educational system but also for successful lifelong learning.

REFERENCES

Ames, C. (1992). Achievement goals and the classroom motivational climate. In D. H. Schunk & J. L. Meece (Eds.), *Student perceptions in the classroom* (pp. 327–348). Hillsdale, NJ: Erlbaum.

Bandura, A. (1965). Influence of models' reinforcement contingencies on the acquisition of imitative responses. *Journal of Personality and Social Psychology, 1,* 589–595.

Bandura, A. (1986). *Social foundations of thought and action: A social cognitive theory.* Englewood Cliffs, NJ: Prentice Hall.

Bandura, A. (1991). Self-regulation of motivation through anticipatory and self-reactive mechanisms. In R. A. Dienstbier (Ed.), *Perspectives on motivation: Nebraska Symposium on Motivation* (Vol. 38, pp. 69–164). Lincoln: University of Nebraska Press.

Bandura, A. (1997). *Self-efficacy: The exercise of control.* New York: Freeman.

Bandura, A., Grusec, J. E., & Menlove, F. L. (1967). Some social determinants of self-monitoring reinforcement systems. *Journal of Personality and Social Psychology, 5,* 449–455.

Bandura, A., & Jeffery, R. W. (1973). Role of symbolic coding and rehearsal processes in observational learning. *Journal of Personality and Social Psychology, 26,* 122–130.

Bandura, A., & Schunk, D. H. (1981). Cultivating competence, self-efficacy, and intrinsic interest through proximal self-motivation. *Journal of Personality and Social Psychology, 41,* 586–598.

Beimiller, A., Shany, M., Inglis, A., & Meichenbaum, D. (1998). Factors influencing children's acquisition and demonstration of self-regulation on academic tasks. In D. H. Schunk & B. J. Zimmerman (Eds.), *Self-regulated learning: From teaching to self-reflective practice* (pp. 203–224). New York: Guilford Press.

Blumberg, P. (2000). Evaluating the evidence that problem-based learners are self-directed learners: A review of the literature. In D. H. Evensen & C. E. Hmelo (Eds.), *Problem-based learning: A research perspective on learning interactions* (pp. 199–226). Mahwah, NJ: Erlbaum.

Boerkaerts, M., & Niemivirta, M. (2000). Self-regulated learning: Finding a balance between learning goals and ego-protective goals. In M. Boekaerts, P. R. Pintrich, & M. Zeidner (Eds.), *Handbook of self-regulation* (pp. 417–451). San Diego, CA: Academic Press.

Borkowski, J. G., & Thorpe, P. K. (1994). Self-regulation and motivation: A life-span perspective on underachievement. In D. H. Schunk & B. J. Zimmerman (Eds.), *Self-regulation of learning and performance: Issues and educational applications* (pp. 45–74). Mahwah, NJ: Erlbaum.

Brody, G. H. & Flor, D. (1997). Maternal psychological functioning, family processes, and child adjustment in rural, single-parent African-American families. *Developmental Psychology, 33,* 1000–1011.

Brody, G. H. & Flor, D. (1998). Maternal resources, parenting practices, and child competence in rural single-parent African American families. *Child Development, 69,* 803–816.

Brown, I. Jr., & Inouye, D. K. (1978). Learned helplessness through modeling: The role of perceived similarity in competence. *Journal of Personality and Social Psychology, 36,* 900–908.

Bussey, K., & Bandura, A. (1984). Gender constancy, social power, and sex-linked modeling. *Journal of Personality and Social Psychology, 47,* 1292–1302.

Butler, D. L. (1998). A strategic content learning approach to promoting self-regulated leaning by students with learning disabilities. In D. H. Schunk & B. J. Zimmerman (Eds.), *Self-regulated learning: From teaching to self-reflective practice* (pp. 160–183). New York: Guilford Press.

Cleary, T., & Zimmerman, B. J. (2000). Self-regulation differences during athletic practice by experts, non-experts, and novices. *Journal of Applied Sport Psychology, 13,* 61–82.

Cleary, T. J. & Zimmerman, B. J. (2003). *From dependence to self-sufficiency: An empowerment model to enhance self-regulated and self-motivated cycles of student learning.* Manuscript submitted for publication.

Corno, L. (1993). The best-laid plans: Modem conceptions of volition and educational research. *Educational Researcher, 22*(2), 14–22.

Deci, E. L. (1975). *Intrinsic motivation.* New York: Plenum Press.

De Corte, E., Verschaffel, L., & Op'T Eynde, P. (2000). Self-regulation: A characteristic and a goal of mathematics education. In M. Boekaerts, P. R. Pintrich, & M. Zeidner (Eds.), *Handbook of self-regulation* (pp. 687–727). San Diego, CA: Academic Press.

Dolmans, D. H. J. M., & Schmidt, H. G. (2000). What directs self-directed learning in a problem-based curriculum? In D. H. Evensen & C. E. Hmelo (Eds.), *Problem-based learning: A research perspective on learning interactions* (pp. 251–262). Mahwah, NJ: Erlbaum.

Dweck, C. S. (1988). Motivational processes affecting learning. *American Psychologist, 41,* 1040–1048.

Ellis, D., & Zimmerman, B. J. (2001). Enhancing self-monitoring during self-regulated learning of speech. In H. Hartman (Ed.), *Metacognition in teaching and learning* (pp. 205–228). New York: Kluwer Academic.

Evensen, D. H. (2000). Observing self-directed learning in a problem-based context: Two case studies. In D. H. Evensen & C. E. Hmelo (Eds.), *Problem-based learning: A research perspective on learning interactions* (pp. 263–298). Mahwah, NJ: Erlbaum.

Evensen, D. H., & Hmelo, C. E. (2000). *Problem-based learning: A research perspective on learning interactions.* Mahwah, NJ: Erlbaum.

Garcia, T., & Pintrich, P. R. (1994). Regulating motivation and cognition in the classroom: The role of self-schemas and self-regulatory strategies. In D. H.

Schunk & B. J. Zimmerman (Eds.), *Self-regulation of learning and performance: Issues and educational applications* (pp. 127–153). Hillsdale, NJ: Erlbaum.

Graham, S., & Harris, K. R. (1989a). Components analysis of cognitive strategy instruction: Effects on learning disabled students' compositions and self-efficacy. *Journal of Educational Psychology, 81,* 353–361.

Graham, S., & Harris, K. R. (1989b). Improving learning disabled students' skills at composing essays: Self-instructional strategy training. *Exceptional Children, 56,* 201–214.

Graham, S., Harris, K. R., & Troia, G. A. (1998). In D. H. Schunk & B. J. Zimmerman (Eds.), *Self-regulated learning: From teaching to self-reflective practice* (pp. 20–41). New York: Guilford Press.

Grolnik, W. S., & Ryan, R. M. (1989). Parent styles associated with children's self-regulation and competence in school. *Journal of Educational Psychology, 81,* 143–154.

Harackiewicz, J. M., Barron, K. E., Pintrich, P. R., Elliot, A. J., & Thrash, T. M. (2002). Revision of achievement goal theory: Necessary and illuminating. *Journal of Educational Psychology, 94,* 638–645.

Hidi, S. A. (1995). A reexamination of the role of attention in learning from text. *Educational Psychology Review, 7,* 323–350.

Hmelo, C. E., & Lin, X. (2000). Becoming self-directed learners: Strategy development in problem-based learning. In D. H. Evensen & C. E. Hmelo (Eds.), *Problem-based learning: A research perspective on learning interactions* (pp. 227–250). Mahwah, NJ: Erlbaum.

Humphrey, L. L. (1982). Children's and teachers' perspectives on children's self-control: The development of two rating scales. *Journal of Consulting and Clinical Psychology, 50,* 624–633.

Kitsantas, A., & Zimmerman, B. J. (2002). Comparing self-regulatory processes among novice, non-expert, and expert volleyball players: A microanalytic study. *Journal of Applied Sport Psychology, 14,* 91–105.

Kitsantas, A., Zimmerman, B. J., & Cleary, T. (2000). The role of observation and emulation in the development of athletic self-regulation. *Journal of Educational Psychology, 91,* 241–250.

LaBerge, D. (1981). Unitization and automaticity in perception. In J. H. Flowers (Ed.), *Nebraska Symposium on Motivation* (Vol. 28, pp. 53–71). Lincoln: University of Nebraska Press.

Lepper, M. R., & Hodell, M. (1989). Intrinsic motivation in the classroom. In C. Ames & R. Ames (Eds.), *Research on motivation in education* (Vol. E, pp. 255–296). Hillsdale, NJ: Erlbaum.

Locke, E. A., & Latham, G. P. (1990). *A theory of goal setting and task performance.* Englewood Cliffs, NJ: Prentice-Hall.

Martinez-Pons, M. (1996). Test of a model of parental inducement of academic self-regulation. *Journal of Experimental Education, 64,* 213–227.

Meichenbaum, D. (1977). *Cognitive-behavior modification: An integrative approach.* New York: Plenum Press.

Meichenbaum, D. & Beimiller, A. (1990). *In search of student expertise in the classroom: A metacognitive analysis.* Paper presented at the annual conference on Cognitive Research for Instructional Innovation, University of Maryland, College Park.

Neves, D. M., & Anderson, J. R. (1981). Knowledge compilation: Mechanisms for the automatization of cognitive skills. In J. R. Anderson (Ed.), *Cognitive skills and their acquisitions* (pp. 463–562). Hillside, NJ: Erlbaum.

Newman, R. (1994). Academic help-seeking: A strategy of self-regulated learning. In D. H. Schunk & B. J. Zimmerman (Eds.), *Self-regulation of learning and performance: Issues and educational applications* (pp. 283–301). Hillsdale, NJ: Erlbaum.

Nicholls, J. (1984). Achievement motivation: Conceptions of ability, subjective experience, task choice, and performance. *Psychological Review, 91,* 328–346.

Pintrich, P. R., Smith, D. A., Garcia, T., & McKeachie, W. J. (1991). *A manual for the use of the Motivated Strategies Learing Questionnaire (MSLQ).* Ann Arbor, MI: National Center for Research to Improve Postsecondary Teaching and Learning.

Pressley, M. (1977). Imagery and children's learning: Putting the picture in developmental perspective. *Review of Educational Research, 47,* 586–622.

Pressley, M., El-Dinary, P. B., Wharton-McDonald, R., & Brown, R. (1998). Transactional instruction of comprehension strategies in the elementary grades. In D. H. Schunk & B. J. Zimmerman (Eds.), *Self-regulated learning: From teaching to self-reflective practice* (pp. 42–56). New York: Guilford Press.

Pressley, M., Woloshyn, V., & Associates (Eds.). (1995). *Cognitive strategy instruction that really improves children's academic performance* (2nd ed.). Cambridge, MA: Brookline.

Pressley, M.. Woloshyn, V., Lysynchuk, L. M., Martin, V., Wood, E., & Willoughby, T. (1990). A primer of research on cognitive strategy instruction: The important issues and how to address them. *Educational Psychology Review, 2,* 1–58.

Purdy, N., & Hattie, J. (1996). Cultural differences in the use of strategies for self-regulated learning. *American Educational Research Journal, 33,* 845–871.

Purdy, N., Hattie, J., & Douglas, G. (1996). Student conceptions of learning and their use of self-regulated learning strategies: A cross-cultural comparison. *Journal of Educational Psychology, 88,* 87–100.

Roa, N., & Sachs, J. (1999). Confirmatory factor analysis of the Chinese version of the motivated strategies for learning questionnaire. *Educational and Psychological Measurement, 59,* 1016–1030.

Rosenthal, T. L., & Zimmerman, B. J. (1976). Organization and stability of transfer in vicarious concept attainment. *Child Development, 44,* 606–613.

Rosenthal, T. L., & Zimmerman, B. J. (1978). *Social learning and cognition.* New York: Academic Press.

Rosenthal, T. L, Zimmerman, B. J., & Durning, K. (1970). Observational induced changes in children's interrogative classes. *Journal of Personality and Social Psychology, 16,* 681–688.

Sawyer, R. J., Graham, S., & Harris, K. R. (1992). Direct teaching, strategy instruction, and strategy instruction with explicit self-regulation: Effects on the composition skills and self-efficacy *of* students with learning disabilities. *Journal of Educational Psychology, 84,* 340–352.

Schunk, D. H., (1981). Modeling and attributional effects on children's achievement: A self-efficacy analysis. *Journal of Educational Psychology, 73,* 93–105.

Schunk, D. H. (1987). Peer models and children's behavioral change. *Review of Educational Research, 57,* 149–174,

Schunk, D. H. (1989). Social cognitive theory and self-regulated learning. In B. J. Zimmerman & D. H. Schunk (Eds.), *Self-regulated learning and academic achievement: Theory, research and pratice* (pp. 83–110). Mahwah, NJ: Erlbaum.

Schunk, D. H. (2001). Social cognitive theory and self-regulated learning. In B. J. Zimmerman & D. H. Schunk (Eds.), *Self-regulated learning and academic achievement: Theoretical perspectives* (2nd ed., pp. 125–151). Mahwah, NJ: Erlbaum.

Schunk, D. H., & Hanson, A. R. (1985). Peer models: Influence on children's self-efficacy and achievement. *Journal of Educational Psychology, 77*, 313–322.

Schunk, D. H., & Rice, J. M. (1984). Strategy self-verbalization during remedial listening comprehension instruction. *Journal of Experimental Education, 53*, 49–54.

Schunk, D. H., & Swartz, C. W. (1993). Goals and progress feedback: Effects on self-efficacy and writing achievement. *Contemporary Educational Psychology, 18*, 337–354.

Schunk, D. H., & Zimmerman, B. J. (1994). *Self-regulation of learning and performance: Issues and educational applications.* Mahwah, NJ: Erlbaum.

Schunk, D. H., & Zimmerman, B. J. (1997). Social origins of self-regulatory competence. *Educational Psychologist, 32*, 195–208.

Weiner, B. (1979). A theory of motivation for some classroom experiences. *Journal of Educational Psychology, 71*, 3–25.

Weinstein, C. E., & Mayer, R. E. (1986). The teaching of learning strategies. In M. C. Wittrock (Ed.), *Handbook of research on teaching* (3rd ed., pp. 315–327). New York: Macmillan.

Weinstein, C. E. Schulte, A. C., & Palmer, D. R. (1987). *LASSI: Learning and study strategies inventory.* Clearwater, FL: H. & H. Publishing.

Winne, P. H. (1997). Experimenting to bootstrap self-regulated learning. *Journal of Educational Psychology, 89*, 397–410.

Yussen, S. (1974). Determinents of visual attention and recall in observational learning by preschoolers and second graders. *Developmental Psychology, 10*, 93–100.

Zimmerman, B. J. (1989). A social cognitive view of self-regulated academic learning. *Journal of Educational Psychology, 81*, 329–339.

Zimmerman, B. J. (2000). Attaining self-regulation: A social cognitive perspective. In M. Boekaerts, P. R. Pintrich, & M. Zeidner (Eds.), *Handbook of self-regulation* (pp.13–39). San Diego, CA: Academic Press.

Zimmerman, B. J., & Kitsantas, A. (1996). Self-regulated learning of a motoric skill: The role of goal setting and self-monitoring. *Journal of Applied Sport Psychology, 8*, 69–84.

Zimmerman, B. J., & Kitsantas, A. (1997). Developmental phases in self-regulation: Shifting from process to outcome goals. *Journal of Educational Psychology, 89*, 29–36.

Zimmerman, B. J., & Kitsantas, A. (1999). Acquiring writing revision skill: Shifting from process to outcome self-regulatory goals. *Journal of Educational Psychology, 91*, 1–10.

Zimmerman, B. J. & Kitsantas, A. (2002). Acquiring writing revision proficiency through observation and emulation. *Journal of Educational Psychology, 94*, 660–668.

Zimmerman, B. J., & Koussa, R. (1975). Sex factors in children's observational learning of value judgments of toys. *Sex Roles: A Journal of Research, 1*, 121–133.

Zimmerman, B. J., & Koussa, R. (1979). Social influences on children's toy preferences: Effects of model rewardingness and affect. *Contemporary Educational Psychology, 4,* 55–66.

Zimmerman, B. J., & Lebeau, R. B. (2000). A commentary on self-directed learning. In D. H. Evensen & C. E. Hmelo (Eds.*), Problem-based learning: A Research perspective on learning interactions* (pp. 299–313). Mahwah, NJ: Earlbaum.

Zimmerman, B. J., & Martinez-Pons, M. (1986). Development of a structured interview for assessing student use of self-regulated learning strategies. *American Educational Research Journal, 23,* 614–628.

Zimmerman, B. J., & Martinez-Pons, M. (1988). Construct validation of a strategy model of student self-regulated learning. *Journal of Educational Psychology, 80,* 284–290.

Zimmerman, B. J., & Martinez-Pons, M. (1990). Student differences in self-regulated learning: Relating grade, sex, and giftedness to self-efficacy and strategy use. *Journal of Educational Psychology, 82,* 51–59.

Zimmerman, B. J., & Ringle, J. (1981). Effects of model persistence and statements of confidence on children's self-efficacy and problem solving. *Journal of Educational Psychology, 73,* 485–493.

Zimmerman, B. J., & Rosenthal, T. L. (1972). Observation, repetition, and ethnic background in concept attainment and generalization. *Child Development, 43,* 605–613.

Zimmerman, B. J., & Rosenthal, T. L. (1974). Observational learning of rule governed behavior by children. *Psychological Bulletin, 81,* 29–42.

Zimmerman, B. J., & Schunk, D. H. (2004). Self-regulating process and outcomes: A social cognitive perspective. In D. Y. Dai & R. J. Sternberg (Eds.) *Motivation, emotion, and cognition: Perspectives on intellectual development and functioning* (pp. 323-349). Mahwah, NJ: Erlbaum.

CHAPTER 8

EXPECTANCY VALUE THEORY IN CROSS-CULTURAL PERSPECTIVE

**Allan Wigfield, Stephen Tonks,
and Jacquelynne S. Eccles**

INTRODUCTION

Jason is a high school student who is in the process of deciding which elective classes to take during the fall semester in his senior year of high school. As he looks at the list of courses in different subject areas he thinks about what kinds of subjects he has done well in and how he expects to do in these subjects in the future. He always has done well in math, and so is confident that he could manage even the higher-level math courses he has not yet taken. He also thinks about which subject areas interest him, or may be useful to him in the future. Because he had a wonderful history teacher in his sophomore year, he has developed a strong interest in history and wants to learn more about it. He tentatively is thinking about majoring in engineering in college, and so he knows additional mathematics classes would be useful to him for this field, both to help him gain acceptance to college and also to be ready for the college engineering curriculum. Based

Big Theories Revisited
Volume 4 in: Research on Sociocultural Influences on Motivation and Learning, pages 165–198.
Copyright © 2004 by Information Age Publishing, Inc.
All rights of reproduction in any form reserved.
ISBN: 1-59311-053-7 (hardcover), 1-59311-052-9 (paperback)

on his reflections about these issues, Jason decides on two electives: He chooses a history course on the topic of the 18th century in American and European history, and also an introduction to calculus course. Ultimately, his decisions were influenced by how well he expected to do in the classes available to him, his sense of the usefulness of the classes, and (particularly for his choice of the history course) his interest in the classes.

Chapter Overview

Jason's decision-making process shows how individuals' expectancies and values influence their choices of activities, in this case elective coursework during high school. This example captures some of the important constructs and principles of expectancy value theory, the theoretical perspective we discuss in this chapter. At the broadest level, expectancy value theory attempts to account for individuals' choices of activities to do, and performance on them. We present the theory as researchers and theorists in the United States, Europe, and Australia have developed it, and then discuss various cultural influences on the constructs and principles of the theory.

We focus in this chapter primarily on the contemporary expectancy value model developed by Eccles, Wigfield, and their colleagues (Eccles, 1984a, 1984b; 1993; Eccles et al., 1983; Wigfield & Eccles, 2000, 2002). We focus specifically on three of the model's constructs that have received the most research attention: beliefs about ability, expectancies for success, and achievement task values. We review research done in Western cultures on the development of individuals' ability, beliefs, expectancies, and values, and also how they influence choice and performance in different areas, with a focus on academic choice and performance. We then turn to a discussion of possible cultural influences on expectancies and values, and different research approaches used in cross-cultural research on these constructs.

It is important to note that in Eccles and colleagues' (1983) model certain cultural influences have always been considered. In particular, these theorists have written about how gender, cultural stereotypes about different subject areas and occupations, and the broader cultural milieu in which individuals grow up influence their expectancies and values (e.g., Eccles, 1984a, 1984b, 1993; Eccles et al., 1983). We consider cultural influences beyond this set, with a special focus on how the meaning of important constructs in the model might vary across culture. We review the relatively scant extant research on how expectancies and values develop in different cultures, then discuss how the meaning of these constructs may vary across culture, and consider the implications of this work for expectancy value theory.

EXPECTANCY VALUE MODELS

Expectancy value models have a relatively long history in the achievement motivation field (for historical overviews, see Weiner, 1992; Wigfield & Eccles, 1992). The expectancy and value constructs themselves initially were defined by theorists such as Lewin (1938) and Tolman (1932). Murray's (1938) notion of various human needs, and specifically the need for achievement, influenced expectancy value theorists. John Atkinson (1957, 1964) developed the first formal expectancy value model in an attempt to explain different kinds of achievement-related behaviors, such as striving for success, choice among achievement tasks, and persistence. Atkinson (1957) postulated that achievement behaviors are determined by achievement motives, expectancies for success, and incentive values. Atkinson defined expectancies for success as the individual's expected probability for success on a specific task, a value that goes from zero to one. He defined incentive value as the relative attractiveness of succeeding on a given achievement task, and also stated that incentive value is inversely related to the probability for success. He and his colleagues did an extensive body of research on individuals' achievement strivings under different probabilities for success (for further discussion, see Atkinson, 1964; Wigfield & Eccles, 1992).

Modern Expectancy Value Models

Modern expectancy value theories (e.g., Eccles, 1987, 1993; Eccles et al., 1983; Feather, 1982, 1988; Pekrun, 2000; Wigfield, 1994a; Wigfield & Eccles, 1992, 2000, 2002) are based on Atkinson's work in that they link achievement performance, persistence, and choice most directly to individuals' expectancy-related and task value beliefs. However, they differ from Atkinson's (1964) expectancy value theory in several ways. First, both the expectancy and value components are defined in more elaborate ways, and are linked to a broader array of psychological and social/cultural determinants. Second, these models have been tested in real-world achievement situations rather than with the laboratory tasks often used to test Atkinson's theory.

FEATHER'S WORK: EXPANDING THE SUBJECTIVE VALUES CONSTRUCT

Feather (e.g., Feather, 1982, 1988, 1992) broadened Atkinson's conceptualization of value, in large part by drawing on the work of Rokeach and tying that work to expectancy value theory. Rokeach (1973, 1979) focused on values as broad-based, general psychological characteristics of the individual (for descriptions of broad human values, see Rohan, 2000; Schwartz, 1992). He believed these values serve as standards or guides for action, and so argued that personal values might affect behavioral choices such as which occupation to pursue. Interestingly, Rokeach viewed these values as universal; values differ across cultures only in the extent to which they are emphasized in the culture. Since he viewed values as central to the individual's belief system, he saw them as relatively stable and encompassing, and thought they influenced behavior by providing meaning to that behavior. Rokeach defined two kinds of these broad values. Terminal values are the beliefs about life's ultimate goals or desired end-states, and instrumental values are the desirable ways of achieving the terminal values. Terminal values include such things as desiring a comfortable life, freedom, equality, and happiness. Instrumental values include courage, capability, ambition, and independence.

Drawing on this work, Feather (1982, 1988) defined values as a set of stable, general beliefs about what is desirable. He proposed that these beliefs come from both society's norms and the individual's psychological needs and sense of self. He integrated Rokeach's approach to values into the expectancy value approach by positing that values are a class of motives that affect behavior by influencing the attractiveness of different possible goals and thus the motivation to attain these goals. Feather studied how individuals' instrumental values and specific task values related to their choices of different kinds of activities. He found that both kinds of values predicted individuals' choices such as which political action group to join and what academic major to choose.

Eccles and Colleagues' Expectancy Value Model

Eccles and her colleagues developed and tested an expectancy value model of achievement-related choices (e.g., Eccles, 1987, 1993; Eccles et al., 1983; Eccles & Wigfield, 1995; Meece, Wigfield, & Eccles, 1990; Wigfield, 1994a; Wigfield & Eccles, 1992, 2000, 2002). They elaborated the definitions of each construct and also studied a variety of influences on each. Eccles and her colleagues have focused on the social psychological influences on choice, persistence, and performance, as well as the developmental course of children's expectancies and values. They initially developed the model to help explain gender differences in mathematics beliefs and choices of mathematics courses and majors. They broadened the model to other activity areas, most notably sport and physical skill activities (e.g., Eccles & Harold, 1991).

Figure 8.1 depicts a recent version of this model. Moving from right to left in the model, expectancies and values directly influence performance and task choice. Expectancies and values themselves are influenced by task-specific beliefs such as perceptions of competence, perceptions of the difficulty of different tasks, and individuals' goals and self-schema, along with their affective memories for different achievement-related events. These beliefs, goals, and affective memories are influenced by individuals' perceptions of other peoples' attitudes and expectations for them, and by their own interpretations of their previous achievement outcomes. Children's perceptions and interpretations are influenced by a broad array of social and cultural factors. These include socializers' (especially parents and teachers) beliefs and behaviors, their specific achievement experiences and aptitudes, and the cultural milieu in which they live. As mentioned earlier, Eccles and colleagues primarily have focused on gender role stereotypes, cultural stereotypes about subjects such as math and reading, and occupations in their discussion of cultural milieu.

Eccles and her colleagues' research provides support for many of the postulates of the model, and we review some of this research in detail below. To summarize briefly the major findings from this research, Eccles and her colleagues found that individuals' expectancies for success and valuing of mathematics predict their performance in mathematics and their choices of whether to continue studying math. Children's expectancies for success and valuing of achievement are influenced by their previous performance and their self-concepts of ability. Parents' and teachers' beliefs about students predict students' own expectancies and values. Variations in classroom environments influence children's expectancies and values in positive and negative ways. Finally, there are gender differences in children's beliefs and values about different activities that tend to conform to gender stereotypes about the activities (for review of this work, see Eccles, 1993; Eccles et al., 1983; Eccles, Wigfield, & Schiefele, 1998; Jacobs & Eccles, 2000; Wigfield & Eccles, 1992, 2000).

Because the Eccles and colleagues model was originally designed to explain a sociocultural phenomenon, we believe it is particularly well suited for a cultural analysis of motivation and activity choices. We expect that cultural differences in a wide array of activity and behavioral choices, particularly in the achievement domain, reflect cultural differences in success expectations and subjective task value-related beliefs, which, in turn, likely result from cultural differences in the wide range of social experiences that shape human development. The work we and our colleagues have done on gender within the United States provides comprehensive examples of just how these cultural processes can work (for review, see Eccles, 1984a, 1984b; Wigfield & Eccles, 2002). This work shows that parents differentially socialize their children's expectancies and values, and that children's expectancies and values for different activities vary across gender.

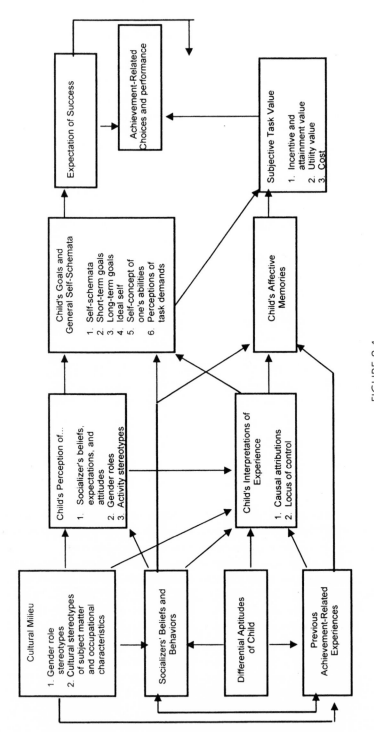

FIGURE 8.1.

General model of achievement choices

As noted earlier, in this chapter we focus on three constructs from the model that have received extensive research attention by Eccles, Wigfield, and their colleagues: expectancies for success, beliefs about ability or competence, and subjective task values. We briefly define each of these constructs, review research on them, and then provide a theoretical analysis of the relevance of these constructs for a cultural analysis of behavior.

Defining the expectancy, value, and ability belief constructs. Eccles and colleagues broadened Atkinson's (1957) original definitions of both the expectancy and value constructs. They define expectancies for success as children's beliefs about how well they will do on an upcoming task (e.g., how well do you think you will do in math next year?). They distinguished conceptually expectancies for success from the individual's beliefs about ability. These beliefs refer to children's evaluations of their competence or ability, both in terms of their assessments of their own ability and also how they think they compare to other students. Ability beliefs are prominent in many motivation models; Wigfield and Eccles (2000) discuss different definitions of this construct in these models. To return to our vignette, Jason's beliefs about his ability in different subjects come from many years of experience with them and reflect his assessment of his current skills in these subjects. His expectancies refer to how he thinks he will do in the future in the next level of these subjects, and he bases his expectancies primarily on his beliefs about his ability in a given subject area.

Eccles and her colleagues' have focused extensively on individuals' valuing of particular tasks or activities, rather than broader values such as those defined by Rokeach (1973). Much of this work has been grounded in the sociocultural processes linked to gender-role socialization (see Eccles, 1993). Consequently, this set of values should be particularly relevant to cultural analysis.

Eccles and colleagues (1983) proposed four major components of subjective values: attainment value or importance, intrinsic value, utility value or usefulness of the task, and cost (for more detailed discussion of these components, see Eccles et al., 1983; Wigfield & Eccles, 1992). Building on Battle's (1965, 1966) work on attainment value, Eccles and colleagues defined attainment value as the importance of doing well on a given task. Attainment value incorporates identity issues; tasks are important when individuals view them as central to their own sense of themselves, or allow them to express or confirm important aspects of self.

Intrinsic value is the enjoyment one gains from doing the task. This component is similar in certain respects to notions of intrinsic motivation and interest (see Renninger, 2000; Ryan & Deci, 2000; Schiefele, 2001), but it is important to acknowledge that these constructs come from different theoretical traditions. When children intrinsically value an activity, they often become deeply engaged in it and can persist at it for a long time.

Utility value or usefulness refers to how a task fits into an individual's future plans, for instance, taking a math class to fulfill a requirement for a science degree. In certain respects utility value is similar to extrinsic motivation, because when doing an activity out of utility value the activity is a means to an end rather than an end in itself (see Ryan & Deci, 2000). However, the activity also could tie to some important goals that the person holds deeply, such as attaining a certain occupation. In this sense utility value also ties to personal goals and sense of self.

Cost refers to what the individual has to give up to do a task (e.g., Do I do my math homework or call my friend?), as well as the anticipated effort one will need to put into task completion. Is working this hard to get an A in math worth it? Eccles and colleagues emphasized that cost is especially important to choice. Choices are influenced by both negative and positive task characteristics and all choices are assumed to have costs associated with them because one choice often eliminates other options. If Jason, from the above scenario, follows his inclinations and chooses to pursue an engineering major once he enters college, that means he will not be able to pursue other possible majors. Despite the theoretical importance of cost to choice, to date, cost has been the least studied of the different components of subjective values (see Battle & Wigfield, 2003, for a study of students' perceptions of the costs associated with graduate school).

Jason's choices of which classes to take reflect these different aspects of value. He chose a math class primarily because of its potential usefulness to him, as he plans to be an engineer. By contrast, he chose the advanced history course primarily because he likes history, rather than because it is useful to him. Sometimes these choices can reflect more than one aspect of value; in fact, Jason enjoys math to a degree and so his choice of a math class reflects both interest and usefulness. Thus the influence of an individual's valuing of an activity on the choice to pursue it or not is a complex process.

Culture and the Expectancy Value Model: Some General Considerations

How might culture relate to the Eccles and colleagues model? Conversely, how might the model help us understand cultural influences on achievement-related behavioral choices? We discuss these questions more comprehensively later in the chapter. At this point, we draw an analogy with the work we have done on gender to illustrate how our approach might be useful to a cultural analysis.

Like gender-role socialization, the processes associated with cultural socialization should influence the ways in which members of cultural groups see themselves as well as the goals and values they develop for their lives. In addition, experiences in different types of learning environments should influence the emotional experiences associated with different activities. Finally, cultures and countries should vary greatly in the opportunities provided to try different types of activities as well as in the range of activities made available and salient to various individuals living within the group. Each of these processes should lead to both cultural group differences and within-culture individual differences in expectancies, ability self-concepts, and subjective task values. We say more about this later.

At an even more basic level, cultures differ in the extent to which individuals have "choice" over such achievement-related behaviors as educational focus, careers, and leisure activities. Western cultures pride themselves on allowing individuals to make these choices for themselves, even though choice still continues to be heavily socialized in these Western cultures (see Jacobs & Eccles, 2000). Other cultures place less emphasis on individual choice, particularly individual choice based on maximizing self-fulfillment and self-actualization. For example, in interviews with young professionals in China, Eccles found that career choices were based much more on the needs of the community for particular types of skills than on the needs of the individual to find a job that maximized the fit of one's occupation with one's talents and interests. In most cases, an individual's occupation was determined for them by their community, or by the state. Similarly, in interviews with Japanese students, Eccles found that choices about future occupations were based more on the quality of the company than on the fit of the particular job category with the individual's talents and interests. In this case, the individuals were given more power to select their future occupation; but the criteria for their choice was quite different from the criteria advocated in vocational counseling in the United States.

Does this mean that the expectancy value model is not a useful theoretical tool for such cultures? We think not. It does mean that we need to consider the full complexity of the Eccles and colleageus model—its cultural as well as its psychological components. We need to pay particular attention to the sociocultural forces that underlie individual differences in expectancies, ability self-concepts, and subjective task value, as well as the relative predictive power of each of these constructs for the various achievement-related choices available to the individuals. In both of the Chinese and Japanese cases discussed above, the subjective value of various occupation categories was based on more communal considerations than is typical among European American adolescents. In addition, the relevance of ability self-concepts for choice should be less than it is for European American adolescents. These hypotheses, however, have not been tested. We return to these points later.

Equally important, cultures will differ in the range of options provided and the freedom of choice allowed. Eccles (1987, 1994) argued that these two sociocultural characteristics are key to understanding gender differences in occupational choice in the United States. Individuals are only exposed to a narrow range of options available to them in any achievement domain. Cultures differ greatly in the kinds of day-to-day activities to which their children are exposed. For example, urban children in the United States are not likely to be exposed to playing cricket, African drums, or Balinese dancing for a leisure activity, or to farming as an occupational choice. Consequently, it is not surprising that American children are unlikely to choose these activities.

RESEARCH ON EXPECTANCIES AND VALUES IN WESTERN CULTURE

We review in this section work on the development of children's competence beliefs, expectancies for success, and achievement values, their relations to performance and choice, and how children of different ages may understand these constructs differently. Because this work has been reviewed in detail elsewhere (e.g., Eccles et al., 1998; Wigfield, 1994b; Wigfield & Eccles, 1992, 2002), we present a relatively brief summary here.

The Structure of Expectancy Beliefs and Values

One important developmental question with respect to these beliefs and values is whether the structure of these constructs is the same in younger and older children. The expectancy value model presumes that these are distinct constructs, but that may not be the case for younger children. Factor-analytic studies of children's competence beliefs (done within the framework of this model and by other researchers studying ability beliefs) have found that even during the early elementary school years children distinguish different domains of competence, including math, reading, general school, physical ability, physical appearance, peer relations, parent relations, and general self-concept (e.g., Eccles & Wigfield, 1995; Eccles, Wigfield, Harold, & Blumenfeld, 1993; Harter, 1982; Marsh, 1989; Marsh, Craven, & Debus, 1991, 1998).

Eccles and Wigfield (1995) and Eccles et al. (1993) looked at whether children ranging from first through 12th grade have distinct competence beliefs and expectancies for success, as is proposed in the Eccles and colleagues (1983) model. Results of confirmatory factor analyses showed that at all ages children's competence beliefs and expectancies for success load on the same factor; hence these components are not empirically distinct. Therefore, two of the constructs proposed as separate in the model (competence beliefs, expectancies for success) are not empirically distinguishable when assessed in this way.

In their factor analyses Eccles and Wigfield (1995) and Eccles and colleagues (1993) also examined whether children's competence beliefs and values form separate factors, and found that they do, in children as young as first grade. This finding is crucial for the expectancy value model, because is shows that two of the central constructs are empirically distinct, even in young children. Although competence-expectancy beliefs and values formed different factors, the different components of task value are less differentiated during the elementary school years, becoming differentiated during early adolescence (Eccles & Wigfield, 1995; Eccles et al., 1993).

Changes in the Mean Level of Expectancies and Values

Several researchers have found that children's competence beliefs and expectancies for success for different tasks decline across the elementary school years and into the middle school years (for review, see Dweck & Elliott, 1983; Eccles et al., 1998; Stipek & Mac Iver, 1989). To illustrate, cross-sectional and longitudinal studies of children's competence beliefs in a variety of academic and nonacademic settings in the United States and Australia show that these beliefs decline (e.g., Eccles et al. 1993; Marsh, 1989; Wigfield et al., 1997). These declines, particularly for math, often continue into and through secondary school (Eccles et al., 1983, 1989; Jacobs, Lanza, Osgood, Eccles, & Wigfield, 2002; Wigfield et al., 1991). Researchers looking at changes in the mean level of children's values generally show that children value certain academic tasks less as they get older (Jacobs et al., 2002; Wigfield et al., 1997; for complete reviews, see Eccles et al., 1998; Wigfield & Eccles, 1992, 2002).

The negative changes in children's expectancy-related beliefs and achievement values found in the United States have been explained in two ways. One explanation involves children's growing sophistication at understanding, interpreting, and integrating the evaluative feedback they receive. They also engage in more social comparison with their peers, particularly once they begin school. These processes help children to become more accurate or realistic in their self-assessments, leading some to become relatively more negative about their ability and also about how much they value different achievement activities (see Dweck & Elliott, 1983; Nicholls, 1984; Stipek & Mac Iver, 1989). Returning to our example of Jason, he began school thinking he was quite good at many different activities. From the feedback he received and his comparisons with others, he began to realize he had stronger skills in some areas than others. Although his sense of competence declined to a degree, Jason was a good student, especially in math and science, and so continued to believe he could do well in these and other areas. Thus he was willing to continue to take additional math courses.

The second explanation has to do with changes in classroom and school environments and conditions. In the United States, school environments often change in ways that make evaluation more salient and competition between students more likely. As high-stakes assessments become more prevalent, such practices are on the increase. This focus on evaluation, performance, and competence make it more likely for some children's expectancies and values to decline as they go through school (see, e.g., Eccles & Midgley, 1989; Wigfield, Eccles, & Pintrich, 1996). These kinds of changes are characteristic of certain cultural approaches to schooling. In cultures outside the U.S. such changes in school environments may or may not occur, which has implications for how children's expectancies and values may change in these different cultures.

Relations of Expectancies and Values to Performance and Choice

In the expectancy value model presented in Figure 8.1, individuals' expectancies for success and subjective values directly predict their achievement outcomes, including their performance, persistence, and choices of which activities to do (e.g. Eccles, 1993; Eccles et al., 1983, 1998). Empirical support for these proposed linkages has been found in longitudinal studies of children ranging in age from 6 to 18. Even when level of previous performance is controlled, students' competence beliefs strongly predict their performance in different domains, including math, reading, and sports. Students' subjective task values predict both intentions and actual decisions to keep taking mathematics and English and to engage in sports. The relations appear in children as young as first grade, although the relations strengthen across age (Eccles, 1984a, 1984b; Eccles et al. 1983; Eccles & Harold, 1991; Meece et al., 1990; Wigfield, 1997; for more detailed review of these studies, see Wigfield, 1994a; Wigfield & Eccles, 2002).

There is one important difference between these findings and the links predicted in the model: In the model competence-related beliefs and values were posited to predict the same outcomes. In the empirical work children's competence-related beliefs have their strongest direct effects on performance, while achievement values have their strongest direct effects on choice. The positive relations of competence-related beliefs and values, however, means that each does have indirect effects on the other achievement outcome as well: expectancies to choice and values to performance. Jason's choices of the advanced math and history courses described earlier reflect both his expectations for future success and his valuing of the different courses he is choosing, rather than simply reflecting one or the other.

If he did not think he could handle the work in the math class, he would be less likely to choose it. As well, if he did not see much value in that class (in this case for his future), he also would likely not choose it.

Changes in Children's Conceptions of What Expectancies and Values Mean

Another kind of change in children's beliefs and values concerns change in the meaning these constructs have for children across their development. The research on this topic has focused primarily on children's conceptions of ability and intelligence. Children of different ages appear to have different conceptions of what ability is, with consequent influences on their motivation. This kind of change is particularly relevant to a chapter on cultural influences, as these constructs also may have different meanings in different cultures. We return to this latter point in a later section.

Much of this work comes from outside the expectancy value tradition, but we include it here because it deals with central constructs in the model. Nicholls and his colleagues extensively examined children's conceptions of ability (e.g., Nicholls, 1978, 1984, 1990; Nicholls & Miller, 1984; Nicholls, Patashnick, & Mettetal, 1986). These researchers asked children of different ages various questions about ability, intelligence, effort, and task difficulty, and how different levels of performance can occur when children exert similar effort. Focusing first on the work on ability and effort, their analyses of children's responses show four relatively distinct levels of reasoning about how ability and effort are differentiated (see Nicholls, 1990, for a more complete review of this work). At the first level (occurring in children ages 5 to 6), effort, ability, and performance are not clearly differentiated in terms of cause and effect. At the second level (dominant in children ages 7 to 9), effort is seen as the primary cause of performance outcomes; however, effort and ability are not differentiated as causes. At level 3 (ages 9 to 12), children begin to differentiate ability and effort as causes of outcomes, but they do not always apply this distinction. Finally, at level 4, which emerges between the ages of 10 and 13, children clearly differentiate ability and effort, and understand the notion of ability as capacity. That is, children conceive that one's ability can limit the effects additional effort can have on performance, and that if success requires a great deal of effort, it may mean the individual lacks ability.

Dweck and her colleagues (e.g., Dweck, 2002; Dweck & Bempechat, 1983; Dweck & Elliott, 1983; Dweck & Leggett, 1988) have discussed how some children view ability as unchangeable. In their view, children hold one of two views of intelligence or ability. Children holding an *entity* view of intelligence believe that intelligence is a stable trait. Children holding an *incremental* view of intelligence believe that intelligence is changeable, so that it can be increased through effort. It appears that the entity view of intelligence is similar to the view of "ability as capacity" that Nicholls discussed. However, Nicholls (1990) argued that Dweck and her colleagues equate "ability" and "intelligence" in their work, thus glossing over important differences between the two constructs.

Despite the differences in their approaches to defining and assessing the construct of intelligence, both Nicholls (1984, 1990) and Dweck and her colleagues (e.g., Dweck, 2002; Dweck & Elliott, 1983; Dweck & Leggett, 1988) have discussed how children's conceptions of ability and intelligence can have important motivational consequences. A sense of ability as capacity means that failure is more debilitating. Some children holding this view will believe they have little chance of ever doing well, because their ability cannot be improved. In contrast, believing effort can improve performance in important ways should mean that children will continue to try even if they are not doing well on a given task (for further discussion, see Dweck & Leggett, 1988; Nicholls, 1984, 1990).

Freedman-Doan and colleagues (2000) built on this work by examining how much children thought their ability could improve in different areas, such as academics, sports, and music/art. First-, second-, and fourth-grade children responded to questions about whether they could get better at the activity they currently did worst, and also if they could be *best* at their current worst activity. Children were optimistic that they could improve and even become best at their current worst activity, especially in the academic and sports domains. There was some evidence that the younger children believed this more strongly than did older children, but the older children also remained optimistic that they can improve. Thus, through the elementary school years children see their ability at particular activities to be malleable.

This work has important implications for the expectancy value model, in particular that the way an individual's beliefs about ability relate to their performance may change depending upon their understanding of what ability is. It also has implications for task choice. With the belief that effort cannot improve ability, individuals may be less likely to choose to do activities at which they believe they are not very good, because they may think they will fail. Individuals believing they can improve their ability through effort may be more likely to choose challenging tasks as a way to build their ability in that area.

CHANGES IN CONCEPTIONS OF SUBJECTIVE TASK VALUES

Researchers have not yet addressed changes in the meaning of the components of task value identified by Eccles and colleagues (1983), although there likely are age-related differences in children's conceptions of what it means to value different tasks. This may be particularly true for the utility of different activities. Young children likely do not have a clear sense of how different school subjects such as math or reading may be useful to them in the present or future. A clear sense of both the meaning of usefulness as well as a sense of which activities are most useful to children likely emerges later in children's development, as they begin to think about which careers or jobs to pursue, and other aspects of their lives. To date this possibility has not been addressed (see Wigfield, 1994a, for further discussion of how children's conceptions of task value may vary across age).

This reasoning also suggests that young children's involvement in different activities may be based more on their interest in the activity rather than its usefulness. As children get older usefulness likely becomes a stronger predictor of children's involvement in different activities (see Wigfield, 1994a, for further discussion). For instance, as a high school student, Jason has thought about what he wants to do after he completes his secondary education. His choice of the calculus class reflects his sense that it is potentially useful for his pursuit of an engineering degree in college. He also might be interested in calculus, but even if he isn't he still would register for the course because of its perceived utility to him. Early in his school career he likely did not have a clear sense of how calculus might be useful to him.

CROSS-CULTURAL RESEARCH ON EXPECTANCIES AND VALUES

In this section, we discuss key issues in cross-cultural psychology research, and consider how they relate to examining the expectancy value model from a cultural perspective. The definition of what cross-cultural research is, of course, is complex; Poortinga (1997) provides a discussion of the term as it applies in psychological research. For the purposes of this chapter we use this term to mean research comparing individuals who live in different countries rather than subgroups living within one country (see Tonks & Wigfield, 2003, for further discussion).

Following the discussion of important issues in cross-cultural research, we review extant work from different cultures on how expectancies and values develop. We organize the research review as in the previous section: factor structure of children's expectancy-related beliefs and values, mean level differences, relations of beliefs and values to student outcomes, and the meaning of the constructs in different cultures.

Much has been written about the distinction between etic and emic research in cross-cultural research, and which approach is more appropriate (e.g., Berry, 1989; Poortinga, 1997; Yu & Wolters, 2001). An etic approach to cross-cultural research assumes that constructs have the same meaning across cultures. For example, an etic model of expectancies and values would assume that students of all cultures interpret these constructs in the same way, or that these are universal constructs. When testing such a model, researchers might look for cross-cultural similarities and differences in the strength to which math expectancies and values predict math achievement. A goal of this approach might be to develop a universal expectancy value model, which would have applicability across cultures.

In contrast, an *emic* approach assumes that constructs take on different meanings in different cultures. An emic model is culture-specific and cannot be generalized to other cultures. Researchers using this approach might address the meanings of expectancies and values within one specific culture by employing qualitative methods such as interviews and ethnographies. The end-product of such research would be a detailed characterization of the construct meanings and their relations to performance and choice within the specific context.

Cross-cultural work of both of these types has been done within the expectancy value framework, and we turn to that work next.

CROSS-CULTURAL RESEARCH ON THE DEVELOPMENT OF EXPECTATIONS AND VALUES

The Structure of Expectancy-Related Beliefs and Values

A number of researchers have examined for children in different cultures the factor structure of their beliefs about their ability. These researchers have used measures developed in Western cultures, such as Harter's (1982) Perceived Competence Scale (PCS) and Marsh's (1989) Self-Description Questionnaire (SDQ), to measure children's perceptions of ability. One purpose of such work is to see if the factor structure of children's ability beliefs found in Western culture replicates in other cultures. Researchers have found that the factor structure indeed does replicate, although the work has been confined primarily to students from Eastern cultures, particularly China.

To illustrate, Hau, Kong, and Marsh (2000) gave a Chinese version of the SDQ to a large sample of adolescents in Hong Kong. Using confirmatory factor analyses, they found that the factor structure of the Hong Kong adolescents' responses to the SDQ was nearly identical to that reported by Marsh and his colleagues (e.g., Marsh, 1990) in administrations of the SDQ in Australia. As discussed earlier, in the Australian (and U.S.) studies children's ability beliefs form separate factors in each domain assessed. The same occurred in the Hong Kong sample.

Stigler, Smith, and Mao (1985) gave the PCS to fifth-grade students in Taiwan and the U.S. They used exploratory factor-analytic procedures similar to those used by Harter (1982) in her study of American children, and found that the Taiwanese students' responses produced a factor structure very similar to the factor structure reported by Harter (1982). Stigler and colleagues were careful to conclude that although their results show that Taiwanese students, like American students, have differentiated beliefs about competence, there could be other ways in which the two groups' beliefs about competence differ. These include other possible domains of competence not measured by the PCS that may be relevant in one culture but not the other, and different areas of emphasis within shared domains of competence.

Given the similarity in factor structure in children's ability beliefs across cultures, it might be argued that the construct does not vary in different cultures. One problem with drawing this conclusion is that the questionnaire measures used in these studies do not get at children's understandings of what their ability is. Instead, children simply respond to investigator-generated items, which were first developed in the West. Interview methods are necessary for the purpose of assessing whether the actual meaning of a construct like sense of ability or subjective values differ across culture. We return to this point below.

We know of no work that has examined the factor structure across cultures of children's subjective task values. Given the results for ability beliefs just reported, we might expect that the factor structure of children's responses to scales measuring task values may also be similar across cultures. However, it is possible that values, more so than ability beliefs, are influenced by culture, as values seem inherently influenced by culture. Parents and institutions within a given culture have the major responsibility to teach their children values of different kinds, including the value of academics. Given this, perhaps, the factor structure of children's subjective values may vary more across culture than the factor structure of children's ability beliefs appears to. To address this issue, researchers need to do two things. First, they should factor analyze for children in different cultures responses to the existing scales measuring subjective task values to see how similar or different the factor structure is using existing measures. Second (and perhaps even more important) researchers need to interview children from different cultures to get at the meaning values has for them. We return to this point later.

Change in the Mean Level of Expectancies and Values

We reviewed work earlier showing that in the United States and Australia children's beliefs about ability and expectancies for success decreased over the school years. Researchers are beginning to address whether this is true in other cultures as well. Chang, McBride-Chang, Stewart, and Au (2003) examined second- and eighth-grade Hong Kong students' beliefs about their competence, using the PCS. They found that younger children had more positive beliefs about their academic and sport self-competence than did the older children. They concluded that like American adolescents, adolescents in Hong Kong face various challenging school, social, and biological transitions, which may lower their sense of competence in different areas. However, the sample size of this study was quite small, and in two areas (social competence beliefs and general self-esteem) there were no age differences. Clearly, more work is needed to see whether the patterns of decline in competence beliefs observed in studies in the United States and Australia occur in other cultures.

To date there has been very little work on how students from different cultures subjective values change across age, at least in terms of the specific kinds of values measured by Eccles, Wigfield, and their colleagues. Recall that the pattern found by Eccles and colleagues is that children's subjective values for academic activities tend to decrease over time. Henderson, Marx, and Kim (1999) studied U.S., Korean, and Japanese children's interest in different activities, including numbers, words, ideas, things, people, and being alone. The first three were categorized as academic activities. The children in each country were in grades 2 through 5, and interest was measured with a single-item indicator. They predicted a decrease across age in interest in the academic activities, and the prediction was supported for words and numbers but not ideas. This study provides some preliminary evidence that there is a decline in interest in academic activities in two Eastern countries as there is in the West, but the instrument used to measure interest is limited and the design was cross-sectional. More research is needed on how children's subjective values change over time in different countries. Researchers could begin this work by using measures developed in the West and seeing if observed changes in children's subjective task values are similar or different from the changes reviewed above. This etic approach should be supplemented with emic work looking at the nature of subjective values in different cultures, and how these values may change across development.

Mean-Level Differences in Expectancy-Related Beliefs and Values across Culture

A number of researchers have compared mean levels of ability beliefs in different cultures, with the comparisons done primarily between students in the West and East. These researchers generally find that American, Canadian, and English students have higher perceptions of their competence in different subject areas than do students from Eastern cultures and Russia (e.g., Eaton & Dembo, 1997; Elliott, Hufton, Illushin, & Lauchlan, 2001; Kwok, 1995; Kwok & Lytton, 1996; Stevenson et al., 1990; Stigler et al., 1985; Whang & Hancock, 1994; for more complete review, see Hufton, Elliott, & Illushin, 2002a; Zusho & Pintrich, 2003). Interestingly, the Asian students often perform better on the achievement measures given in these studies (e.g., Stevenson & Lee, 1990).

The differences in perceived competence favoring Western students are often discussed in terms of their tendency to self-enhance, and Asian students' tendency to be modest in their self-presentations. These tendencies themselves are explained in terms of the characterization of Western culture as individualistic, and Eastern cultures as collective (Markus & Kitayama, 1991). However, Zusho and Pintrich (2003) argue that such explanations may be too general, and that more work is needed on how students calibrate their responses in each culture, and also how students construe ability in each culture, to know if the measures given are seen in the same way and responded to in the same way (see also Hufton et al., 2002a). In one study looking at how students from different cultures calibrate their responses, Chen, Lee, and Stevenson (1995) found that American students more often used the extreme ends of the answer scale, and students from Asian cultures used the midpoints more frequently, suggesting that there are differences in calibration across culture.

Are there cultural differences in children's valuing of different activities? This question has been examined in two ways. One approach is to study individuals' broader valuing of education. Feather (1975) studied how the broader values defined by Rokeach (1973) varied across cultures and found some interesting differences in different cultural groups. (We do not review that work because it is outside the scope of this chapter.)

Researchers have looked at differences across culture in children's interest in different school-related activities, one of the components of task value in the expectancy value model. Results of this work present a somewhat mixed picture. Stevenson and colleagues (1990) examined first- and fifth-grade children from Chicago and Beijing to rate their interest in math. They found that a higher percentage of Chinese children (85%) than American children (72%) reported liking math, but as can be seen, these percentages both are high. Furthermore, when children were asked what they would like to learn if they had the opportunity to learn something new, more American children spontaneously mentioned math.

In the study of cross-cultural differences in interest described above, Henderson and colleagues (1999) also looked at how the Asian and American children differed in their interest in different activities. They predicted that the Asian children would express more interest in academic activities, but there was little evidence for this. There also were few culture-by-grade interactions. In a study of 11th-grade students' interest in math (measured with two items analogous to measures used by Eccles,

Wigfield, and their colleagues) in Germany and Japan, Randel, Stevenson, and Witruk (2000) found that the German students reported liking math more.

Thus the findings with respect to one component of subjective values, children's interest in different activities, clearly are mixed. The work to date is limited because different researchers used quite different measures, and so it is difficult to reach any firm conclusions about how children's valuing of different activities varies across cultures. These researchers also did not address whether the interest construct they assessed varied in meaning across cultures. Clearly, more research is necessary in this area, both to look at the different components of task value identified by Eccles and their colleagues, and also to assess other possible aspects of task value.

Relations of Expectancies and Values to Performance and Choice

This issue has been addressed in different ways. As Zusho and Pintrich (2003) point out, the fact that Asian students generally perform very well but rate their ability relatively lower may mean their beliefs and performance don't relate that strongly, or at least that Asian students underestimate their ability and American students overestimate theirs.

Other researchers examined directly the relations of ability beliefs and performance. Marsh, Hau, and Kong (2002) assessed in a large sample of adolescents from Hong Kong causal relations of academic self-concept of ability (SCA) and verbal and numeric performance during high school. Based on earlier research done in Australia by Marsh and Yeung (1997), they predicted that achievement and SCA would relate reciprocally to one another. They found that this indeed was the case, and the strength of these relations was similar in the two studies. Marsh and colleagues concluded (cautiously) that these results provide preliminary support that the reciprocal effects model is universal.

How about the relations of students' achievement values to achievement? Researchers measuring students' interest in different activities using items similar to those used by Eccles and her colleagues in their work have looked at relations of interest to achievement. Stevenson and Lee (1990) report cross-cultural similarities in the relations between interest and achievement among elementary school students in samples from Taiwan, Japan, and the United States. The researchers found significant positive correlations between one item measuring interest in math and achievement in math among students in Grades 1 and 5. In another study, Randel and colleagues (2000) combined this interest item with an item about liking math to form the composite math attitude, which correlated positively with achievement among Grade 11 students in Japan, but not among

Grade 11 students in Germany. So overall these researchers have found that interest measured by items similar to those used by Eccles, Wigfield, and their colleagues relates to children's achievement. More such studies are needed, including work looking at how the other components of task values relate to performance or achievement.

Recall that Meece and colleagues (1990) found that children's ability beliefs and expectancies directly predicted their subsequent performance in math and were themselves influenced by previous performance, similar to the findings of Marsh and colleagues (2002) just reviewed. In the Meece and colleagues study, children's valuing of mathematics predicted their intentions to take more mathematics courses. There has been little cross-cultural work on values' relations to intentions and choice. One exception is Elliott, Hufton, and colleagues' work (see Hufton et al., 2002a, for a summary). These researchers report that Russian students appear to accept schoolwork as valuable in its own right and for the purposes of becoming an educated citizen, rather than for its relations to later careers, perhaps indicating that their specific valuing of different tasks does not relate as strongly to course choice as is found in studies of American samples.

Asakara and Csikszentmihalyi (2000) conducted a study of adolescents' judgments of the importance of different activities to their future goals. They reported stronger correlations of these ratings to happiness and self-esteem in Asian American students compared to Caucasian students, although it should be noted that the correlations in both groups generally were low. The researchers interpreted these results as indicating that the Asian American students have internalized values relevant to achievement more strongly than the Caucasian students, because these values relate to other important psychological characteristics more strongly in the Asian American group. In terms of our expectancy value focus, these findings can be extrapolated to mean that the Asian American students' sense of importance of achievement may predict more strongly their choice of achievement activities, given the stronger internalization of values in this group. This possibility needs to be tested directly, particularly in light of the low correlations reported in this study.

Differences in the Meaning of the Ability and Value Constructs Across Cultures

Most of the work just reviewed takes the etic approach to cross-cultural research, in that constructs and measures developed in Western cultures are given to children in other cultures, and comparisons made of the responses. The factor-analytic studies perhaps can be considered a mixture of the etic and emic approaches (see also McInerney, 1995). This research

provides much interesting information, but does not help us to understand fully similarities and differences in the constructs across culture.
Emic approaches are required for this task. We already know from research
reviewed earlier done primarily by Dweck, Nicholls, and their colleagues
that even within American culture younger and older children appear to
have different understandings of what ability and intelligence mean.
Nicholls and his colleagues' work, summarized above, suggests developmental differences in children's ideas about what constitutes ability, with
younger children seeing effort and ability working together, and older children seeing them as inversely related. Dweck's work suggests individuals
differences, with some children believing intelligence is changeable and
others not.

Conceptions of Ability

A number of researchers have looked at how conceptions of ability differ
across culture. Like the Western research on ability beliefs, some cross-cultural work in this area has focused on the meaning of intelligence.
Quihuis, Bempechat, Jimenez, and Boulay (2002) specifically addressed
Dweck and Legget's (1988) model of entity and incremental views of intelligence in a group of 10th- through 12th-grade Mexican American students, using both questionnaire and interview methods. They found that
when students who were classified as holding entity views of intelligence in
all domains (i.e., general intelligence, mathematics, science, and English)
elaborated on their answers, many held incremental views as well. Some
students held entity views in some domains and incremental views in others, while other students were shown to hold both views within domains.
The authors attribute this finding to the fact that interviews afforded a context for achievement views that decontextualized questionnaires did not.
In relating their responses to their day-to-day learning, interviewees were
able to consider social, structural, and internal (to the person) factors in
their answers. One shortcoming of this study, however, is that the authors
did not specifically discuss these students' particular culture and how it
might influence their beliefs.

  Hufton, Elliott, and Illushin (2002a) conducted surveys and interviews
with pupils in England, Russia, and the United States to investigate a variety of factors related to motivation and engagement, including meaning of
ability. They report that subtle differences in the meaning of ability do
exist between students in these locations. American students' notion of
"smart" seems to designate something that can be increased by effort, reminiscent of Dweck and Leggett's (1988) incremental view of intelligence. In
England, students see intelligence as somewhat less changeable and Russian students contrast having a talent with not having a talent in a subject
area. The authors took these differences to indicate that notions of ability

do not transcend cultures, and stated that instruments used to measure students' concepts of ability need to reflect such culturally specific meanings.

Another study by the same researchers (Hufton et al., 2002b) painted an even more complex picture of student-constructed meanings of ability. To investigate further their earlier finding that English and American students were more likely to attribute success to effort over ability, yet exerted less academic effort than the Russian students, they interviewed 15-year-olds from each location. Pupils in all locations viewed ability less as an innate quality and more as determined by effort and teaching. Russian students were the most likely to see ability as an outcome of effort, which may indicate that these students saw the most overlap between the effort and ability constructs. Although survey data indicate that English and American students attribute success to effort rather than ability more so than the Russian students, interviews reveal that the Russian students' concept of ability may include a higher degree of effort. As for the Russian pupils' notion of talent as part of intelligence, the authors explain that all Russian students in the study were exerting high amounts of effort. In such a culture, pupils see natural talent as the quality that distinguishes the very top students.

There is a large literature on how students' attributions differ across culture. Although attribution theory is not the topic of this chapter, this work is relevant to how individuals construe ability, and so we mention it briefly here. The prevailing findings in this work are that Asian students emphasize effort relatively more in explaining their achievement outcomes than students in the West (see Holloway, 1988; Stevenson & Lee, 1990). This work may suggest that Asian students take a more incremental view of their ability than do students in the West, given their focus on effort as essential to their achievement.

How are these cultural differences in concepts of ability explained? Holloway (1988) and others have argued that socialization practices may produce these differences. She discussed how Japanese culture emphasizes cooperation and integration into the social group as key aspects of socialization. Holloway reviewed research showing that Japanese adults emphasize social competence in their definition of intelligence more so than Americans, who separate social and intellectual competence to a greater degree. These findings fit with Markus and Kitayama's (1991) notion that the Japanese have a more interdependent view of the self. She further discussed how in Japanese culture parents and teachers emphasize the development of learning and understanding for its own sake, use control strategies that are less authoritarian, and evaluate children in ways that emphasize effort as ways in which children are socialized to believe effort is what is key to success. Certainly, the belief that effort is crucial is rooted in American culture as well, but may be more so in other cultures, particularly Asian cultures.

Another possible cultural difference in ability beliefs concerns cultural differences in the stereotypes of different abilities. Some cultures believe that individual differences in math and sports ability reflect individual differences in practice and learning. Others believe these individual differences are due primarily to innate aptitude. It is likely that the conclusions the children in these different types of cultures draw from their success and failure experiences in math and sports about their ability will differ—leading to cultural differences in ability self-concepts for different academic domains. Such differences also could have implications for participation in different activities.

One methodological implication of this body of research is that etic methods alone cannot get at the complex meanings that students construct around concepts such as ability and intelligence, as Bempechat and colleagues (Bempechat & Boulay, 2001; Bempechat & Drago-Severson, 1999) have pointed out. They contend that emic methods are needed in order to better understand how students in any culture construct their own meanings regarding motivation constructs. Furthermore, they warn against reducing complex constructs down to dichotomies (e.g., entity vs. incremental or effort vs. ability), which end up limiting how the constructs are studied and interpreted.

This work on the differences in the meaning of ability across cultures has important implications for expectancy value theory. Recall that one important finding in expectancy value research is that individuals' expectancies for success and ability beliefs predict their performance. We reviewed some evidence earlier suggesting these links hold in other cultures as well (although that research is scant). However, the interpretation of these findings across cultures may vary, given the differences in the meaning of ability in different cultures. Beliefs about ability may predict performance in different cultures, but we should not necessarily assume that children view ability in the same way in these cultures. Furthermore, in cultures where effort appears a more important explanation for success than ability, perhaps links between student effort and outcomes would be stronger than those between students' expectancies for success and outcomes.

Conceptions of Task Value

To date, there has been little research on how the meaning of the values construct may vary across cultures. One such study was the Hufton and colleagues (2002b) study described above. They also assessed Russian students' achievement values, and reported that these students did not appear to view the values of tasks in terms of the components of task value identified by Eccles and her colleagues. These findings suggest a different conceptualization of values across cultures, but they are preliminary.

As noted earlier, we believe it is quite possible that culture may impact values even more than conceptions of ability, as a major cultural obligation is the socialization of children's values, both broadly and more specifically defined. We have focused in this chapter on attainment value or importance, utility, and interest as the three main components of children's valuing of academic activities. How might the meaning of each component of values vary in different cultural settings? Here are some possibilities.

Attainment value, for example, should be very culturally embedded. The value of various identity components, activities, and behaviors is a central component of culture. To the extent that individuals within a culture internalize the culturally proscribed identity components, these individuals will place greater importance (attainment value) on those behaviors and activities that are consistent with these identity components. Similarly, to the extent that individuals have internalized the culturally proscribed identity components, the lower value, and the higher cost, they will attach to activities and behaviors that are inconsistent or antithetical with the culturally proscribed identity components.

In the Eccles and colleagues' model, importance is defined in terms of self and identity issues; tasks that are important to the individual confirm or relate to central aspects of their own identities (see Eccles, 1993; Eccles et al., 1983). For children in Western cultures, this focus on identity may imply how important the task is to one's independent, individualistic self. Eastern cultures often are characterized as collective, with people focused on how one fits into the collective whole (or at least a social group) rather than on the individual self (Markus & Kitayama, 1991; but see Pintrich & Zusho, 2003, and Triandis, 2001, for a critique of this view). In such cultures, importance could reflect this different emphasis. Thus, rather than confirming aspects of one's own identity, importance of an activity may confirm one's relation to the group, and individuals would judge the importance of a task based on these considerations as well as how the task relates to one's own separate identity.

A similar point may apply to usefulness, defined by Eccles and colleagues (1983) in terms of the utility of the activity to the individual. In cultures characterized as collective utility may reflect not just the usefulness of the activity to the individual but also to one's larger social group. The concern about the group actually could outweigh the utility to the individual. To go back to the example of Jason from the beginning of this chapter, if living in a collective culture, Jason might judge the usefulness of the calculus course more on how it would help him fit into and contribute to his group, rather than its utility solely to him personally.

If various adult roles are valued differently across cultures, then the utility value of those activities and behaviors likely to be instrumental to achieving these adult roles will also vary across cultures and subcultural groups. Similarly, the cost of engaging in activities or behaviors that reduce the likelihood of achieving these adult roles will vary across cultures. In addition, cultures will vary in their tolerance and encouragement of non-traditional and non-normative behavioral choices. As the tolerance and encouragement go down, the cost of non-normative and nontraditional choices goes up—in some cases to the point of death.

How about interest? Interest often is defined in terms of personal interest or situational interest (see Schiefele, 2001). Personal interest is a deep-seated interest resting within the individual, whereas situational interest is a temporary interest generated by the activity one is doing. In collectivist cultures, interest also may reflect social aspects to a greater extent, so that individuals judge their personal interest based more on group rather than just individual standards or considerations.

Finally, females and males in all cultures, as well as other cultural subgroups within a culture, engage in quite different activities both as children and adults. In part, these differences are likely to reflect differences in the choices to which females and males are exposed; in part, these differences reflect the impact of sociocultural processes on the development of females' and males' ability self-perceptions and subjective task values. Interview methods could be used to ask children from different cultures about how they view these value constructs, to begin to understand more clearly the nature of subjective task values in different cultures, and how they influence individuals' choices of activities to pursue.

Such emic research would help us understand some of the important relations posited in the expectancy value model. As noted earlier, in research done in the West, children's ability beliefs directly predicts their performance, and values predict their intentions and choices of activities. We reviewed earlier cross-cultural research on how children's ability-related beliefs relate to their performance. Researchers now need to assess the relations of values to intentions and choice in other cultures. Having an understanding of what the different subcomponents of values mean to children in different cultures would be very beneficial for interpreting the results of these studies, particularly if the relations were different than those found in the studies done in the West.

Clearly, there is much yet to be done on cross-cultural differences in children's valuing of different activities, both in terms of the meaning this construct has for children, how values relate to choice of activities, and the kinds of activities children find most valuable to them. Such work is crucial in order for us to understand how the expectancy value model may operate in different cultures.

CONCLUSION

In this final section we close with some implications of the cross-cultural work we reviewed for expectancy value theory. It is important to reiterate that this model was developed originally to address a sociocultural phenomenon, gender differences in mathematics performance and choice, and so it is particularly well suited for a cultural analysis of motivation and activity choices. Having said that, there is a great deal of research that needs to be done to assess the model cross-culturally, and in this final section we provide some additional suggestions for what some of this research should be.

Returning to the model in Figure 8.1, our view is that many, if not all, of the links proposed in the model likely would be found in full tests of the model in other cultures. We base this contention on the cross-cultural research reviewed in this chapter. This work indicates that individuals' beliefs about their ability relate to their performance, and their values have an impact on activity choice. Children's previous performance influences their beliefs about their abilities. Although not reviewed here, there is cross-cultural research showing how parents and teachers influence children's ability beliefs, expectancies, and values.

Thus many of the basic linkages in the model have received some preliminary research support from cross-cultural research. However, much more work is needed to look more carefully at the strength of the relations proposed in the model, to see how much they vary across culture. It is conceivable that there could be variations in the strength of these relations in different cultures, even if the linkages all are present. One reason for this could be differences in how the different constructs are defined across cultures, which, as we have seen, does occur. Cultural emphases on one construct (e.g., valuing of achievement) rather than others (beliefs about ability) could be another reason why the strength of the linkages proposed in the model could vary across cultures. For instance, if the value of achievement was emphasized in a given culture, irrespective of how able a child is, then subjective values may more strongly predict both performance and choice in that culture. Furthermore, as noted above, other direct links may need to be added, such as a link between beliefs about effort and achievement outcomes.

Work examining these linkages likely would be characterized as etic, if existing measures developed in the West were used to study them in individuals from different cultures. To understand clearly what the linkages mean, emic work needs to be done to investigate the nature of the crucial constructs in the model before examining linkages among them. We suggest that this work should start with explorations of individuals' ability beliefs, expectancies for success, and subjective task values. The work on values may be especially important. As reviewed above, there has been some work on how individuals in different cultures characterize ability. There is very little such work done on the values construct. Once this work has been done, perhaps new measures of ability beliefs and values could be developed for use in different cultures, and linkages of these beliefs and values to performance and choice be examined.

Furthermore, it also is quite possible that additional constructs need to be included in the model for it to account more fully for cultural influences. The cultural milieu block (see Figure 8.1) clearly is one place where this needs to occur. That block focuses on two major things: gender role stereotypes and cultural stereotypes about activities. These likely are important things to consider in all cultures, but other aspects of the cultural milieu in different cultures should be added to this block. The particular constructs included here likely could vary greatly across cultures.

Another example is in the socializers' beliefs and behaviors block. We need a better understanding of both of these things to understand fully how socializers influence children in different cultures (see also Jacobs & Eccles, 2000). An example of this is teachers' behavior. We reviewed briefly work suggesting that changes in students' ability beliefs and values is due in part to changes in teachers' instructional practices across the school years. Whether and how this occurs in other cultures is an important topic for research, and would help us understand changes in children's ability-related beliefs and values in these cultures.

One of the challenges in understanding cultural influences is to go beyond cross-cultural comparisons and look at variations *within* cultures. Studies of expectancies and values done in the West have done this by examining gender and developmental differences, and variations in expectancies and values across both gender and age have been found (see Wigfield & Eccles, 2002). Researchers have also examined variations in achievement beliefs and values within a given group in a culture, such as African American children in the United States (Graham, 2002). Less of this work has been done in other cultures, to examine the complex interplay of culture, gender, ethnicity, and development and how they influence individuals' expectancies and values, and their performance and choice. It seems likely that in some cultures gender may have a stronger influence on individuals' beliefs and values than occurs in the West, depending on how gender is defined within that culture. In other cultures, gender differences could be less pronounced. Broadly, within-cultural variation may be produce greater differences than cross-cultural variation in some cases. Expectancy value models have promise to help us understand these variations, but much more research is needed to understand them fully.

REFERENCES

Asakawa, K., & Csikszentmihalyi, M. (2000). Feelings of connectedness and internalization of values in Asian American adolescents. *Journal of Youth and Adolescence, 29*, 121–145.

Atkinson, J. W. (1957). Motivational determinants of risk taking behavior. *Psychological Review, 64*, 359–372.

Atkinson, J. W. (1964). *An introduction to motivation.* Princeton, NJ: Van Nostrand.

Battle, A., & Wigfield, A. (2003). College women's value orientations toward family, career, and graduate school. *Journal of Vocational Behavior, 62,* 56–75.

Battle, E. (1965). Motivational determinants of academic task persistence. *Journal of Personality and Social Psychology, 2,* 209–218.

Battle, E. (1966). Motivational determinants of academic competence. *Journal of Personality and Social Psychology, 4,* 534–642.

Battle, E. (1966). Motivational determinants of academic competence. *Journal of Personality and Social Psychology, 4,* 534–642.

Bempechat, J., & Drago-Severson, E. (1999). Cross-national differences in academic achievement: Beyond etic conceptions of children's understandings. *Review of Educational Research, 69,* 287–314.

Berry, J. W. (1989). imposed etics-emics-derived etics: The operationalization of a compelling idea. *International Journal of Psychology, 24,* 721–735.

Chang, L., McBride-Chang, C., Stewart, S. M., & Au, E. (2003). Life satisfaction, self-concept, and family relations in Chinese adolescents and children. *International Journal of Behavioral Development, 27,* 182–189.

Chen, C., Lee, S., & Stevenson, H. W. (1995). Response style and cross-cultural comparisons of rating scales among East Asian and North American students. *Psychological Science, 6,* 170–175.

Dweck, C. S. (2002). The development of ability conceptions. In A. Wigfield & J. S. Eccles (Eds.), *Development of achievement motivation.* (pp. 57–88). San Diego, CA: Academic Press.

Dweck, C. S., & Bempechat, J. (1983). Children's theories of intelligence. In S. Paris, G. Olsen, & H. W. Stevenson (Eds.), *Learning and motivation in the classroom* (pp. 239–256). Hillsdale, NJ: Erlbaum.

Dweck, C. S., & Elliott, E. S. (1983). Achievement motivation. In P. H. Mussen (Ed.), *Handbook of child psychology* (3rd ed., Vol. 4, pp. 643–691). New York: Wiley.

Dweck, C. S., & Leggett, E. (1988). A social-cognitive approach to motivation and personality. *Psychological Review, 95,* 256–273.

Eaton, M. J., & Dembo, M. H. (1997). Differences in the motivational beliefs of Asian American and non-Asian students. *Journal of Educational Psychology, 89,* 433–440.

Eccles, J. S. (1984a). Sex differences in achievement patterns. In T. Sonderegger (Ed.), *Nebraska Symposium on Motivation* (Vol. 32, pp. 97–132). Lincoln: University of Nebraska Press.

Eccles, J. S. (1984b). Sex differences in mathematics participation. In M. Steinkamp & M. Maehr (Eds.), *Advances in motivation and achievement* (Vol. 2, pp. 93–137). Greenwich, CT: JAI Press.

Eccles, J. S. (1987). Gender roles and women's achievement-related decisions. *Psychology of Women Quarterly, 11,* 135–172.

Eccles, J. S. (1993). School and family effects on the ontogeny of children's interests, self-perceptions, and activity choice. In J. Jacobs (Ed.), *Nebraska Symposium on Motivation, 1992: Developmental perspectives on motivation* (pp. 145–208) Lincoln: University of Nebraska Press.

Eccles, J. S. (1994). Understanding women's educational and occupational choices: Applying the Eccles et al. model of achievement-related choices. *Psychology of Women Quarterly, 18,* 585–609.

Eccles, J. S., Adler, T. F., Futterman, R., Goff, S. B., Kaczala, C. M., Meece, J. L., & Midgley, C. (1983). Expectancies, values, and academic behaviors. In J. T. Spence (Ed.), *Achievement and achievement motivation* (pp. 75–146). San Francisco: W. H. Freeman.

Eccles, J. S., & Harold, R. D. (1991). Gender differences in sport involvement: Applying the Eccles' expectancy-value model. *Journal of Applied Sport Psychology, 3*, 7–35.

Eccles, J. S., & Midgley, C. (1989). Stage/environment fit: Developmentally appropriate classrooms for early adolescents. In R. Ames & C. Ames (Eds.), *Research on motivation in education* (Vol. 3, pp. 139–181). New York: Academic Press.

Eccles, J. S., & Wigfield, A. (1995). In the mind of the achiever: The structure of adolescents' academic achievement related-beliefs and self-perceptions. *Personality and Social Psychology Bulletin, 21*, 215–225.

Eccles, J., Wigfield, A., Flanagan, C., Miller, C., Reuman, D., & Yee, D. (1989). Self-concepts, domain values, and self-esteem: Relations and changes at early adolescence. *Journal of Personality, 57*, 283–310.

Eccles, J. S., Wigfield, A., Harold, R., & Blumenfeld, P. B. (1993). Age and gender differences in children's self- and task perceptions during elementary school. *Child Development, 64*, 830–847.

Eccles, J. S., Wigfield, A., & Schiefele, U. (1998). Motivation to succeed. In W. Damon (Series Ed.) & N. Eisenberg (Volume Ed.), *Handbook of child psychology* (5th ed., Vol. 3, pp. 1017–1095). New York: Wiley.

Elliott, J. G., Hufton, H., Illusin, L., & Lauchlan, F. (2001). Motivation in the junior years: International perspectives on children's attitudes, expectations, and behaviour and their relationship to educational achievement. *Oxford Review of Education, 27*, 37–68.

Feather, N. T. (1975). *Values in education and society.* New York: Free Press.

Feather, N. T. (1982). Expectancy-value approaches: Present status and future directions. In N. T. Feather (Ed.), *Expectations and actions: Expectancy-value models in psychology* (pp. 395–420). Hillsdale, NJ: Erlbaum.

Feather, N. T. (1988). Values, valences, and course enrollment: Testing the role of personal values within an expectancy-value framework. *Journal of Educational Psychology, 80*, 381–391.

Feather, N. T. (1992). Values, valences, expectations, and actions. *Journal of Social Issues, 48*, 109–124.

Freedman-Doan, C., Wigfield, A., Eccles, J., Blumenfeld, P. B., Arbreton, A., & Harold, R. D. (2000). What am I best at? Gender and grade differences in elementary school-age children's beliefs about their abilities at different activities. *Applied Developmental Psychology, 21*, 379–402.

Harter, S. (1982). The Perceived Competence Scale for Children. *Child Development, 53*, 87–97.

Hau, K.-T., Kong, C.W., & Marsh, H. W. (2000, October). *Chinese student self concept: Validation of measurement and extension of theoretical models.* Paper presented at Inaugural Self-Concept Enhancement and Learning Facilitation (SELF) Research Centre International Conference, Sydney, Australia.

Henderson, B. B., Marx, M. H., & Kim, Y. C. (1999). Academic interests and perceived competence in American, Japanese, and Korean children. *Journal of Cross-Cultural Psychology, 30*, 32–50.

Holloway, S. D. (1988). Concepts of ability and effort in Japan and the United States. *Review of Educational Research, 58*, 327–345.

Hufton, N., Elliott, J. G., & Illushin, L. (2002a). Achievement motivation across cultures: Some puzzles and their implications for future research. In J. Bempechat & J. G. Elliott (Eds.), *Learning in culture and context: Approaching the complexities of achievement motivation in student learning* (Vol. 96). New York: Wiley.

Hufton, N. R., Elliott, J. G., & Illushin, L. (2002b). Educational motivation and engagement: Qualitative accounts from three countries. *British Educational Research Journal, 28*, 265–289.

Jacobs, J. E., & Eccles, J. S. (2000). Parents, task values, and real-life achievement choices. In C. Sansone & J. M. Harackiewicz (Ed.), *Intrinsic and extrinsic motivation: The search for optimal motivation and performance* (pp. 405–439). San Diego, CA: Academic Press.

Jacobs, J., Lanza, S., Osgood, D. W., Eccles, J. S., & Wigfield, A. (2002). Ontogeny of children's self-beliefs: Gender and domain differences across grades one through 12. *Child Development, 73*, 509–527.

Kwok, D. C. (1995). The self-perception of competence by Canadian and Chinese children. *Psychologia, 38*, 9–16.

Kwok, D. C., & Lytton, H. (1996). Perceptions of mathematics ability versus actual mathematics performance: Canadian and Hong Kong Chinese children. *British Journal of Educational Psychology, 66*, 209–222.

Lewin, K. (1938). *The conceptual representation and the measurement of psychological forces*. Durham, NC: Duke University Press.

Markus, H. R., & Kitayama, S. (1991). Culture and the self: Implications for cognition, emotion, and motivation. *Psychological Review, 98*, 224–253.

Marsh, H. W. (1989). Age and sex effects in multiple dimensions of self-concept: Preadolescence to early adulthood. *Journal of Educational Psychology, 81*, 417–430.

Marsh, H. W. (1990). A multidimensional, hierarchical self-concept: Theoretical and empirical justification. *Educational Psychology Review, 2*, 77–172.

Marsh, H. W., Craven, R. G., & Debus, R. (1991). Self-concepts of young children 5 to 8 years of age: Measurement and multidimensional structure. *Journal of Educational Psychology, 83*, 377–392.

Marsh, H. W., Craven, R. G., & Debus, R. (1998). Structure, stability, and development of young children's self-concepts: A multicohort-multioccasion study. *Child Development, 69*, 1030–1103.

Marsh, H. W., Hau, K.-T., & Kong, C-K. Multilevel causal ordering of academic self-concept and achievement: Influence of language instruction (English compared with Chinese) for Hong Kong students. *American Educational Research Journal, 39*, 727–763.

Marsh, H. W., & Yeung, A. S. (1997). Causal effects of academic self-concept on academic achievement: Structural equation models of longitudinal data. *Journal of Educational Psychology, 89*, 41–54.

McInerney, D. M. (1995). Achievement motivation and indigenous minorities: Can research by psychometric? *Cross-Cultural Research, 29*, 211–239.

Meece, J. L., Wigfield, A., & Eccles, J. S. (1990). Predictors of math anxiety and its consequences for young adolescents' course enrollment intentions and performances in mathematics. *Journal of Educational Psychology, 82*, 60–70.

Murray, H. A. (1938). *Explorations in personality.* New York: Oxford University Press.

Nicholls, J. G. (1978). The development of the concepts of effort and ability, perceptions of academic attainment, and the understanding that difficult tasks require more ability. *Child Development, 49,* 800–814.

Nicholls, J. G. (1984). Achievement motivation: Conceptions of ability, subjective experience, task choice, and performance. *Psychological Review, 91,* 328–346.

Nicholls, J. G. (1990). What is ability and why are we mindful of it? A developmental perspective. In R. J. Sternberg & J. Kolligian (Eds.), *Competence considered.* New Haven, CT: Yale University Press.

Nicholls. J. G., & Miller, A. T. (1984). The differentiation of the concepts of difficulty and ability. *Child Development, 54,* 951–959.

Nicholls, J. G., Patashnick, M., & Mettetal, G. (1986). Conceptions of ability and intelligence. *Child Development, 57,* 636–645.

Pekrun, R. (2000). A social cognitive, control-value theory of achievement emotion. In. J. Heckhausen (Ed.), *Motivational psychology of human development* (pp. 143–163). Oxford, UK: Elsevier.

Poortinga, Y. H. (1997). Towards convergence? In J. W. Berry, Y. H. Poortinga, & J. Pandey (Eds.), *Handbook of cross-cultural psychology: Vol 1. Theory and method* (pp. 347–387). Boston: Allyn & Bacon.

Quihuis, G., Bempechat, J., Jimenez, N. V., & Boulay, B. A. (2002). Implicit theories of intelligence across academic domains: A study of meaning making in adolescents of Mexican descent. In J. Bempechat & J. G. Elliott (Eds.), *Learning in culture and context: Approaching the complexities of achievement motivation in student learning* (Vol. 96). San Francisco: Jossey-Bass.

Randall, B., Stevenson, H. W., & Witruk, E. (2000). Attitudes, beliefs, and mathematics achievement of German and Japanese high school students. *International Journal of Behavioral Development, 24,* 190–198.

Renninger, K. A. (2000). Individual interest and its implications for understanding intrinsic motivation. In C. Sansone & J. M. Harackiewicz (Eds.), *Intrinsic and extrinsic motivation: The search for optimal motivation and performance* (pp. 373–404). San Diego, CA: Academic Press.

Rohan, M. J. (2000). A rose by any name? The values construct. *Personality and Social Psychology Review, 4,* 255–277.

Rokeach, M. (1973). *The nature of human values.* New York: Free Press.

Rokeach, M. (1979). From individual to institutional values with special reference to the values of science. In M. Rokeach (Ed.), *Understanding human values* (pp. 47–70). New York: Free Press.

Ryan, R. M., & Deci, E. L. (2000). Intrinsic and extrinsic motivation: Classic definitions and new directions. *Contemporary Educational Psychology, 25,* 54–67.

Schiefele, U. (2001). The role of interest in motivation and learning. In J. M. Collis & S. Messick (Eds.), *Intelligence and personality: bridging the gap in theory and measurement* (pp. 163–194). Mahwah NJ: Erlbaum.

Schwartz, S. H. (1992). Universals in the content and structure of values: Theoretical advances in empirical tests in 20 countries. In M. P. Zanna (Ed.), *Advances in experimental social psychology* (Vol. 24, p. 1–65). San Diego, CA: Academic Press.

Stevenson, H. W., Chen, C., & Uttal, D. H. (1990). Beliefs and achievement: A study of black, white, and Hispanic children. *Child Development, 61,* 508–523.

Stevenson, H. W., & Lee, S. (1990). Contexts of achievement. *Monographs of the Society for Research in Child Development* (Serial No. 221, Vol. 55, Nos. 1-2). Chicago: University of Chicago Press.

Stevenson, H. W., Lee, S., Chen, C., Lummis, M., Stigler, J., Fan, L., & Ge, F. (1990). Mathematics achievement of children in China and the United States. *Child Development, 61,* 1053–1066.

Stigler, J. W., Smith, S., & Mao, L. (1985). The self-perception of competence by Chinese children. *Child Development, 56,* 1259–1270.

Stipek, D. J., & Mac Iver, D. (1989). Developmental change in children's assessment of intellectual competence. *Child Development, 60,* 521–538.

Tolman, E. C. (1932). *Purposive behavior in animals and men.* New York: Appleton-Century-Crofts.

Tonks, S., & Wigfield, A. (2003). *Cultural influences on aspects of motivation.* Manuscript in preparation.

Triandis, H. C. (2001). Individualism and collectivism. In D. Matsumoto (Ed.), *The handbook of culture and psychology* (pp. 35–50). Oxford, UK: Oxford University Press.

Weiner, B. (1992). *Human motivation: Metaphors, theories, and research.* Newbury Park, CA: Sage.

Whang, P. A., & Hancock, G. R. (1994). Motivation and mathematics achievement: Comparisons between Asian American and Non-Asian students. *Contemporary Educational Psychology, 19,* 302–322.

Wigfield, A. (1994a). Expectancy-value theory of achievement motivation: A developmental perspective. *Educational Psychology Review, 6,* 49–78.

Wigfield, A. (1994b). The role of children's achievement values in the self-regulation of their learning outcomes. In D. H Schunk & B. Zimmerman (Eds.) *Self-regulation of learning and performance: Issues and educational applications* (pp. 101–124). Hillsdale, NJ: Erlbaum.

Wigfield, A. (1997, April). *Predicting children's grades from their ability beliefs and subjective task values: Developmental and domain differences.* Paper presented at the biennial meeting of the Society for Research in Child Development, Washington, DC.

Wigfield, A., & Eccles, J. (1992). The development of achievement task values: A theoretical analysis. *Developmental Review, 12,* 265–310.

Wigfield, A., & Eccles, J. S. (2000). Expectancy-value theory of motivation. *Contemporary Educational Psychology, 25,* 68–81.

Wigfield, A., & Eccles, J. S. (2002). The development of competence beliefs, expectancies for success, and achievement values from childhood through adolescence. In A. Wigfield & J. S. Eccles (Eds.), *Development of achievement motivation.* (pp. 91–120). San Diego, CA: Academic Press.

Wigfield, A., Eccles, J., Mac Iver, D., Reuman, D., & Midgley, C. (1991). Transitions at early adolescence: Changes in children's domain-specific self-perceptions and general self-esteem across the transition to junior high school. *Developmental Psychology, 27,* 552–565.

Wigfield, A., Eccles, J. S., Pintrich, P. R. (1996). Development between the ages of eleven and twenty-five. In D.C. Berliner & R.C. Calfee (Eds.), *The handbook of educational psychology* (pp. 148–185). New York: MacMillan.

Wigfield, A., Eccles, J. S., Yoon, K. S., Harold, R. D., Arbreton, A., Freedman-Doan, C., Blumenfeld, P. C. (1997). Changes in children's competence beliefs and subjective task values across the elementary school years: A three-year study. *Journal of Educational Psychology, 89*, 451–469.

Yu, S. L., & Wolters, C. A. (2001). Issues in the assessment of motivation in students from ethnic minority populations. In P. R. Pintrich & M. L. Maehr (Eds.), *Advances in motivation and achievement* (pp. 349-380). Greenwich, CT: JAI.

Zusho, A., & Pintrich, P. R. (2003). A process-oriented approach to culture: Theoretical and methodological issues in the study of culture and motivation. In F. Salili & R. Hoosain (Eds.), *Teaching, learning, and motivation in a multicultural context.* Greenwich, CT: Information Age.

CHAPTER 9

MOTIVATIONAL MESSAGES FROM HOME AND SCHOOL
How Do They Influence Young Children's Engagement in Learning?

Nancy E. Perry and Philip H. Winne

INTRODUCTION

Scott Paris and Richard Newman have described how some children, arriving for their first day of school, are "filled with great expectations and ambitions" while others need to be "tugged reluctantly and cajoled into going despite their apprehensions" (Paris & Newman, 1990, p. 89). What influences children's attitudes toward school and engagement in learning activities? What attitudes and actions result in more or less success in learning? Can attitudes be shaped to encourage actions that support learning? These questions stimulate theories and research described throughout this volume.

In this chapter, we examine expectancy value theories of motivation that explain how individuals' beliefs, values, and expectations influence their

Big Theories Revisited
Volume 4 in: Research on Sociocultural Influences on Motivation and Learning, pages 199–222.
Copyright © 2004 by Information Age Publishing, Inc.
All rights of reproduction in any form reserved.
ISBN: 1-59311-053-7 (hardcover), 1-59311-052-9 (paperback)

actions. These theories have a long history in research on motivation, and current expectancy value models have strong empirical support in educational settings (Graham & Weiner, 1996; Pintrich & Schunk, 2002; Wigfield & Eccles, 2002). We specifically highlight how sociocultural models of learning can enrich expectancy value theories of motivation by examining how home and classroom factors are reflected in young students' (ages 6 and 7) beliefs about learning and their subsequent engagements in school.

Perry's research provides the backdrop for our analyses. Since 1995, she has focused on (a) how tasks, structures of authority, and evaluation practices in elementary school classrooms influence young children's beliefs, values, expectations, and actions; and (b) how teachers can be helped to design tasks and interact with students to promote independent, academically effective approaches to learning, self-regulated learning (SRL) (Perry, 1998; Perry & VandeKamp, 2000; Perry, VandeKamp, Mercer, & Nordby, 2002). Specifically, we draw on examples from classrooms Perry observed to highlight how particular features of the task environment, including what teachers say and do, can promote or curtail academically effective attitudes and approaches to learning. In addition, we describe data that examines how motivational messages can vary across home and school contexts and how those differences are reflected in students' approaches to learning (Perry, Nordby, & VandeKamp, 2003). These examples will be supplemented and supported with examples from the wider research literature.

We begin with a brief overview of expectancy value theories of motivation and of sociocultural models of learning and motivation. Following this overview we map out three sections. The first section introduces two students who participated in Perry's research and offers predications about their learning outcomes given their achievement and motivation profiles. The second and third sections, respectively, introduce information about both students' classroom environments and one student's home environment to demonstrate how knowledge of these social contexts can enrich understandings about their beliefs, expectations, and actions. We conclude by analyzing the contributions that sociocultural models of learning make to theory and research about motivation in general and to expectancy value theories of motivation in particular.

EXPECTANCY VALUE THEORIES OF MOTIVATION

The basic tenets of expectancy value theories of motivation align with everyday views of motivated behavior (Graham & Weiner, 1996). In general, these theories assume that motivation to behave in a particular way is influenced by a person's estimate of the likelihood a successful outcome can be achieved—an expectation; and the perceived significance or utility of that outcome—its value (Graham & Weiner, 1996; Pintrich & Schunk, 2002; Wigfield & Eccles, 2002). These theories originated in the 1930s when Tolman (1932) suggested that, over trials, animals formed cognitive expectations about consequences they expected to follow particular behaviors. He claimed that expectations of reward or punishment, rather than habits, increased or decreased the likelihood an animal would engage in a behavior in the future. Thus, cognitive expectations replaced notions of unconscious habits in theories of motivation, achieving a better fit to a growing acceptance of cognitive versus behavioral views of learning (Pintrich & Schunk, 2002).

In the 1950s and 1960s, Atkinson (1957, 1964) expanded this model to embrace individual differences in achievement motivation. According to his theory, a person's decision about whether to approach an achievement-related goal is the product of three interrelated factors: (1) the person's achievement motives, (2) the probability of reaching the goal, and (3) the incentive for reaching the goal. In Atkinson's model, achievement motives refer to a person's relatively stable and general disposition to strive for success or avoid failure. The expected probability of success or failure is linked to specific situations and tasks. Finally, incentives refer to the degree to which success at a given task is valued. Atkinson predicted people would assign more value to difficult tasks because success at such tasks would intrinsically generate a greater sense of accomplishment. Furthermore, he predicted that success-oriented students would be most motivated by moderately challenging tasks—tasks for which it is reasonable to expect success but success is not certain. In contrast, if students fear failure, he predicted they would likely choose easy tasks, ensuring their success; or very difficult tasks on which few people could be expected to succeed, thus decreasing the shame and humiliation that typically result from failure. Research generally supports Atkinson's predictions (Pintrich & Schunk, 2002; Weiner, 1992). Most people choose tasks that are moderately challenging, but success-oriented individuals are more likely to engage in such tasks than individuals who fear failure.

Early research on expectancy value theories of motivation helped reshape the discourse about motivation in educational psychology. Rather than relying on stimulus–response paradigms to explain behavior, researchers and theorists began to think about and study motivation in more rational and cognitive terms (Pintrich & Schunk, 2002; see Winne & Marx, 1989, for an example). These more cognitive models illuminated the importance of people's subjective beliefs and values as mediators of their behavior in particular task environments.

Many contemporary theories of motivation include expectancy and value constructs, but the expectancy value model developed by Eccles and Wigfield and their colleagues (Eccles, 1993; Wigfield & Eccles, 2002; Wigfield et al., 1997) has generated the most theory and research on achievement motivation in classrooms (Pintrich & Schunk, 2002). Like its predecessors, this model identifies students' expectations for success and their values for tasks as key predictors of their achievement-related behaviors. This model is noteworthy because it increases the level of specificity at which these constructs are measured, elaborates notions of task value, and recognizes aspects of students' social world that influence their achievement-related behaviors (Wigfield & Eccles, 2002). In Wigfield and Eccles' (2002) model, expectations for success are children's beliefs about how well they will do on a particular task, termed *competency beliefs*. Competency beliefs are generated on the basis of previous experiences with similar tasks. They can vary depending on the domain of study (e.g., math, reading, sports) and whether the situation surrounding the task brings out students' sense of their own competence or their competence in relation to others. Values reflect students' subjective reasons for participating in particular tasks (or not). Wigfield and Eccles identified four major components of subjective task values: (1) attainment value (How important is it, generally, to do well in this domain or on tasks like this?), (2) intrinsic value (How important is it to me to do well in this domain or on this task?), (3) utility value (How will success on this task help me in the future?), and (4) cost (What costs are associated with engaging in this task and do they outweigh the potential benefits?). Finally, Eccles and Wigfield recognized that students' competency beliefs, expectations for success, and values they assign to success in particular domains and activities are influenced by the beliefs and values of the various communities to which they belong (e.g., classroom, family, and peer-group).

Eccles, Wigfield, and their colleagues have conducted many studies to test this model (e.g., Eccles, 1993; Eccles & Wigfield, 1995; Wigfield, 1994; Wigfield et al., 1997). These investigations consistently have indicated that students' competency beliefs and expectations are strong predictors of their future grades in domains such as English and math, even stronger than measures of ability, such as prior grades. However, students' interests in and beliefs about the importance and utility of tasks and subject matter are the best predictors of whether they will continue studies in these domains. Not surprisingly, students' valuing of tasks and subject matter is linked to their competency-related beliefs.

Most of the studies conducted by Eccles and Wigfield have targeted students in the upper elementary and middle grades. However, more recent cross-sectional and longitudinal investigations (Eccles & Wigfield, 1995; Wigfield et al., 1997) have included students in the early elementary grades (grades 1 and 2). These studies found even very young students' competence beliefs are differentiated across domains of study (reading, math, sports, and music). Furthermore, in these studies, young students distinguished components of subjective task values. Eccles and Wigfield's findings are generally consistent with other research that indicates students' competency beliefs and subjective task values become more differentiated as they advance in school, and that young children tend to be more optimistic about their potential than older students (Paris & Newman, 1990; Turner, 1995). However, these studies are notable in that they indicate students begin differentiating these constructs much earlier than was previously thought.

Wigfield and Eccles (2002) explained the downward trends of beliefs about competence and values in two ways. First, as children advance through the grades, they become better at understanding and integrating evaluative feedback into their approaches to classroom tasks. As well, they engage in more social comparison with select peers. These advances provide information upon which to construct more accurate and realistic beliefs about competence. For many children, new perceptions of competence are lower than before. Second, as children shift from lower to higher grade levels, school environments change. Evaluation becomes more salient and involves more social comparison. For students who do well, this elevates their competency beliefs and, most likely, the value they assign to school-related activities. For low-achieving students, these changes lower beliefs about competence, depress expectations for success, subtract value from school-related tasks, and decrease productive achievement-related behavior.

We believe expectancy value models of motivation have added much to understandings about what influences children's attitudes toward learning and school, and how beliefs and values can lead to forms of engagement that enhance or undermine academic achievements. A particular contribution of expectancy value models is that an individual's cognitions are highlighted in motivation. Also, as these research programs have advanced, recognition that motivation is context-sensitive has emerged.

In the past decade, contextual factors that previously had been at the periphery of models of motivation have moved to center stage (Perry, 1998; Perry et al., 2003; Turner, 1995; Turner, Meyer, Midgley, & Patrick, 2003). Researchers recognize that individuals' cognitions exist in historical, cultural, and institutional contexts and, to be ecologically valid and practically relevant, research needs to attend to the dynamic interplay between the individual and the social (Anderman & Anderman, 2000; Goodenow, 1992; Solomon, 1995; Wertsch, Tulviste, & Hagstrom, 1993). We turn next to the nature of this significant conceptual revision in models of motivation.

SOCIOCULTURAL MODELS OF LEARNING AND MOTIVATION

McCaslin (2003), in her introduction to a recent special issue of *The Elementary School Journal,* compared current research on motivation with research on motivation in 1984, the year in which *The Journal* last devoted an issue to research on motivation:

Context is far more important to authors in this issue.... It is no longer acceptable to equate the attributions of hypothetical teachers with actual teachers' beliefs, and "college" is not a minor signifier of "student." The authors in this special issue have taken considerable care to understand [and, we add, portray for readers] the contexts of their research participants, typically using multiple methods in the process (p. 315).

Recent special issues of *Educational Psychologist* (Anderman & Anderman, 2000; Perry, 2002) and several edited volumes (McInerney & Van Etten, 2001; Urdan, 1999; Volet & Jarvela, 2001) are further evidence of the growing interest in how social perspectives on learning and engagement are keys to understanding students' motivated behavior (Hickey, 2003).

Theories that adopt social perspectives on motivation share, in varying degrees, a contextualist worldview (Hickey, 2003). In this view, events of learning and motivated behavior are entwined with the context in which they unfold. Hickey (2003) distinguished between modest applications of social-perspective theories (e.g., social-cognitive and social-constructivist theories) and more strident views of the interplay between learners and environments in which they operate (e.g., situated and sociocultural theories of learning). More strident applications assert the relevance of Vygotsky's (1978) view that learners gain knowledge by interacting with the social and material world, by participating in the knowledge practices of a community, and with the support of others in the community who are more knowledgeable than themselves (Hickey, 2003; Lave & Wenger, 1991; McCaslin & Hickey, 2001; Serpell, 1997). Also, they emphasize that people are not products of their environments but help to create environments in a reciprocal manner, as Bandura described (Bandura, 1986, 1997).

McCaslin and colleagues (McCaslin & Good, 1996; McCaslin & Hickey, 2001) have developed a distinctly sociocultural model of motivation. It stresses "the fundamental and reciprocal relationship between the social/instructional environment and individual cognitive and affective processes in [both] the moment to moment of classroom life and in aggregation" (McCaslin & Good, 1996, p. 662). McCaslin and Good (1996) label this reciprocal relationship the "arena of coregulation." They argue that a model of coregulated learning incorporates intrapersonal processes of motivation, enactment, and evaluation in an environment where the individual is involved with others, structural supports, and affording opportunities. Specifically, in such a model, motivation includes predecisional wishes, attributions, beliefs, and expectations about the situated self; and decisions concerning goals, goal relationships, and their coordination. Enactment involves applying strategies that advance toward goals while coordinating demands encountered on that path with (a) one's emotions and capabilities, and (b) the participant and setting resources of the social/instructional environment. Finally, evaluation involves calibrations of self with others' evaluation. Learners use evaluative information to assess their current status in relation to the goal they have set and then decide whether to continue, modify, or cease efforts to reach that goal in the same way that Winne (2001) characterizes for self-regulated learning. According to McCaslin and Good, evaluative information about the "degree of goal attainment or nonattainment becomes part of the autobiographical record that informs motivation" (p. 662) and, we add, regulation. Thus, coregulated learning assumes socially constructed beliefs, values, and expectations contribute to motivation for learning (Hickey, 2003).

A critical issue confronting sociocultural theorists is the extent to which beliefs, values, and expectations are bound to the context in which they are co-constructed (Hickey, 2003) versus generalizable. In McCaslin and Good's (1996) model, learning and motivation are co-regulated at the start, but once learners internalize the structural social supports in the environment, the learners are capable of relatively self-regulated learning in that domain, as Winne (2001) describes it. In this way, coregulated learning is the process by which socially shaped instructional environments support individuals toward autonomous activity in a context of relationships among teachers, peers, objects and setting, and self in the classroom. More strident sociocultural models of motivation might posit that beliefs, values, and expectations are so tightly bound to the context in which they are co-constructed that notions of internalization and generalization, which are essential for self-regulation, are not relevant (Hickey, 2003).

Adopting a situated and sociocultural perspective on learning and motivation has implications for how we, as researchers, study these phenomena. Clearly, these perspectives on motivation require that investigations of motivation and self- and coregulation occur in naturalistic settings—real contexts and real time—in events rather than as aptitudes (Winne & Perry, 2000). They indicate the need to use and adapt methods and measures to unique characteristics of particular teaching and learning contexts (Paris & Paris, 2001; Randi & Corno, 2000), and to use of more in-depth, online investigations of interactions among facets of the social/instructional environment and students' engagement and learning. This typically involves the use of multiple methods and measures.

In this vein, Perry's research (Perry, 1998; Perry et al., 2002, 2003) is anchored by social-cognitive and sociocultural theories of learning and motivation and, in Hickey's (2003) terms, can be characterized as a moderate application of social-perspective theories. Her studies of SRL use observations, in the form of running records, to describe how classroom activities unfold and to reflect what teachers and students actually do versus what they may recall they did or believe they do. These observations have helped to link teachers' and students' behaviors to contexts and conditions, and have guided the development of a framework for working with teachers to design tasks and interact with students to support intrinsic motivation and self-regulation. Additionally, her fine-grained analyses of the discourse in classrooms have illuminated what teachers say to support (or curtail) students' motivation and regulation, and how students respond. Questionnaires and interviews with parents shed light on the continuity between students' home and school environments, and semistructured and retrospective interviews reveal aspects of kindergarten to grade 3 students' cognition and motivation that are not readily observable.

Here we introduce two students from Perry and colleagues' research and examine what observations and interviews reveal about whether and how their beliefs, values, expectations, and actions reflect those that are promoted in their school and, for one student, home environments. While Perry's data do not map directly onto Wigfield and Eccles's model of motivated learning (Eccles, 1983; Wigfield & Eccles, 2002), both research programs include young children and provide evidence concerning their competence beliefs and expectations for success. Perry's data do not offer evidence of students' task values according to the four components Wigfield and Eccles identified. Attainment and utility values for individual participants are not measured in Perry's studies. However, Perry and colleagues chose literacy as a context in which to study young children's motivation and self-regulation because it is an area assumed to hold high attainment and utility value for students in kindergarten through grade 3. In general, young children believe learning to read and write is important and will serve them well in the future. Intrinsic value in Perry's studies reflects students' expressions of interest in reading and writing activities and the reasons they give for engaging in literacy activities in particular ways. Cost is reflected in observations of negative affect during task completion or in response to criticism, preference for easy or challenging tasks, and employment of academically fruitful or debilitating strategies.

Both research programs have interest in environmental influences on students' engagement in learning. However, Perry's research provides a much more detailed portrayal of the contexts in which students participate (the tasks, authority structures, and evaluation practices). In fact, documenting and interpreting the interactions of teachers and students, students and students, and students and parents in context is the primary objective of Perry's research.

THE CASES

Greg participated in Perry and colleagues' 2003 study. At the time of the investigation, he was 6 years old and in grade 1. He was the youngest of three children (siblings were 12 and 15 years of age). His parents lived together and both had completed a 2-year college/diploma program. His father was a developer of commercial property and his mother worked part time as the property manager. This family is English-Canadian and, at the time of the investigation, lived in a fairly homogeneous and mostly mid-dle-class community.

Rajah was 7 years old and in grade 2 when she participated in Perry's 1998 study. We don't have as much demographic information about Rajah's family because it was not collected for the study. (Rajah is included in this chapter because her classroom context and motivational profile provide a good contrast with Greg's.) The family is Indo-Canadian and, at the time of the study, lived in a homogeneous English-Canadian and mostly middle-class community. Rajah spoke English fluently and was not receiving English as a second language instruction at school.

The teachers of both students characterized them as low-achieving read-ers and writers. Greg participated in the Reading Recovery Program in his school and Rajah received remedial instruction in her school's Learning Assistance Program. Given these difficulties, we might expect these students to be motivationally "at risk" when engaged in reading and writing activities. Theoretically, they should perceive themselves as having low abil-ity for reading and writing, and expect to do poorly on reading and writing assignments. They should perceive reading and writing as having high attainment and utility value; however, according to theory, they should downplay the intrinsic value of being successful at reading and writing because the perceived cost of low levels of success or failure is high.

In fact, both students indicated during interviews that they were not good at writing. According to Greg, "Most of my [writing is] bad." Simi-larly, Rajah commented that sometimes her writing is "dumb." Also, both students admitted they often found writing difficult. However, Greg had a more constructive view of challenges he faced than Rajah. He believed that "no one could do writing perfect." Furthermore, he valued the feedback he received from his teacher because "it answers my question, 'What do I do? *What do I do?*'" He fully expected his writing would improve over time: "Lots of people I know get better ... we get better from our teachers ... [this year,] a little bit better than last year ... [next year,] a little bit better again ... because I learn more stuff every year." Rajah was more sensitive about errors she made and sometimes hid her work so peers would not see it. She was defensive when they pointed to an error she had made. "I know, I know, [you] make mistakes in your life." Her comments during interviews indicated she preferred easy to challenging tasks "because they were easier and they were something I knew." Greg preferred moderately challenging tasks "because [they are] just in the middle."

Greg's beliefs and expectations match those considered optimal for learning and engagement, whereas Rajah's are consistent with descriptions of more debilitating academic and motivational orientations (Paris & New-man, 1990; Pintrich & Schunk, 2002; Wigfield & Eccles, 2002). What accounts for these differences? Social-perspective theories suggest we look for answers to this question in the social/instructional environments in which these learners participate. More specifically, using the data we have, we ask: (a) What are the literacy practices in these learners' classrooms? (b) What motivational messages do learners receive in these contexts? (c) How are features of each classroom context reflected in the learners' descriptions about how they approach reading and writing tasks? (d) And, for Greg, how complementary are his literacy experiences at home and at school?

The Classrooms

Greg's classroom. Greg was one of 17 students in Ms. Madelay's kindergarten-grade 1 class. The classroom was located in an elementary school (kindergarten–grade 5) in a large suburban school district outside Vancouver, British Columbia, Canada, that served a fairly homogeneous community. Only 8% of students in attendance spoke English as a second language, compared with the district's average of more than 33%. Although the full range of SES was represented in the student body, the majority of families were middle class.

Ms. Madelay's classroom has been described elsewhere by Perry (see Perry et al., 2002, 2003) as a "high-self-regulated learning (high-SRL)" environment, supporting children's development of metacognition, intrinsic motivation, and strategic action. Consistent with other descriptions of highly engaging, high-SRL environments (Perry, 1998; Turner, 1995; Turner et al., Cinto, 1998), children in Ms. Madelay's class were engaged in complex, cognitively demanding activities that incorporated a variety of processes and purposes. Typically, reading and writing activities extended over multiple reading and writing periods, and reading and writing were almost always integrated in the same activities (e.g., students wrote an alternate ending for a story they read). Students in Ms. Madelay's class had opportunities to make choices, control challenge, and evaluate their learning. They received instrumental support from their teacher and peers, scaffolding their development of domain and strategy knowledge, helping them to make good choices, and encouraging them to attempt challenging tasks to expand their developing abilities. Assessment and evaluation were embedded in daily reading and writing routines, constructive criticism was part of the classroom discourse, and students were encouraged to take errors in stride, using them as evidence for what they needed to learn next.

A typical writing activity in Ms. Madelay's kindergarten and grade 1 class began with reading and discussing a story intended to support students' generation of ideas for their writing. After reading a story about a boy who lived on a farm and lost his pet, Ms. Madelay prompted students to compare the farm in the book with a farm they visited recently. Also, she asked students if they had ever lost a pet "or something you really like? How did you feel when you lost your …? How did you feel when you found it?" Then they planned their stories, using a simple story grammar to generate ideas about characters, setting, beginning, middle, and end. Ms. Madelay recorded students' ideas on chart paper and students elaborated these ideas in illustrations prior to writing text (their pictures were their plans). Finally, students wrote their stories from their pictures.

Before they began to write, Ms. Madelay asked, "How can we begin our stories?" Students didn't understand, responding with the titles and topics of their stories. Ms. Madelay prompted, "If you open the cover [of a book and begin to read] ..." Students understood and began to generate various story starters (e.g., Once upon a time ... There once was ... One day ...). "I can think of one," says Ms. Madelay and asks students if she can add it to their list. "I think we'll leave this here ... add to it ... once we get into [writing] more stories," referring to the list as an aid for students' writing. The class also discussed where they would write and whether they would use "book spelling or kid's spelling today." In a subsequent observation, Perry observed Ms. Madelay discussing "kid's spelling" with her class. "Who can tell me what kid's writing is?" When a student responded, "It's just writing what you think the word is like," she asked, "Is it just guessing? ... Is it smart guessing? ... Sometimes you know more about a word than other times ... Where can you look?" While students worked, Ms Madelay circulated. Toward the end of the writing period, she asked students to make sure they finished "at least one sentence today . . . Once you finish, read it back to yourself. See if it's the way you want it.

Low-achieving readers and writers like Greg were well supported or coregulated (McCaslin & Good, 1996) in Ms. Madelay's classroom. In the activity just described, the teacher and students generated ideas for writing by reading and discussing a story having a topic similar to their writing topic. As they read, Ms. Madelay asked students to make connections between the story and their experiences (e.g., going to a farm, losing a pet or something of personal significance). On other occasions, Ms. Madelay asked students to "discuss [ideas] with a neighbor ... I want everyone to come up with at least one idea." After students had shared ideas with one another, and before they began their writing, she asked each student to tell her their idea. Students who didn't have an idea stayed and worked with Ms. Madelay until they did. "[Student] stay here for a moment. I'm not sure about that one." Often students' ideas were posted like the story starters in this activity. Strategies for coping with difficult vocabulary were posted all around the room, and Ms. Madelay checked with students to make sure they knew what to do when they got stuck. "Where could you look? ... What could you do?" Students had opportunities to tailor tasks and the task environment to suit their individual achievement levels and working preferences. In this activity, students could choose to use book spelling or kid spelling. Also, Ms. Madelay made herself available as students worked. "[Student] would it help you to concentrate if you work here, or can you work there?" The student chose to stay but increased his attention to the writing task. Later, Ms. Madelay followed up by commenting, "I like the way you are focused now." Finally, Ms. Madelay made students accountable for thinking and learning (e.g., "I would like you to finish one sentence today."), but in a nonthreatening way. Most assignments in her classroom didn't lend themselves to assessment that reports "the number correct." Students typically received anecdotal feedback from Ms. Madelay in the context of a class discussion or personal interview. Mistakes were discussed as a natural part of most instructional events. "Everyone makes mistakes ... everyone needs help sometimes, and everyone learns by helping."

Greg's approach to writing in his classroom. Greg's responses to interview questions indicate he felt supported in this environment and shared the beliefs and values expressed in it. He did not interpret errors as evidence of poor writing ability, "No one could do writing perfect," and he expected that his writing would improve with effort and experience.

Researcher: "Do you sometimes find writing difficult?"
Greg: "Yes, lots of times."
Researcher: "Do you think you will always have difficulties writing?"
Greg: "No, I'll get better at it."
Researcher: "Do you ever have to make changes to your story over and over again?"
Greg: "Yes."
Researcher: "How does that make you feel?"
Greg: "I feel sad that it keeps going back and forth."
Researcher: "What do you do when that happens?"
Greg: "Just keep on trying."

Furthermore, the instrumental support that characterized Ms. Madelay's interactions with students was reflected in Greg's description of how she helps him, "She gives me clues ...," and how he helps his classmates, "I ...try to give [them] clues. 'Can you see that something is wrong with that word?... Your letters are good but some are capitals that aren't supposed to be capitals.'" In this context, although admittedly "a bit afraid to do it," Greg was willing to attempt moderately challenging tasks that would extend his writing skills. "It's not like I always have to do hard work, right?" [Adding], "Some things are easier than I thought." When asked to evaluate a particular piece of his writing, Greg gave himself a rating of 4 on a 5-point scale. Asked if he thought it was a good story and why, he responded, "To me it is. I like that it's ... I tried to put a lot of effort in it. I spent a lot of time [on] it." He had a realistic view of his competence and a reasonable expectation that, with the support he was receiving, his writing would improve.

Rajah's classroom. Rajah was one of 20 grade 2 and 3 students in Peter's class. The classroom was located in a different elementary school (kindergarten–grade 5), but in the same school district, as Ms. Madelay's class-room. This school served a fairly homogeneous, middle-class community, although the population was more ethnically diverse than the one attend-ing Ms. Madelay's school (the number of students attending who spoke English as a second language approximated the district's average, 33% at the time of the study).

Mr. Baxter's classroom, originally described in Perry (1998), was charac-terized as a low-SRL classroom. In contrast to the practices in Ms. Made-lay's classroom, students in Mr. Baxter's classroom engaged in reading and writing activities that were brief (10 min.) and disconnected. Tasks focused on specific skills apart from a more general theme/project (e.g., correct-ing spelling and punctuation errors in a sentence the teacher wrote on the board versus writing connected discourse about a topic of interest or under study in another part of the curriculum). Students' choices were more limited in these activities, and the teacher controlled the degree of difficulty tasks presented and set the criteria for evaluation, which typically were the same for all students. Mr. Baxter did ask students to evaluate their own work, but the focus of their self-reflection was directed toward the mechanical aspects of reading and writing (e.g., correct spelling and punc-tuation, neat printing). Support from the teacher and peers focused on the procedural aspects of tasks (e.g., giving directions, distributing materi-als, correcting an answer) rather than scaffolding students' construction of meaning and strategic learning. Teacher evaluation offered more opportu-nities for social comparison (e.g., stickers in books, star charts on the wall, group points based on individuals' performance), and students were inter-ested to see if they received a "good mark" and to compare their score and stickers with their neighbor.

The "sentence fix-up" activity was typical of writing tasks in Mr. Baxter's classroom. Each morning students copied a sentence Mr. Baxter had writ-ten on the blackboard into their language notebooks. The sentence con-tained errors and the number of errors was posted beside the sentence. Students' task was to find Mr. Baxter's mistakes and correct them. Later, the class went over the sentence together, correcting errors. Mr. Baxter called on students to offer corrections and explain why they were needed. Once all the errors had been identified and the sentence on the board was correct, Mr. Baxter asked students to "double-check" their version of the sentence with the one on the board. At the end of this activity, students submitted their notebooks to Mr. Baxter so he could check their work. If they successfully corrected the errors in the sentence and did "neat print-ing," their notebooks were returned the following day with a sticker beside the entry.

When Mr. Baxter engaged students in "story writing," they had more control over content and opportunities to seek support from peers. How-ever, he encouraged them to limit their help-seeking to students sitting close to them and to the procedural aspects of the task (e.g., clarifying directions, spelling, cutting and pasting). Students were discouraged from sharing ideas, "If you have an idea, I know you are excited, but keep it to yourself." Also, in contrast to Ms. Madelay's student-centered coregulating approach to writing instruction, story writing in Mr. Baxter's class was a fairly "teacher-directed" (his description), linear, and nonrecursive process. Although students engaged in prewriting and drafting activities, Mr. Baxter did not ask them to consider possible purposes for those activities, nor make explicit links between the planning phase and the drafting phase. Consequently, when asked what they were planning for, students typically responded, "I don't know." Furthermore, students in Mr. Baxter's class did not edit their own or each other's writing. Mr. Baxter collected students' drafts of stories, edited them, and then returned them to students so that they could make the changes on their final version. This resulted in lost autonomy and opportunities to apply editing skills they were acquiring through the sentence fix-up activity, and to reflect on and revise other meaning-related qualities of their writing (e.g., organization and clarity of ideas). When Rajah was asked whether she checked her writing before turning it into the teacher, she indicated that she didn't. "I don't have to ... mistakes are checked by the teacher."

In this context, low-achieving readers and writers, like Rajah, were less likely to develop beliefs, values, expectations, and actions associated with intrinsic motivation and self-regulated learning than were students in Ms. Madelay's class. Most of the writing activities in Rajah's class did not require the production of extended discourse and, for those that did, the teacher assumed much of the responsibility for navigating the phases of the writing process, controlling challenge, editing, and revising. Instances of the kind of coregulated learning observed in Greg's class were much less common in Rajah's class, and when students were given the choice to work collaboratively, they often decided against it.

Rajah's approach to reading in her classroom. The following excerpt from a retrospective interview with Rajah offers evidence of the lack of support students provided one another to complete tasks and the attention paid to performance standards as opposed to understanding a task's purpose for learning. Theory and research would predict that, for a low-achieving reader such as Rajah, this environment would reinforce, likely promote, low efficacy—a belief that competence is low and success is unlikely.

Researcher: "[Mr. Baxter] said you could count paragraphs with other people on your team or you could do it by yourself. How did your team make the choice?"

Rajah: "We just decided ourselves."

Researcher: "Did you talk about it?"

Rajah: "No, because we knew recess was coming up soon."

Researcher: "What would you have chosen if you didn't feel like recess was coming?"

Rajah: "I would choose to work with the team."
Researcher: "Why?"
Rajah: "Because the team doesn't really ever work together...help each other out."

On the rare occasions when students did offer feedback, it was typically not the kind of support that would build Rajah's competency-related beliefs or solve a writing problem.

Researcher: "Did [student] help you count the paragraphs?"
Rajah: "She said that is the wrong number."
Researcher: "Did she help you to count the other ones?"
Rajah: "Nope."

Rajah understood her teachers' evaluations of her writing better than she understood the difficulties she was having and how to fix them.

Researcher: (*pointing at the grade on Rajah's paper*) "What does that tell you?"
Rajah: "I got two wrong and 12 take away two equals 10. So that would make 10 right and I didn't get 12 right."
Researcher: "What do you think you learned from doing this?"
Rajah: "I don't know."
Researcher: "How can it help you with your writing?"
Rajah: "I'm not sure."

In fact, Perry's (1998) observations and interviews indicate that both the high- and low-achieving students in Mr. Baxter's class were concerned with getting a "good mark." However, for the low-achieving writers, this concern reflected a fear of the very real possibility that their notebook would be returned without a sticker or their low mark would be posted on a chart at the front of the class. In interviews, Rajah made comments reflecting perceptions of low competence, low expectations for success in writing, and desire to avoid failure. She also described engaging in self-handicapping behaviors, such as choosing work that is "easier" and hiding work, "so no one else would see."

HOMES AND FAMILIES

Some teachers participating in Perry's research have expressed concerns that their goal of promoting intrinsic motivation and self-regulation may not be shared by their students' parents/families (Perry et al., 2003). During student-led conferences, Ms. Madelay observed that parents recommended a much more limited range of strategies for solving reading and writing difficulties (e.g., "sound it out" was the principle recommendation for dealing with difficult words) than she did and discouraged early attempts at literate behavior that she judged were developmentally appropriate (e.g., using invented spellings, engaging in picture-governed attempts at reading). Other teachers who invited parents into their classrooms to read with students observed that parents tended to offer procedural rather than instrumental support for learning to read and write (e.g., correcting children's reading miscues instead of asking them what they might do to solve a reading problem and then helping them to work it out).

These observations are consistent with research about how home and school literacy contexts can differ, especially for children from low-SES or culturally and linguistically diverse communities (Heath, 1982; McCaslin & Murdock, 1991; Serpell, 1997). Serpell (1997) and Baker, Scher, and Mackler (1997) compared the literacy practices of middle- and low-SES American families in terms of the theoretical likelihood they would promote motivation for reading. A key difference between these communities was the relative emphasis given to reading as entertainment versus reading as important and serious business. Middle-class families spent more time engaged in reading for entertainment and their children were more likely to incorporate literacy behavior in their play activity. Serpell made the point that play is highly motivated behavior that is sustained over time. Thus, a focus on reading and writing as entertainment or play may elevate young children's interest in becoming literate and may increase time engaged in literate activities. In contrast, these researchers found that low-SES parents were more likely to view learning to read and write as "serious business," emphasizing the development of specific skills and engaging their children in activities that are more like work than play. Similarly, Anderson and Gunderson (1997) interviewed Chinese, Iranian, and Indo-Canadian parents about their beliefs and preferences for the teaching and learning of literate behaviors. In contrast to the emergent and meaning-based models of literacy development that many teachers in North America support, these parents emphasized accuracy from early on and were critical of practices such as invented spelling and emergent storybook reading (Sulzby, 1985). They wanted teachers to provide more direct instruction, give students more homework, and ask them to memorize more facts.

According to Serpell (1997), schools constitute a community of practice that reflects a particular set of beliefs, values, and expectations—those of mainstream society. Similarly, students come from homes that constitute their own beliefs and practices, and that may or may not present a "close cultural match" with the schools'. For this reason, Serpell and others (e.g., McCaslin & Murdock, 1991; Perry et al., 2003) have emphasized that researchers and educators need to consider the prior and ongoing influences of home and other social/instructional environments in a child's experience to understand students' beliefs, values, expectations, and actions at school. Home environments, like classroom environments, may differ in the extent to which they value and promote attitudes and actions associated with intrinsic motivation and self-regulation. For some parents and students, Ms. Madelay's high-SRL teaching practices may be unfamiliar. They may need to learn the routines and participation structures she employs and, in Corno's (1989) words, become "literate about [high-SRL] classrooms."

Greg's Home

Greg's parents described a home literacy environment that had much in common with the reading and writing practices of middle-class families we described above, and literacy practices in his classroom. His parents believed that reading at home was important and made time for it every day. Like Ms. Madelay, they believed that a child's first reading experiences should focus on the message, not on reading the exact words, and that children should not be corrected as soon as they make a reading mistake. They also believed that reading aloud to Greg would improve his ability to read on his own. Consistent with descriptions of environments that motivate children to read, Greg's parents reported keeping "a good assortment" of books in their home that they acquired from bookstores, the library, and school. They gave Greg choices about what to read and their descriptions of reading time conjured images of enjoyable family time. Greg's mother said, "We choose a story that we can both agree on (usually his choice). Then we cuddle up and take turns reading." Similarly, they appeared to engage Greg in writing for authentic purposes (e.g., writing cards, filling out notices); however, writing received much less attention than reading, a finding that was representative of literacy practices in the majority of the homes in Perry and colleagues' (2003) study.

Although much was mutually reinforcing about Greg's home and school literacy context, there were some key differences. In addition to the difference concerning opportunities for developing writing skills, Greg's parents indicated more traditional, bottom–up views about how children learn to read than were reflected in Ms. Madelay's style of teaching. His parents believed children should learn the sounds of the letters before learning to read and that learning to read requires learning skills in a particular order. Also, Greg's parents believed that "sounding out" is the first strategy to suggest when children are experiencing difficulties reading a word. The value they placed on these more traditional methods reflects the majority opinion in Perry and colleagues' (2003) parent sample. In the case of Greg's parents, this belief may be influenced by what they perceive will help Greg (who finds reading words challenging) to improve in reading. Depending on how much emphasis is placed on the development of specific skills when Greg reads at home (i.e., his parents indicated that they have purchased computer software and workbooks to promote Greg's word-reading ability), he may interpret that reading and writing are, in Serpell's (1997) words, more like work than play and, as a consequence, become less motivated to engage in literacy activities.

Overall, we judge there was a good deal of congruency between Greg's home and school literacy contexts. As well, there was balanced attention in both contexts to helping Greg build specific skills that will improve his reading and writing skills while keeping him engaged in learning to read and write (i.e., willing to try moderately challenging tasks and "keep trying" when difficulties present themselves). Some of Greg's judgments about what constitutes "good" writing reflect a focus on specific skills and an awareness that his writing is, at times, not good. Judging one assignment, he commented, "It's sloppy. I was writing too big and I tried to help it but it just didn't work." However, he also indicated that he felt supported by his teacher and intended to "just keep trying," believing "[he'll] get better." Similarly, Greg's parents were pleased with the amount of contact they had with Ms. Madelay and the progress that Greg had made in reading and writing that year. "He has learned to read just since the fall. It just clicked! And we will continue to reinforce it."

Rajah's Home

Since Perry's 1998 study did not examine students' home contexts, we do not know what motivational messages Rajah was receiving at home or how they compared with those she received in her classroom. If (not assuming) Rajah's parents' beliefs and values concerning reading and writing instruction were similar to those expressed by the Indo-Canadian parents in the Anderson and Gunderson (1997) study, we might expect a fair degree of overlap in the motivational messages she received at home and school. Her parents, like Mr. Baxter, might emphasize accuracy and discourage developmental practices, such as invented spelling. They might appreciate Mr. Baxter's teacher-directed approach to instruction and his focus on mastering discrete skills apart from more authentic reading and writing tasks. Also, they might appreciate Mr. Baxter's evaluation practices, which provided numeric and comparative information. Unfortunately, with Rajah's achievement profile, it could be that the emphasis parents and teachers place on accuracy and getting good grades would exacerbate Rajah's perceptions of low competence and low expectations for success in reading and writing and actually promote Rajah's use of academically self-handicapping strategies for reading and writing (Covington, 1992; Paris & Newman, 1990).

CONCLUSIONS AND FUTURE DIRECTIONS

We chose to highlight how sociocultural models of learning can enrich expectancy value theories of motivation, which examine how individuals' beliefs, values, and expectations influence their actions (Graham & Weiner, 1996; Pintrich & Schunk, 2002; Wigfield & Eccles, 2002). Specifically, we presented evidence from Perry's research on young children's motivation and self-regulation that connects features of classroom and home contexts to students' expressions of beliefs about their learning abilities (competence), values related to reading and writing, and expectations for success in these domains. Expectancy value theories have a long history in research and strong empirical support in educational settings (Pintrich & Schunk, 2002). The expectancy value model developed by Wigfield and Eccles has generated a significant volume of theory and research on achievement motivation in classrooms. Their theory and program of empirical studies are noteworthy because they have elaborated notions of task value and assessed students' expectations for success and task values across time (developmentally) and in different domains. Also, like many contemporary theories of motivation, their model and research recognize and attend to aspects of students' social world that influence their achievement-related behaviors.

One way in which contemporary theories and research on motivation can be distinguished is by the manner and degree to which they attend to the contexts in which learners operate. According to Hickey (2003), some theories and research programs reflect modest applications of social perspectives on motivation while others reflect more strident views of the interaction between learners and their environments. Historically, expectancy value theories have been associated with predominantly cognitive models of motivation. We align Wigfield and Eccles's model of motivation with social cognitive theories, which, in Hickey's terms, are modest applications of social perspectives on motivation. While acknowledging it is difficult to draw conclusions about students' motivations without considering classroom contexts in which they find themselves (Wigfield & Eccles, 2002), their research activities primarily focus on the thoughts and actions of the individual. As a contrast, we have presented Perry's research on young children's motivation and self-regulation. We would not go so far as to claim this research exemplifies the most strident applications of sociocultural theories to studies of motivation. However, we believe this work reveals some of what can be learned about expectancy value constructs when the social/instructional context, rather than the individual, is the primary focus of the research.

Consistent with sociocultural approaches to studying learning and motivation, Perry's research is situated in naturalistic contexts and blends qualitative with quantitative research tools. Observations, in the form of running records, and semistructured, retrospective interviews provide detailed descriptions of what teachers and students are saying and doing in classrooms. We believe these research tools have several important strengths as measures of students' motivation and self-regulation (Winne & Perry, 2000). First, by documenting learning and behavior in situ and real time, running records can mark instances of motivational messages and opportunities to engage in self-regulated learning and link them directly to students' responses. These linked events provide a basis for then asking students what they thought or how they felt in a follow-up interview. Second, observations reflect what learners actually do versus what they say they do as these may be colored by fallible and reconstructive memory (Winne, Jamieson-Noel, & Muis, 2001). This has proven particularly beneficial for studying young children's motivation and self-regulation. Observations ameliorate some difficulties associated with assessing young children's motivation and self-regulation through structured, self-report inventories (e.g., positive response bias and limited language for describing cognitive processes). Also, they illuminate the nature and degree of support young children require to be self-regulating, as per Vygotsky's view of learning and McCaslin and Good's view of coregulated learning, which leads to insights about teaching practices that promote (or curtail) young children's SRL. Perry's descriptions of Ms. Madelay's classroom, for example, demonstrate how teachers can encourage learners to view errors as opportunities to learn ("Everyone makes mistakes, everyone needs help sometimes, and everyone learns by helping), prompt their use of strategies to solve problems ("Where could you look? What could you do?"), and create opportunities for students to support one another ("Discuss it with a neighbor."). Finally, observations can reveal how teachers engage in "on the spot thought experiments" (Brunning, Schraw, & Ronning, 1995), change goals, adapt instruction, and adjust expectations in response to students and other environmental factors (e.g., an unexpected assembly, a cancelled field trip). In this way, we see evidence of the "reciprocal relationship between the social/instructional environment and individual cognitive and affective processes in the moment to moment of classroom life" (McCaslin & Good, 1996, p. 662).

There is a small but growing body of research applying social-perspective theories to investigations of children's motivation and self-regulation (see the special issues of *Elementary School Journal* and *Educational Psychologist* we mentioned earlier). However, we perceive that much of this research reflects mild to moderate applications. Future research needs to continue making connections between features of contexts and students' motivation and self-regulation, perhaps with more strident applications of sociocultural theories. We look forward to the insights these efforts provide.

In addition to recognizing the strengths of sociocultural theories and observational methods, we believe it is important to address several limitations. First, it is important to recognize that some aspects of motivation and self-regulation are impossible to observe (e.g., metacognitive processes such as planning and monitoring may be carried out in people's minds) unless specific provision is made to trace (Winne, 1982; Winne & Perry, 2000) these activities. Also, it is important for researchers to recognize that what is observed reflects a selective view about what is important to observe. Perry's observations are framed by her interest in SRL, her understandings about what supports SRL, and her knowledge of what the teachers participating in her studies are trying to accomplish with their students. Although Perry and her colleagues make every effort to be open to emergent categories, no recording medium of which we are aware, human or technological, can capture everything teachers say and do, and every student's response, and the nuances of these interactions in a running record. Second, as research becomes more and more situated, it is possible to lose sight of the forest by focusing too much on the trees. We believe additional insight can be gained by constantly making adjustments to grain size; that is, moving back and forth between detailed descriptions of the elements of single events involving particular people and reconstructions of those occurrences at aggregated levels within and across classrooms over time. McCaslin and Good (1996) also recommend that researchers compare the "moment to moment of classroom life" and the aggregate. Finally, observations and semistructured interviews may not yield answers to specific questions. Students may not use or may not be able to use language that maps onto motivational and other constructs of interest to theory. But a lack of expression is not a priori interpretable as an absence of thought. The human mind is both selective and summative. These cognitive qualities can, without awareness, delete and mask particulars that once played a key part in experience. In our judgment, no one view, no single methodological approach, is a panacea. We urge researchers to adopt multiple views and methods of inquiry in striving to develop thorough understandings of students' achievement motivation and SRL.

REFERENCES

Anderman, L. H. & Anderman, E. M. (2000). Considering contexts in educational psychology: Introduction to the special issue. *Educational Psychologist, 35,* 67–68.

Anderson, J., & Gunderson, L. (1997). Literacy learning from a multicultural perspective. *Reading Teacher, 50,* 514–516.

Atkinson, J. W. (1957). Motivational determinants of risk-taking behavior. *Psychological Review, 64,* 359–372.

Atkinson, J. W. (1964). *An introduction to motivation.* Princeton, NJ: Van Nostrand.

Baker, L., Scher, D., & Mackler, K. (1997). Home and family influences on motivations for reading. *Educational Psychologist, 32,* 69–82.

Bandura, A. (1986). *Social foundations of thought and action: A social cognitive theory.* Englewood Cliffs, NJ: Prentice Hall.

Bandura, A. (1997). *Self-efficacy: The exercise of control.* New York: Freeman.

Bruning, R. H, Schraw, G. J., & Ronning, R. R. (1995). *Cognitive psychology and instruction* (2nd ed.). Englewood Cliffs, NJ: Merrill-Prentice Hall.

Corno, L. (1989). What it means to be literate about classrooms. In D. Bloome (Ed.), *Learning to use literacy in educational settings* (pp. 29–52). New York: Ablex.

Covington, M. V. (1992). *Making the grade: A self-worth perspective on motivation and school reform.* New York: Cambridge.

Eccles, J. S. (1993). School and family effects on the ontogeny of children's interests, self-perceptions, and activity choice. In J. Jacobs (Ed.), *Nebraska Symposium on Motivation: Developmental perspectives on motivation* (pp. 145–208). Lincoln: University of Nebraska Press.

Goodenow, C. (1992). Strengthening the links between educational psychology and the study of social contexts. *Educational Psychologist, 27,* 177–196.

Graham, S., & Weiner, B. (1996). Theories and principles of motivation. In D. C. Berliner & R. C. Calfee (Eds.), *Handbook of educational psychology* (pp. 63–84). New York: Simon & Schuster Macmillan.

Heath, S. B. (1982). Questioning at home and at school: A comparative study. In G. Spindler (Ed.), *Doing the ethnography of schooling* (pp. 102–129). New York: Holt, Rinehart, and Winston.

Hickey, D. T. (2003). Engaged participation versus marginal nonparticipation: A stridently sociocultural approach to achievement motivation. *Elementary School Journal, 103,* 401–429.

Lave, J., & Wenger, E. (1991). *Situated learning: Legitimate peripheral participation.* Cambridge: Cambridge University Press.

McCaslin, M. (2003). Introduction. *Elementary School Journal, 103,* 313–316.

McCaslin, M., & Good, T. L. (1996). The informal curriculum. In D. C. Berliner & R. C. Calfee (Eds.), *Handbook of educational psychology* (pp. 622–670). New York: Simon & Schuster Macmillan.

McCaslin, M., & Hickey, D. T. (2001). Educational psychology, social constructivism, and educational practice: A case of emergent identity. *Educational Psychologist, 36,* 133–140.

McCaslin, M. & Murdock, T. (1991). The emergent interaction of home and school in the development of students' adaptive learning. In M. Maehr & P. Pintrich (Eds.), *Advances in motivation and achievement* (Vol. 7, pp. 213–259). Greenwich, CT: JAI Press.

McInerney, D. M., & Van Etten, S. (Eds.). (2001). *Research on sociocultural influences on motivation and learning.* Greenwich, CT: Information Age.

Paris, S. G. & Newman, R. S. (1990). Developmental aspects of self-regulated learning. *Educational Psychologist, 25,* 87–102.

Paris, S. G., & Paris, A. H. (2001). Classroom applications of research on self-regulated learning. *Educational Psychologist, 36*, 89–102.

Perry, N. E. (1998). Young children's self-regulated learning and contexts that support it. *Journal of Educational Psychology, 90*, 715–729.

Perry, N. E. (2002). Introduction: Using qualitative methods to enrich understandings of self-regulated learning. *Educational Psychologist, 37*, 1–3.

Perry, N. E., Nordby, C. J., & VandeKamp, K. O. (2003). Promoting self-regulated reading and writing at home and school. *Elementary School Journal, 103*, 317–338.

Perry, N. E., & VandeKamp, K. O. (2000). Creating classroom contexts that support young children's development of self-regulated learning. *International Journal of Educational Research, 33*, 821–843.

Perry, N. E, VandeKamp, K. O., Mercer, L. K., & Nordby, C. J. (2002). Investigating teacher-student interactions that foster self-regulated learning. *Educational Psychologist, 37*, 5–15.

Pintrich, P. R., & Schunk, D. H. (2002). *Motivation in education: Theory, research, and applications.* Upper Saddle River, NJ: Merrill Prentice Hall.

Randi, J., & Corno, L. (2000). Teacher innovations in self-regulated learning. In P. Pintrich, M. Boekaerts, & M. Zeidner (Eds.), *Handbook of self-regulation* (pp. 651–685). Orlando, FL: Academic Press.

Serpell, R. (1997). Literacy connections between school and home: How should we evaluate them? *Journal of Literacy Research, 29*, 587–616.

Solomon, G. (1995). Reflections on the field of educational psychology by the outgoing journal editor. *Educational Psychologist, 30*, 105–108.

Tolman, E. C. (1932). *Purposive behavior in animals and men.* New York: Appleton-Century-Crofts.

Turner, J. C. (1995). The influence of classroom contexts on young children's motivation for literacy. *Reading Research Quarterly, 30*, 410–441.

Turner, J.C., Meyer, D. K., Cox, K. C., Logan, C., DiCintio, M., & Thomas, C. T. (1998). Creating contexts for involvement in mathematics. *Journal of Educational Psychology, 90*, 730–745.

Turner, J. C., Meyer, D. K., Midgley, C., & Patrick, C. (2003). Teacher discourse and sixth graders' reported affect and achievement behaviors in two high-mastery/high-performance mathematics classrooms. *Elementary School Journal, 103*, 357–382.

Urdan, T. C. (Ed.). (1999). *Advances in motivation and achievement: The role of context* (Vol. 11). Stamford, CT: JAI Press.

Volet, S., & Jarvela, S. (Eds.). (2001). *Motivation in learning contexts: Theoretical advances and methodological implications.* Amsterdam: Pergamon-Elsevier.

Vygotsky, L. S. (1978). *Mind in society: The development of higher-order psychological processes.* Cambridge, MA: Harvard University Press.

Weiner, B. (1992). *Human motivation: Metaphors, theories, and research.* Newbury Park, CA: Sage.

Wigfield, A. (1994). Expectancy value theory of motivation: A developmental perspective. *Educational Psychology Review, 6*, 49–78.

Wigfield, A. & Eccles, J. S. (2002). The development of competence beliefs, expectancies for success, and achievement values from childhood through adolescence. In A. Wigfield & J. S. Eccles (Eds.), *Development of achievement motivation* (pp. 91–120). San Diego, CA: Academic Press.

Wigfield, A., Eccles, J. S., Yoon, K. S., Harold, R. D., Arbreton, A., Freedman-Doan, C., & Blumenfeld, P. C. (1997). Changes in children's competence beliefs and subjective task values across the elementary school years: A three-year study. *Journal of Educational Psychology, 89,* 451–469.

Winne, P. H. (1982). Minimizing the black box problem to enhance the validity of theories about instructional effects. *Instructional Science, 11,* 13–28.

Winne, P. H., Jamieson-Noel, D. L., & Muis, K. (2002). Methodological issues and advances in researching tactics, strategies, and self-regulated learning. In P. R. Pintrich & M. L. Maehr (Eds.), *Advances in motivation and achievement: New directions in measures and methods* (Vol. 12, pp. 121–155). Greenwich, CT: JAI Press.

Winne, P. H., & Marx, R. W. (1989). A cognitive processing analysis of motivation within classroom tasks. In C. Ames & R. Ames (Eds.), *Research on motivation in education* (Vol. 3, pp. 223–257). Orlando, FL: Academic Press.

Winne, P. H. & Perry, N. E. (2000). Measuring self-regulated learning. In P. Pintrich, M. Boekaerts, & M. Zeidner (Eds.), *Handbook of self-regulation* (p. 531–566). Orlando, FL: Academic Press.

CHAPTER 10

THE INFLUENCE OF SOCIOCULTURAL THEORY ON OUR THEORIES OF ENGAGEMENT AND MOTIVATION

Daniel T. Hickey and Jeremy B. Granade

INTRODUCTION

Most of the chapters in this volume address sociocultural influences on the motivational beliefs and values of individuals. Taking a different approach, this chapter looks at the influence of sociocultural *theory* on theories of motivation. Rejecting the prevailing assumption that the goals and values that motivate engagement are acquired "whole cloth" from the participation in sociocultural contexts, we start with the fundamental sociocultural assumption that participation in knowledgeable activity transforms that knowledge and any associated goals and values. Furthermore, we apply the assumption that all knowledge is socially defined, so that *all* such participation (with or without actual collaboration) transforms that knowledge and

Big Theories Revisited
Volume 4 in: Research on Sociocultural Influences on Motivation and Learning, pages 223–247.
Copyright © 2004 by Information Age Publishing, Inc.
All rights of reproduction in any form reserved.
ISBN: 1-59311-053-7 (hardcover), 1-59311-052-9 (paperback)

associated values (and therefore contributes to it). Taken in full, this analysis argues that the values and goals that support engagement in learning are defined by and resident in the practices of knowledgeable communities, rather than the hearts and minds of individuals. We advance the notions of "engaged participation" and "maladaptive nonparticipation" as alternatives to intrinsic and extrinsic motivation. We also raise the complex issue of reconciliation between the individual and the social context, contrasting the prevailing "aggregative" approach with a "dialectical" approach that follows from sociocultural perspectives. We conclude by suggesting that this new view of engagement suggests new ways of addressing the seemingly intractable debate over the use of extrinsic rewards to support learning.

THE INFLUENCE OF SOCIOCULTURAL THEORY ON OUR THEORIES OF ENGAGEMENT AND MOTIVATION

This book represents the fourth volume in a series on sociocultural influences on motivation. The series is a testimonial to the interest in sociocultural influences among motivation theorists. These same forces are illustrated in other considerations of "motivation in context" as exemplified in a special issue of *Educational Psychologist* (Anderman & Anderman, 2000) and several edited volumes (Urdan, 1999; Volet & Järvelä, 2001; Zimmerman & Schunk, 2001). This is an important development for educational research, because it is helping create a robust body of practical knowledge and principles for creating learning environments that both motivate learners and prepare learners for less-ideal contexts.

The diversity of motivational theories supports a broad characterization of sociocultural contexts and their influence on the goals and values of individuals. However, this recent "broadening" of motivation theory still relies largely on individually-oriented notions such as intrinsic motivation, interest, self-regulation, goal orientation, or self-determination. As we will attempt to show, starting with individually-oriented constructs leads theorists to characterize sociocultural contexts using "aggregates" of those same individually-oriented constructs. The title of this volume reflects this conventional approach, in that it highlights the influence of sociocultural factors, presumably on the motivation of individuals. The title of our chapter highlights our interest in the relationship between sociocultural *theory* and modern views of motivation. Specifically, we are referring to the core theories about knowing and learning that are widely associated with the Soviet theorist Vygotsky. Our perspective on these assumptions is most strongly influenced by contemporary "participatory" theories of cognition (e.g., Greeno et. al., 1998), learning (e.g., Brown, 1994), instruction (e.g., Collins, Brown, & Newman, 1989), and educational research (e.g. Collins, 1999).

The majority of the contributions in the present series make no reference to sociocultural theories of knowing and learning. With the exceptions of Sivan (1985) and McCaslin (1989), sociocultural theory had largely been ignored by modern motivation theorists. The exceptions are useful for helping orient readers to our contribution. In Volume 2, Pressick-Kilborn and Walker (2002) reconceptualize the construct of interest, using sociocultural theory to integrate the traditionally separate notions of situational and individual interest. Rather than focusing on one or the other (as in previous research), they advocate an approach that examines the interrelationships between the individual and the environment. Thus, they argue that the development of interest

> needs to be explained in the context of participation in a community of practice that values community activities and supports interest in the process of learning. Personal value and the construction of meaning have social origins and these canalize or channel the development of interest. (p. 171)

Likewise, Thomas (2002) uses a sociocultural perspective to consider how classroom, school, and community factors mediate the metacognition of individuals.

In Volume 1, Rueda, Macgillivray, Monzó, and Arzubiaga (2001) broaden the discussion of motivation to engage in reading by considering sociocultural factors such as parental reading habits and the meaning of literacy in the community. These factors are examined in terms of their effect on individuals' engagement in reading. Although situated within the broader social context, motivation is conceptualized in terms of students' perceptions of themselves as readers and the value they place on reading. A 20-item self-report reading survey measures these aspects of motivation and the effect of cultural factors (such as immigration, nurturance, instrumental knowledge, culture and language, and workload) on motivation.

Clearly, all three of these contributions use ideas from sociocultural theory to understand the influence of sociocultural factors, and presume that motivation is partly bound to context. However, they all appear to presume that the values and goals that support engagement ultimately reside in individuals. In other words, while acknowledging the influence of sociocultural theory, each of these analyses *start* with conventional individually-oriented models of motivation. There is one exception. As will be elaborated below, Vadeboncoeur and Portes's (2002) chapter advances a view of identity that appears to start from core assumptions of sociocultural theory, leading them to question the very notion of internalization. Our chapter attempts to extend such a consideration of identity and broaden it to the entire notion of achievement motivation.

Put differently, we ask what kind of motivation theory emerges from a stridently sociocultural view of knowing and learning. We summarize the ideas set forth in several previous analyses (Hickey, 2003; Hickey & McCaslin; McCaslin & Hickey 2001a, 2001b) in an attempt to outline such a theory. In particular, we attempt to show how the "dialectical" reconciliation of the individual and the social context that follows from sociocultural perspectives differs from the prevailing "aggregative" reconciliation. We then explore how such a model of engagement might lead to principles of motivation that are more useful for the central challenge of understanding and improving learning environments. Along the way, we use examples from ongoing efforts to enhance engagement and learning in a secondary science classroom, where students are learning introductory genetics (e.g., Hickey, Kindfield, Horwitz, & Christie, 1999, 2003).

As a caveat, we point out that we are exploring the implications of sociocultural perspectives that others have developed and defended. Readers interested in the more general merits of these ideas are invited to consult the resources cited throughout. Our arguments are limited to the value of these perspectives for improving teaching and learning. As a final introductory point, we reiterate that we are considering a commonly overlooked assumption of sociocultural theory. The fact that many scholars, who reference sociocultural theory, overlook this assumption suggests that the assumption is complex. Those of us who embrace this assumption appreciate the puzzlement of others who do not. As will be shown, this assumption and its implications can be confusing or simply irrelevant when considered in isolation.

Sociocultural Theories of Knowing and Learning

Any consideration of motivation to learn is premised on one's assumptions about learning; one's assumptions about learning are in turn rooted in one's assumptions about the nature of knowledge. Thus, it is necessary to first review sociocultural theories of knowing and learning, as most generally associated with Lev Vygotsky. Vygotksy's efforts to address the educational challenges created by the Russian revolution were consistent with what Pepper (1942/1970) called a *contextualist* worldview. This led him to focus on knowledge in terms of historical events and culture. This in turn led him to characterize learning as the internalization and transformation of socially defined knowledge (1978). This emphasis on learning as participation (rather than acquisition) is why sociocultural perspectives are sometimes referred to as "participatory" views.

From this perspective, knowledge is inextricably bound to the context of its use. A knowledgeable individual is one who participates successfully in sociocultural rituals and uses socially defined tools—what might best be called *knowledge rituals* and *knowledge tools*, or inclusively, *knowledge practices*. Referring to our example of introductory genetics, the knowledge that makes up a domain, such as genetics, is "stretched across" the physical and social contexts of use in which that knowledge is continually being refined. Reflecting an inherently contextualist worldview, every aspect of the context in which understanding of genetics is developed is, at some level, part of that understanding. From this perspective, "knowledge" is represented in the regularities of successful activity. This regularity is possible because the "knowledgeable" individual has become attuned to the constraints (that bound participation) and affordances (that scaffold participation) of the environment in which successful activity occurs. This means that participants in knowledgeable activity are increasingly able to use physical and social tools to maximize successful participation and overcome the limitations of individual human minds. Thus, to be knowledgeable about a domain such as introductory genetics would mean being able to participate in the meaningful use of some of the language, tools, and concepts that scientists have constructed in their collective efforts to understand inheritance.

When knowledge is viewed as distributed across the social and physical context in which it is developed, learning is characterized as increasingly regular and successful participation in practices in which that knowledge resides. Through this participation, individuals strengthen their respective ability to further participate in this activity. Vygotsky's theories of learning yielded notions, such as the *zone of proximal development* (ZPD), that have become widely known to Western educators and researchers. The ZPD is a hypothetical zone within a continuum of increasingly successful participation, relative to an individual's personal limitations. It begins at the point where an individual requires some form of assistance to participate more successfully. The zone continues as the assistance allows the individual to participate with increasing success. The zone ends at the point when the assistance no longer leads to increased success. Learning is presumed to occur as the individual internalizes the assistance that enabled more successful participation. Thus, in our example of introductory genetics, an individual might only be capable of using the familiar 2 x 2 Punnett square to solve simple inheritance problems (e.g., involving a single autosomal trait); with some assistance, this same individual could participate meaningfully in solving more complex problems, such as ones involving multiple or sex-linked traits. This assistance might come in the form of hints from a more knowledgeable individual, but it might also come from other sources. For example, that same individual might very well be able to solve dihybrid (two-gene) inheritance problems with the assistance of a 4 x 4 matrix. The point is that learning occurs as the individual internalizes the assistance that scaffolded their increasingly successful participation.

Partial interpretations of sociocultural theory. Notions such as ZPD have found wide appeal among Western educators. But, observers have repeatedly pointed out that many scholars and educators mistakenly cite Vygotsky to argue that mental functioning is derived "whole cloth" from participation in social interaction (Bruner, 1984; Davydov & Radzikhovskii, 1985;

Webb & Palincsar, 1996; Wertsch, 1991; Zinchenko, 1985). For example, many education textbooks characterize ZPD using very conventional cognitive views of learning, ignoring the fundamentally participatory view of knowing and learning that it embodies. Thus, ZPD is widely assumed to represent the right amount of assistance that more capable others should give to learners to help them learn formalized knowledge, such as in "cooperative learning" settings. In such characterizations, the ritualized interactions that define cooperation are presumed to be separate from the content knowledge that the individuals are expected to acquire from those interactions.

This misunderstanding appears to be the result of considering learning via the internalization of socially defined knowledge without considering the *transformation* of that same knowledge. Wertsch (1985) describes internalization as "a process involved in the transformation of social phenomena into psychological phenomena" (p. 63). What is internalized, then, is not an exact replica of external social activity. More to the point, when one assumes that knowledge is both constructed *and* resides in the context of its use, it can't also reside in the minds of individual knowers. In the words of V. P. Zinchenko, "the notion that external and internal activity are identical makes the concept of internalization meaningless" (1985, p. 106). Rather than the acquisition of knowledge as the result of social interaction, internalization requires participation in the creation of socially defined knowledge. As such, internalization is better understood as continued participation in the creation of socially defined knowledge. At this point, we should stress that we are not arguing whether internalization actually occurs. We view such a question as unscientific and ultimately unanswerable. Rather, we are arguing that treating internalization as an epiphenomenal artifact of conventional assumptions about knowing and learning leads to valuable new insights for improving education. When coupled with accepted benchmarks of educational improvement (such as increased evidence of learning using accepted educational outcomes) this leads to more scientific questions that can ultimately be answered using accepted educational research conventions.

POLITICAL AND PHILOSOPHICAL
ROOTS OF SOCIOCULTURAL THEORY

The widespread ignorance of a key aspect of sociocultural theory appears partly due to the extraction of Vygotksy's ideas from their fundamentally Marxist origins. Bruner cautions, "We must not lose sight of Vygotsky's philosophical commitment to Marxism, or more specifically, of Vygotsky's commitment to a psychology based on Marxist premises" (1984, p. 93). During his short life, Vygotsky attempted to forge a Marxist view of psychology by elaborating on Engels's (1890/1972) argument that human labor and tool use are the means by which humans change nature, and in doing so, change humankind. Primarily focusing on language, but including symbol systems more broadly (such as number systems), Vygotsky extended Engels's argument that using tools of physical labor changes humankind to argue that using tools like language changes the human *mind*. Rather than merely employing such tools and internalizing their function, Vygotsky argued that any participation in the use of these tools necessarily changes those tools. Just as Engels argued that an economy was comprised of the collective contributions of every worker, Vygotsky argued that culturally defined knowledge such as language was comprised of the collective participation of the members of that culture. This commitment to Marxist theory is particularly evident with regard to the zone of proximal development. According to Bruner, "the ZPD is a direct expression of the way in which the division of labor expresses itself in a collectivist society" (1984, p. 94). Thus, the internalization of socially defined knowledge requires participation in the use of that knowledge, which in turn transforms it.

From this view, knowledge does not originate in the structure of the objective world or in spontaneous efforts to make sense of that structure. Nor does knowledge originate in the individual's interaction with the objective world, as Piaget maintained (Case, 1996). Rather, knowledge originates in the interaction of social and material worlds, and resides in socially defined tools and ways of interacting (Lave & Wenger, 1991). Such a characterization of knowledge assumes that *all* learning takes place *by definition* in the ZPD, as individuals use social and physical tools to participate more successfully than they could otherwise. In this dynamic, knowledge is not located in the mind of knowledgeable individuals. Nor is it "out there" in the environment waiting to be imprinted on the minds of learners. Instead, knowledge is "stretched across" the social and physical contexts of its use (Cole, 1991; Pea, 1985).

The initial assumption that learning occurs via the internalization of knowledge represented in social interaction is generally consistent with modern cognitive/rationalist theories of knowing and learning (Hickey, 2003). These are the same cognitive/rationalist views that underlie mainstream views of motivation and goal orientation. As such, this initial assumption has relatively modest implications for modern motivation theories that are consistent with this view of learning. Indeed, the widening of existing theoretical lenses represented by this volume (metaphorically stepping back from the individual to also include sociocultural contexts) seems precisely like an effort to respect this assumption. This is not the case with the more fundamental assumption that internalization is best characterized as increasingly successful participation in the creation of socially defined knowledge. Because this participation (including ostensibly solitary engagement) transforms that knowledge, the knowledge can't actually be located in the minds of individual knowers. From this perspective, to be engaged in learning is to be participating in the meaningful use of knowledge practices. This alternative view of engagement calls for different models of practice for motivating engagement and leads to a dramatically different set of principles for motivating engagement in learning.

Sociocultural Views of Motivation

As outlined above, three of the contributions in Volumes 1 and 2 use sociocultural perspectives to conceptualize the motivation of individuals (Pressick-Kilborn & Walker, 2002; Rueda et al., 2001; Thomas, 2002). In key respects, these views are consistent with McCaslin's model of *coregulated learning* (CRL; McCaslin & Good, 1996a, 1996b; McCaslin & Hickey, 2001b). As CRL is one of the most well developed and studied of this class of models, it presents a useful basis for considering the issues of internalization. CRL has been advanced as an alternative to the conventional notion of self-regulated learning (SRL). CRL focuses on the relationships, social supports, opportunities, and emergent interactions that empower the individual to seek new challenges within that scaffolded environment. Students are presumed to internalize those supports in a manner that is expected to further enhance their ability to participate in worthwhile school activity. Whereas self-regulated learning focuses on changing individuals to make existing instructional tasks and learning more meaningful, McCaslin and Good argue that motivation and learning are "not merely individual struggles" (1996a, p. 660). This class of approaches assumes that the standards and values that motivate learning are socially constructed. Therefore, these models go beyond interactive models that assume merely that motivation is influenced by the social context.

Once we assume that standards and values are socially constructed, we must ask how fully those standards and values are bound to the contexts in which participants co-construct them. Coregulated learning assumes that domain-specific goals and values ("social support structures") are ultimately internalized, leaving learners "capable of relatively self-regulated learning in that particular domain" (McCaslin & Good, 1996a, p. 660). In essence, such characterizations advance a fundamentally sociocultural view of the creation of standards and values, then assume that these standards and values are internalized by the individuals via their participation in the interactions that gave rise to them—without directly addressing the issue of where the standards and values reside.

We argue that the internalization of standards and values that motivate learning is a key question of sociocultural motivation theorists in much the same way as the internalization of knowledge has been a key question for sociocultural learning theorists. Strident sociocultural theories of cognition assume that knowledge ultimately resides in the context of its use, and that the apparent internalization of knowledge is epiphenomenal (e.g., Wenger, 1998). The question we are exploring is whether a sociocultural theory of motivation should also assume that the standards and values associated with that knowledge ultimately reside alongside that knowledge and in the context of it's use. In other words, might the apparent internalization of standards and values also be epiphenomenal? Obviously, there is no empirical means to resolve this question. As we see it, the central question is not whether standards and values are actually internalized. Rather, it seems to us that as one's model of motivation becomes increasingly sociocultural, the standards and values that motivate engagement become increasingly bound to the context in which they were constructed, until the notion of internalization becomes irrelevant.

To reiterate, mainstream views of sociocultural influences on motivation (i.e., the majority of contributions in this volume) suggest that individuals internalize the standards and values of the contexts in which they participate; explicitly sociocultural views of motivation (as best exemplified by coregulated learning) emphasize how individuals participate in the co-construction of standards and values that they subsequently internalize. To use contemporary situative terms, the former implies that individuals become "attuned" to the standards and values in learning contexts; the latter implies that individual learners also co-construct the standards and values by their participation, and then become "attuned" to them. As argued elsewhere (Hickey, 2003), the assumption that standards and values are internalized seems partly responsible for the apparent reconceptualization and trivialization of the instructional implications of coregulated learning as little more than group instructional strategies for developing intrinsically motivated, self-regulated learners. Frankly, we worry that the similar contributions in this series will be similarly misunderstood. This is another reason why we believe that a more strident sociocultural approach to motivation provides a useful anchor for understanding these shifts. As described next, such an approach requires directing attention away from *motivation* and toward *engagement*.

A Sociocultural Theory of Engagement

Given that the term motivation itself seems laden with assumptions, we organize our thinking around the more theoretically neutral term of *engagement*. From our perspective, collective and continuing participation in the co-construction of standards and values means that they are constantly being negotiated in learning contexts. If so, the standards and values seem more appropriately characterized as residing alongside the knowledge practices in the contexts where they were constructed. In situative terms, this implies that the context becomes attuned to the standards and values of the collective participants who define that context, rather than the other way around. This fundamentally contextualist assumption seems to have profound implications for any educational research that is concerned with learning in complex social contexts. As Greeno and colleagues point out, a fundamentally contextualist approach addresses the issues of generalizability confronting individually-oriented approaches:

> Without analyzing the larger systems thoroughly, we risk arriving at conclusions that depend on the specific features of activities that occur in the special circumstances that we arrange, and that these specific features will prevent generalization to the domains of activity that we hope to understand. (1998, p. 7)

From a sociocultural perspective, an analysis of learning contexts that does not emphasize how contexts are attuned to the standards and values of the participants seems to present such a risk. In other words, emphasizing (or perhaps even acknowledging) that individuals are ultimately attuned to contexts may preclude a thorough analysis of the larger sociocultural systems in which motivated activity occurs.

A sociocultural view of learning supports a characterization of engagement as meaningful participation in a context where to-be-learned knowledge is valued and used (Wenger, 1998). This participation involves the maintenance of interpersonal relations and identities in that community, as well as satisfying interactions with the environments in which the individual has a significant personal investment (see Greeno, Collins, & Resnick, 1996, p. 26). Rather than a function of internalized goals and values, engagement is a function of the degree to which participants in knowledgeable activity are attuned to the constraints and affordances of social practices and *identity*.

> Regarding motivational issues, the situative perspective emphasizes ways that social practices are organized to encourage and support *engaged participation* by members of communities and that are understood by individuals to support the continuing development of their personal identities. (Greeno et al., 1998, p. 11, emphasis added)

In our view, this notion of *engaged participation* is at the core of a sociocultural theory of motivation. Viewing motivation as engaged participation in knowledge practices places the burden for motivating engagement on those practices, rather than the environment (in a traditional behaviorist view) or individuals (as in a modern cognitive view).

In other words, the standards and values that motivate engagement are a function of the same negotiations between the social and material worlds that gave rise to other knowledge. Thus, they are also part of that knowledge. Engaged participation is about negotiating one's identity with different and potentially conflicting and competing communities of practice. This participation necessarily involves both conformity to and alienation from prevailing standards and values because *these standards and values are a function of the knowledge communities those practices represent.* As such, what is typically construed as internalization is really better understood as continued (and increasingly regular) participation in the negotiations whereby those standards and values are continually refined and applied.

We acknowledge the complexity of this approach. In light of conventional emphasis on parsimonious theories, we appreciate that some theorists may view this as a puzzling step *backward.* Our reconceptualization of internalization is bolstered by contemporary views of educational research that place the advancement of useful educational practices over traditional concerns with theoretical coherence and parsimony (e.g., Brown, 1992; Collins, 1999). From this perspective, such issues should be resolved in light of the practical implications of competing theoretical explanations. We believe that the strident sociocultural theory of engagement may ultimately resolve heretofore intractable practical problems in education. For example, we find in this view a powerful alternative explanation of why so many students seem to lack the motivation to learn in classroom environments. Our perspective points out that if the "community" in a classroom does not value participation in knowledge practices associated with the intended curriculum, it will be difficult for any individual to participate in those practices. Rejecting what we see as a common misconception by modern motivation theorists, we do not presume that such students are not *learning*; by virtue of their presence in the classrooms, *all* students are participating in sociocultural rituals, and therefore learning. The critical point is that the knowledge practices that learners are participating in are often unrelated or antagonistic to the intended practices. We believe that efforts to improve teaching and learning will be better served if we redirect at least some of our attention away from individuals and toward the domain knowledge practice that our classrooms intend for them to participate in.

Identity and engagement. Sociocultural views characterize identity as a function of our practices, of our lived experiences of participation in specific communities (and therefore our competencies), rather than our beliefs or values (Penuel & Wertsch, 1995). And if identity is negotiated within the social context, it can also reside there: "Identity in this sense is an experience and a display of competence that requires neither an explicit self-image nor self-identification with an ostensible community" (Wenger, 1998, p. 152). As indicated above, the chapter in Volume 2 of this series by Vadeboncoeur and Portes (2002, after Portes, 1996) illustrates how individually-oriented constructs fundamentally are reconceptualized when one starts from core assumptions in sociocultural theory. In their analysis of students who are at risk of school failure, they advance a view of identity as dialectically constituted in the social relations of the community, such that the values and beliefs that locate the community within a particular status domain in the cultural hierarchy are imposed by others on the subject as a result of group membership and inter-group relations. (2002, p. 95)

From this view, identity is dynamic and shifts over time. As such, an attempt to define identity as an individual status is incomplete at best, if not impossible. Instead, a sociocultural view of identity "emphasizes the mutually constitutive relationship of the individual and the social context" (Vadeboncoeur & Portes, 2002, p. 92). Reflecting Vygotskian influences, this approach considers mediated activity as a unit of analysis and the process through which identity is negotiated. This characterization is consistent with a view of internalization as "an activity of the giving and incorporation of meaning, not a process of impression in which the individual stays passive" (Miedenna & Wardekker, 1999, pp. 79–80).

The notions of *legitimate peripheral participation* and *trajectories* (Lave & Wenger, 1991; see also Brown & Duguid, 1993) are useful for understanding the dynamic, temporal nature of a sociocultural view of identity. In an *inbound* trajectory, one's competence relative to a given community of practice negotiates legitimate participation on the periphery of a community, but with a clear trajectory toward a more central role in the co-construction of that community's practices. This negotiates an identity that is very different from the identity negotiated around an *outbound* trajectory leading *away* from the practices of a given community. Identities associated with some outbound trajectories (such as from childhood or toward graduation from high school) are natural and desirable, while others (such as premature separation from formal schooling) are undesirable. Importantly, however, such reified milestones are not the only (or even primary) way that identity trajectories are defined. By their very participation, the more central members of a community of practice create the possibilities for more peripheral newcomers. These so-called "paradigmatic" trajectories embody the history of the community, actual people as well as composite stories; they may not be represented at all in what is actually said, taught, prescribed, or recommended (Wenger, 1998). From this perspective, identity is not the *result* of reconciliation. Instead, identity is continually negotiated as participants reconcile membership in competing communities. Even highly interactive models of motivation and identity presume a clear distinction between individual and community. Yet Wenger (1998, p. 146) argues, "each act of participation or reification, from the most public to the most private, reflects the mutual constitution between individuals and collectivities," so that the separate notions of the individual and the community "are reifications whose self-contained appearance hides their mutual constitution."

Nonparticipation. A useful practical implication of participatory views of identity and engagement is the resulting characterization of *nonparticipa-*

tion, highlighting the issue of exclusion as well as inclusion. Ostensibly, the most important communities in classrooms are defined by knowledge practices that make up the "official" curriculum. Domains such as science, language, and math are defined by specific knowledge practices that students, by gaining competence with, negotiate an identity with. But the many constraints of classrooms and schools mean that the knowledge practices that students actually enact via their interaction with teachers, texts, and tests have a dubious relationship with their authentic practice outside of the classroom. This creates yet another community of practice that must be reconciled. Meanwhile, there are the many non-academic practices associated with youth culture, many of which are inherently antithetical to the intended practices of school. To complicate matters even more, there are a variety of conflicting contingencies in the environment that reward or punish participation and nonparticipation in individual practices—an additional constraint on activity as various participants in the many various overlapping communities of practice negotiate identity formation.

While nonparticipation in some knowledge practices is inevitable, it is not neutral relative to identity formation. Many unnoticed experiences of nonparticipation are so removed from the individual and the community of practice that they are irrelevant. The more crucial experiences of nonparticipation are those that serve to define identity, and therefore, participation. Managing to participate in absent-minded doodling during study hall supports a very different identity than during biology; doodling during biology supports a different view of identity than doodling during a high-stakes achievement test. Wenger (1998) distinguishes between *peripheral* and *marginal* nonparticipation. Peripheral nonparticipation is associated with an inbound trajectory. It is enabling because it conveys both opportunity and expectation for fuller participation. Marginal nonparticipation in the knowledge practices of a community is associated with an outbound trajectory relative to that community. It conveys neither opportunity nor expectation for fuller participation. From our perspective, marginal nonparticipation anchors the maladaptive end of the continuum that defines a stridently sociocultural model of engagement.

Marginal nonparticipation illuminates the complex motivational reality of the disadvantaged students who often get identified as being at risk of school failure (e.g., Bempechat, 1998; Csikszentmihalyi, Rathunde, & Whalen, 1993; McCombs & Pope, 1997). By the time students are labeled "at risk," their mutually constituted trajectory may be so misaligned with the knowledge practices of formal schooling that it is impossible to redirect it. Eckert (1989) showed how nonparticipation by "jocks" *and* "burnouts" plays a central role in identifying the practices that define the boundaries of both communities. In the case of antisocial practices among students (such as defiance, bullying, drug use, delinquency, truancy, etc.), the communities that form around these practices are defined by their opposition to the intended prosocial practices of the school community—

and vice versa. Membership in one such community by definition implies marginalization in the others. If so, crossing boundaries can be exceedingly difficult. Negotiating membership in both communities or attempting to cross boundaries entirely presents the further risk of double marginalization.

The utility of this perspective for understanding nonparticipation is not limited to *acknowledged* nonparticipation. The seemingly contradictory notion of *legitimate nonparticipation* offers a powerful framework for understanding typical educational practices. Consider the science education phenomenon Duschl (Jimenez-Alexandre, Rodriguez, & Duschl, 2000) called "doing the lesson." Relative to the knowledge practices associated with scientific domains, Duschl argues that the vast majority of activity in science classrooms is consistent with what Bloome, Puro, and Theodoru (1989, p. 272) called *procedural display:* "procedures that themselves count as accomplishment of a lesson…not necessarily related to the acquisition of intended academic or nonacademic content or skills." In other words, instead of learning to "do the science," most of the knowledge practices in school science involve coping with the demands of the class and still getting a good grade, regardless of whether the actual knowledge practices of science are involved (see Schauble, Glaser, Duschl, Schulze, & John, 1995). The important point is that the students' nonparticipation in the knowledge practices of the domain is entirely legitimized by prevailing curricular practices. The pressures of time, accountability, and resources that are cited to justify these activity structures are pervasive and potentially inevitable; the legitimacy of such nonparticipation is obviously open to interpretation. Regardless, the point remains that for many students whose identity includes successful participation in school science practices, their nonparticipation in authentic scientific practices is an essential (but almost entirely unnoticed) element of that identity.

One of the major implications of sociocultural views is that *all* learning involves using (and therefore changing) socially defined knowledge and values about that knowledge. Everyday characterizations of ZPD as an instructional strategy overlook the assumption that students are always participating in *something* (even when they choose not to participate in the intended curricular activities) and are therefore always functioning in a ZPD. A conservative interpretation of sociocultural theory may conclude that movement through ZPD is only accomplished with the direct help of more capable others (such as teachers and parents). However, physical tools such as books and computers also provide assistance that can define ZPDs because socially constructed knowledge is represented in books, lab materials, computers, and other physical artifacts. Solitary engagement with those artifacts *can* support meaningful engagement in the knowledge practices of a larger community. Conversely, participants in collaborative learning activities can be completely disengaged from the larger community to which they are ostensibly being acculturated (e.g., the practices of scientists). A more complete, participatory characterization of ZPD seeks to understand why learners are participating in practices (i.e., functioning in ZPDs) other than the desirable, intended practices (e.g., Wenger, 1998).

RECONCILIATION BETWEEN INDIVIDUAL AND SOCIAL ACTIVITY

The notion of engaged participation emphasizes the reconciliation of participation in the knowledge practices of multiple and potentially competing knowledge communities. Another kind of reconciliation involves the relation between competing views of knowing and learning. Reflecting the analyses provided by Case (1996) and Greeno and colleagues (1996), we presumed that most conceptualizations of knowing and learning can be associated with behavioral/empiricist, cognitive/rationalist, or situative/sociohistoric perspectives associated with theories advanced by Skinner, Piaget, and Vygotsky, respectively. Despite the claim that clarifying the relations between different perspectives is a critical issue for educational psychology (Greeno et al., 1996), there has been little explicit consideration of theoretical reconciliation in current efforts to broaden achievement motivation. Given the competing views of knowing and learning held by educators, researchers, and policymakers, clarification should help advances in motivation research enhance educational practice. Following is an abbreviated consideration of this issue as outlined in Hickey and McCaslin (2001) and Hickey (2003).

A relatively straightforward approach to reconciliation follows what Greeno and Moore (1993) labeled the "levels-of-aggregation" approach. Such approaches use aggregated individual-level constructs to characterize and understand broader physical and social contexts.

As embodied in influential motivation textbooks (e.g., Pintrich & Schunk, 2002), one can assign behavioral views a relatively trivial role of explaining the simple behavior of isolated individuals. One can then characterize broader sociocultural contexts using the same cognitive constructs developed to explain individual information processing. This approach to reconciliation is consistent with the "pragmatic" approach I have previously argued for (Hickey, 1997). As outlined in Hickey (2003) and Hickey and McCaslin (2001), it is also consistent with most efforts to broaden motivation theory to address sociocultural influences and contexts, as well as Bandura's theory of *collective efficacy* (1995). In perhaps the most explicit characterization of aggregative reconciliation, Bandura (2000, p. 76, emphases added) argues that "collective efficacy resides in the minds of the group members" and that social activity is "people acting coordinatively on a shared belief, *not a disembodied group mind* that is doing the cognizing, theorizing, aspiring, motivating, and regulating." Highlighting the incompatibility of the sociocultural model of motivation and aggregative reconciliation, Bandura assumes that there "is no emergent entity that operates independently of the beliefs and actions of the individuals" and that while "beliefs of collective efficacy include emergent aspects, they *serve functions similar to those of personal efficacy beliefs and operate through similar processes.*" Indeed, it seems that the "disembodied group mind" that Bandura rules out *is* an appropriate characterization of the standards and values residing alongside the knowledge practices in the model of engaged participation above.

Consistent with Vygotsky's philosophical orientation, an alternative reconciliation of the individual and the social context is rooted in a Hegelian cycle of thesis–antithesis–synthesis. As suggested by Greeno and Moore (1993), this approach first characterizes empiricism as the initial thesis, then characterizes rationalism as empiricism's antithesis. This characterization emphasizes their incompatibility and highlights the futility of considering the validity of one perspective from the other. A dialectical reconciliation then characterizes socioculturalism as a higher-order synthesis that combines the strengths and minimizes the weaknesses of behavioral/empiricist and cognitive/rationalist perspectives. Such a view "supports an expectation of theoretical developments that will show how principles of individual behavior and information processing can be understood as special cases of more general principles of interactive function" (Greeno et al., p. 40). In this approach to reconciliation, *both* the specific behaviors of individual organisms and the typical patterns of human cognition are characterized as fundamentally situated activity that can't be fully understood outside of the context where it occurred. As such, both behavior and cognition can only be fully explained in terms of the physical and social constraints and affordances that simultaneously bound and scaffold activity in the context where it occurs. It follows that typical individual-level characterizations of both behavior and cognition are, at best, incomplete characterizations of isolated activity.

From a dialectical approach to reconciliation, empirical data about the way organisms respond to environmental contingencies or the way humans typically think are considered epiphenomenal artifacts of the specific setting and methods that allowed the data to be collected. This has long been a concern about self-report Likert-scale items that have been the mainstay among motivation researchers (see Hidi & Harackiewicz, 2000). Most importantly, though, a dialectical approach argues that simply using observations and interviews alongside or in lieu of self-report methods (as in many recent studies of contextual motivation) will not address this problem. The essence of the dialectical approach is captured by the label *competitive* applied by Greeno and colleagues (1996). A dialectical approach assumes that situated sociocultural activity provides an ideal window for understanding individual behavior and cognition, but not vice versa. Consider Eraut's (2000, in Turner, 2001, p. 99) insistence that "the situative perspective must be able to explain how individuals enter, engage in, and leave shared experiences with a shared construction of reality while retaining individuality." A dialectical approach does so by explaining "individuality" as a special case of the shared experience, wherein "individual" (i.e., socially isolated) activity is wholly coregulated because it involves the use of socially-defined concepts, tools, standards, and values.

This dialectical approach offers several potential advantages that seem to merit consideration. It offers a more clearly specified characterization of the relationship between individual behavior, human cognition, and sociocultural activity. This appears to offer researchers a way out of the potentially endless interactions—the "hall of mirrors" warned of by Cronbach (1975; see Linnenbrink & Pintrich, 2001). A dialectical approach offers a way to prioritize efforts to collect, interpret, and report multilevel data. This is particularly important given the resources demanded by event-based data (as described below). By anticipating conflicting results, a dialectical approach provides a valid framework for presenting selected results to particular audiences or for warranting particular arguments. It also provides a more coherent framework for presenting complex findings to divergent audiences.

A dialectical approach also promises to help resolve tensions between empiricist and rationalist assumptions regarding specific educational practices, particularly the seemingly intractable debate over extrinsic rewards and intrinsic motivation (cf. Cameron & Pierce, 1994, 1999; Cameron, Banko, & Pierce, 2001; Lepper & Greene, 1978; Lepper, Henderlung, & Gingras, 1999; Lepper, Keavney, & Drake, 1996). The sociocultural model of motivation outlined above characterizes engagement as a function of the standards and values that reside alongside the knowledge practices co-constructed in the context of their use. As outlined in Hickey and McCaslin (2001), a dialectical reconciliation treats engagement presumed to be motivated either by intrinsically human sense-making processes or by extrinsic contingencies in the environment as special cases of engaged participation. This offers a relatively objective viewpoint for judging engagement that is ostensibly motivated by either "intrinsic" or "extrinsic" factors.

STUDYING PARTICIPATION AND RECONCILIATION

The preceding section suggests value in comparing aggregative and dialectical approaches to reconciliation. The nature of the issue precludes direct empirical comparisons. Rather, interpretive studies are needed that use different perspectives to collect and compare data from the same event. A study involving introductory genetics (Hickey, 2000; Hickey, Krueger, Fredrick, Schafer, & Zuiker, 2003) is doing just that. Three teams of researchers are simultaneously studying engagement during formative feedback activities from empiricist, rationalist, and sociocultural perspectives. In addition to engagement, learning is also being documented from each perspective. Consistent with an empiricist perspective, students are completing a multiple-choice test made of standardized genetics items before and after instruction. Consistent with a rationalist perspective, students also complete a genetics performance assessment before and after instruction. This assessment requires students to solve a series of increasingly complex problems and provide rationales for their answers (Hickey, Wolfe, & Kindfield, 2000). Finally, consistent with a sociocultural perspective, video-based ethnography is examining the transfer of curricular and domain knowledge practices from the formative feedback activity to the subsequent computer-supported collaborative learning activities.

In order to compare motivation and learning from three different perspectives, we must carefully define how engagement should be conceptualized and measured from each perspective. A significant part of the characterization of engaged participation outlined above was conceptualized after this study was initiated. Efforts to measure engagement from a sociocultural perspective are guided by a decade of effort by sociocultural instructional theorists. For example, Barab, Hay, & Yamagata-Lynch (2001) have refined a method known as CNA-RE (Constructing Networks of Action-Relevant Episodes) that structures the process of identifying important interactions and building activity networks that represent the historical development of knowledge practices. We are now trying to use these methods to document how standards and values associated with domain knowledge are constructed, how standards and values associated with knowledge practices antagonistic to the domain knowledge practices are constructed, and how both kinds of knowledge relate to engaged participation and marginal nonparticipation in the domain knowledge practices. Along the way we are exploring new digital video technologies that allow researchers to capture, compress, chunk, and code event-based data in real time (Hay, Hickey, Elliot, Kim, & Hand, 2002). Particularly tantalizing is the elimination of both tape and transcripts from event-based research. The publication of an entire corpus of coded raw event-recording data on the Internet promises to allow outside researchers to readily interrogate coded primary event data to reach an independent interpretation.

The discussion so far has focused more on the practical implications that *do not* follow from sociocultural views of motivation. When viewed through a dialectical lens, the sociocultural perspective, as outlined by Greeno, is ultimately "agnostic" regarding the particular educational practices that should be adopted (see Greeno et al., 1998, p. 14). Prior behavioral and cognitive approaches to motivation advanced well-defined (but antithetical) principles of practice for motivating engagement in learning. While some principles for motivating engaged participation were alluded to above, the perspective outlined here is just that—a perspective, a new way for understanding educational issues that have generally been referred to as "motivational." The agnosticism of this perspective lies in its fundamentally different way of characterizing knowledge, and therefore learning and engagement. This leads to new ways of characterizing prior approaches to instruction, and new solutions to practical problems that may have eluded prior considerations. Hickey (2003) outlines the general implications of this approach, offering new ways of understanding the impact (or lack thereof) of "cognitive" motivational interventions and reconciling their conflicts with behavioral interventions. As highlighted by Yowell and Smilie (1999), educators need to better counter the motivational effectiveness of the many nonacademic communities of practice available to school learners. The most problematic practices (i.e., "sex, drugs, and rock and roll") offer powerful visceral rewards and emerge in intimate social contexts that offer an obvious trajectory from the periphery to the center. In this light, motivational strategies based on intrinsic desire to make sense of school content seem rather impotent, particularly given seemingly inevitable curricular forces that reduce domain knowledge practices to the mastery of numerous disconnected associations.

A more specific implication of engaged participation concerns the use of extrinsic rewards. This perspective is neutral regarding the motivational appeal of such practices. The standards and values that motivate engagement are a function of the knowledge practices. As such, they are a fundamental part of the constraints and affordances that define those practices. This means that tangible extrinsic rewards are neither inherently detrimental for learning (e.g., Kohn, 1993), nor essential for some kinds of learning (e.g., Chance, 1992). Rather, the appropriateness of extrinsic rewards is considered in light of specific knowledge practices, as they are co-constructed by students, teachers, policymakers, test developers, domain experts, and other participants in the development and use of those practices. In the case of motivating students to attain fluency by repeatedly rehearsing lower-level associations (e.g., phonics, arithmetic facts), it seems of little consequence that engagement in these practices will decline when the incentive is removed. Some of the new fluency will remain and be used (and likely further developed) in contexts for which the practice was originally constructed. Furthermore, such practices are wed to the constraints of formal classroom settings. This means that "meaningful" engagement in these practices is inherently illegitimate relative to the actual sociocultural context that gave rise to this knowledge. Therefore, the distortion in participation caused by rewards seems less likely to affect the legitimacy and meaningfulness of participation (with obvious exceptions such as cheating). In other words, learners never really had the opportunity to construct value around these practices in the first place. Therefore, the ego-protecting task disengagement that rewards can cause seems less likely to occur.

On the other hand, offering salient extrinsic rewards for participation in practices where value is constructed can lead to problematic distortions. Consider motivating language arts students to participate in the practice of writing creative essays. This activity presents many opportunities to co-construct new knowledge and value for that knowledge. As such, a salient extrinsic reward (e.g., publishing the "best" essays in the school paper) may distort participation in such practices. Students who value such a reward but do not think they can succeed are likely to disengage. Conversely such rewards might have positive consequences for the participation of some students, especially those who think they have a chance and understand the criteria. To be sure, a careful examination of collective participation is required, rather than merely judging the outcome or asking students to judge how motivated they were to engage.

SUMMARY

The many arguments made in this chapter can be summarized in terms of the three core assumptions: (1) learners internalize knowledge and values via participation in social interaction; (2) using knowledge and values necessarily changes both learners and the knowledge; and (3) all participation in knowledgeable activity (including solitary activity) involves using—and therefore contributing to or otherwise changing—socially defined knowledge and values. The assumption that learners internalize knowledge through social interaction has modest implications for achievement motivation, relative to more purely rationalist approaches that do not emphasize the role of social interaction. The assumption that using knowledge transforms or changes both learners and the knowledge, however, has more profound implications for achievement motivation. It follows that both the knowledge and the value associated with that knowledge reside in the context of their use. We have attempted to show how this assumption supports a distinct, participatory view of knowing, learning, and engagement. The potential implications of a sociocultural view of engagement are further highlighted by the third core argument, that *all* participation in knowledgeable activity involves socially defined knowledge and values. Thus, all learning is presumed to occur in a zone of proximal development, where individuals are participating in some meaningful activity more successfully than they could otherwise. This assumption seems to have potential for understanding and enhancing engagement and learning in all conceivable types of learning environments.

Acknowledgments: The chapter and research it describes were supported by Nation Science Foundation Grant REC-0196225 to the University of Georgia. The opinions presented here belong to the authors and do not necessarily represent the positions of the University of Georgia or the National Science Foundation. Co-investigators on the GenScope Assessment Project were Ann Kruger, Laura Fredrick, and Nancy Schafer, of

Georgia State University; Ann Kindfield of Educational Designs Unlimited and Paul Horwitz of the Concord Consortium made significant contributions to that project as well. We thank the editors for their helpful suggestions. Amy Ourso assisted in the preparation of this manuscript.

REFERENCES

Anderman, L. H., & Anderman, E. M. (Eds.). (2000). The role of social context in educational psychology: Substantive and methodological issues [Special issue]. *Educational Psychologist, 35*(2).

Bandura, A. (1995). Exercise of personal and collective efficacy in changing societies. In A. Bandura (Ed.), *Self-efficacy in changing societies* (pp. 1–45). Cambridge: Cambridge University Press.

Bandura, A. (2000). Exercise of human agency through collective efficacy. *Current Directions in Psychological Science, 9,* 75–78.

Barab, S. A., Hay, K. E., & Yamagata-Lynch, L. C. (2001). Constructing networks of activity: An in-situ research methodology. *Journal of The Learning Sciences, 10*(1&2), 63–112.

Bempechat, J. (1998). *Against the odds: How 'at-risk' children exceed expectations.* San Francisco: Jossey-Bass.

Bloome, D., Puro, P., & Theodoru, E. (1989). Procedural display and classroom lessons. *Curriculum Inquiry, 19,* 265–291.

Brown, A. L. (1992). Design experiments: Theoretical and methodological challenges in creating complex interventions in classroom settings. *Journal of the Learning Sciences, 2,* 141–178.

Brown, A. L. (1994). The advancement of learning. *Educational Researcher, 23*(8), 4–12.

Brown, J. S., & Duguid, P. (1993). Stolen knowledge. *Educational Technology, 33*(3), 10–15.

Bruner, J. S. (1984). Vygotsky's zone of proximal development: The hidden agenda. *New Directions for Child Development, 23,* 92–97.

Cameron, J., Banko, K., & Pierce, W. D. (2001). Pervasive negative effects of rewards on intrinsic motivation: The myth continues. *Behavior Analyst, 24,* 1–44.

Cameron, J., & Pierce, W. D. (1994). Reinforcement, reward, and intrinsic motivation. A meta-analysis. *Review of Educational Research, 64,* 363–423.

Cameron, J., & Pierce, W. D. (1999). The debate about rewards and intrinsic motivation. Protests and accusations do not alter the results. *Review of Educational Research, 66,* 39–51.

Case, R. (1996). Changing views of knowledge and their impact on educational research and practice. In D. R. Olson & N. Torrance (Eds.), *The handbook of education and human development,* (pp. 75–99). Cambridge: Blackwell.

Chance, P. (1992). The rewards of learning. *Phi Delta Kappan, 74,* 200–207.

Cole, M. (1991). On socially shared cognitions. In L. Resnick, J. Levine, & S. Behrend (Eds.), *Socially shared cognitions* (pp. 398–417). Hillsdale, NJ: Erlbaum.

Collins, A. (1999). The changing infrastructure of educational research. In E.C. Lagemann & L. B. Schulman (Eds.), *Issues in educational research: Problems and possibilities* (pp. 289–298). San Francisco: Jossey-Bass.

Collins, A., Brown, J. S., & Newman, S. E. (1989). Cognitive apprenticeship: Teaching the craft of reading, writing, and mathematics. In L. B. Resnick (Ed.), *Knowing, learning, and instruction: Essays in honor of Robert Glaser* (pp. 453–494). Hillsdale, NJ: Erlbaum.

Cronbach, L. J. (1975). Beyond the two disciplines of scientific psychology. *American Psychologist, 30*, 116–127.

Csikszentmihalyi, M., Rathunde, K., & Whalen, S. (1993). *Talented teens: The roots of success and failure.* Cambridge: Cambridge University Press.

Davydov, V., & Radzikhovskii, L. (1985). Vygotsky's theory and the activity-oriented approach in psychology. In J. Wertsch (Ed.), *Culture, communication, and cognition: Vygotskian perspectives* (pp. 35–65). Cambridge: Cambridge University press.

Eckert, P. (1989). *Jocks and burnouts: Social categories and identity in the high school.* New York: Teachers College Press.

Engels, F. (1972). Socialism: Utopian and Scientific. In R. C. Tucker (Ed.), *The Marx-Engels reader* (pp. 605–639). New York: Norton. (Original work published 1890)

Eraut, M. (2000). Non-formal learning and tacit knowledge in professional work. *British Journal of Educational Psychology, 70*, 113–136.

Greeno, J. G., and the Middle School Mathematics through Application Project. (1998). The situativity of knowing, learning, and research. *American Psychologist, 53*, 5–26.

Greeno, J. G., Collins, A. M., & Resnick, L. (1996). Cognition and learning. In D. Berliner & R. Calfee (Eds.), *Handbook of educational psychology* (pp. 15–46). New York: MacMillan.

Greeno, J. G., & Moore, J. L. (1993). Situativity and symbols: A response to Vera and Simon. *Cognitive Science, 17*, 49–60.

Hay, K. E., Hickey, D. T., Elliot, D., Kim, B., & Hand, B. (2002, January). *Integrated temporal multimedia data research system: The present and future of digital tools for research.* Presentation at the 15th Annual Conference on Interdisciplinary Qualitative Studies, Athens, GA.

Hickey, D. T. (1997b). Motivation and contemporary socio-constructivist instructional perspectives. *Educational Psychologist, 32*, 175–193.

Hickey, D. T. (1999, Augustc). *Epistemological reconciliation and the future of motivation research.* Paper presented at the 8th annual meeting of the European Association for Research on Learning and Instruction, Göteborg, Sweden.

Hickey, D. T. (2000). *Assessment, motivation, & epistemological reconciliation in a technology-supported learning environment.* Grant No. REC-0196225 from the National Science Foundation, Division on Research, Evaluation, and Communication to the University of Georgia.

Hickey, D. T. (2001b, August). *Alternative approaches to broadening achievement motivation: Insights from our own practices.* Paper presented at the 9th annual meeting of the European Association for Research on Learning and Instruction, Fribourg, Switzerland.

Hickey, D. T. (2003). Engaged participation versus marginal non-participation: A stridently sociocultural approach to achievement motivation. *Elementary School Journal, 103,* 401–429.

Hickey, D. T., Kruger, A. C., Fredrick, L. D., Schafer, N. J., & Zuiker, S. (2003, April). *Design experimentation using multiple perspectives: The GenScope Assessment Project.* Paper presented at the annual meeting of the American Educational Research Association, Chicago.

Hickey, D. T., & McCaslin, M. (2001). A comparative and sociocultural analysis of context and motivation. In S. Volet & S. Järvelä (Eds.), *Motivation in learning contexts: Theoretical and methodological implications* (pp. 33–56). Amsterdam: Pergamon/Elsevier.

Hickey, D. T., Wolfe, E. W., & Kindfield, A. C. H. (2000). Assessing learning in a technology-supported genetics environment: Evidential and consequential validity issues. *Educational Assessment, 6,* 155–196.

Hidi, S., & Harackiewicz J. M. (2000). Motivating the academically unmotivated: A critical issue for the 21st century. *Review of Educational Research, 70,* 151–179.

Jiménez-Aleixandre, M. P., Rodríguez, A. B., & Duschl, R. A. (2000). "Doing the lesson" or "Doing science": Argument in high school genetics. *Science Education, 84,* 757–792.

Kohn, A. (1993). Rewards versus learning. A response to Paul Chance. *Phi Delta Kappan, 74,* 783–787.

Lave, J., & Wenger, E. (1991). *Situated learning: Legitimate peripheral participation.* Cambridge: Cambridge University Press.

Lepper, M. R., & Greene, D. (Eds.). (1978). *The hidden cost of reward.* Hillsdale, NJ: Erlbaum.

Lepper, M. R., Henderlong, J., & Gingras, I. (1999). Understanding the effects of extrinsic rewards on intrinsic motivation—Uses and abuses of meta-analysis. *Psychological Bulletin, 125,* 669–676.

Lepper, M. R., Keavney, M., & Drake, M. (1996). Intrinsic motivation and extrinsic rewards: A commentary on Cameron & Pierces' meta-analysis. *Review of Educational Research, 66,* 5–32.

Linnenbrink, E. A., & Pintrich, P. R. (2001). Multiple goals, multiple contexts: The dynamic interplay between personal goals and context goal stresses. In S. Volet & S. Järvelä (Eds.), *Motivation in learning contexts: Theoretical advances and methodological implications* (pp. 251–269). Amsterdam: Pergamon-Elsevier.

McCaslin, M. (1989). Self regulated learning and academic achievement: A Vygotskian view. In B. Zimmerman & D. Schunk (Eds.), *Self-regulated learning and academic achievement: Theory, research, and practice* (pp. 143–168). New York: Springer.

McCaslin, M., & Good, T. (1996a). The informal curriculum. In D. Berliner & R. Calfee (Eds.), *Handbook of educational psychology* (pp. 622–673). New York: Macmillan.

McCaslin, M., & Good, T. (1996b). *Listening in classrooms.* New York: HarperCollins.

McCaslin, M., & Hickey, D. T. (2001aa). Educational psychology, social constructivism, and educational practice: A case of emergent identity. *Educational Psychologist, 36,* 133–140.

McCaslin, M., & Hickey, D. T. (2001bb). Self-regulated learning and academic achievement: A Vygotskian view. In B. Zimmerman & D. Schunk (Eds.), *Self-reg-*

ulated learning and academic achievement: Theory, research, and practice (2nd ed., pp. 227–252). Mahwah, NJ: Erlbaum.

McCombs, B. L., & Pope, J. E. (1994). Motivating hard to reach students. Washington, DC: American Psychological Association.

Miedema, S., & Wardekker, W. L. (1999). Emergent identity versus consistent identity: Possibilities for postmodern repoliticization of critical pedagogy. In T. S. Popkewitz & L. Fendler (Eds.), Critical theories in education: Changing terrains of knowledge and politics. New York: Routledge.

Pea, R. (1985). Beyond Amplification. Using the computer to reorganize mental functioning. Educational Psychologist, 20, 167–182.

Penuel, W. R., & Wertsch, J. V. (1995). Vygotsky and identity formation: A sociocultural approach. Educational Psychologist, 30, 215–234.

Pepper, S. C. (1970). World hypotheses: A study in evidence. Berkeley: University of California Press. (Original work published 1942)

Pintrich, P. R., & Schunk, D. H. (2002). Motivation in education: Theory, research, and application (2nd ed.). Englewood Cliffs, NJ: Prentice Hall.

Portes, P. R. (1996). Ethnicity and culture in educational psychology. In D. Berliner & R. Calfee (Eds.), Handbook of educational psychology (pp. 331–357). New York: MacMillan.

Pressick-Kilborn, K., & Walker, R. (2002). The social construction of interest in a learning community. In D. M. McInerney & S. Van Etten (Eds.), Research on sociocultural influences on motivation and learning (Vol. 2, pp. 153–182). Greenwich, CT: Information Age.

Rueda, R., Macgillivray, L., Monzó, L., & Arzubiaga, A. (2001). Engaged reading: A multi-level approach for considering sociocultural factors with diverse learners. In D. M. McInerney & S. Van Etten (Eds.), Research on sociocultural influences on motivation and learning (Vol. 1, pp. 233–264). Greenwich, CT: Information Age.

Schauble, L., Glaser, R., Duschl, R., Schulze, S., & John, J. (1995). Students' understanding of the objectives and procedures of experimentation in the science classroom. Journal of the Learning Sciences, 4, 131–166.

Sivan, E. (1985). Motivation in social constructivist theory. Educational Psychologist, 21, 209–233.

Thomas, G. P. (2002). The social mediation of metacognition. In D. M. McInerney & S. Van Eten (Eds.), Research on sociocultural influences on motivation and learning (Vol. 2, pp. 225–247). Greenwich, CT: Information Age.

Turner, J. C. (2001). Using context to enrich and challenge motivation theory. In S. Volet & S Järvelä (Eds.), Motivation in learning contexts: Theoretical advances and methodological implications (pp. 85–104). Amsterdam: Pergamon-Elsevier.

Urdan, T. C. (Ed.). (1999). Advances in motivation and achievement: The role of context (Vol. 11). Greenwich, CT: JAI Press.

Vadeboncoeur, J., & Portes, P. (2002). Students "At Risk": Exploring identity from a sociocultural perspective. In D. M. McInerney & S. Van Etten (Eds.), Research on sociocultural influences on motivation and learning (Vol. 2, pp. 89–127). Greenwich, CT: Information Age.

Volet, S., & Järvelä, S. (Eds.). (2001). Motivation in learning contexts: Theoretical advances and methodological implications. Amsterdam: Pergamon-Elsevier.

Vygotsky, L. S. (1978). Mind in society: The development of higher-order psychological processes. Cambridge, MA: Harvard University Press. (Original work published 1934)

Webb, N. M., & Palincsar, A. S. (1996). Group processes in the classroom. In D. Berliner & R. Calfee (Eds.), *Handbook of educational psychology* (pp. 841–873). New York: Macmillan.

Wenger, E. (1998). *Communities of practice: Learning, meaning, and identity.* Cambridge: Cambridge University Press.

Wertsch, J. V. (1985). *Vygotsky and the social formation of mind.* Cambridge, MA: Harvard University Press.

Wertsch, J. V. (1991). *Voices of the mind: A sociocultural approach to mediated action.* Cambridge, MA: Harvard University Press.

Yowell, C. M., & Smylie, M. A. (1999). Self-regulation in democratic communities. *Elementary School Journal, 99,* 469–490.

Zimmerman, B. J., & Schunk D. H. (Eds.). (2001). *Self-regulated learning and academic achievement: Theoretical perspectives* (2nd ed.). Mahwah, NJ: Erlbaum.

Zinchenko, V. P. (1985). Vygotsky and units for the analysis of mind. In J. Wertsch (Ed.), *Culture, communication, and cognition: Vygotskian perspectives* (pp. 94–118). Cambridge: Cambridge University press.

CHAPTER 11

COREGULATION OF OPPORTUNITY, ACTIVITY, AND IDENTITY IN STUDENT MOTIVATION
Elaborations on Vygotskian Themes

Mary McCaslin

INTRODUCTION

In this chapter I make a case for the importance of a notion of an individual within a sociocultural perspective that honors the emergent interaction of historical and cultural events in the development of individual identity. My particular focus is on motivational features of individual identity. My goal is to portray the emergent interaction of opportunity and interpersonal validation that coregulate the activities that individuals engage, come to value, and pledge commitment. Recognition of individual identity highlights the role of opportunity; thus, in making a case for the individual I

Big Theories Revisited
Volume 4 in: Research on Sociocultural Influences on Motivation and Learning, pages 249–274.
ISBN: 1-59311-053-7 (hardcover), 1-59311-052-9 (paperback)

also make a case for informative social policies and educational practices. Individual identity also underscores processes of interpersonal validation; thus, in making a case for the individual, I also make a case for prior and ongoing social influences in emergent interaction with personal development.

In this chapter, research on the individual is presented within the contexts of ongoing influences of parents, teachers, and peers in students' realization of opportunity and emergent identity. The analysis begins with a brief overview of Vygotsky's original theory followed by a more recent conceptualization that stresses the dynamic interplay—the coregulation—of opportunity, activity, and identity formation in personal development. Four strands of research are presented to illustrate the potential of coregulation within Vygotsky's "zone of proximal development" for understanding student motivation: (1) the function of task opportunity and the enhancement of self-directed activity and motivational beliefs, (2) the affordances of teacher classroom management for student-learning cultural rules of responsibility and citizenship, (3) the influence of parent beliefs and behavior on children's emergent identity and negotiation of personal commitments in school, and (4) the power of peer participation in student-valuing curriculum tasks, learning motivation, and motivation to learn.

A BRIEF OVERVIEW OF VYGOTSKIAN THEORY

Vygotsky's ideas were the product of unique circumstances marked by rapid social change and very high stakes (for more complete discussion, see McCaslin Rohrkemper, 1989; McCaslin & Hickey, 2001; Wertsch, 1985). Vygotsky was an avowed Marxist and three tenets associated with Marxist theory are evident in his work: (1) language developed as a result of human activity and the need for cooperative labor (Engels, 1890); (2) consciousness is the result of gradual accumulation of small changes and is an active constructor of experience that organizes and allows self-control of behavior, and thus enables socially meaningful activity (Marx, 1972; see also Gray, 1966); and (3) movement, or progress, is the result of the conflict of opposites that merge and transcend into a higher truth in a dialectic hierarchy (Hegel, 1807/1949).

Vygotsky formulated his ideas on the social mediation of learning and the role of consciousness with Luria and Leontiev at the Institute of Psychology in Moscow. Luria (1979) recalled:

> In Vygotsky's hands, Marx's methods of analysis did serve a vital role in shaping our course. Influenced by Marx, Vygotsky concluded that the origins of higher forms of conscious behavior were to be found in the individual's

social relations with the external world. But man is not only a product of his environment, he is also an active agent in creating that environment.... We needed, as it were, to step outside the organism to discover the sources of specifically human forms of psychological activity. (p. 43)

Developmental Focus

Vygotsky took a developmental approach to individual mediation of cultural experience. Experience is cultural because it represents socially structured tasks and tools. It is historical because it reflects the "storehouse" of knowledge of humankind that "enormously expanded man's powers, making the wisdom of the past analyzable in the present and perfectible in the future" (Luria, 1979, p. 44). It is personal because individual development, particularly biological readiness and opportunity, enable the individual to refine his capacity for self-direction and, hence, meaningful social contribution.

Functions of Language

Mediation for Vygotsky is best illustrated with his position on language. He accepted Engels's position that language is a uniquely human characteristic and elaborated upon Pavlov's (1927) distinctions between a first signal system of perception, which is shared with nonhumans, and a uniquely human second signal system of language, which allows mastery of the environment rather than control by its stimuli. Humans evolve from a dominance of the first signal system at birth to facility with the second signal system, which allows mastery of nature and thus mastery of the self (Leontiev & Luria, 1968, p. 342).

Vygotsky focused on the development of multiple functions of language that fused Engels's premise on language with Marx's position on consciousness: the ability to communicate with others is distinct from but also informs the ability to self-direct one's conscious thinking. The functions of speech differ such that speech that communicates with others requires transforming thoughts to words; in contrast, self-directive speech involves transforming words to thoughts (Vygotsky, 1962, p. 131). The developmental sequence of these functions is from social or interpersonal to self-directive or intrapersonal; however, the social environment is the source of each. Language, the second signal system that makes us distinctly human, is embedded in the cultural, historical, and social language environment. Vygotsky, in the manner of Hegel, collapsed the distinction between biological development and environmental control. The contrast of opposites that dominated the psychology of his day—biology versus environment—was transcended. To find the mind, Vygotsky went outside the body to the social world. Language was the key.

Processes of Internalization

The developmental sequence of language development—from the first to second signal system and from interpersonal, communication with others to intrapersonal self-directive speech—locates the emergent capacity for "self-regulation" in the interpersonal realm. Luria (1969) explained that Vygotskian theory "conceives of mind as the product of social life and treats it as a form of activity which was earlier shared by two people (originated in communication), and which only later, as a result of mental development, became a form of behavior within one person" (p. 143). Higher psychological processes begin in the social world.

Perhaps the most well-known representation of this process is the "zone of proximal development" (ZPD). Vygotsky identified this area as a sort of gap between what a learner can do alone compared with what can be done with help. The basic idea is that learners learn more than the "answer"—the surface level—of the assistance, they also learn to incorporate the underlying structure—the deep level—of the assistance. For example, consider "the case of the lost keys." Help finding them can be more than a matter of their location (the surface level), it can also be about strategies for how to go about finding them—perhaps a memory strategy that allows more effective metacognition and behavioral organization (the deep level). One result is a learner who can now accomplish the task with higher accuracy and deeper understanding. The relationship between the participants in the ZPD is central; the dynamic is of mutual regulation (compared with unidirectional top–down control). The goal of the assistance in the ZPD is to connect the cultural knowledge of the teacher or more capable peer with the learner's everyday understandings and opportunities. Relationships within the ZPD are personal. "It is within close personal relationships marked by support of student autonomy, intersubjectivity, and intelligent sympathy that effectively scaffolded interactions between teachers and students can occur" (Yowell & Smylie, 1999, p. 475). Scaffolding in the ZPD requires knowledge of the individual learner, not merely knowledge of the learner's knowledge. In this conception, both participants are enriched by mutual regulation; culture is rendered more meaningful for each. (See Yowell & Smiley, 1999, for an excellent discussion of optimal functioning in the zone of proximal development.)

The ZPD is a central construct in the four research illustrations that follow. Each highlights a potential feature of the zone that may or may not serve to optimize student learning and emergent identity: (a) task difficulty; (b) social mediation and personal development; (c) parent authority and child autonomy; and (d) peer participation and individual identity.

Integration of Affective and Intellectual in Consciousness

As the discussion of ZPD suggests, Vygotsky considered affective and intellectual a false dichotomy:

> We have in mind the relation between intellect and affect. Their separation as subjects of study is a major weakness of traditional psychology since it makes the thought process appear as an autonomous flow of "thoughts thinking themselves," segregated from the fullness of life, from the personal needs and interests, the inclinations and impulses, of the thinker. (1962, p. 8)

One expressed goal of integrating affect and intellect was to trace the path from need to thought to activity. Vygotsky thought it futile to study any facet in isolation; however, direct study of the integration of the affect and intellectual was not part of his research program.

ELABORATIONS ON VYGOTSKIAN CONSTRUCTS: OPPORTUNITY, ACTIVITY, AND IDENTITY FORMATION

Vygotsky's focus on multiple functions of language, its social origins, and the call to merge the affective with the intellectual were at once provocative and found wanting. Vygotsky believed the basic unit of analysis, "that which retains all the properties of the whole and which cannot be further divided" (1962, p. 132), was word meaning. Wertsch (1985) and Zinchenko (1985) challenged this position and argued instead for a construct of "activity" that embodies tool-mediated, goal-directed action. Activity theory, as it is known, posits human activity rather than word meaning as the basic unit of analysis that links the individual and society—a return of sorts to Engels's basic premise of the evolution of human activity, the need for cooperative labor, and the development of language—in the present tense.

Activity theory presumes that motives and goals emerge and exist within the sociocultural realm, rather than as a property of the individual (see, e.g., Kozulin, 1986; Leontiev, 1974–1975; 1978). Wertsch (1985) extended activity theory to the interpsychological and intrapsychological plane and has argued its use as a framework for mediation (p. 208). Most theorists within the Vygotskian tradition consider "tool-mediated (the Engels part), goal-directed (the Marx part), action (the neo-Vygotskian part)" as the basic unit of meaningful analysis for understanding higher psychological processes. This position has replaced Vygotsky's original stance on word meaning. The activity perspective differs from the modern cognitive perspective on human action as purposeful cognition and behavior in the context of a goal. Activity theory locates and coregulates human activity in the social realm rather than envisioning activity solely as a characteristic of an individual. Activity theory also differs from a traditional behavioral perspective. In activity theory, human activity represents individual and collective mediation of participation in opportunity rather than a direct effect of opportunity. For example, a subsequent case study illustrates one child's—Julio's—negotiation of noncompatible home and school learning that is profoundly affected by his immigrant parents' beliefs in the power of education to make a better life. Julio's struggles are about more than completing tonight's homework; completing homework is all about realization of future goods for himself and his family and justification of his parents' past decisions.

One result of an emphasis on coregulated activity has been an interest in types of opportunities that might illuminate, refine, and promote the integration of the affective and the intellectual in human consciousness, an arena about which Vygotsky theorized but did not explore. An example of the impact of a core construct of activity in educational research in the Vygotskian tradition can be seen in a research program I conducted in the 1980s (McCaslin Rohrkemper, 1989; Rohrkemper, 1986; Rohrkemper & Bershon, 1984; Rohrkemper, Slavin, & McCauley, 1983). The guiding principle of this work was to identify the features of student "adaptive learning"—a healthy integration of the affective and the intellectual in coping with classroom stress—for the purpose of enhancing it through classroom interventions. Adaptive learning involves the internalization of goals; the motivation to commit, challenge, or reform them; and the competence to enact and evaluate those commitments. It involves a certain "hardiness." In one instance adaptive learning may involve taking charge of the frustration of difficult learning; in another it may mean overcoming the tedium of boredom (McCaslin & Murdock, 1991; Rohrkemper & Corno, 1988).

Subsequently, I termed the opportunities and interpersonal relationships within students' range of experience "coregulated learning." My research had suggested that I had biased my original construction of ZPD as, by definition, positive promotion of student learning and development. Meaningful learning, by definition, does occur within the learner's ZPD, and ZPD is all about coregulation among participants and opportunity; however, the ZPD is not by definition healthy and helpful to the learner. Coregulation in the ZPD may enhance or impede students' adaptive learning; in either case, the individual mediates these relationships. Participation in the mutual regulation of the ZPD does not supplant the individual; it renders the individual more attuned to cultural participation and thus, theoretically and ideally, enabled to make a cultural contribution.

OPPORTUNITY, ACTIVITY, AND IDENTITY FORMATION:
FOUR RESEARCH ILLUSTRATIONS

Abbreviated illustrations from four research programs are presented to suggest the utility of a Vygotskian approach to understanding student motivation. These illustrations, like the historical presentation and modern representations, have been selected from previous publications. Interested readers can locate the original work in the appended references.

1. TASK DIFFICULTY, SOLVING PROBLEMS,
AND LEARNER BELIEFS

In this series of studies on adaptive learning, opportunity was defined by math tasks of varied difficulty, the activity of interest was problem solving, and identity formation focused on student beliefs about themselves as learners. Studies represented here varied in method, such that students spontaneously reported on their general beliefs about what they say to themselves in differing task conditions (Rohrkemper & Bershon, 1984), used a thought-matching procedure in specific, just-completed problem solving (Rohrkemper, 1986), participated in a structured interview of beliefs about fictional classmates' ability and motivation (Rohrkemper, 1985), discussed their experiences guided by a structured questionnaire (Rohrkemper et al., 1983), or engaged in think-aloud problem solving interviews (McCaslin Rohrkemper, 1989). Reported self-directive inner speech served as core data in each study.

Reported Self-Directive Inner Speech

Affective and intellectual cognition were represented by categorizing reported inner speech as self-involved or task-involved inner speech. Task-involved inner speech reflected student control over the task through reported algorithms, problem-solving strategies, solutions, or modification of the task representation. Students reported task-involved inner speech shared common elements within classrooms, which was expected given the teacher/instructional origins of problem-solving strategies. Self-involved inner speech proved much more complicated. Self-involved inner speech ideally is about control over the self through enhancing motivational and affective support of one's activity. Theoretically, these self-statements can be judged positive ("Congratulate your brains!") or negative ("I can't do this") (Rohrkemper & Bershon, 1984), but in reality students' reported self-involved inner speech was much more complex, varied, and difficult to judge.

Task Difficulty and Problem-Solving Activity

Vygotsky predicted self-directive inner speech in nonautomatic "effortful" cognition and suggested that it would be both affectively and "intellectually" charged. Affectively charged inner speech was considered self-involved in that opportunities for automatic and nonautomatic, effortful cognition in this research program were represented by math problems identified by the classroom teacher as most apt to be of high, moderate, and low difficulty (thought to afford highly effortful, moderately effortful, and essentially automatic problem solving) for participating students. Case studies of student problem-solving-in-progress were the most informative for understanding the role of problem difficulty in affording the integration of the affective and intellectual in self-directive inner speech. In this study, students engaged in process-tracing interviews during problem solving. Of all the methods used in this research program, only this procedure would likely meet Vygotsky's approval for capturing inner speech and even that is likely confounded by the interview situation. Turning words into thoughts with an attentive listener likely differs from self-direction in solitude in important ways; however, classrooms are not private places and thinking aloud for a teacher is fairly common practice.

Students perceive problem difficulty somewhat differently than their teachers. Teacher beliefs (and researcher hypothesis) about what would "objectively" be relatively hard or moderate math problems, based on curriculum coverage and particular student achievement, did not result in the expected inner speech reports. Students reportedly experience moderately difficult problems—those problems that they think they should know, but do not—as the most difficult. As one student reported: "I don't believe we just did this and I don't know how to do it" (McCaslin Rohrkemper, 1989, p. 161). It appears that recognizing a problem as familiar can increase its demand characteristics, which increases anxiety, which makes reasonable problem-solving strategies even more accountable—and illusive. This suggests that moderately difficult problems may afford optimal opportunities for enacting and enhancing students' task- and self-involved inner speech. That is, (subjectively) moderate difficult problems may be an essential feature of an optimizing ZPD. These are opportunities for integration of the affective and intellectual in consciousness; hence, these are opportunities for the development and display of "adaptive learning" within the students' ZPD. Subsequent research (to be described) appears to challenge this conclusion, however, and suggests instead that the challenge of new work is a more informative feature of an optimizing ZPD in classroom learning.

In contrast, teacher-defined difficult problems were perceived by students as too difficult, and not taken all that seriously. Too-difficult problems apparently reside outside the student's ZPD, at least in research contexts that include resources like textbooks but lack personal instruction. The same student who struggled to solve familiar but unsolved problems simply noted she had no idea on the objectively difficult ones. With this realization, she transformed objectively difficult problems into something else, settling for "done" rather than striving for correctness—a strategy that can be adaptive. Constructs like "mastery orientation" based on students' dogged persistence when confronted with insolvable tasks or uninformative failure are not by definition optimal nor adaptive in this perspective. Adaptive learning is all about judgments of relative worth, knowing when you need help, and when it is time to quit and do something else.

Finally, student behavior in conditions of easy problems aligned with expectations. Students solve problems they consider easy automatically. These problems may increase habit strength, but they do not increase mindfulness, the conscious awareness and enhancement of effortful cognition, and harnessing of one's motivation and emotion. For example, in this condition our problem-solver reported no inner speech at all, but noted these problems were boring "because I already know them. And sometimes I like to move on."

Taken together, these data support activity theorists' (e.g., Wertsch, 1985, p. 208) assertion that "tool-mediated goal-directed action" is the basic unit of psychological analysis. Reported inner speech differentially mediates tasks and tasks differentially mediate reported inner speech. Moderately difficult tasks appear to provide especially fruitful opportunities. They require and challenge the integration and enhancement of the affective and the intellectual in the mediation of goal-directed action. Moderately difficult tasks are opportunities to promote adaptive learning, in part because students impose an expectation of successful solution on familiar but not automatic tasks. Students invest in them.

Task Difficulty and Learner Beliefs

Across studies, students' beliefs about themselves as learners and their likely approach to solving problems portrayed students who were more confronted *by* tasks than *confronting* tasks. In general, students reported similar relationships between task difficulty and self-involved inner speech in their approach to problem solving. Namely, for most students, subjectively difficult problems are frustrating and stressful. Students' strategic self-involved inner speech within that general self-knowledge differed in instructive ways, however. Consider these examples of two sixth-grade girls' reports of their typical self-involved inner speech in stressful situations—in this case due either to the frustration of difficulty or the tedium of boredom—reported in McCaslin Rohrkemper (1989):

> A lot of times I get sick of things so I just want to stop. And I do . . . I always, whenever I'm working and I just get sick of working and I just stop because I can't stand it anymore. I think of things that are, I like to do. Like in school, I'm going to play with my friends. I think, "Um, all the things that are fun that we do, and stuff. But I have to get this done and *right* before I can go and do that."

Compared with:

> Well, I think I'm going to get them all wrong. And I kind of feel like I have to get up and walk around and think about it. I feel like I have to stop and work on something else for a little bit. I might get up and work on spelling for a minute 'cause that's pretty easy and I don't have to think about it, 'cause spelling I just know the answers and they're right there. I can think about the math and what I'm going to do. . . . [It's time for a break] when I get pretty frustrated and think to myself you can't do this and I start tearing, I start biting my pencil then I know I have to get up and do something else. I just I get so frustrated with it I can't think. . . . I start to fiddle with my hands, go like that. I know I have to do something else. 'Cause I really get mad. I don't take a real long [break] time, maybe just ten minutes. Then I come back to work again. Just to get it out of my mind for a minute. (p. 155)

These students are classmates. The interviews occurred during the spring semester of sixth grade. Their reports capture the variation in students' reported self-involved inner speech when confronting stressful learning. They suggest that students uniquely mediate and negotiate stressful learning as part of their participation in classroom work. Participation in this classroom apparently promotes a common commitment to task completion; how individuals negotiate that commitment has important implications for coregulation of emergent identity.

Reported inner speech is aligned with student beliefs about themselves as learners. These studies renewed an interest in the social origins of student beliefs about themselves as students that I had explored previously in research on classroom management. The emphasis of the earlier work was on the influence of teacher socialization style, defined as predictability of teacher behavior and explanation of that behavior in classroom management systems, on (a) student self- and other-understandings and (b) the relationships among these understandings and reported emotion and behavior (Rohrkemper, 1984, 1985).

2. CLASSROOM MANAGEMENT, LEARNING RESPONSIBILITY, AND CITIZENSHIP

Wertsch and Stone (1985) coined the term "emergent interaction" to capture the mediation and internalization of interpersonal relationships and opportunities within a Vygotskian perspective. McCaslin and Murdock (1991) elaborated upon emergent interaction to highlight the unique integration of multiple social/instructional environments in students' experiences within the context of unfolding developmental processes and understandings. In this perspective, internalization is inherently social; it blurs the distinction between self and other. The individual is a part of the perceived social world; thus self-knowledge is not independent of knowledge of others. Emergent interaction asserts that self-knowledge is an ongoing process that is uniquely negotiated, integrated, and reconstructed through interpersonal engagement and meaningful opportunity. In the language of activity theory, self-knowledge is all about "tool-mediated, goal-directed, activity."

One implication of this perspective is that what mainstream American psychology may consider characteristic of individuals, a Vygotskian theorist would consider a continuous negotiation between cultural-, other-, and self-knowledge. Attribution theory, for example, presents a theory about individuals' answers to "why" questions about events and persons in their lives. Individuals' answers or causal ascriptions can be understood by the dimensional understandings that underlie them. It is the underlying attributional dimensions that predict self and other affect and behavior (see Weiner, Chapter 2, this volume). As many as five attributional dimensions have been studied: locus of causality, stability (over time), globality (over situations), controllability (in general), and intentionality (in this instance) (e.g., Abramson, Seligman, & Teasdale, 1978; Carrol & Payne, 1977; Weiner, 1986). Attributional dimensions combine into three categories of judgments individuals can make: source, constancy, and responsibility that inform how they think, feel, and behave.

Consider the occasion of a friend's rejection. Attribution theory predicts that, painful as it is, the individual will ask, "Why did my friend not want to be with me?" Let's assume the answer is "because we don't have good stuff to play with at my house." The importance of that answer to an attribution theorist lies in the attributional understandings it represents. In this case, the speaker likely believes that the reason for the rejection is internal in locus of cause (my family is poor), constant, that is, it is stable over time and generalized over situations ("We are and always will be poor"), and not her responsibility, that is, it is uncontrollable and unintentional ("My mom can't get a good job"). Attribution theory would predict these understandings lead to shame, sadness, and withdrawal of the rejected friend.

In the Vygotskian perspective, these personal beliefs and behavior are understood as a result of the emergent interaction between the developing individual and opportunities to learn the interpersonal rules of the culture. Cultural rules become personally meaningful. Rohrkemper (1984, 1985) studied these dynamics within the context of elementary school classrooms of teachers known for their management expertise, but who differed in management style. Socioeconomic status (and therefore typical language patterns at home [Hess, 1970; Kohn, 1977]) of the elementary schools was balanced so that half of the students in each type of teacher management system were from lower-class and half from middle-class neighborhoods. Half of the classroom teachers enacted a highly verbal, explanatory management system based on intention; the other half enacted a highly predictable, rule-driven management system based on behavior. Rohrkemper conceptualized teaching as a manifestation of culturally sanctioned helping behavior; hence, classroom management was considered an especially potent vehicle for teaching sociocutural roles and rules associated with helping, neglecting, or punishing behavior. These constructs are illustrated in research on the potential of classroom management to teach cultural rules of interpersonal and personal responsibility. In this study, opportunity is defined by the type of classroom management system used by expert teachers; the activity of interest is student learning about responsibility and societal expectations for affect, behavior, and fairness; and the focus of identity development is citizenship.

In brief, results suggested that student learning of sociocultural roles and rules of responsible behavior was most meaningfully organized by their teacher's management style, especially in interaction with student developmental level: Younger students were more influenced by teacher management style than their older peers. Individual differences among students (which ranged from a continuum of problem students to those who were easy and pleasurable to teach) were the least useful in organizing student reports, with one exception: hyperactive students. Most notably, student-reported understandings illustrated the power of the social language environment established by the teacher in student prediction and understanding of and response to peer behavior that "objectively" represented behavior across the responsibility continuum. Students whose teachers focused on rationales for their rules and expectations evidenced attributional knowledge in their predictions consistent with cultural principles for responsibility. In comparison, students of teachers who focused on behavior and consequences primarily focused on behavior and consequence rules in their predictions. These students were better predictors of teacher behavior than students in highly explanatory classrooms.

Developmental Differences

Teacher management systems interacted with student developmental level in student understandings. Of all participants, younger students in management classrooms based on behavior exhibited the least understanding of attributional principles that our culture employs and expects individuals to use in self-control and the interpretation and judgment of others. In contrast, younger students in management classrooms based on explanations of intention displayed attributional understandings aligned with that of older students in both types of management style classrooms. These data mesh nicely with Vygotsky's notions of the ZPD: teacher explanations for behavior and expectations and rationales for discipline scaffolded younger students' interpersonal understanding beyond the level of understanding associated with their developmental level. These students' teachers were able to meaningfully connect cultural norms about responsibility and accountability at a higher level of understanding than the everyday understandings and behavior–consequence experiences of their students. These teachers transformed the routines that managing groups of students allows into opportunities for explicit instruction and modeling of interpersonal expectations consistent with cultural norms of responsibility. Student negotiation of cultural expectations in these classrooms was particularly evident in their use of attributional principles within the context of differentiated perspectives. Students, it turns out, have to negotiate two points of view simultaneously—if they are to be in both teacher and peer good graces—and can do so within the cultural framework of responsibility. These data suggest the viability of mediation within the ZPD that can enrich cultural understandings and empower individuals beyond the affordances of their personal development.

Students in behavior management classrooms knew the rules and how their teacher would respond to student problem behavior; they were more attuned to prediction than interpretation. Younger students in these management conditions were markedly unaware of attributional interpretations important for understanding responsibility and accountability. In a Vygotskian perspective, responsive contingency—a basic tenet of behaviorism—is essential to the development of higher psychological processes because it enables prediction of predictable events (McCaslin & Hickey, 2001). Prediction of sequences of student behavior–teacher response and student behavior–student response in this perspective lays the foundation for subsequent learning of cultural rules of responsibility, which older students in these management conditions do exhibit. It is useful to note that prediction of behavior sequences does not imply understanding of the underlying cultural structure that renders those sequences meaningful. This seems especially important when considering the possible effects of modern school-wide management systems that stress rules and consequences. They may well overestimate student cultural understandings of control, intent, and responsibility and hence, inappropriately hold students accountable for as-yet-unrealized understanding of cultural attributional principles.

Individual Differences

Individual differences among students to emerge in this study were mostly absent. Students who were targets of teacher management directives and those who presumably seldom, if ever, directly experienced the downside of classroom management policies similarly understood the sociocultural roles and rules of their classrooms. The one exception to these common understandings concerns hyperactive students. Hyperactive students were noted for the discrepancy between their beliefs about hyperactivity—and thus, the appropriate affective and behavioral response to it—and the beliefs and responses of their peers. Hyperactive students attributed hyperactivity to uncontrollable and unintentional actions and expected the support that that judgment demands in our culture. In contrast, these students' classmates considered hyperactivity controllable and intentional; thus, a blamable and punishable offense.

It appears that there is much common ground in negotiation and integration of cultural understandings within classrooms and classrooms are communities that can differ in important ways. Developmental differences among students were more potent than categories of individual differences among them, with little exception. Both seem submerged beneath the context of teacher management/socialization style. In this arena—the opportunity to learn about cultural responsibility and societal expectations for citizenship via classroom management—the context is the more meaningful unit of analysis with minor exception. Unless, of course, you are one of the exceptions (i.e., hyperactive).

Individual negotiation of acculturation and individuation may be better illustrated with case studies of individual identity formation rather than the development of group/cultural functioning with group comparison research designs. Vygotsky did not study identity formation directly; however, recent work on identity has found this perspective quite useful.

3. PARENTING STYLES, CHILDREN'S EMERGENT IDENTITY, AND PERSONAL COMMITMENTS

Penuel and Wertsch (1995) advanced identity formation within a sociocultural perspective that aligned closely with Erikson's (1968) notions of identity development. Erikson, like Vygosky, embedded sociocultural, historical, and psychological contexts in his psychosocial theory of development. Penual and Wertsch argued that human action is the starting point of identity formation. This assertion also is compatible with Erikson's stage progression wherein the crisis of "industry or inferiority" precedes the identity crisis stage. What we do—the opportunities we engage—are intimately related to what we value and to whom we make commitments.

McCaslin and Murdock (1991) illustrated the evolving dynamics of emergent interaction through a case study comparison of a sixth-grade Hispanic male, "Julio," and his classmate, a white female, "Nora." Julio and Nora's case comparisons add to the literature that some social/instructional environments (SIE) are more supportive, informative, and appropriately challenging than others; and some combinations of home and school SIE are more congruent than others (Corno, 1989; Heath, 1982). McCaslin and Murdock argued that understanding the prior and ongoing influences of home (and other SIE in a child's experience, e.g., child care, school, friends) are part of understanding the values, goals and self-regulation students enact in school (p. 216). Home influence is represented with parent beliefs about child autonomy and managerial style. Students' home learning was expected to influence their mediation of school such that student participation in classroom opportunities was expected to illustrate unique coregulation processes. Student resource management—their own and others'—were of particular interest. Help-seeking and self-reliance in school were considered for manifestations of home learning mediating school opportunities and doing homework was considered one manifestation of school learning at home.

Student Background

Julio and Nora's families occupy the same socioeconomic status (SES) category. Both are children of two high school educated (or GED-certified) working-parent families of similar income. They differ in home language. Julio's parents speak Spanish as a first language. Julio's mother has very limited English proficiency; Julio's father is bilingual and stresses spoken English with his children. Nora's family is English-speaking only. Both students have one (Julio) or more (Nora) younger siblings, home responsibilities, and parents who keep up with and care about their school performance. Julio's father and Nora's mother went to considerable lengths involving rearranged work schedules and child care to participate in this study.

Julio and (especially) Nora perform relatively well on standardized tests of academic achievement. In April of their sixth-grade year, test results in math were strong for both Julio and Nora (Julio: grade equivalent 8.4, national percentile 86; Nora: grade equivalent 9.0, national percentile 93). Reading scores differed notably. Julio's achievement in reading measured a grade equivalent of 7.3, national percentile of 60; Nora scored a grade equivalent of 8.5, national percentile of 81. Although the subject matter of interest in these case studies was problem solving in math, language facility is clearly a relevant issue. So, too, is the emergent capacity for self-regulation learned at home.

Parenting Style

Parenting styles research has generally been conducted within the perspective that parents are the authorities whose task it is to manage their children (e.g., Baumrind, 1971, 1987). This perspective differs considerably from the Vygotskian premise of mutual or coregulation in the ZPD between expert parent and novice child. Even so, constructs from the parenting styles literature provide a useful framework for understanding differences in the approach to childrearing in the homes of Julio and Nora that inform the personal resources for self-regulation each brings to school.

Parent management of children is primarily about their approach toward emergent child autonomy and child involvement in rules and explanations. The approach to management in both Julio's and Nora's homes involves a certain level of authoritarianism. In general, authoritarian parents exert considerable control over decision making and their children. A child's emergent capabilities and capacities for independence are typically not part of the control equation.

Although both Julio's and Nora's homes include authoritarian parenting, they differ in important ways. Julio's parents exhibit "authoritative-restrictive" parenting; in contrast, Nora's parents implement a "traditional" parenting style (Baumrind, 1987). The difference between these approaches is about eventual recognition of and structural support for children's emergent self-regulation and independence as they get older. Authoritarian-restrictive families keep their children in a role subordinate to the parent; they do not share power or loosen controls as the child develops. Authoritarian-restrictive parents continue to tell the child who he/she is and what that means.

Traditional families also have a strong belief system that they inculcate in their children early on through authoritarian approaches in an attempt to ensure later identity as a family member. They differ from authoritarian-restrictive parents when they extend increasing authority to their children consistent with their emerging ability to take responsibility. Traditional parents do this to enable self-discipline rather than sheer control by others (e.g., parents, peers). Traditional parents do not keep children in a subordinate role; as children reach certain "markers" (for Nora, babysitting younger siblings after school), child autonomy and privileges increase.

Neither authoritarian-restrictive nor traditional homes are necessarily punitive. However, in Julio's authoritarian-restrictive home, when punishment occurs, it is linked to something he did or did not do—overt behavior. In contrast, in Nora's traditional home, punishment is all about perceived intention and failure to take responsibility. These differences in punishment criteria are similar to differences in instructional features of teacher classroom management systems in the research described previously. Recall that teacher management systems were especially powerful with younger children's developing understandings but less so with older students. Julio's and Nora's case studies hint at the dynamics of continuous mediation of rules of conduct and responsibility in home learning that appear to matter in their negotiation of school.

Julio

Julio: Home learning in school. In Julio's home you are judged by your actions. You are expected to respect and obey your parents. Beliefs about learning also are based on what you apparently do: work or misbehave. If you work you learn; if you misbehave you don't. In school the telling is in the grades. Good behavior gets good grades. And Julio did get good grades until now. His first-grade teacher predicted high achievement and college in his future. Father holds onto those predictions for sixth-grader Julio and reacts quickly and decisively at any suggestion that Julio is "falling off track" to success in college and a good job. Home learning hasn't changed over the years, but what it means to learn in school has. The obedience strategies required at home that initially were useful in school no longer serve Julio well in sixth grade. His teacher considers his "good boy" help-seeking strategies immature. She expects a certain level of self-regulation and self-reliance from sixth-grade students and suspects Julio's questions are disingenuous if not passive-aggressive. Julio believes he works hard and is confused when that is not good enough. He does what he is told to do, asks for help if he needs it, and is gratified when the teacher says his work is right. It has not occurred to Julio that it could be wrong to ask for help or that he should evaluate his work on his own. Home learning is not helping sixth-grade Julio negotiate school as his parents and Julio expect; however, neither is school helping Julio negotiate at home.

Julio: School learning at home. In Julio's family, homework is an important bridge between the authority of home and school. Homework sessions at the kitchen table demonstrate parent commitment to student learning and extra homework assignments given by the teacher or requested by the parents are evidence of a "united front" between home and school should Julio even think differently. The problem with homework for Julio, however, is that he cannot get appropriate help at home. And Julio believes he needs time and work and help if he is to get things right. Obediently trying to do homework at home isn't good enough for the criteria at school. Julio's willing parents are not capable students; thus, extra homework meant to teach a lesson, whether it be academic or disciplinary, often does neither. Instead, Julio typically returns to school with homework judged careless and wrong. He responds with frustration and anger. Parents are contacted and the extra-homework-united-front cycle continues. More than errors are practiced in this process.

Nora

Nora: Home learning in school. In Nora's home you are your commitments; you are valued for striving, for doing the best you can to meet them. Nora's home learning is all about being responsible and setting priorities. It begins with effort and organization. Effort is all about thinking through and following through, and being organized protects priorities that are essential to meeting commitments. Innate ability is not particularly valued at home. The fact that Nora learns easily troubles her mother who would prefer that Nora had to "work a little harder at it." Home learning serves Nora very well in school. She doesn't need much study to succeed in sixth grade, but Nora keeps that to herself. Nora hides her considerable talents behind displays of effort. When Nora does confront difficult tasks and failure, however, she knows what to do about it. Nora reconfigures task failure as an opportunity for increased effort and different strategies, which she believes will ultimately be successful. Failure for Nora is transitional, not the final word. Effortful successes are the small wins she brings home; Nora does not talk about learning easily. Like Julio, Nora presents herself at school as the child raised at home. She is effortful and responsible and meets commitments. Her teacher tells Mother what an enjoyable child she is. Home learning serves Nora well in school, even though Nora is not able to acknowledge her considerable ability for school learning.

Nora: School learning at home. In Nora's home, homework is just one more responsibility. Occasionally Nora fails to meet that responsibility. Mother does not intervene in the school consequences that result or in Nora's feeling bad about them. Nora responds to an F with resetting priorities, getting better organized, and working on it. An F on homework or long-term projects to Nora is not so much a "Failure to learn" as it is an Incomplete or a "Failure to get started in time." She knows how to fix that.

Teacher Mediation of Julio and Nora

Home learning is an essential feature of school learning for both students and school learning enters their homes. Teacher beliefs about Julio and Nora are part of this coregulation. Recall these students' test performance data. His teacher describes Julio as relatively low in ability and mixed in his motivation to learn: sometimes he seems overwhelmed, doesn't care, or gives up, but mostly he "endures." Julio's report card grades mostly covary judgments of achievement with displayed effort. Overall, Julio is judged an effortful B student whose grades dip to a C when improvement in effort is needed or surge to an A with evidence of outstanding effort. Satisfactory ratings of Julio's "personal growth" in the first two quarters were replaced with "needs improvement" in the last two. Julio's report card appears to support the maxims of home learning. If Julio worked harder, he would be (more) successful and his personal growth scores are all about getting off track.

Nora's teacher believes that she is a moderate-ability learner who is positively motivated and "enjoys" schoolwork. Report card grades reveal an A student whose effort is judged outstanding throughout the year. Nora's personal growth scores changed from a single "satisfactory" in the first marking period to all "outstanding" ratings. Nora's report card supports home learning. Both home and school agree that Nora is an outstandingly effortful and, hence, successful student.

Recall Julio and Nora's standardized test performance data. These data differ from teacher beliefs. They also are limited in their representations of Julio and Nora as students and what that means for them. Julio and Nora each have internalized the value of effort promoted at home. Their homes differ in what effort means and how it is known. In Julio's home, effort is known *by* the outcome; in Nora's home, effort *is* the outcome. Julio and Nora have mediated home beliefs about effort uniquely. For Julio, effort is endurance, staying on track; for Nora effort includes monitoring and modifying one's efforts. Both students want to achieve in school; however, their constructions of what that means and the self-regulatory skills they bring to it differ in ways that likely will continue to increase the discrepancy between their successes in school. Home learning coregulates student negotiation of the opportunities of school, their mediation of activities and commitments, and the validation of the person they might become. Students participate in a shared classroom life; it is an important opportunity in their emergent identity, but it does not obviate that identity.

4. CURRICULUM TASKS, LEARNING MOTIVATION, AND MUTUAL VALIDATION

One outcome of appreciating Julio and Nora was an interest in how students negotiate the world of peer relationships, especially around ability conceptions, within the expectations of classroom learning and behavior. The result was an emphasis on emergent identity concerning peer relationships, especially within a hierarchical school system, namely, tracking. A focus on peers shifted attention from the social origins of emergent identity afforded by research with the adults in students' lives to a notion of continuous coregulation of activity and consciousness among peers.

McCaslin and Burross (2002) explored the motivational linkages between activity and identity development among early adolescent students who, in terms of personal development, are particularly vulnerable to identity struggles. In this study, opportunity was defined as curriculum tasks, the activity of interest was learning motivation, and identity formation was informed through validation within track placement. An experience-sampling journal method (Csikszentmihalyi & Larson, 1984) was used to study seventh-grade students' ($N = 158$) adjustment to junior high school. The data described here concern the function of track placement in students' reported achievement motivation and apparent emergent identity.

In addition to being a major school transition in terms of sheer size and number of students, this also was students' first exposure to systemic ability tracking. We considered that, although students are novices in new learning (and in negotiating this new context), they are experts in understanding the implicit demands and unique contingencies of curriculum tasks (e.g., "review" suggests that this task should be known). We expected these understandings to coregulate student motivation and emotion. Thus, we considered the possibility that curriculum task demands serve as opportunities for both learning curriculum content—the intended goal—and for learning motivation—as yet an unintended goal. In the language of scaffolding in the ZPD, we viewed learning curriculum content as the surface level of the curriculum tasks and learning motivation as the deeper level of understanding.

When viewed as basic coregulation opportunities for the learning and enhancement of students' motivational dynamics, curriculum tasks are involved in motivating student learning and in students learning motivation. This is because they provide students with basic motivational opportunities in which to learn and practice their motivational knowledge, skill, and affect. Curriculum opportunity, then, is a primary vehicle for teaching and learning motivation. Motivation requires meaningful opportunity, both for arousal and for practice learning motivation. Differential learning opportunities have been associated with track placements; we wondered if motivational opportunities also might differ.

We have seen that motivation is part of emergent identity; thus, it is historical. It may be expressed in the present moment but it is linked to the individual's past and informs her future. Coregulation of motivation and opportunity contribute to developing motive dispositions and skills. Developing motive dispositions inform what we value and to what and whom we make commitments; that is, motive dispositions inform student identity, including the development and display of motivational competence. Motivation also involves the community that participates in and validates personal striving and commitments. We were especially interested in the possibility of differential opportunity and validation associated with participation in unique track placements.

Student-reported motivation to engage curriculum tasks was captured within an expectancy value framework—the perceived value of a task in relation to perceived ability to complete it. For nine days in October, when signaled to do so, students completed journal entries that included identifying the type of task in which they were engaged (free time, discussion, new work, practice, review, test) and ratings on two scales designed to tap student expectancy for, and two to tap student value of, that task. Task difficulty ratings represented student expectation for success and student confidence in procedural knowledge ratings—knowing "what" to do—represented student efficacy. We included both self-assessments because previous research has convinced us that, while not all students are concerned with being successful or avoiding failure, most are concerned with knowing how to go about doing assignments (Rohrkemper & Bershon, 1984). There are a lot of tasks on a given day and at times it is enough just to get them done. Student ratings of how much they liked the engaged task and their subject experience of time passing represented the value the student held for the task. Although we did not expect flow-like experiences (Czikszentmihalyi, 1999), we thought it reasonable to augment student-reported liking with time/task immersion to represent student value of the curriculum tasks they engage.

Student Curriculum Expertise and Motivation

Overall, student reports validated their expert knowledge of curriculum task demands and differential task demands coregulated student-reported motivation. Student expectations for success were distinct from valuing that success. Students valued new work of perceived relative difficulty and they were up to the challenge of new learning. Practice reports indicated that the initial repetition of new work—the learning by doing part of new learning—is as good as it gets in curriculum tasks. Student reports in practice opportunities were the most "mastery-" and "flow"-like of their reported curriculum experiences (ignoring free time).

We suspect that new work is the curriculum opportunity that best connects with students' achievement disposition, which results in motivation that directs and energizes practice learning and with it the satisfaction of mastery. New learning and practice opportunities appear to function as "approach" motivational conditions. They allow the opportunity for students to see and enjoy themselves at their motivational best.

In contrast, student reports when engaged in review for, and then taking, tests suggest that students are no longer motivated in the manner

coregulated by new learning. Now perceived difficulties co-occur with relative dislike and time in slow motion—not the coregulation of expectancy
and value likely to enhance motivated test performance or the promotion
of a positive motivational identity. Rather, review and testing opportunities
appear to function as "avoidance" motivational conditions. They allow
opportunities for students to learn about themselves at motivational disadvantage when the difficulty harnessing the motive to achieve renders the
task even more difficult.

The struggle for competence within a Vygotskian perspective is all about
the conflict of opposites—the headiness of success and the dread of failure—and their transcendence. Our learner must know the motivational
dynamics of success and failure if she is to become an adaptive learner who
maintains self-confidence and realistic self-appraisals. The role of opportunity in the coregulation of motivational competence—the proportion of
approach and avoidance curriculum opportunities that might promote an
adaptive motivational identity—is one feature of the school curriculum yet
to be fully mined.

Track placement and motivational identity. Erikson (1968) proposed that
the major developmental crisis for this age group is the struggle between
industry and inferiority—taking chances and risking failure—that is
resolved with beliefs about personal competence. In the language of activity theory, identity begins with activity. We have suggested that curriculum
opportunity is essential for learning motivation and informing identity. In
schools that use tracking to group students of similar achievement, track
placement is all about learner identity. Track placement may play an even
greater role in the development of student identity if it is associated with
different kinds of curriculum opportunity.

The new work and practice opportunities that students value and find
energizing were differentially available across tracks in this study, even
though teachers taught multiple tracks. The lowest track (in this study, i.e.,
track six of eight in the school) and highest track classes had the most
exposure to new work and practice opportunities, but the lowest track valued them more. More than all students, track six students reportedly experienced a personally challenging curriculum that they enjoyed. These
students had more opportunities to learn about themselves confronting
and overcoming task challenge with mastery than did their peers.

A within-track analysis revealed that reported expectancy is most appropriate for understanding—and differentiating—the motivation of students
with a history of relatively high or low achievement. High-achieving students appear to resolve the developmental competence dilemma Erikson
described by valuing the curriculum opportunities that reaffirm their talents—not exactly the balance of success and failure that promotes adaptive
learning. In contrast, low-achieving students value difficult task opportunities in which they display effort. Low-achieving students know about failure

and appear to resolve the competence dilemma through display of what they can control: effort.

Expectancy value reports did not meaningfully capture the motivation of middle track—moderate ability—students. This is not particularly surprising, given the extreme-group comparison origins of achievement motivation research and theory. There are more moderate ability learners among us than not, however, and we would do well to learn more about their motivational identities. Tracking systems and the curriculum opportunities that they provide are not connecting with these students' motivational identities. This seems an especially important area for further study if we are to optimally coregulate the majority of our students so that they might become adaptive learners who value achievement and make socially meaningful contributions to their future.

OPPORTUNITY, ACTIVITY, AND IDENTITY: CLOSING COMMENTS

One goal in writing this chapter was to make a case for the individual within a sociocultural approach to the study of student motivation. Research illustrations of the emergent interaction of opportunity and interpersonal validation that coregulates the activities individuals engage and come to value (or not) was presented. Four strands of research were represented. The importance of opportunity was prominent in each research strand; interpersonal validation, when studied, was compelling. The most convincing case for the centrality of the individual in understanding student motivation is the study of the coregulation of home and school for Julio and Nora. The least compelling case for the individual arguably emerged from the tracking study of curriculum opportunity. In this latter study, similar to the study on classroom management systems, between-classroom differences are the more powerful organizer of student reports. It is useful to distinguish the apparent source of the interpersonal validation within them, however. Teachers' classroom management systems organize students' understandings of cultural roles and rules. In contrast, classroom peers appear to mutually validate each others' motivational dynamics.

Taken together, the four studies suggest that a useful distinction might be made between the "being a student" part of schooling—the one who understands classroom management expectations and the demands of curriculum tasks—and the "being a learner" part of schooling—the one who harnesses motivation, confronts difficult tasks, and brings home learning to school. At minimum, it seems that some opportunities in school afford the integration of student and learner roles. It is important that all students have the opportunity to lose themselves in tasks that challenge them.

New work challenge appears to promote optimal motivational self-knowledge while it furthers curricular goals. New work and its mastery are the essential achieving opportunities of classrooms. I suspect that it is from these opportunities—if they connect with student emergent identity and motive disposition and result in an array of relative success and failure outcomes that are validated by valued others—that students will learn to trust themselves when faced with the challenges of failure and the seduction of success. Mindful acculturation of motivated achievement for the promotion of the social good seems an important outcome of schooling. A sociocultural approach toward realization of that goal is promising.

REFERENCES

Abramson, L. V., Seligman, M. E. P., & Teasdale, J. D. (1978). Learned helplessness in humans: Critique and reformulation. *Journal of Abnormal Psychology, 87,* 49–74.

Baumrind, D. (1971). Current patterns of parental authority. *Developmental Psychology Monographs, 4*(No. 1, Part 2).

Baumrind, D. (1987). A developmental perspective on adolescent risk taking in contemporary America. In. C. Irwin, Jr. (Ed.), *Adolescent social behavior and health.* San Francisco: Jossey Bass.

Carroll, J. S., & Payne, J. W. (1977). Judgments about crime and the criminal: A model and a method for investigating parole decisions. In B. D. Sales (Ed.), *Prospectives in law and psychology. Vol. 1: The criminal justice system.* New York: Plenum Press.

Corno, L. (1989). What it means to be literate about classrooms. In D. Bloome (Ed.), *Learning to use literacy in educational settings.* Norwood, NJ: Ablex.

Czikszentmihalyi, M. (1999). If we are so rich, why aren't we happy? *American Psychologist, 54,* 821–827.

Czikszentmihalyi, M., & Larson, R. (1984). *Being adolescent.* New York: Basic Books.

Engels, F. (1890). Socialism: Utopian and scientific. In R. C. Tucker (Ed.), (1972). *The Marx-Engels reader* (pp. 605–639). New York: Norton.

Erikson, E. (1968). *Identity: Youth and crisis.* New York: Norton.

Gray, J. (1966). Attention, consciousness, and voluntary control of behavior in Soviet psychology. In N. O'Connor (Ed.), *Present-day Russian psychology* (pp. 1–38). London: Pergamon.

Heath, S. B. (1982). Questioning at home and at school: A comparative study. In G. Spindler (Ed.), *Doing the ethnography of schooling.* New York: Holt, Rinehart, and Winston.

Hegel, G. W. F. (1949). *The phenomenology of the mind.* London: G. Allen & Unwin. (Original work published 1807)

Hess, R. (1970). Social class and ethnic influences upon socialization. In P. Mussen (Ed.), *Carmichael's manual of child psychology* (3rd ed., Vol. 2). New York: Wiley.

Kohn, M. (1977). *Class and conformity* (2nd ed.). Chicago: University of Chicago Press.

Kozulin, A. (1986). The concept of activity in Soviet psychology: Vygotsky, his disciples, and critics. *American Psychologist, 41,* 264–274.

Leontiev, A. N. (1974–1975, Winter). The problem of activity in Soviet psychology. *Soviet Psychology,* 4–33.

Leontiev, A. N. (1978). *Activity, consciousness, and personality.* Englewood Cliffs, NJ: Prentice Hall.

Leontiev, A. N., & Luria, A. R. (1968). The psychological ideas of L. S. Vygotsky. In B. B. Wolman (Ed.), *Historical roots of contemporary psychology* (pp. 338–367). New York: Harper & Row.

Luria, A. R. (1969). Speech development and the formation of mental processes. In M. Cole & L. Maltzman (Eds.), *A handbook of contemporary Soviet psychology* (pp. 121–162). New York: Basic Books.

Luria, A. R. (1979). *The making of mind: A personal account of Soviet psychology* (M. Cole & S. Cole, Eds.). Cambridge, MA: Harvard University Press.

Marx, K. (1972). *Capital.* In R.C. Tucker (Ed.), *The Marx-Engels reader* (pp. 191–327). New York: Norton.

McCaslin Rohrkemper, M. (1989) Self-regulated learning and academic achievement: A Vygotskian view. In B. Zimmerman & D. Schunk (Eds.), *Self-regulated learning and academic achievement: Theory, research and practice* (pp. 143–168). New York: Springer.

McCaslin, M., & Burross, H. L. (2002*). Expectancy-value relationships in 7th grade students' understandings of curriculum tasks: Learning motivation.* Manuscript submitted for publication.

McCaslin, M., & Hickey, D. T. (2001). Educational psychology, social constructivism, and educational practice: A case of emergent identity. *Educational Psychologist, 36,* 133–140.

McCaslin, M., & Murdock, T. B. (1991). The emergent interaction of home and school in the development of students' adaptive learning. In M. L. Maehr & P. R. Pintrich (Eds.), *Advances in motivation and achievement* (pp. 213–259). Greenwich, CT: JAI Press.

Pavlov, I. (1927). *Conditioedl reflexes.* London: Oxford University Press.

Penuel, W. R., & Wertsch, J. V. (1995). Vygotsky and identity information: A sociocultural approach. *Educational Psychologist, 30,* 215–234.

Rohrkemper, M. (1984). The influence of teacher socialization style on students' social cognition and reported interpersonal classroom behavior. *Elementary School Journal, 85,* 245–275.

Rohrkemper, M. (1985). Individual differences in students' perceptions of routine classroom events. *Journal of Educational Psychology, 77,* 29–44.

Rohrkemper, M. (1986). The functions of inner speech in elementary students' problem solving behavior. *American Educational Research Journal, 23,* 303–313.

Rohrkemper, M., & Bershon, B. (1984). The quality of student task engagement: Elementary school students' reports of the causes and effects of problem difficulty. *Elementary School Journal, 85,* 127–147.

Rohrkemper, M., & Corno, L. (1988). Success and failure on classroom tasks: Adaptive learning and classroom teaching. *Elementary School Journal, 88,* 299–312.

Rohrkemper, M., Slavin, R., & McCauley, K. (1983, April). *Investigating students' perceptions of cognitive strategies as learning tools.* Paper presented at the annual meeting of the American Educational Research Association, Montreal.

Vygotsky, L. S. (1962). *Thought and language.* Cambridge, MA: MIT Press.

Vygotsky, L. S. (1978). *Mind in society: The development of higher-order psychological processes.* Cambridge, MA: Harvard University Press. (Original work published 1934)

Weiner, B. (1986). *An attributional theory of motivation and emotion.* New York: Springer-Verlag.

Wertsch, J. (Ed.). (1985). *Culture, communication, and cognition: Vygotskian perspectives.* New York: Cambridge University Press.

Wertsch, J., & Stone, C. (1985). The concept of internalization in Vygotsky's account of the genesis of higher mental functions. In J. Wertsch (Ed.), *Culture, communication, and cognition: Vygotskian perspectives.* New York: Cambridge University Press.

Yowell, C. & Smylie, M. (1999). Self-regulation in democratic communities. *Elementary School Journal, 99,* 469–490.

Zinchenko, V. P. (1985). Vygotsky's ideas about units for the analysis of mind. In J. Wertsch (Ed.), *Culture, communication, and cognition: Vygotskian perspectives.* New York: Cambridge University Press.

CHAPTER 12

METACOGNITIVE THEORY
Considering the
Social-Cognitive Influences

Douglas J. Hacker and Linda Bol

SOMETHING NEW IS NEEDED

I am sorry to say that the chapter you are holding in your hands may be extremely unpleasant. It tells an unhappy tale about the unfortunate state of affairs that some believe to be true and complete. It is my sad duty to write down this unpleasant tale, but there is nothing stopping you from putting this chapter down at once and reading something happy, if you prefer that sort of thing.[1]

INTRODUCTION

In the spirit of Lemony Snicket (1999), who served as the model for these opening words, we would like to begin with a cautionary remark about the state of affairs concerning metacognitive theory. With a few notable excep-

Big Theories Revisited
Volume 4 in: Research on Sociocultural Influences on Motivation and Learning, pages 275–297.
Copyright © 2004 by Information Age Publishing, Inc.
All rights of reproduction in any form reserved.
ISBN: 1-59311-053-7 (hardcover), 1-59311-052-9 (paperback)

tions, during the past 40 years of research on metacognition, results have provided a very lukewarm appraisal of people as metacognizers. Cognitive psychologists, armed with a large variety of metacognitive measures (e.g., confidence judgments, calibration, judgments of learning, judgments of comprehension, feeling of knowing, ease of learning, serial recall, and allocation of study effort), have consistently found that at best the accuracy with which people can judge what they know has consistently been 50/50 or slightly better, with better accuracy being correlated with better performance (e.g., Arbuckle & Cuddy, 1969; Barnett & Hixon, 1997; Bol & Hacker, 2001; Butterfield, Nelson, & Peck, 1988; Cavanaugh, 1999; Dembo & Jakubowski, 2003; Druckman & Bjork, 1994; Glenberg & Epstein, 1987; Grimes, 2002; Hacker, Bol, Horgan, & Rakow, 2000; Hart, 1965; Kruger & Dunning, 1999; Lichtenstein & Fischhoff, 1977; Maki, 1998; Pressley & Ghatala, 1989; Winne & Jamieson-Noel, 2002). In our own studies, we have found that even over prolonged trials to improve metacognitive accuracy, many students remain inaccurate in their judgments of test performance, with low performance strongly associated with overconfidence (Bol & Hacker, 2001; Bol, O'Shea, Hacker, & Allen, 2003; Hacker et al., 2000; Hacker & Hamilton, 2003; Horgan, Bol, & Hacker, 1997).

Moreover, Nelson, Leonesio, Landwehr, and Narens (1986) found in their comparisons of individuals' feeling of knowing, normative feeling of knowing, and base-rate item difficulty that simply knowing the normative difficulty of a test item was a better predictor of performance than individuals' own judgments of performance. If this is the case, we are just as well off asking someone else what it is we know! All of this is reminiscent of the story told of the two radical behaviorists who just got off the ferris wheel at the local county fair and asked one another, "That was great fun for you, but was it fun for me?" Can it be true that people are so poor at assessing their own knowledge?

Despite these depressing outcomes pointing to inaccuracy in performance judgments, there are still many researchers and practitioners who remain firmly convinced that metacognitive monitoring and control are essential processes to aid in self-regulated learning (e.g., McCombs, 1989; Schunk, 1994; Zimmerman, 2000). We share these same convictions. Our thesis for this chapter is mirrored in Ruth Maki's (1998) alternative viewpoint stated below:

> The low accuracy of text predictions may mean that students cannot predict performance well, and that prediction is not a teachable skill. Alternatively, low predictive accuracy may indicate that our measurement of metacomprehension accuracy is too unreliable for us to detect changes. (p. 142)

We are proposing that results showing chance to slightly above chance accuracy in metacognitive judgments are due to measurement difficulties and not to people's inabilities to take stock of what they know or what they are currently doing. As early cognitive psychologists argued with radical behaviorists that thinking does play a fundamental role in behavior, we are arguing that thinking about thinking also plays a fundamental role in behavior, but we unfortunately have not devised appropriate or complete measures of it. We propose that some of these measures must include the social-cognitive and cultural factors of learning. In this chapter, we describe various aspects of metacognition that have made it a worthwhile area of study for researchers and practitioners, provide a brief discussion of the cognitive factors that have been considered in the investigation of metacognition, argue for a need to consider social-cognitive and cultural factors, provide a review of some recent representative studies that have linked social-cognitive variables to cognition and metacognition, and finally provide implications for research and practice.

METACOGNITION DEFINED À LA LEMONY SNICKET

Metacognition is generally defined as knowledge of one's knowledge, cognitive processes, and cognitive and affective states and the ability to consciously and deliberately monitor and regulate one's knowledge, cognitive processes, and cognitive and affective states (Hacker, 1998). Thus, while engaged in reading the opening remarks of this chapter, there are potentially at least six ways in which "metacognitive" knowledge and processing could be used.

First, knowledge of one's knowledge could include your knowledge of past chapters of scientific information that you have read, knowledge of Lemony Snicket, or knowledge of past pleasant or unpleasant states that you have experienced. Second, knowledge of one's cognitive processes could include knowing that you will require reading processes and perhaps rereading or problem solving to process the quandary to continue reading the chapter or to put it down in favor of something else. Third, knowledge of one's cognitive states could include knowing that some cognitive conflict has been caused by the disparity between how the typical scientific article begins and how this one begins. Fourth, knowledge of one's affective states could include the disquieting feelings that you are experiencing about the cognitive conflict. Fifth, deliberate monitoring would entail your online monitoring of your comprehension that is generated as you read. And finally, deliberate regulation would be your decision to continue reading the unpleasant tale or to put the chapter down and select something happy to read—perhaps Dr. Zimmerman's chapter on self-regulation of learning.

From this simple analysis of the potential impact that metacognitive knowledge and processing can have on reading comprehension (and similar scenarios can be written concerning writing, mathematical problem solving, historical analysis, etc.), it is easy to understand why researchers have been so intensely interested in studying the multifaceted and complex nature of metacognition, and why practitioners have been so compelled to foster metacognitive thinking in their classrooms. But, like any complex cognitive process, the study of metacognition has created theoretical debates, methodological quandaries, and general uncertainties about whether such inherent complexities may defy measurement and analysis.

WHAT'S MISSING?

The vast majority of research on metacognition has focused on isolating and measuring the cognitive states and processes that enable a person to engage in metacognitive activities. The list of cognitive factors is continually expanding and includes such things as the accessibility of information stored in memory (Dunlosky & Nelson, 1994), ease of recall (Mazzoni & Nelson, 1995), cue familiarity (Reder, 1987), retrieval fluency (Benjamin & Bjork, 1996), topic knowledge (Hacker et al., 2000), type of test item (Bol & Hacker, 2001), item difficulty (Schraw & Roedel, 1994), inferential processing (Koriat, 1997), and study conditions (Dunlosky & Nelson, 1994).

Noticeably missing from this list are socially based factors. Social influences on metacognition have long been recognized. At the very outset of metacognitive theory, Flavell (1971) emphasized the important influence that self-knowledge and *knowledge of others* can have on one's own thought processes; and later, he more fully described the developmental aspects of metacognition and stressed the roles that metacognitive knowledge and experiences play in a person's social-cognitive enterprises, for example, perspective taking and monitoring of one's behavior in response to differing social contexts (Flavell, 1981). Ericsson and Simon (1980), in their landmark volume on verbal protocol analysis, acknowledged that the social dynamics between researcher and subject could influence the quality of a verbal protocol. They found that the simple physical placement of the researcher in proximity to the subject could affect the protocol, with the researcher placed behind and out of sight of the subject helping to ensure more accurate reporting of cognition. Social influences on metacognition are likely very real, but unfortunately, as Karabenick (1996) has summarized, "Although there have been no studies of whether others' actions affect one's own monitoring judgments, the ubiquity of socially situated learning warrants examining whether such effects do, in fact, occur" (p. 690).

The lack of attention to socially based factors is particularly surprising in light of Levine, Resnick, and Higgins's (1993) argument that greater understanding of cognition can be gained only by focusing on the situations or contexts of learning. This focus on situations or contexts has "led cognitive scientists to recognize the importance of relations among cognition, motivation, and broader processes of social influence and engagement" (p. 587). Levine and colleagues further argue that a new field of study called sociocognition is needed to more completely understand cognition in the "real world" in which "emotions, social meanings, social intentions, and social residues" (p. 604) are intertwined with one's cognitive activity.

Not only have social-cognitive factors been largely unexplored in the study of metacognition, but cultural effects have received even less attention. All social-cognitive activities occur within a cultural context, and there is evidence to suggest that differences in culture can cause differences in social-cognitive activities (Lundeberg, Fox, Brown, & Elbedour, 2000; Rogoff & Chavajay, 1995; Schneider, Borkowski, Kurtz, & Kerwin, 1986). There are likely small cultural differences when metacognitive processes are used in social-cognitive activities that involve contextually organized materials, for example, manipulating spatial arrangements (Rogoff & Chavajay, 1995); however, because metacognition is so highly linked to the kinds and amounts of a person's knowledge, it is reasonable to assume that different societies with different educational environments in home and school will produce differences in metacognition (Schneider et al., 1986). "Theoretically salient environment factors in the home and school need to be measured and then related to personal, motivational, and metacognitive factors to create more accurate and comprehensive models of cognitive performance in different cultural settings" (p. 333). Although there are few studies of the influence of cultural factors on metacognition, we will attempt to incorporate relevant findings from the few studies that we were able to find.

WHY CONSIDER SOCIAL-COGNITIVE COMPONENTS?

Now that we have discussed potential limitations of metacognitive research due to the lack of attention given to social-cognitive and cultural components, we turn more directly to arguments about why these components need to be considered. We focus on three arguments that we believe to be more fundamental to metacognitive processing. These three arguments focus on the public versus private aspects of self-concept, high versus low self-monitoring ability, and people's metamemorial belief systems.

Public Self versus Private Self

In his landmark work, William James (1890) proposed that self-concept consists of a social self (i.e., self-as-known) and a private self (i.e., self-as-knower). Within the concept of self, these two self-aspects always coexist (Fenigstein, Scheier, & Buss, 1975), and although the two are not always equally weighted in terms of their impact on self-concept, one can never divorce the public self from the private self. Cognitions, no matter how private, are to some extent always influenced by the social experiences of one's life, and the social experiences of one's life are inevitably influenced by one's private cognitions. Mead (1934), Cooley (1902), and Vygotsky (1978) further extended this view by proposing that self-concept is, in fact, created from social interactions. Thus, according to these researchers, reflection upon the self is made possible by and always contains some element of a person's social interactions.

Although with not quite as long a history as James, Mead, Cooley, or Vygotsky, researchers within the field of social psychology have been arguing since the 1980s for greater emphasis on social factors in examining self-concept and the intentions, motivations, and judgments that are generated by that self-concept. Conceptualizations of self-concept as consisting of a public self and a private self have persisted, with greater definition and expansion on how, when, and why the two components of the self-concept interact. Public self has been operationalized in a variety of ways, including such factors as social recognition for a desired attribute, social relationships, family relationships, desire to please others, or competitive motivation to be the best; private self also has been operationalized in a variety of ways, including personal traits, dispositions, or talents, a person's specific abilities, the attitudes or values they hold, or what interests they pursue (Brown, 1991).

Evidence is strongly supportive of the general notion that even when a person's behavior is not being directly observed, and there is no opportunity for interaction with others, the mere fact that others are present can affect how the public and private self are weighed and affect self-relevant behavior (Levine et al., 1993). People appear to differ in their sensitivity to self-relevant stimuli and to differ in how they process these stimuli, but such sensitivity and processing can occur even without their awareness (Markus & Wurf, 1987).

Carver and Scheier (1985) argue that a person's intentions and judgments "are a joint product of personal attitudes toward whatever act is being contemplated, and perceptions of the operative social norms with respect to that act" (p. 154). People's judgments are made by weighing these two influences and combining their relative weights. For most people, self-concept is, of course, holistic in that both public and private components are present in their intentions, judgments, and resultant behaviors. However, greater focus on the private self should promote one kind of self-perception, whereas focus on the public self should promote a very different kind of self-presentation (Carver & Scheier, 1985).

Although somewhat speculative, indirect evidence has suggested that people with a focus on the public self tend to express more moderate opinions, are highly motivated to avoid appearing deviant, conform whenever possible to an incorrect social majority when there is risk of standing out, and make use of reference-group positions to help determine their opinions (Carver & Scheier, 1985). People with a focus on the private self tend to disregard majority opinions and express instead their own values, place greater reliance on their own personal attitudes and beliefs, and exhibit more egocentric behaviors (Carver & Scheier, 1985).

Thus, metacognitive judgments concerning upcoming or past performance can depend on whether the focus of the judgment is to public or private aspects of the self. For some people, a strong focus on the public self may serve to moderate their judgments of their knowledge even though their knowledge of a topic could be relatively high. Numerous studies have shown that for many high-achieving students, moderation or underconfidence has been shown consistently in their self-judgments (e.g., Hacker et al., 2000). In contrast, because a great deal of research has shown that many people are influenced by the social motive to appear favorably to others (e.g., Ellis, 1997), they tend to harbor unrealistic positive views of their self-concept (Brown, 1991). For these people, a strong focus on the public self may serve to escalate judgments of their knowledge even when their knowledge of a topic is low.

Also, culture can differentially impact how people weigh public and private aspects of self and combine the relative weights to arrive at judgments. In a cross-cultural study conducted by Lundeberg and colleagues (2000), participants from the United States, the Netherlands, Israel, Palestine, and Taiwan were asked to make discrimination judgments about what they knew or did not know. The results showed that participants from Taiwan exhibited the lowest confidence ratings of all the participants, but they also exhibited the greatest discrimination accuracy. In contrast, the Palestinian participants exhibited the greatest confidence ratings of all the participants but the least discrimination accuracy. The authors speculate that the Palestinian participants were more public-self oriented and more likely to adopt strategies that maintain positive social impressions, whereas the Taiwanese participants were more private-self oriented and discriminated more accurately irrespective of the social situation.

Finally, although a study conducted by Hacker, Plumb, Butterfield, Quathamer, and Heineken (1994, Experiment 1) showed little differences between German and United States students in their metacognitive abilities, a study conducted by Schneider and colleagues (1986) showed that public aspects of self-concept (defined by social comparisons in academic and nonacademic areas) for United States children were strongly correlated with measures of metamemory. For the German children, however, there was no correlation between self-concept and metamemory. Rather, for the German children, self-concept was more highly related to individuals' strategy use to solve problems on a pretest. These results suggest that United States children may place stronger emphasis on public aspects of self-concept, while German children may place stronger emphasis on private aspects of self-concept that pertain to their own specific cognitive abilities.

High versus Low Self-Monitoring

In addition to public versus private components of self-concept and the differential impact each can have on one's intentions, judgments, and behaviors, another factor to consider in regards to metacognition is whether a person is a high or low self-monitor (Snyder, 1979). According to some theorists, self-monitoring is a social and cultural construction (e.g., Alexander & Lauderdale, 1977; Vygotsky, 1978). These theorists have proposed that each social setting or interpersonal context creates within the individual a particular pattern of behavior that conveys an identity (i.e., situated identity) that is specific to that social situation (Snyder, 1979). People, in general, tend to engage in behaviors that are consistent with their situated identities and succeed in these behaviors, in large part, to the extent to which they can self-monitor their thoughts and behaviors. Thus, self-monitoring can serve as a social-psychological function that assists people in establishing and maintaining an appropriate situated identity.

People vary in their abilities to self-monitor their situated identities, ranging in a continuum from high to low. People who are high self-monitors are particularly sensitive to social and interpersonal cues and to interpersonal appropriateness (Snyder, 1979). Knowing the characteristics of their situations and controlling their situations would be the best ways to predict their behaviors. The psychology of high self-monitors is the psychology of their social situations (Snyder & Swann, 1976).

In contrast, those who are low self-monitors of their situated identities can be characterized as reflecting personal attitudes, affective states, and dispositions regardless of social situations (Snyder, 1979). They are generally unresponsive to the appropriateness of a situation. Influencing their present attitudes would be the best way to predict and control their behaviors. The psychology of low self-monitors is the psychology of their attitudes, dispositions, and other inner states (Snyder, 1979).

Researchers and practitioners should expect varying degrees in the accuracy of metacognitive judgments based on where a person falls on the continuum from high to low self-monitoring. Knowing and manipulating the characteristics of social situations for high self-monitors would be necessary to gain a better understanding of their metacognitive accuracy. As mentioned earlier, Ericsson and Simon's (1980) work on verbal protocol analysis recommends that a slight change in the social situation (i.e., placing the researcher behind and out of sight of the subject) can ensure more accurate reporting of cognition.

Manipulating the personal attitudes or dispositions of low self-monitors would be necessary to better understand metacognitive accuracy. Although attempts to change attitudes and dispositions for low self-monitors may be difficult, the researcher or practitioner may not need to focus on changing them as much as simply being aware of them. If the attitudes and dispositions indicative of low self-monitoring can be identified, the researcher or practitioner can at least take this information into account when asking research participants or students to make self-monitoring judgments.

Metamemorial Belief Systems

One other social-cognitive factor that we believe may impact the accuracy of people's metacognitive judgments is the belief system that each person holds about his or her memory (Cavanaugh, 1999). Cavanaugh, Kramer, Sinnott, Camp, and Markley (1985) proposed that metamemorial self-evaluations are not made solely on the basis of direct input from one's content knowledge and knowledge about his or her memory processes and functions, but rather are mediated through one's beliefs about their memory. This position is similar to Bandura's (1986) concept of self-efficacy but applied specifically to memory (i.e., how effective is one at remembering certain types of knowledge or cognitive processes). People's self-judgments about their knowledge or cognitive processes, therefore, are influenced by such factors as whether a person can retrieve the correct knowledge, whether they can correctly assess that knowledge in response to the tasks in which they are engaged, *and* on their beliefs about themselves as rememberers (Cavanaugh, Feldman, & Hertzog, 1998).

Memory self-efficacy is a complex social-cognitive structure that can have profound effects on judgments of memory and on behavioral performance as well. How people view themselves as rememberers depends on how and which stored judgments are being accessed (Cavanaugh, 1999), and on the social circumstances under which the judgments are being made. Considering that all of these elements can change each time a person is asked to provide a self-judgment, perhaps it should not be surprising that metacognitive judgments have shown such low reliability within and across studies of metacognition.

For some people, memory self-efficacy can be a relatively stable attribute, but for others a relatively changeable one (Ross, 1989). The stability of memory self-efficacy depends, in part, on the degree to which people's underlying cognitive structures are flexible and context specific, and, in part, on the kinds of judgments being asked of them, and the subsequent social feedback they receive in response to their judgments. For example, on one hand, some people may consider themselves consistently poor rememberers when it comes to remembering other people's names, and if they continually get names wrong, their negative memory self-efficacy in this specific context is socially reinforced and likely to become relatively stable. On the other hand, some people may believe that they are quite good at remembering people's names when those people are in a specific context (e.g., a classroom). When they consistently get the names correct, their positive memory self-efficacy is socially reinforced, which contributes to a stable self-attribute in that context. However, if these same people are good rememberers of names only in a specific context but cannot remember names in other contexts, the social reinforcement will likely be far less and the stability of the self-attribute will be questioned.

Thus, memory self-efficacy is, in part, a socially based factor that can affect not only how people make self-judgments but how accurately they can make those judgments. Although memory self-efficacy is a complex construct, the degree to which people are socially reinforced for their accurate judgments and discouraged for their inaccurate judgments should help people become more efficacious in their self-judgments. Unfortunately, data from current metamemory studies with adults have shown that self-efficacy beliefs are often inaccurate and that self-efficacy judgments and performance are only moderately correlated (Hertzog & Dixon, 1994; West & Berry, 1994). And to make matters even more complicated, memory self-efficacy may be influenced by whether one's self-judgments focus on aspects of the public self versus the private self, and by whether one is a high or low self-monitor.

Summary

These three social constructs only touch the surface of an ocean of social-cognitive factors that could be considered in metacognitive judgments. The point we are stressing is that a start must be made to incorporate social-cognitive and cultural components in research focused on how people make self-judgments concerning what they know and how they are cognitively processing that knowledge. In the next section, we describe a few studies that have done just that.

STUDIES LINKING SOCIAL VARIABLES IN COGNITION AND METACOGNITION

In the previous sections, we have argued for the need to consider social-cognitive and cultural variables to better understand metacognition. In this section, we review empirical research that has linked social variables to cognition, metacognition, and more specifically to metacognitive judgments (e.g., judgments of learning, ease of learning, feelings of knowing). Some of these studies have included a focus on public versus private self, high versus low self-monitoring, and metamemorial belief systems, although the surface on these three lines of research has barely been scratched. A comprehensive review of the body of studies linking social variables to metacognition, in general, is beyond the scope of this chapter. Rather, we have selected representative studies that include some of our own exploratory investigations in progress. We begin by providing a review of research that has connected social variables and cognition. We then extend this review to illustrative studies that have connected social variables and metacognition. Finally, we further extend our review to the relatively few studies that have examined the influence of social variables on metacognitive judgments more specifically.

Social Influences on Cognition

In their chapter on social foundations of cognition, Levine and colleagues (1993) organized and reviewed related studies into five main areas: (1) the mere presence of others; (2) social roles, positions, and identities; (3) mental representations of others; (4) social interaction and cognitive change; and (5) cognition as social collaboration. Studies representative of the first main area suggest that the mere presence of others can have a widely variable effect on one's cognition. In some cases, the presence of others can have an energizing effect that serves to enhance performance, but in other cases, it can have a debilitating effect. For example, social loafing is a debilitating effect that may occur when students work together on a task.

The second area of research includes studies investigating how different expectations about social roles, positions, and identities influence cognition and behavior. This line of inquiry is related to self-fulfilling prophecies where assigning a person to a social position leads research participants to think about themselves and others in ways congruent with a particular role or identity.

The third area of research has shown that mental representations of others can affect cognition even when others are not physically present. The implied versus actual presence of others is an important social factor predicting cognition and behavior. Studies have indicated that individuals adopt various roles and make social comparisons even in the absence of actual evaluation or expected evaluation by others.

The fourth and fifth areas both deal with social interactions, with the fourth including studies of cognitive change through social interaction, and the fifth concerned with cognition as a form of social collaboration. Investigations in the fourth area have focused on social conflict as a way to spark cognitive growth, with majority versus minority differences exerting influences on cognition and group decision-making processes. The last area has focused on the use of social interactions in group collaboration to stimulate cognitive interaction and shared cognitions. Studies in this area have shown differences between individual and group work, but differences in the quality of performance depends primarily on the task and the types of interactions that occur.

Social Influences on Metacognition

There also have been a number of studies investigating the effects of social influences on metacognition, in this case, self-regulation of learning. Many of these studies are aligned with theories about the impact of others on metacognitive processing. Zimmerman's (1989) social-cognitive model of self-regulated learning sparked a series of studies highlighting the importance of providing modeling and verbal persuasion to positively affect the self-regulatory processes of others.

Zimmerman and Ringle (1981) investigated the effects of modeling puzzle-solving behaviors on young elementary students. In one condition, models made optimistic statements while solving puzzles, and in the other condition, the models made pessimistic statements. Research participants who were exposed to optimistic statements significantly increased their self-efficacy perceptions. In contrast, there was a significant decrease in self-efficacy perceptions for children exposed to the pessimistic statements. The increase or decrease in self-efficacy perceptions was, in turn, related to increases or decreases in self-regulation, respectively.

Zimmerman and Rocha (1987) also found that a model's motoric and verbal elaborations enhanced children's performance on an associative learning task and also increased their use of elaborative strategies on a transfer task. Children who observed the nonelaborative model did not perform as well and demonstrated relatively few elaborative strategies on the transfer task in comparison to the children who observed the elaborative model. Thus, modeling and verbal persuasion can be powerful social factors affecting self-efficacy and self-regulated learning.

Vygotsky's theory of social learning has served as a theoretical basis for studies on how strategies, such as reciprocal learning and group learning, can influence metacognitive processes (Brown & Palincsar, 1989; Carr & Jessup, 1997; Goos, Galbraith, & Renshaw, 2002; Kuhn, Shaw, Felton, 1997). For example, Carr and Jessup (1997) reported gender differences in first-grade students' use of strategies when solving math problems individually and in groups. Individually, girls used more overt strategies (e.g., counting on fingers), whereas boys used more covert strategies (e.g., retrieval from memory). Both girls and boys used more covert strategies when working in groups, suggesting that the boys' preferred strategies dominated the group work. Moreover, both metacognitive and social rationales were correlated with strategy use in groups, such as boys were more likely than girls to provide rationales for their strategic behaviors related to competitiveness and social comparisons.

Goos and her colleagues (2002) also investigated mathematical problem solving but at the senior high school level rather than the elementary level. They explicitly relied on Vygotsky's conception of collaborative zones of proximal development to identify patterns of students' social interactions that mediated metacognitive activities. Successful outcomes in collaborative groups were associated with developing challenging ideas, discarding ideas judged to be unhelpful, and adopting more useful strategies, all indicative of effective metacognitive processing. Unsuccessful outcomes in collaborative groups were characterized by poor decisions and a lack of critical engagement with one another's thinking, both indicative of poor metacognitive processing.

The impact of social variables on metacognition is further illustrated in a series of four experiments conducted by Karabenick (1996). He examined the effects of co-learner questioning on comprehension monitoring measured while participants watched videotaped messages. The co-learners were not actually present, but the participants were told that another person or "co-learner" was in an adjacent room watching the videotape. Participants also were told that the co-learner was in the "question condition" and would signal whenever he or she had questions. The manipulation entailed varying the number of simulated co-learner questions. Participants were asked to signal by pressing a button whenever they were confused (the measure of comprehension monitoring).

Karabenick (1996) found that the presence of simulated co-learner questions increased the amount of self-reported confusion as participants monitored the message in real time, with more co-learner questions associated with more confusion. Karabenick concluded that the presence of other learners' questions facilitated externalization of cognitive dissatisfaction, an interpretation that might also apply to other collaborative learning contexts. However, his data did not support the prediction that the absence of questioning by others would cause less confusion. He speculated that the absence of co-learner questions did not reduce confusion because the co-learners were not actually present in his experimental procedure. Nor did he find any significant effects of co-learner questions when participants retrospectively rated their confusion compared to when they monitored their comprehension online while viewing the messages. This introduces the possibility that social factors may impact comprehension monitoring online but not retrospectively. Other researchers also have suggested differences in online assessment of monitoring versus retrospective reports of comprehension and strategy use (e.g., Winne & Jamieson-Noel, 2002).

Social Influences on Metacognitive Judgments

In contrast to the number of studies linking social variables to cognition and metacognition, relatively few studies have investigated the impact of social-cognitive factors on metacognitive judgments specifically. A notable exception is provided in two studies conducted by Carvahlo and Yuzawa (2001).

In the first study (in press and described in Carvalho & Yuzawa, 2001), the researchers manipulated social cues by presenting some participants with information concerning the mean percentage of correctly answered questions that a fictitious group of students had received. This information was presented prior to participants making their own prospective metacognitive judgments on their performance. Participants were divided into high and low metacognitive groups based on the accuracy of their confidence judgments. The authors assessed the impact of social cues on several prospective judgments, including ease of learning (EOL), judgments of learning (JOL), and feelings of knowing (FOK) on the questions. The results showed that social cues did impact the magnitude of metamemory judgments, with greater magnitude in judgments associated with social cues indicating higher performance. Significant differences also were found depending on the metacognitive abilities of participants: Social cues had more impact on participants with low self-monitoring ability compared to participants with high self-monitoring ability across all three judgments.

Carvalho and Yuzawa (2001) used a similar experimental manipulation in their second study. Participants judged their confidence by rating the number of items about Japanese literature they believed that they had answered correctly for each of six tests (i.e., a retrospective judgment) in either high social cue (79% and 90% of the questions answered correctly by a fictitious group of students) or low social cue conditions (35% and 46% of the questions answered correctly). Metacognitive monitoring was operationally defined as the mean accuracy of these confidence judgments, and participants were again divided into high and low metacognitive groups based on these scores. The authors found that social cues significantly influenced the magnitude of overall confidence judgments, but only for low monitors. The low monitors increased their confidence in the high social cue condition, but decreased their confidence in the low social cue conditions. Therefore, the results of both studies indicate that social cues significantly influenced prospective (Study 1) and retrospective (Study 2) judgments among students with low metacognitive ability. The authors concluded that participants who have little confidence in their judgments may be particularly susceptible to social influences.

These studies begin to illuminate how social variables influence metacognitive judgments. However, they were conducted in laboratory settings with contrived tasks and with the simulated presence of others who provided fictitious social comparative data. Although the studies afforded a good deal of experimental control, they may lack ecological validity. We now turn to some of the studies that were conducted in real classroom settings. What these studies lose in internal validity, they gain in external validity.

As noted earlier, studies suggest that students are largely inaccurate in their metacognitive judgments and that these judgments are resistant to change. Studies also indicate that low-achieving students are less accurate and overconfident when compared to their high-achieving peers who tend to be somewhat underconfident (Barnett & Hixon, 1997; Bol & Hacker, 2001; Grimes, 2002; Hacker et al. 2000; Kruger & Dunning, 1999). In our more recent studies, we have begun to investigate whether these patterns of findings might be at least partially explained by different attributional styles. We have developed an "attribution for calibration accuracy" questionnaire asking students to rate statements explaining the discrepancy between their predictions and their actual scores (Bol et al., 2003). We found that high-achieving students rated "student-centered" explanations (i.e., students attribute discrepancies primarily to factors internal to their self) significantly higher than low-achieving students. Though the difference did not reach statistical significance, we observed for low-achieving students a higher mean on "task-centered" explanations (i.e., students attribute discrepancies primarily to factors external to the self) than high-achieving students.

These findings point to different explanatory styles by achievement group that persist even in the face of contradictory information. Hacker and colleagues (2000) found that students anchored their calibrations on previous calibrations, not previous performance scores. Schraw (1997) also found that confidence judgments on a particular test were related to confidence judgments on unrelated tests, supporting a domain-general hypothesis for explaining metacognitive judgments. Low-achieving students may demonstrate a self-serving attributional style, repeatedly overestimating their performance to protect their self-worth or their image of themselves as relatively good students in comparison with others. High achievers, on the other hand, are more likely to attribute their success to student-centered variables, but are slightly underconfident perhaps because they do not want to appear immodest or overconfident in the implied or actual presence of the instructor and other students. At this point these results are merely speculative and await further empirical confirmation.

We are not the only researchers who have proposed or collected data to support this interpretation of the tenacity of students' metacognitive judgments. Dembo and Jakubowski (2003) recently conducted a study in a college classroom in which they had students make predictions about their performance on a series of five quizzes. For a homework assignment, they also asked students to write about their accuracy in test predictions and what this information told them about their motivation and study behaviors. As was reported in other studies, low-achieving students were less accurate in their predictions than students in the medium or high achievement groups. Moreover, there was no significant improvement across the five quizzes regardless of achievement level. Unlike other researchers, they did not find that low-achieving students significantly overestimated their performance compared to students in the other achievement groups. The authors discussed the possibility that restriction of range on previous achievement (matched on SAT scores) and prediction (10-point quizzes) measures might have obscured this effect.

More importantly, however, distinct patterns of explanations emerged from their analysis of the qualitative data, and some of these explanations were clearly social in nature. Student responses reflected a deliberate over- or underreporting of efficacy (predictions) as a self-protective mechanism. Students reported underestimating because they did not want to appear conceited. They also used underestimation as a motivational strategy to not "jinx" themselves or to avoid disappointment. Students reported overestimating to motivate themselves to exert more effort, or in hopes of influencing the teaching assistants who graded the quizzes. Still others adopted a strategy of consistently predicting the average in order to "play it safe" or "give them room for error" (p. 9). These findings suggest that students used, at least in part, self-protection strategies to make their predictions rather than more objective data such as past test performance.

Summary

We began this section with a broad overview of the research linking social-cognitive factors to cognition and metacognition and provided a description of representative studies exemplifying these lines of inquiry. The influence of models, verbal persuasion, collaborative learning, and co-learner questions on metacognition has been empirically demonstrated for a wide variety of age groups across a wide variety of tasks. In contrast, there has been a dearth of studies examining the impact of social variables on metacognitive judgments more specifically. Carvahlo and Yuzawa's studies (2001) showed that social cues influenced metacognitive judgments, especially among students with low metacognitive abilities and confidence. In our own research, we also have found differences in metacognitive judgments as a function of student achievement levels and have more recently gathered evidence linking achievement level, calibration accuracy, and explanatory style (Bol et al., 2003). Similar findings were recently reported by Dembo and Jakubowski (2003) who identified explanations about calibrations as self-protective mechanisms. Beyond these few studies we could not find any others linking social-cognitive factors to metacognitive judgments. Given the glaring gap in the literature, our next section presents implications for research with this gap in mind.

IMPLICATIONS FOR RESEARCH AND PRACTICE

One obvious area for future research is to gather more data on students' explanatory styles and how they affect metacognitive judgments. The possibility that explanatory styles serve to protect one's social self-image may help account for the fact that metacognitive judgments are resistant to improvement (Bol et al., 2003; Dembo & Jakubowski, 2003) and not anchored on past performance or more objective feedback as one would expect (Hacker et al., 2000; Kruger & Dunning, 1999). Students' self-protection strategies may be even more persistent under conditions of implied or social presence of others, such as classroom situations. The presence of social comparisons, co-learner questions, or feedback provided by instructors or other students may differentially affect explanatory styles, which in turn affect metacognitive judgments.

Another area of investigation is how social factors affect various types of metacognitive judgments. Some evidence suggests that online monitoring of judgments is more sensitive to social interventions than retrospective judgments (Karabenick, 1996). Retrospective judgments may be more susceptible to the influence of domain-general perceptions like explanatory style, whereas judgments made online may be anchored more on task characteristics and direct social manipulations. We might investigate the role of social influences on further distinctions among types of judgments labeled differently by different researchers (e.g., judgments of learning, ease of learning, feelings or knowing, confidence, efficacy, calibration, predictions, postdictions). This line of inquiry brings us back to Maki's (1998) quote, presented earlier in the chapter, questioning the reliability of how we measure metacomprehension. Part of the difficulty in reliably measuring this type of metacognition may be attributable to omission of social-cognitive variables.

The consistent finding that calibration accuracy differs as a function of student ability level implies that we may need to design and study the effects of various interventions by type of student (e.g., high vs. low achievement, high vs. low self-monitoring, high vs. low metamemory efficacy, or high public vs. high private self-concept). Some of these interventions might be social in nature. In terms of practical implications, we should be more concerned about the lowest-achieving students who are inaccurate and usually far too confident when judging their performance. Realizing that you have not mastered knowledge or processes should presumably lead one to self-corrective strategies, such as spending more time studying material that you did not understand. The vexing question is how to facilitate more accurate judgments without harming self-efficacy and achievement motivation. One strategy might be to incorporate more group work in a classroom climate where questions, mistakes, and corrections are not only accepted but expected. This is reminiscent of Brown and Campione's (1996) call for communities of metacognitive practice.

Different patterns of results may be obtained in laboratory versus classroom settings. For instance, low-achieving students may more vigorously protect their self-image in real-world classrooms compared to laboratory situations. High-achieving students may be more concerned about appearing immodest in classroom settings versus lab settings. The findings obtained from studies manipulating the simulated or fictitious presence of others (Carvahlo & Yuzawa, 2001; Karabenick, 1996) may not generalize to more ecologically valid contexts. Conversely, lack of control in real classrooms makes it difficult to isolate particular social variables and causally link those variables to metacognition. To further obfuscate this distinction, technological advances make it easier to control conditions and collect data when instruction is Web-based. In other words, the computer environment is frequently becoming the classroom or at least components of the classroom. Social influences and interactions are transformed in these virtual classroom contexts and may differentially affect metacognition. More realistically, researchers need to move back and forth along a continuum of contexts in order to replicate and extend findings illuminating the relationship between social influences and metacognitive judgments.

CONCLUSION

At the outset of this chapter we warned the reader that our message may be an unhappy tale for researchers and practitioners who are convinced that metacognitive monitoring and control are essential processes in self-regulated learning. These people are hard pressed to remain optimistic about the prospects of fostering metacognitive processing in contexts of learning when faced with the plethora of studies that would dampen the optimism of even the most optimistic proponent of metacognition. Our goal was to propose to the reader that current studies on metacognitive judgments are not providing a complete picture of people as metacognizers. We have further proposed that a more complete and accurate picture may be gained by considering the social and cultural influences on metacognitive judgments.

Glaring gaps between the social-cognitive and metamemory literatures exist (Cavanaugh, 1999). Filling those gaps points to many potentially fruitful areas of research that can provide a much more complete picture of the social and cognitive processes and conditions that lead to greater metamemory accuracy. This is *not* to advocate for a complete discarding of the cognitive research that has so thoroughly investigated many critical aspects of metacognition. Rather, our hope is that in addition to the cognitive factors, researchers and practitioners will augment current studies with investigations of the social and cultural factors influencing metacognition, some of which were suggested in this chapter.

There are many difficulties to ponder when we consider how well the human species has survived for the past 100,000 years or so if we were indeed so poor at knowing our own thoughts and thought processes. Perhaps, following Levine and colleagues' (1993) advice, we need to consider metacognition as a sociocognitive process that must be studied in the "real world." Investigations of people in more naturalistic contexts can tell us much about how people use their social and cultural environments as tools to augment and supplement the cognitive processing that occurs in working and long-term memories (Glenberg, 1999; Varela, Thompson, & Rosch, 1999). Our hope—if you have not already forsaken our chapter for something happy—is that this chapter will not be perceived as an unhappy tale, but rather a tale that will encourage new lines of research and educational practice.

NOTE

1.   Our thanks to Emily Hacker for informing us of the wisdom of Lemony Snicket and for suggesting this segment from the Lemony Snicket books for our chapter.

REFERENCES

Alexander, C. N., Jr., & Lauderdale, P. (1977). Situated identities and social influence. *Sociometry, 40,* 225–233.

Arbuckle, T., & Cuddy, L. L. (1969). Discrimination of item strength at time of presentation. *Journal of Experimental Psychology, 81,* 126–131.

Bandura, A. (1986). *Social foundations of thought and action: A social cognitive theory.* Englewood Cliffs, NJ: Prentice-Hall.

Barnett, J. E., & Hixon, J. E. (1997). The effects of grade level and subject student test score predictions. *Journal of Educational Research, 90,* 170–174.

Benjamin, A. S., & Bjork, R. A. (1996). Retrieval fluency as a metacognitive index. In Lynne R. Reder (Ed.), *Implicit memory and metacognition* (pp. 309–338). Hillsdale, NJ: Erlbaum.

Bol, L., & Hacker, D. (2001). The effect of practice tests on students' calibration and performance. *Journal of Experimental Education, 69,* 133–151.

Bol, L., O'Shea, P., Hacker, D. J., & Allen, D. (2003, April). *The influence of practice, achievement level, and explanatory style on calibration accuracy.* Paper presented at the annual meeting of the American Educational Research Association, Chicago.

Brown, J. D. (1991). Accuracy and bias in self-knowledge. In C. R. Snyder & D. F. Forsyth (Eds.), *Handbook of social and clinical psychology: The health perspective* (pp. 158–178). New York: Pergamon Press.

Brown, A. L., & Campione, J. C. (1996). Psychological learning theory and the design of innovative environments: On procedures, principles and systems. In L. Shauble & R. Glaser (Eds.). *Contributions of instructional innovation to understanding learning.* Hillsdale, NJ: Erlbaum.

Brown, A., L., & Palincsar, A. S. (1989). Guided cooperative learning and individual knowledge acquisition. In L. B. Resnick (Ed.), *Cognition and instruction: Issues and agendas* (pp. 393–451). Hillsdale, NJ: Erlbaum.

Butterfield, E. C., Nelson, T. O., & Peck, V. (1988). Developmental aspects of the feeling of knowing. *Developmental Psychology, 24,* 654–663.

Carr, M., & Jessup, D.L (1997). Gender differences in first grade mathematics strategy use: Social and metacognitive influences. *Journal of Educational Psychology, 89,* 318–328.

Carvalho, M. K. F., & Yuzawa, M. (2001). The effects of social cues on confidence judgments mediated by knowledge and regulation of cognition. *Journal of Experimental Education, 69,* 325–343.

Carver, C. S., & Scheier, M. F. (1985). Aspects of self, and the control of behavior. In B. R. Schlenker (Ed.), *The self and social life* (pp. 146–174). New York: McGraw-Hill.

Cavanaugh, J. C. (1999). Metamemory as social cognition: Challenges for (and from) survey research. In N. Schwarz, D. C. Park, B. Knäuper, & S. Sudman (Eds.), *Cognition, aging, and self-reports* (pp. 145–162). Ann Arbor, MI: Taylor & Francis.

Cavanaugh, J. C., Feldman, J. M., & Hertzog, C. (1998). Memory beliefs as social cognition: A reconceptualization of what memory questionnaires assess. *Review of General Psychology, 2,* 48–65.

Cavanaugh, J. C., Kramer, D. A., Sinnott, J. D., Camp, C. J., & Markey, R. J. (1985). On missing links and such: Interfaces between cognitive research and everyday problem solving. *Human Development, 28,* 146–168.

Cooley, C. H. (1902). *Human nature and social order.* New York: Scribners.

Dembo, M. H., & Jakubowski, T. G. (2003, April*). The influence of self-protective perceptions on the accuracy of test prediction.* Paper presented at the annual meeting of the American Educational Research Association, Chicago.

Druckman, D., & Bjork, R. A. (1994). Illusions of comprehension, competence, and remembering. In D. Druckman & R. A. Bjork (Eds.), *Learning, remembering, believing: Enhancing human performance* (pp. 57–80). Washington, DC: National Academy Press.

Dunlosky, J., & Nelson, T. O. (1994). Does the sensitivity of judgments of learning (JOLs) to the effects of various study activities depend on when the JOLs occur? *Journal of Memory and Language, 33,* 545–565.

Ellis, S. (1997). Strategy choice in sociocultural context. *Developmental Review, 17,* 490–524.

Ericsson, K. A., & Simon, H. A. (1980). Verbal reports as data. *Psychological Review, 87,* 215–251.

Fenigstein, A., Scheier, M. F., & Buss, A. H. (1975). Public and private self-consciousness: Assessment and theory. *Journal of Consulting and Clinical Psychology, 43,* 522–527.

Flavell, J. H. (1971). First discussant's comments: What is memory development the development of? *Human Development, 14,* 272–278.

Flavell, J. H. (1981). Cognitive monitoring. In W. P. Dickerson (Ed.), *Children's oral communication skills* (pp. 35–60). New York: Academic.

Glenberg, A. M. (1999). Why mental models must be embodied. In G. E. Stelmach (Ed.), *Advances in psychology* (pp. 77–90). Amsterdam: Elsevier.

Glenberg, A. M., & Epstein, W. (1987). Inexpert calibration of comprehension. *Memory and Cognition, 15*, 84–93.

Goos, M., Galbraith, P., & Renshaw, P. (2002). Socially mediated metacognition: Creating collaborative zones of proximal development in small group problem solving. *Educational Studies in Mathematics, 49*, 193–223.

Grimes, P. W. (2002). The overconfident principals of economics student: An examination of metacognitive skill. *Journal of Economic Education, 33*, 15–30.

Hacker, D. J. (1998). Definitions and empirical foundations. In D. J. Hacker, J. Dunlosky, & A. C. Graesser (Eds.), *Metacognition in educational theory and practice* (pp. 1–23). Mahwah, NJ: Erlbaum.

Hacker, D. J., Bol, L., Horgan, D. D., & Rakow, E. A. (2000). Test prediction and performance in a classroom context. *Journal of Educational Psychology, 92*, 1–11.

Hacker, D. J., & Hamilton, C. (2003). *Discriminating between what is known and not known in the classroom: Critical issues for self-regulated learning.* Manuscript under review.

Hacker, D. J., Plumb, C., Butterfield, E. C., Quathamer, D., & Heineken, E. (1994). Text revision: Detection and correction of errors. *Journal of Educational Psychology, 86*, 65–78.

Hart, J. T. (1965). Memory and the feeling-of-knowing experience. *Journal of Educational Psychology, 56*, 208–216.

Hertzog, C., & Dixon, R. (1994). Metacognitive development in adulthood and old age. In J. Metcalfe & A. P. Shimamura (Eds.), *Metacognition: Knowing about knowing* (pp. 227–251). Cambridge, MA: MIT Press.

Horgan, D., Bol, L., & Hacker, D. J. (1997, August). *Interrelationships among self, peer, and instructor assessments.* Paper presented at the Symposium on New Assessment Methods, 7th Annual Conference of the European Association for Research on Learning and Instruction, Athens, Greece.

James, W. (1890). *Principles of psychology.* New York: Holt.

Karabenick, S. A. (1996). Social influences on metacognition: Effects of colearner questioning on comprehension monitoring. *Journal of Educational Psychology, 88*, 689–703.

Koriat, A. (1997). Monitoring one's own knowledge during study: A cue-utilization approach to judgments of learning. *Journal of Experimental Psychology: General, 126*, 349–370.

Kruger, J., & Dunning, D. (1999). Unskilled and unaware of it: How difficulties in recognizing one's incompetence lead to inflated self-assessments. *Journal of Personality and Social Psychology, 77*, 1121–1134.

Kuhn, D., Shaw, V., & Felton, M. (1997). Effects of dyadic interaction on argumentative reasoning. *Cognition and Instruction, 15*, 287–315.

Levine, J. M., Resnick, L. B., & Higgins, E. T. (1993). Social foundations of cognition. *Annual Review of Psychology, 44*, 585–612.

Lichtenstein, S., & Fischhoff, B. (1977). Do those who know more also know more of how much they know? The calibration of probability judgments. *Journal of Experimental Psychology: Learning, Memory, and Cognition, 16*, 464–470.

Lundeberg, M. A., Fox, P. W., Brown, A. C., & Elbedour, S. (2000). Cultural influences on confidence: Country and gender. *Journal of Educational Psychology, 92,* 152–159.

Maki, R. H. (1998). Test predictions over text material. In D. J. Hacker, J. Dunlosky, & A. C. Graesser (Eds.), *Metacognition in educational theory and practice* (pp. 117–144). Mahwah, NJ: Erlbaum.

Markus, M., & Wurf, E. (1987). The dynamic self-concept: A social psychological perspective. *Annual Review of Psychology, 38,* 299–337.

Mazzoni, G., & Nelson, T. O. (1995). Judgments of learning are affected by the kind of encoding in ways that cannot be attributed to the level of recall. *Journal of Experimental Psychology: Learning, Memory, and Cognition, 21,* 1263–1274.

McCombs, B. L. (1989). Self-regulated learning and academic achievement: A phenomenological view. In B. J. Zimmerman & D. H. Schunk (Eds.), *Self-regulated learning and academic achievement: Theory, research, and practice* (pp. 51–82). New York: Springer-Verlag.

Mead, G. H. (1934). *Mind, self, and society.* Chicago: University of Chicago Press.

Nelson, T. O., Leonesio, R. J., Landwehr, R. S., & Narens, L. (1986). A comparison of three predictors of an individual's memory performance: The individual's feeling of knowing versus the normative feeling of knowing versus base-rate item difficulty. *Journal of Experimental Psychology: Learning, Memory, and Cognition, 12,* 279–287.

Pressley, M., & Ghatala, E. S. (1989). Metacognitive benefits of taking a test for children and young adolescents. *Journal of Experimental Child Psychology, 47,* 430–450.

Reder, L. M. (1987). Strategy selection in question answering. *Cognitive Psychology, 19,* 990–998.

Rogoff, B., & Chavajay, P. (1995). What's become of research on the cultural basis of cognitive development? *American Psychologist, 50,* 859–877.

Ross, M. (1989). Relation of implicit theories to the construction of personal histories. *Psychological Review, 96,* 341–357.

Schneider, W., Borkowski, J. G., Kurtz, B. E., & Kerwin, K. (1986). Metamemory and motivation: A comparison of strategy use and performance in German and American children. *Journal of Cross-Cultural Psychology, 17,* 315–336.

Schraw, G. (1997). The effect of generalized metacognitive knowledge on test performance and confidence judgments. *Journal of Experimental Education, 65,* 135–146.

Schraw, G., & Roedel, T. D. (1994). Test difficulty and judgment bias. *Memory and Cognition, 22,* 63–69.

Schunk, D. H. (1994). Self-regulation of self-efficacy and attributions in academic settings. In D. H. Schunk & B. J. Zimmerman (Eds.), *Self-regulation of learning and performance: Issues and educational applications* (pp. 75–99). Hillsdale, NJ: Erlbaum.

Snicket, L. (1999). *A series of unfortunate events.* New York: Scholastic.

Synder, M. (1979). Self-monitoring processes. In L. Berkowitz (Ed.), *Advances in experimental social psychology* (Vol. 12, pp. 85–128). New York: Academic Press.

Snyder, M., & Swann, W. B., Jr. (1976). Behavioral confirmation in social interaction: From social perception to social reality. *Journal of Experimental Social Psychology, 14,* 148–162.

Varela, F. J., Thompson, E., & Rosch, E. (1999). *The embodied mind: Cognitive science and human experience.* Cambridge, MA: MIT Press.

Vygotsky, L. S. (1978). *Mind in society: The development of higher psychological processes.* Cambridge, MA: Harvard University Press.

West, R. L., & Berry, J. M. (1994). Age declines in memory self-efficacy: General or limited to particular tasks and measures? In J. D. Sinnott (Ed.), *Handbook of adult lifespan learning* (pp. 426–445). New York: Greenwood Press.

Winne, P. H., & Jamieson-Noel, D. (2002). Exploring students' calibration of self reports about study tactics and achievement. *Contemporary Educational Psychology, 27,* 551–572.

Zimmerman, B. J. (1989). A social cognitive view of self-regulated academic learning. *Journal of Educational Psychology, 81,* 329–339.

Zimmerman, B. J. (2000). Attaining self-regulation: A social cognitive perspective. In M. Boekaerts, P. R. Pintrich, & M. Zeidner (Eds.), *Handbook of self-regulation* (pp. 13–39). San Diego, CA: Academic Press.

Zimmerman, B. J., & Ringle, J. (1981). Effects of model persistence and statements of confidence on children's efficacy and problem solving. *Journal of Educational Psychology, 73,* 485–493.

Zimmerman, B. J., & Rocha, J. (1987). Mode and type of toy elaboration strategy training on kindergartners' retention and transfer. *Journal of Applied Developmental Psychology, 8,* 67–78.

CHAPTER 13

WHAT WE HAVE LEARNED ABOUT STUDENT ENGAGEMENT IN THE PAST TWENTY YEARS

Lyn Corno and Ellen B. Mandinach

INTRODUCTION

This chapter looks back 20 years to reconsider our first discussion of the role of student cognitive engagement in classroom learning and motivation (see Corno & Mandinach, 1983). Our perspective has changed in important ways since the publication of the 1983 article.

Models of design have moved from a focus on individual learners and classroom instructional systems to other social environments that engage students cognitively. Researchers now pose questions about students in learning communities outside school that impact long-term academic engagement. Recent theory introduces fresh concepts, enhancing definitions of engagement, and emphasizing new relationships. To convey our improved understanding, this chapter pays special attention to two contexts in which students are increasingly engaged apart from classrooms: in homework and computer technology.

Big Theories Revisited
Volume 4 in: Research on Sociocultural Influences on Motivation and Learning, pages 299–328.
Copyright © 2004 by Information Age Publishing, Inc.
All rights of reproduction in any form reserved.
ISBN: 1-59311-053-7 (hardcover), 1-59311-052-9 (paperback)

OUR ANALYSIS OF STUDENT ENGAGEMENT TWENTY YEARS AGO

Our story begins more than 20 years ago, in the 1970s, when research on teaching put the spotlight on a variable called "time on task." Several large-scale, government-funded studies examining the correlates of academic achievement converged on the conclusion that students who scored well on standardized tests tended to spend more class time successfully completing academic tasks. Although this result seemed rather obvious, an effect of practice with feedback, careful observations showed surprisingly large disparities between classrooms in the amounts of time students spent in task engagement, even at the same grade level in the same school. When similar differences appeared in comparisons between schools within districts and districts across states, researchers began to study what some teachers and school systems did differently to enhance student engagement (see Berliner, 1979, for a summary of this research).

In the early 1980s, our contribution to this agenda was to flesh out the psychological processes underlying student cognitive engagement in classrooms, and to consider how these processes might contribute to classroom learning and motivation (Corno, 1981). We adopted concepts from cognitive information processing theory to define a process we called "self-regulated learning," or SRL (first discussed in Corno, Collins, & Capper, 1982, p. 1). We considered SRL to be the most sophisticated form of engagement that students could display in school-related (academic) activities and events.

In our conception, SRL enhances academic mastery. As opposed to non-academic work, academic-intellectual work is heavily cognitive, requiring combinations of knowledge and reasoning skills (Snow & Lohman, 1984). Effective use of knowledge and reasoning skills such as those defined in SRL shows in standardized test scores.

Cognitive science also discovered that such cognitive processes can be captured in nontest tasks. Studies of chess playing by computers, for example, reveal interesting information about how human memory functions in problem-solving contexts. The strategic thinking of a good human chess player helps to explain how people seek, organize, and transform information (e.g., Chase & Simon, 1973). In the early 1980s research by cognitive scientists was ready to mine for ideas of great potential value in education.

Our initial definition of cognitive engagement further acknowledged that there was more to engagement than the cognitive processes used to acquire and transform information. Productive engagement entails reaching for standards, effortful striving, and a positive affective response that Csikszentmihalyi (1975) called *flow*. Engagement is thus partly cognitive, partly conative (having to do with purposive striving), and partly affective (having to do with feelings or emotions). Accordingly, our 1983 discussion of engagement extended beyond cognitive concepts into the conative and affective domains of human functioning, defining self-regulated learning as a deliberate effort by students to deepen and manipulate the content being covered while concurrently orchestrating and controlling concentration, motivation, and affect (Corno & Mandinach, 1983, p. 95).

To integrate cognitive theory with the then-budding motivation theories in education, we described some contemporary models of academic motivation consistent with our framework and used them to shape hypotheses (process theories of conation, evolving later, wrapped motivation together with volitional processes; see Snow, Corno, & Jackson, 1996). The models of academic motivation we discussed were Bandura's (1977) early explication of the role played by self-efficacy in personal agency, Weiner's (1979) attribution theory for academic situations, and the self-evaluation maintenance model of school motivation proposed by Tesser and Campbell (1982). Following other conceptions of motivation developed in the 1970s, these theorists broke from tradition to hypothesize that the critically important causal mediators of human behavior were cognitive interpretive processes rather than personality constructs such as self-concept or self-esteem (Weiner, 1980). Cognitive interpretive processes include perceptions, appraisals, and self-evaluations that students generate in academic work.

Central concepts in the three motivation theories we discussed were personal beliefs about efficacy or efficacy expectations, performance attributions or ascriptions, and self-assessments or self-evaluations. For efficacy and other personal beliefs, classic motivation theory held that either an excess or a deficiency could be detrimental (see, e.g., Atkinson, 1974). An "optimal level" of efficacy for a task suggests nonlinear relations between motivation and performance outcomes. The new models added the hypothesis that perceptions such as the stability or controllability of a performance attribution influenced as well as followed cognitive engagement, and that attributions were influenced also by the learning environment. Bandura and Weiner both proposed models with reciprocal effects between persons and the environment.

Evidence we presented in the 1983 article showed that processes of self-regulation contribute to academic accomplishments other than tests, such as grades and course promotions. We set out an agenda for future research on SRL in classrooms and considered some situations outside classroom learning that also call upon cognitive skills, such as computer games. Other psychologists, such as Paris and Cross (1983), developed conceptions of self-regulation in education at the same time (see also Winne & Marx, 1982). What these integrative theories of the 1980s had in common was a focus on individual learning or problem solving at the process level, with a primary goal of defining the conceptual schemas, cognitive skills, and motivational strategies that appeared predictive of long-term academic success.

Prominent Research Methods Twenty Years Ago

Looking back two decades at the dominant research paradigms, academic tasks entailed short versions of school-like activities designed specifically for research purposes. Students would, for example, read a passage from a novel or a persuasive text and answer questions assessing recall of the material. Text passages included various instructional features designed to aid comprehension and retention. Of interest was how students used instructional supports to learn; did they, for example, review embedded questions or chapter summaries in preparing for tests? Answers to such research questions could lead to identification of different approaches or styles of learning.

A parallel strand of research looked analytically at classroom teaching, correlating specific teacher behavior with indicators of student achievement. For example, observers coded teachers' use of higher-order questions in relation to student scores on test items measuring both higher- and lower-order thinking. Occasionally, research on teaching looked beyond achievement to assess students' interpretations of tasks and their self-appraisals.

An early study by Stayrook, Corno, and Winne (1978) showed that higher-order questions positively affected student achievement only if students understood that they needed to provide a higher-order response—for example, an answer that analyzed or elaborated the material. However, up to the early 1980s, even the most penetrating classroom observation studies gathered data for just short periods of class time.

A common practice in past decades was to take students from their regular classrooms to a work area where they were engaged in research tasks—for example, alone, in small groups, or with an interviewer, students solved a series of problems of increasing difficulty. By having students "think aloud" while they work, describing their likelihood of success, interviews can yield a combination of data, such as traces of cognitive activity during problem solving, goals, efficacy expectations, and performance scores (see Schunk, 1982; Winne & Marx, 1989).

Even today, in studies that include measures of motivation, self-reports and reports from teachers predominate (e.g., Furrer & Skinner, 2003). Prior to, sometimes during, and immediately following research tasks, students complete structured response scales indicating efficacy, perceived control, attributions, and so on. But the situation remains artificial, and scales can produce socially desirable responses. Moreover, all questionnaire results are decontextualized because they require reflection post hoc. Only gradually have researchers investigating cognition and motivation brought their designs into classrooms or the workplace to study theories as they play out in real time. Our article, concerned primarily with classroom learning, pointed research in the direction of more representative designs that emphasized practical validity (Snow, 1974).

Motivation Confounded with Affect

Theories about affective processes were in their infancy 20 years ago. Indeed, theorists tended to confound processes of affect with motivation. Tesser and Campbell (1982) were among the few motivation theorists who dealt with affect in the 1980s. To take one example from their model, these authors defined the concept of "aspiration" as an expectation accompanied by a strong desire to succeed. The need to set affect apart from motivation—at least conceptually—was not yet well articulated. As we have already indicated, recognition of the volitional (productive striving) aspects of self-regulation was an even later development (Corno, 1989, 2001).

Our 1983 model considered affect just another form of appraisal. We represented affect for school learning as a positive or negative interpretation based on previous experience. Elation over a high grade exemplifies a positive interpretation. (Note that the term *interpretation* stresses the conscious appraisal aspect of affect rather than the pleasure involved in elation.) Debilitating anxiety associated with a given performance is an example of a negative interpretation. Our stance on affect, however narrow, was consistent with the highly cognitive orientation of motivation theory in the 1980s. Bandura (1982), for example, characterized performance anxiety as "repetitive perturbing ideation" (p. 137).

Context as Categories of Variables

To represent instructional context, our model included different categories of variables. However, we depicted the texture of a classroom with none of the nuances seen in today's theory and research. Instead, we stipulated a thin view of the task environment set aside from the larger classroom environment a teacher creates. Level of difficulty was central—that is, did students think the assigned tasks were difficult, or was the challenge about right? Were task requirements new to students, or were the tasks calling upon skills that were relatively polished? Studies had shown that if students perceived assigned tasks to be difficult where requirements were beyond their level of expertise, that raised the likelihood of performance anxiety, and more effort would be needed for success (Snow & Lohman, 1984).

Another category of instructional context variable was the nature of the instruction. In our systematic worldview, the nature of instruction was adequately reflected by three features: the form of instruction used, teacher monitoring, and feedback.

Consider, for example, the form of instruction called "direct" instruction; that is, didactic, teacher-directed lessons, where students were recipients of information handed to them in a structured sequence. At the other extreme is "discovery" learning in which students have to discern concepts and principles for themselves and have to participate in the learning experience. In some iterations of discovery-oriented instruction, students might even be stymied intentionally by a cagey teacher. One hypothesis, based on then-extant research (see Snow, 1977, for a review), was that the entrapment characterizing this sly sort of discovery learning can be deleterious to students with below-average scores on standardized ability tests. Thus, our model posited instructional variations; however, we failed to account for strategic shifts in instruction by teachers during the school day, which we now know to be a regular and important occurrence.

In our model teacher monitoring was the second aspect defining the nature of instruction. Teachers monitor students' learning with various assessments: quizzes, chapter tests, and so forth. But teacher monitoring also takes the form of behavioral supervision and informal assessments of a student's capabilities and performance. We now know that supervision of this type can influence teacher behavior toward students; teachers form opinions and beliefs about students from their daily observations.

The final aspect of the nature of instruction was the feedback provided to students on their work. Did the teacher provide contingent and frequent feedback, correcting mistakes; did the teacher encourage students toward positive performance attributions; or were students simply given "knowledge of results" (e.g., papers marked with numbers of answers correct)? Here, our research suggested that careful monitoring and "encouraging" feedback would result in increased student engagement (Elawar & Corno, 1985). However, this variable said nothing about the goals and overall reward system a teacher establishes to manage and control classroom behavior, which again, we now know to be important.

Twenty years ago, methods for investigating classrooms as coherent groups, methods of observing classrooms that went beyond teacher or student behavior counts, and virtually all forms of qualitative interview and analysis procedures were underdeveloped in educational research. We tried to break new ground by presenting examples from actual teachers and classrooms. We also made forays into content analysis to study teaching effects qualitatively (cf., Reigeluth, 1983 and 1999, on instructional principles).

Nevertheless, our conception of instruction in 1983 failed to take into account influences on student engagement operating in the larger, sociocultural environment beyond classrooms. It lacked a developmental perspective on self-regulated learning. And it gave little sense of the complexities involved when good teachers work to create experiences that fully engage their students with school (Randi & Corno, 2000).

HOW TIMES HAVE CHANGED

Today, the theoretical and methodological landscape for student engagement presents a different picture. First, research on self-regulated learning has advanced over the past 20 years, evolving into several lines of active theory-based investigation in the United States and abroad (see, e.g., Boekaerts, Pintrich, & Zeidner, 2000, for international work). Nowadays many more models than our own exist to characterize SRL, and these models continue to undergo refinements as new hypotheses are tested (Zimmerman & Schunk, 2001, updates their 1989 volume).

Increasingly, theorists interested in SRL are precise about contextual influences. Some even locate context at the center of their theories, giving good evidence that what individual students learn and the processes of learning in which they engage come about because of the layered social and cultural contexts in which they are embedded (cf. McCaslin Rohrkemper, 1989; McCaslin & Hickey, 2003; Paris & Byrnes, 1989; Paris, Byrnes, & Paris, 2003).

Yet another active line of investigation broadens renderings of student engagement in classrooms and coursework. Results of recent studies conducted by motivation theorists align solidly with some of the earliest findings concerning time on task (see, e.g., Patrick, Turner, Meyer, & Midgely, 2003; Reed, Schallert, & Deithloff, 2002). The classroom research of Turner, Schallert, and others is complemented by a growing number of investigations into the academic capabilities that develop from engagement in nonschool experiences, such as in after-school or weekend youth programs (McLaughlin, Irby, & Langman, 1994; Valentine, Cooper, Bettencourt, & Dubois, 2003). Finally, there is a strong foundation for continued research now suggested by sociocultural theory.

We cannot do justice in the space available to the extensive body of sociocultural and ecological theory developed over the past 20 years (see, e.g., Gee, 2000; Michaels & Carello, 1981). But to continue our story we must note sources that contribute to our own thinking. Each central concept that appears in italics throughout the general discussion of sociocultural theory that follows is important to our particular perspective on student engagement in 2003.

Key Concepts from Sociocultural Theory

Going back to Vygotsky (1978), the idea of social appropriation dominates sociocultural theory. Vygotsky held that when students participate in social contexts, they come to incorporate into their own thinking and behavior what they see and do. That is, they appropriate the essential understandings, practices, and mores of those contexts. Mores include values, attitudes, and beliefs as well as social norms.

Schools are not exclusively academic any more than homes and families are nonintellectual, social institutions. Social and emotional issues are significant in school life for teachers as well as students. Peer groups and nonschool activities likewise have both social and academic elements. The discourse, activities, human action, and practices (Wertsch, 1991) of school and home contexts supply a continuous stream of opportunities for students to display interest and build relationships.

Fully participating in school leads students to make sense of explicit curricular material. But taking part and contributing to a curriculum also fosters a sense of the rules and agendas that go unwritten. For example, a student can grasp the subtext of an activity by participating in it, and that experience can be positive or negative. A positive experience might, for example, be a sense of personal identification that spurs further participation—a reading buddy working with a kindergarten child uses that experience to launch an aspiration to teach (Greeno, Resnick, & Collins, 1996). Not every student personally identifies with schoolwork, however, and many report negative experiences. Students who sense unfairness on the part of a teacher may effectively withdraw from school, never raising their hands. Different children will actively challenge the teacher's authority in the same circumstances. Either response reflects avoidance rather than engagement.

The process of apprenticeship intrinsic to schooling ensures that students learn relevant practices of the school culture beyond those derived from participation alone, which they develop as students. Teaching is literally the only profession that is on display as a model for children during several hours weekly beginning at age 5. As students interact with experienced practitioners in structured learning events, the guidance, feedback, and support offered promotes expertise. Without such encouragement there is little chance that students will have positive emotional responses to school (see Collins, Brown, & Newman, 1989). Students also learn to be good students from working alongside others who constantly model what good "studenting" entails. The actual effort to become a good student brings one into the center of an academic community.

Being at the center of a community leads to intrinsic feelings of satisfaction and affiliation rewards. Becoming a good student is not necessarily the end result of the process of participating in multiple academic communities, however. Nor is it, as we may have assumed 20 years ago, evidence that a student has mastered predetermined skills.

Sociocultural theory holds that developing as a student is itself a process of continually discovering learning possibilities in school-related contexts. Even seasoned members of communities still have more to learn. Moreover, growth in individuals theoretically enriches understandings of the collective at hand.

What students learn through participation in social and academic contexts—the contents and processes of their personal repertoires—can be seen in what students and teachers do and say in those contexts. Thus, sociocultural researchers study the social and cultural practices of communities, those conventions and particulars that indicate how participants use the tools that cultural communities make available. Cultural tools include language and discourse, facial expressions and gestures, various forms of technology, and other physical objects and events, all of which can be used as the basis for activity (Meyer & Turner, 2002; Roth, 2001).

For socioculturalists, activity is a fundamental concept, it is the correct unit of analysis for representing the intersection of the individual and the collective. Activity refers to the confluence of academic tasks that teachers plan for their students according to curricular and administrative agendas. Additionally it reflects the way tasks are interpreted by students and the tools and practices that surround task completion (Wenger, 1998).

Ethnographers emphasize the importance of community as a construct influencing individual engagement. Classroom ethnographies use data such as field notes, discourse transcripts, informal and formal interviews, and participant observations to capture how practices in school communities both offer and deny students opportunities to exercise learning and engagement (see, e.g., Olsen, 1997). As some authors note (e.g., Engle & Conant, 2002), a community supports shared beliefs and interdependence on the part of its members, helping to sustain people in the inevitable low or dry times. School learning occurs in community, in the company of others who share common values and goals. The learning of individuals deepens as they share in community life.

At the same time, communities can evoke feelings of exclusivity and conformity, which can be negative. Other negative effects can arise if students are given limited opportunities to display their knowledge in a classroom community, or they feel unwelcome in planned activities. Additionally, if teachers treat students in ways that are age-inappropriate, or if curricular material fails to hold interest, then the very skills teachers hope to polish may actually degrade. Students may then invest cognitive and motivational resources in other, less productive ways.

Neither this language nor these targets of investigation were even on the educational research horizon when we discussed student engagement 20 years ago.

AN ECOLOGICAL PERSPECTIVE: ENGAGEMENT AS EMERGING FROM THE EXERCISE OF ACADEMIC WORK

To clarify our own work in relation to these central constructs of sociocultural theory, we return to our roots as graduate students influenced by

Stanford University's Richard E. Snow. Although our current perspective on student engagement embraces sociocultural elements (this volume), we also build upon the lesser understood theory of situated aptitude envisioned by Snow.

Redefining Aptitude

No serious scholarly discussion of student engagement with school should ignore the role of aptitude. As Snow (1996) wrote, "Aptitude is the most important raw material of education, and its most important product" (p. 537). By this he meant that aptitude equips students to succeed in school while education equips them to succeed in life later on. Nevertheless, Snow recognized that aptitude is a widely misunderstood concept, even among prominent researchers.

In the early 1990s Snow (1991) began the arduous task of recasting traditional "in-the-person" theories of aptitude. He saw a need to rescind the wrong-headed idea that aptitude refers to natural intellectual capacity or endowment. Snow expressed his understanding that aptitude is not exclusively intellectual, and that it is fundamentally situated—that is, it is expressed by the person in some situation.

Snow drew upon modern ecological theory to argue further that aptitude for school learning is something that all persons have the chance to develop. This is because aptitude emerges from transaction, from the interchange between what students bring into academic tasks and the social-educational contexts in which they undertake those tasks and activities. Transaction in this sense assumes a personal agency in students that develops in part from the agencies of others—that is, from parents as well as teachers and peers; hence, within communities (Bandura, 1982).

What a given student "brings" to tasks in school, even in the elementary years, is a set of relatively stable but developing knowledge structures, including skills and beliefs. Built from prior experience, belief structures consist of (perhaps harder to access) values, motives, and goals. More or less, students also bring in plans, preferences, and states of mind—the entire panoply of accumulations from other previously experienced school and school-like events. Evolving continuously throughout life, these accumulations are achievements (Snow, 1996, p. 4), the fruits of experience, only some of which are products of planned instructional events (Stanford Aptitude Seminar, 2002). Like schools, naturally occurring transactions also tune up personal qualities—work habits, for example—even as they degrade others. Shyness or fear of failure, thought to have a neural basis, might degrade to good ends through natural experience.

It is this repertoire of propensities brought to school (Stanford Aptitude Seminar, 2002, p. 47) that establishes students' readiness in the sense of suitability or preparedness to succeed in school learning tasks. Some propensities in the repertoire serve students well when they come into play in school activities and tasks; that is, they function as aptitudes. Other propensities fail to enhance performance on school tasks, and even lead to lackluster effort or work avoidance. These function as inaptitudes. A zeal for reading functions as a school-related aptitude, while extreme performance anxiety—another developed propensity—can impede success in school.

The act of interacting with academic tasks or situations changes a student's initial (pretask) propensities, thus changing the repertoire. So aptitude develops from situations planned and unplanned, from chance encounters with challenging real-world problems, and likewise from tasks that teachers engineer or experiences they make available, however unintentionally. Aptitude, Snow determined, cannot be defined apart from situations; it is an emergent property of person–situation transactions.

Situational Affordances

Snow used the ecological psychologist J. J. Gibson's (1977) notion of affordances to explain how situations activate and develop human potential. In classroom learning, students confront a task or activity, usually one designed or managed by a teacher. There are patterns of action or ways of thinking that astute students sense as necessary for success. Sometimes the teacher is clear about performance expectations; other times an assignment comes with little explanation of how students ought to manage it.

Success occurs when school-savvy students make good use of the situation presented to do their best work. They detect what they need to do, hanging on the teacher's words, picking up meanings from the situation that clue them into the knowledge and skills called for. They manage the endeavor.

Students who are at ease in the company of a work group or a more knowledgeable student take advantage of these external resources as well. And school-savvy students often develop a teacher's mentality; for example, framing questions as a teacher would. In this case, internal, cognitive resources are called for.

Engaging in the process of appraising teacher and task alters the situation at the same time it alters the school-savvy student. There is a resonance of person and environment because teachers respond differently to students who comprehend what they are after. There is an ecological "fit" between student and situation—a person and environment wrapping together that surpasses either the student or the task set apart.

Students finding such a niche for a given activity or learning environment have a different affective experience from those who struggle. When questions come, the struggling student may not be ready; but the comfortable student experiences the feelings of pleasure that go hand in hand with psychological involvement (Csikszentmihalyi, 1975). Students attuned to what a situation offers and the opportunities it affords are then locked into place, absorbing what they can. For the student so engrossed in work, spending mental energy to self-regulate is actually wasteful (Mithaug, 1993). Why buckle down when one can think deeply and playfully, without careful monitoring and control? This is an entirely different conception of engagement from that specified in our 1983 treatise.

Note also that a student can display engagement, even profess engagement (e.g., on research questionnaires), yet garner little satisfaction from a task or activity if the engagement is forced (Reed et al., 2002). Indeed, a keen sense of the rules of engagement could underlie the school-related cynicism commonly observed in adolescents. Certainly, negative affect and external distractions have the potential to interfere with effective cognitive processing (Klinger, 1996); in this case, however, self-regulatory processes or routinized work styles can maintain persistence. For most students on some tasks, engagement is a kind of oblivious carrying out of well-learned procedures.

To take this idea a step further, we now understand that within the norms of schooling students become attuned to react to certain classes of academic affordances and constraints in characteristic ways. School routinely confronts students with some classes of academic situations that are designed to call forth particular propensities. Consider the class of situations that includes tests or test-like events; a quiz means little or no preparation, quick work, and checking answers. Writing assignments represent another class of situations; strategic actions associated with writing include making an outline, using an appropriate format, paying attention to topics, and recalling the rules of grammar and style. Still another class of situations is problem solving. Apart from the formulae, laws, and procedures required for homework problems in, say, algebra or chemistry, problem solving requires careful work habits. Some of these work habits, such as precision in recording mathematical symbols, are unnecessary in other classes of tasks.

Beyond the academic demands of tasks, schooling provides opportunities for students to draw upon their repertoires of stylistic preferences. For example, individuals have different styles of reacting. Confronted with the need to do an essay book review, one student will write easily, automatically incorporating high-level elements of structure and writing style. Another student will refer back to the book frequently, taking more time to complete the same assignment, and then check and recheck before moving on (Strelau, 1983).

Elements of tasks and activities that teachers assign evoke other nonacademic, affective propensities in students as well. A group activity that spurs competition in some students will be totally dispiriting to others.

To the extent that a given propensity is tapped and exercised by school activities, that propensity will develop and mature, even perhaps to the point of overlearning, whether for good or ill. Propensities to engage with school thus have potential to achieve the status of automaticity, occurring almost without acknowledgment and beneath conscious awareness in response to similar future encounters. School engagement emerges from the productive exercise of academic work.

Finally, in Snow's theory, the more affordances that students perceive to be present in a given task, the more meaning can be taken from the experience. "If a...human mind is drawn to something, it is because it expresses something woven into that mind" (Higgins, 2003, p. 6). Frequent meaningful academic experiences accompanied by suitable cognitive effort and positive emotional response lead to greater overall aptitude for school learning.

Snow felt that psychologists were obligated to enlighten public attitudes about human potential by redefining aptitude in these ways, emphasizing its situated, transactional, and emergent properties. He struck out against conventional and commonly assumed views of aptitude as an in-born and fixed intellectual capacity that could be assessed reliably apart from classes of situations (e.g., Herrnstein & Murray, 1994). Snow took his own work in a forceful, new direction.

Recently, at Snow's request, a group of us refined and extended his theoretical writings on aptitude (Stanford Aptitude Seminar, 2002). This effort allowed the two of us to bring our own research on student academic engagement into the new century. Consistent with other contemporary situationist views (Brown, 1994; Greeno, 1998), we reconceptualized aptitude for school learning as a readiness to act in given classes of academic situations.

REMAINING CHAPTER STRUCTURE

The remainder of this chapter continues our story to consider examples of how student engagement develops in two classes of school-relevant activities that take place—or can take place—outside school. In the first case, we discuss the ubiquitous experience of doing homework. Despite a long and controversial history (Gill & Schlossman, 2003), homework is assigned to nearly all school-age children nowadays, beginning as early as kindergarten. Increasingly, American children also have modern computer technology within personal reach. We consider the engagement properties of these two educational contexts—homework and computer learning—and their potential for immersing learners in academic-intellectual situations.

To distinguish our contribution from others in this volume, our examples highlight the volitional aspects of self-regulation (see, e.g., Corno,

2001). Although a variety of processes underlie the ancient concept of conation or purposive striving, current theorizing sets apart the motivational aspects of conation from those that are volitional (e.g., Butler, 2002).

Motivation covers psychological states that precede a commitment to action—including beliefs, desires, expectations, and intentions. Volitional states come into play following commitment, to prepare for and protect goal pursuits, influencing self-appraisals and future motivation. In education, volitional states predominate in work habits and work styles. From neatness and care with written work, to organization and scheduling in homework, teachers reward students who display good work habits all along the age range (Corno, 1993). Our special interest in volitional aspects of self-regulation permits in-depth analysis of the two concrete examples of homework and computer learning. Other chapters in this volume provide good detail on motivational states.

The work habits and work styles that reflect volition can be seen in classroom activities ranging from whole-class, teacher-led instruction, to learning by computer or in small groups. They can also be seen when students complete homework. As students develop accomplished learning routines and productively follow through with academic work, strategic efforts to focus on tasks can be documented. So can the manner by which students regulate affect. In some cases, it makes sense to reestablish links between affect and conation that had been discarded when we wrote about student engagement 20 years ago.

HOW DOES ENGAGEMENT EMERGE AND GET EXERCISE IN ACADEMIC WORK?

Homework and computer technology in some ways reflect contrasting classes of tasks. Homework can be the bane of existence in a household from second grade through middle school. Only on occasion are homework assignments engaging enough to draw children in; nevertheless, some aspects of the classic homework situation exercise engagement in fundamental ways, as we shall see. The case of homework contrasts with the not always realized but seemingly inherent engagement opportunities offered by educational activities in which students use computer technology (Lepper & Malone, 1988). First we discuss homework.

Engagement in Homework

Although students generally complete their homework, this occurs under some duress, at least in the elementary years (Corno, 1996). Even students who enter school with favorable attitudes require assistance as they begin to manage homework assignments. Early homework experiences require levels of management and self-control that challenge the average second grader, often evoking a negative emotional response. As children mature, homework assignments increase in complexity and management issues recede. Many students then begin to struggle with homework's cognitive demands.

By middle school students place homework at the bottom of their list of preferred after-school activities (Leone & Richards, 1989). Studies also show that as they advance in school, students' moods while doing homework generally remain negative, regardless of gender or academic performance (Cooper, 1989). Students rate their levels of positive affect, motivation, and attention during homework lower than similar subjective experiences in other activities (e.g., eating, doing chores, and leisure). Perhaps not surprisingly, middle school students appear most engaged in homework when they complete it in the presence of an adult (usually a parent), rather than with a peer or alone.

Students who accept adult supervision tend to be high achievers (higher grades and test scores are antecedent to supervision rather than, or more clearly than, its consequences) (Leone & Richards, 1989, p. 544). These students also spend increasingly more time on homework as they get older, gradually doing homework entirely on their own

In lieu of parental intervention, students have to muster the volitional control necessary to complete homework, particularly when assignments are boring or difficult. Kuhl (1984) viewed volitional control as synonymous with self-regulation, which he operationalized as learned volitional strategies. Strategies of volitional control that Kuhl identified range from easily observable efforts to arrange and control the environment (e.g., removing oneself to a quiet location to study), to covert processes of self-control such as deliberate concentration, emotion control, and self-instruction. Students use various volitional control strategies to manage time on task, and to bring their attention back to a task when necessary. Volitional strategies are also useful for protecting intentions from the inevitable distractions present in home environments—intrusive siblings, media, or dinnertime bustle. In many ways, homework is a volitional reference task, the kind of situation that is ripe for the study of volitional control.

That was precisely the point of departure for the homework research conducted by Xu and Corno (see Xu, 1994; Xu & Corno, 1998, 2003). Xu observed and interviewed six third graders and their families to compile case studies of students while they did homework. Videotapes and interviews provided qualitative data; both students and parents answered interview questions as they viewed the videotapes of homework sessions.

Results showed that homework provided clear opportunities for children to learn to cope with many of the difficulties of academic effort—

arranging a study environment, managing time, focusing attention, and monitoring motivation. Some students learned these coping strategies from parent suggestion and modeling. Because the homework situation also requires skill in controlling negative emotions and handling distractions, homework experiences can move a child from the status of a novice with academic work to higher levels of skill and self-responsible follow-through (Corno, 2000).

In another study with middle school students (Xu & Corno, 2003) we found support for the position that it is important to help students develop behaviors associated with self-responsible completion of homework even beyond the early grades. Reports from students in grades 6–8 showed benefits to clear teacher expectations regarding when and how homework should be done. In addition, we found it can be helpful to receive direct assistance at home from adults who demonstrate ways to navigate the rough spots of difficult assignments.

This research demonstrates that homework is an emotionally charged process for children and their families (Corno, 1996). Although older students report fluent use of strategies with which beginners struggle, the skill of older students in handling negative emotions during homework remains relatively unsophisticated. Thus, although some areas of self-responsibility can be learned by doing homework, learning how to monitor and control emotions continues to be a volitional challenge into adolescence. These studies converge to suggest that schools and parents can play an important role in helping children refine their self-regulation routines even through the adolescent years. In this way homework can exercise academic engagement.

Engaged Learning in Technology-Based Environments

One of the most interesting venues for the study of academic engagement is the educational computing environment. Increasingly infused into U.S. homes and schools, computer technology is a medium with unique affordances for both teaching and learning (Honey, 2002). Snow and Yalow foresaw this in 1982 when they wrote, "[T]he new technologies can be used to…extend and exercise aspects of intelligence at new and higher levels, thereby strengthening and broadening the scope of intellectual skills already possessed…these technologies can also be used to…do for individuals what they may not be able to do for themselves…to compensate for…information processing limitations" (p. 569).

For example, computers perform lower-level operations such as arithmetic calculations and spelling checks for students, thus freeing up resources that can be used to carry out higher-order thinking. Keyboards do away with handwritten work in many subjects, thus freeing up time. In the best computer-based learning environments, technology and tasks meld to ensure that "Learners generate and test hypotheses in the context of problem solving, check their own knowledge representations, and reflect on their learning in context" (Lajoie & Azevedo, 2002, p. 249).

We can point to four types of research to illustrate the affordances for academic engagement offered by educational technology. First are our own studies of the effects of computer games on student learning and engagement. Second are evaluations of technological innovations for teaching and learning implemented in schools. Third, computer applications are being developed specifically to promote cognitive engagement in users; and theories of self-regulation underlie some of these efforts. Finally, there is research on the Internet as a unique medium for investigating academic studying and self-regulation during homework.

Studies of engagement in a computer game. To look beyond classroom teaching, we conducted studies of strategic planning and self-regulation in a first-generation computer problem-solving environment. A tricky "hunt the hidden monster" game called WUMPUS is one of the early structured software applications in which users apply information-processing skills to handle increasingly complex tasks and memory requirements (see Mandinach, 1984). The game can be played in or outside school.

We collected data as middle school students played WUMPUS during free periods at school. Measures such as error patterns, reaction times, use of feedback, and understanding of game-related strategies were gathered through the structure of the game. We monitored engagement using observations, analyses of student notes, and semistructured interviews (Mandinach & Corno, 1985).

Our results showed that WUMPUS required self-regulation; students who displayed skill in SRL performed best on the game. Successful students actively gathered information, integrated new information with prior knowledge, identified relationships among elements of the game, discriminated relevant from irrelevant stimuli, monitored their performance, and persisted even when they lost. In short, they displayed a combination of cognitive skill and strategic game-playing.

When students received guided instruction as they played the game, performance varied by ability and gender. Lower ability students benefited from guided modeling more than higher ability students, and females benefited more than males.

In addition to these instruction effects, males and females adopted different game-playing styles. Males tended to use active and strong forms of engagement to master the game (i.e., SRL or a close focus on the task). In contrast, while some female players used SRL actively, many more females than males resorted to weaker or more passive engagement that ultimately proved less successful in the game. Females were more likely to adopt one form of engagement and stick to it throughout the various games they played, while more successful game players shifted their engagement strategies according to task demands and feedback from the computer. In other words, when the game demanded active engagement, the successful students responded accordingly. When they were winning and could display a more relaxed form of engagement, then they did so.

To interpret these results using our 2003 language, the game environment (playful, hunting and blasting a monster) afforded opportunities for students to participate in the sort of nonschool activity that strengthens both strategic planning ability and self-regulation. Some students who played the game seized these opportunities in ways that were more productive than others, according to their cognitive and stylistic propensities. There was a better fit between the engagement demands of WUMPUS and the stylistic predilections of males than of females. Students who lacked a propensity for this sort of game (i.e., low ability females) became most engaged when given guided modeling instruction.

Other research on gender differences in response to computer applications complements these findings. Some of this work has led to new games and other computer applications designed to appeal specifically to women. Brunner, Bennett, and Honey (1998) suggested that females respond best to technology that supports existing social settings or other life-related tasks. Females, they argue, look for added value from technology in their daily affairs. Males, on the other hand, tend to seek speed, efficiency, and power in computer applications—features that push the envelope but have potential to take their work to higher levels. Here is an example of how research can inform what might be called the engagement impact of educational innovations (see also Pajares, 2002).

Implementation studies. Another angle on engagement impact can be seen in technology implementation studies, where computers represent a nontraditional approach to classroom teaching. Perhaps the most well-known example of innovative computer use in schools is the Apple Classroom of Tomorrow.

Sandholtz, Ringstaff, and Dwyer (1994, 1997) infused technology into American schools and homes for a select sample of sites. Researchers paid attention to how technology affected student engagement, as measured by teacher reports, audiotapes, journals, and observations. Results showed that students in Apple classrooms expressed more excitement about learning than they did before technology was introduced. Students also spent more time on task, and extra time working on computer-based tasks when they were given the technology. They displayed increased risk-taking and initiative, often going beyond assigned tasks.

However, as students became accustomed to the software, over time their responses became more routine. The software content and task constraints provided insufficient room for experimentation, so students began to lose interest, spending increasing amounts of time on peripheral tasks (such as formatting) rather than concentrating on substantive work.

One interpretation of these results is that increasing expertise with technology leads students to seek other challenges and/or the bells and whistles that maintain engagement. Another plausible interpretation is that increased expertise allows room for higher-level intellectual activity, following Snow and Yalow (1982, p. 869). Relative freedom from complexity decreases need for self-regulation. These researchers did not investigate relationships between individual difference variables such as ability or gender and student response in the Apple classroom, however.

To overcome some of the design and analysis issues raised by the technology implementation studies, Mandinach (1988) designed a more focused study of the impact of technology on student self-regulation. This study piggybacked a larger project whose data included student work products, measures of academic achievement, and measures of SRL in a sample of 53 students in a rural school district over an academic year (Mandinach & Cline, 1994).

Results from the larger project were consistent with related research: Relative to students in control classrooms, students in technology-based classrooms increased in motivation, on-task behavior, and academic engagement. There was also decreased absenteeism. But Mandinach (1988) found that students who exhibited SRL when they worked with technology performed better on academic assignments than other students, including on paper-and-pencil and computer-based problem-solving tasks. There was a direct connection between skillful self-regulation when using the technology and academic performance in the students observed.

Examinations of student responses by ability levels showed a predictable advantage for higher-ability students who became more engaged cognitively as complexity increased. Less able students actually lost ground with increased complexity (see also Stanford Aptitude Seminar, 2002). This result was consistent with our previous finding that certain features of technology promote engagement in some students more than in others (Mandinach & Corno, 1985). Again, we see that successfully promoting engagement leads to gains in volitional competence. The nature of aptitude development is nonlinear, however, benefiting from chance connections and redirections, and depending on functions beneath the level of conscious awareness.

Computer-based tools for cognitive engagement. Azevedo and his colleagues studied SRL in various Web-based and computer software applications. This work is grounded in Winne's (2001) theoretical model of SRL, which targets specific motivational skills such as goal-setting and cognitive qualities, explaining how people study as they learn. To examine goal-setting in the hypermedia environment, college students participated in various forms of assignments and instruction (Azevedo, Guthrie, & Seibert, in press; Azevedo, Ragan, Cromley, & Pritchett, 2002; Azevedo et al., 2002). Data included think-aloud protocols, questionnaires, audio- and videotapes, and work products as measures of cognitive models, goal-setting, and SRL.

Training in goal-setting with the technology enhanced students' mental models as well as their ability to self-regulate. Specifically, students showed evidence of more effective study tactics and learning strategies, better conceptual understanding, and more ability to cope with increasingly difficult tasks. They planned and monitored their own learning, created subgoals, used prior knowledge, and engaged in self-questioning. This targeted technology intervention sufficiently improved the cognitive and motivational skills of less able learners so as to preclude engagement decrements on assignments.

One study in this camp (Azevedo et al., in press) investigated individual differences in students' ability to regulate learning. Data on students' mental models and self-regulation suggested that not all students were capable of regulating their learning or gaining conceptual knowledge from a hypermedia environment. In general, students who did not acquire the conceptual knowledge needed to handle the task also failed to show evidence of skillful self-regulation. The next step in this work is construction of computer-based metacognitive tools for students to use as scaffolds for self-regulation (Azevedo, Cromley, Winters, Xu, & Iny, 2003).

White and Frederiksen (1998) created a curriculum for scientific inquiry centered on a software program called ThinkerTools that builds metacognitive skill and knowledge. The ThinkerTools Inquiry Curriculum, geared to middle school science, addresses Reflective Assessment, defined as the processes by which students reflect on their own and other students' inquiry.

An evaluation of the curriculum in 12 classrooms showed that students who used the metacognitive tool curriculum outperformed controls who received traditional instruction in science. Inquiry curriculum students performed better in both the content area (physics) and on tests of inquiry skills accompanying the program. The curriculum appeared particularly beneficial for low-achieving students.

More recently, White, Shimoda, and Frederiksen (2000) designed SCI-WISE, a software tool that uses embedded "agents" to provide strategic advice on inquiry processes (as in the little guy who pops up on the screen in a word processing program to offer help). SCI-WISE assists students to think about their own cognitive processing, helping to develop knowledge, regulatory skills, and expertise. Such software facilitates appropriate inquiry and SRL by serving as a research instrument at the same time that it scaffolds student skills.

Perhaps the most creative use of computer technology for developing students' cognitive engagement is the software "workshop" of study tools developed by Winne and his colleagues. STUDY (Winne & Fick, 2000) provides tools for students to use as they study textbook or other curricular materials at home. CoNoteS and CoNoteS2 (Hadwin & Winne, 2001;

Winne & Hadwin, 1998) are software applications that support SRL skills, as defined in Winne's (2001) theoretical framework.

CoNoteS2 is an electronic notebook that provides tacit and explicit scaffolding for notetaking and studying. Although it has been tested with textbook materials, CoNotesS2 can be adapted to other contexts such as classroom teaching. Teachers can use it to tutor students in understanding written material and tasks, in setting goals and planning, for study tactics, and to evaluate metacognition. PrepMate (Winne & Jamieson-Noel, 2002) is a yet another software program for text material that provides students with learning objectives and study prompts.

Winne's research group uses these tools not only to assist students in calibrating their actual work habits relative to the ways they purport to study, but also to validate Winne's model of SRL. The software creates a log of study events for each student as interaction occurs. The log then becomes feedback to students, describing their study behavior and assisting them to analyze their own study skills. The research team performs experiments in which calculations from the log represent particular study tactics used, the ways that students organize tactics, and how they coordinate cognitive events with motivational and volitional processes. Additionally, these experiments address hypotheses about how self-regulated studying affects learning.

To date, most of the research with Winne's tools has enhanced the software. But one interesting substantive result is the group's finding that students tend to keep fairly inaccurate records of what and how they study. In addition, many learners in these investigations benefited from the revealing feedback on study habits that tools in the workshop provided. If the promise of computer learning systems is to be realized—that is, if we are really able to document that these systems provide a more effective way to engage new generations of students academically but outside of school—then work such as Winne's has practical as well as theoretical importance.

Research on Internet learning. The Internet presents a unique opportunity for users to engage with content material and in a free exchange with other users for educational or personal purposes at any time of day, in different locations outside school, and at their own pace. It also represents an environment in which many self-regulatory skills are needed for efficient and responsible navigation. As experts on a Web-based Education Commission (2000) noted, the Internet is the most potentially transformative educational technology yet.

The Internet permits access to source material unbound by time and space. Through real-time interactivity, browsing, email, chatrooms, instant messaging, conferencing tools, listservs, and databases, the Internet provides infinite learning opportunities. Students can move outside the limits imposed by social and cultural environments in both the home and school. Exposure to the Internet for diverse groups of adolescent users is increasing (Lenhart, Simon, & Graziano, 2001).

For perhaps the first time, the worldwide access to the Internet means that students from different nations, cultures, and socioeconomic situations can receive instruction in models of self-regulation and academic mastery that are not represented in their home communities. Isolated indigenous groups who gain access to computer technology may be brought closer to the outside world through their exposure to valid models of learning and motivation. As students from many cultural and social backgrounds begin to share similar learning experiences online, tapping into the best websites for instant dialogue about these experiences, the positive possibilities of a global learning community ultimately may be realized. Not incidentally, teachers who join the global learning community will begin to share common understandings of self-regulated learning, and their students will benefit from what they have learned.

In addition, however, the World Wide Web raises the possibility of problems heretofore unseen in education. The Internet is of course a port of access for many inappropriate and undesirable forms of communication and information (Thornburgh & Lin, 2002). Although there are some protections that administrators can provide to avoid hazards, hazards also create new opportunities for creative management, highlighting the importance of self-responsibility and self-regulation by users.

Honey (1999) advocates that students become empowered by teachers and parents to make responsible decisions about the use of Internet technology. She believes that problems that arise when the power of the Internet dangles in front of impressionable youth can be remediated through education. Indeed, accessing inappropriate content, breaching codes of privacy, use of email and online services to send offensive or overly suggestive messages, and plagiarism are increasing (Lewis, 2001). The sort of education needed includes technical information, but also better communications by adults about consequences, development of media literacy, and instruction that pushes students toward sound judgment as self-regulating users. As Shute and Towle (2003) write, "An e-learning program that is replete with bells and whistles, or provides unlimited access to Web-based documents, is no substitute for sound instructional design" (p. 111).

Web-based projects that specifically engender appropriate cognitive engagement skills are beginning to emerge. One such project, AmericaQuest, was highlighted by the Web-based Education Commission (2000). AmericaQuest attempts to foster skills such as finding, recognizing, and evaluating content; analyzing information, weighing different perspectives, determining a solution, and solving problems by integrating clues and information. These skills of cognitive engagement underlie effective navigation of Web-based learning experiences. The "courses, certification, and capability" (3C architecture) proposed by Schutz (2002) is another example. In this system of courses delivered through Internet links, individuals of all ages would learn content material. At the same time, they would have access to personal "expert guides" who serve as counselors and portals for prospective employment, educational opportunities, and certification.

Our story comes full circle with a recent dissertation by Rogers (2001), who attempted to validate our 1983 model of student engagement in a study of Internet navigation. Rogers examined 80 undergraduates' ability to search the Internet for information using the five processes of self-regulated learning we defined in 1983; namely, alertness, selectivity, connecting, planning, and monitoring. Data included observations of students as they searched the Internet, metacognitive and Internet questionnaires assessing SRL obtained prior to and following the study, measures of time spent in searching the Internet, and a test of field perception.

Results showed that students used different search strategies over time. In initial work, students exhibited little evidence of strategic searching. However, as students became more reflective about their search strategies, their objectives shifted with a transition to higher-level processing characteristic of SRL. Some students even used SRL strategically, shifting to weaker forms of engagement as task demands decreased (see also Schofield, 1997).

Rogers (2001) also examined how cognitive engagement processes were manifested in interactions with the Internet. She noted distinct patterns of alertness, selectivity, and connecting, but observed little planning and monitoring in all but the more experienced users. Rogers concluded that planning may be difficult in Internet interactions due to the speed and manner by which information is transmitted. In contrast, monitoring may be a skill that experienced users have made automatic; to the extent that this is correct, monitoring would be difficult to observe.

Rogers did not measure any noncognitive aspects of SRL; she did not examine individual differences among students; nor did she compare Internet use in classrooms with Internet use by individual students working alone.

CONCLUSION

We discussed two contexts for student academic engagement that enhance or extend what takes place in classrooms. Our analysis illustrates important conceptual dimensions that evolve apart from traditional classroom teaching. Academic engagement is not a classroom phenomenon as we thought in 1983, it is sociocultural.

To conclude our story, we revisit an observation that kept appearing as we reviewed the research for this chapter: Students tend to lose focus when left on their own to do academic-intellectual work, regardless of whether the learning environment is designed to engage them or not. When working alone on homework, students are easily distracted by both external and internal events. On a computer, students drift off task toward recreational sites. At home, work on computers includes downloading music and instant messaging (multitasking). When the computer and Internet are used in class and to do homework, drifting away from tasks and multitasking present problems. Classwork and homework situations require focused attention. Thus there remains a need for productive self-regulation during work on computers, regardless of their bells and whistles.

Whether students participate in classroom activities, do homework, or go online, academic-intellectual situations also present a psychological dilemma, a tradeoff between personal autonomy and external control (Deci, 1980). The social and cultural elements common to many educational situations that we described in this chapter—group activity, a press for participation, the availability of tools, and skills appropriated through apprenticeship—afford resources and opportunities for student engagement in and outside school. At the same time, there is an explicitly stated objective or at least a sincere hope that eventually students will fly solo (Scardamalia & Bereiter, 1985). The need for active management of internal resources complements the need to manage external resources.

Teachers, parents, or peers who step in to help when a student struggles in an educational situation become valuable external resources for success. There is a temporary compensation when the skills of someone else, or, alternatively, the capabilities of a computer study tool, can be used to supplant the more onerous requirements of a task (Salomon, 1979). But there are different ways to take advantage of externally available resources. Certainly students can seek help with work that they cannot do alone; but even a tacit decision to do this trades off autonomy. Alternatively, students can retain some personal control by actively managing external resources and taking responsibility for learning.

When adults see students struggle academically, they are predisposed by training if not temperament to make themselves available. Some are all too ready to assume control, often without intention or even awareness. It is just as common for children to take the prospect of adult assistance for granted. But part of long-term development for students is becoming self-regulated, and part of teaching and parenting is letting go. It seems clear that at minimum students have to engage self-regulated learning regularly to incur its advantages.

By actively managing both internal and external resources in academic-intellectual situations encountered in and outside school, students not only expand their knowledge and skill, they also grasp the mores and practices of those nonschool learning experiences that share academic properties with school. The students who capitalize on opportunities provided within education's various social and cultural communities modulate their own self-regulation routines. In this way, they accommodate shifting demands of tasks. The ability to manage both internal and external resources concurrently compels productive self-regulated learning in whatever educational experiences students undertake. Achieving this goal in the development of volitional aptitude moves a student further toward preparation, readiness, and suitability for future academic encounters, equipped for success in education and beyond. All of this we have learned about student engagement in the past 20 years.

REFERENCES

Atkinson, J. W. (1974). Motivational determinants of intellectual performance and cumulative achievement. In J. W. Atkinson & J. O. Raynor (Eds.), *Motivation and achievement* (pp. 389–410). Washington, DC: Winston.

Azevedo, R., Cromley, J. G., Winters, F. I., Xu, L., & Iny, D. (2003). *Is strategy instruction effective in facilitating students' ability to regulate their learning in hypermedia?* Paper presented at the World Conference on AI in Education, Sydney, Australia.

Azevedo, R., Guthrie, J. T., & Seibert, D. (in press). The role of self-regulated learning in fostering students' conceptual understanding of complex systems with hypermedia. *Journal of Educational Computing Research.*

Azevedo, R., Guthrie, J. T., Wong, H., & Mulhern, J. (2001, March). *Do different instructional interventions facilitate students' ability to shift to more sophisticated mental models of complex systems?* Paper presented at the annual meeting of the American Educational Research Association, Seattle.

Azevedo, R., Ragan, S., Cromley, J. G., & Pritchett, S. (2002, April). *Do different goal-setting conditions facilitate students' ability to regulate their learning of complex science topics with RiverWeb?* Paper presented at the annual meeting of the American Educational Research Association, New Orleans.

Azevedo, R., Seibert, D., Guthrie, J. T., Cromley, J. G., Wong, H., & Tron, M. (2002, April). *How do students regulate their learning of complex systems with hypermedia?* Paper presented at the annual meeting of the American Educational Research Association, New Orleans.

Bandura, A. (1977). Self-efficacy: Toward a unifying theory of behavioral change. *Psychological Review, 84,* 191–215.

Bandura, A. (1982). Self-efficacy mechanism in human agency. *American Psychologist, 37,* 122–148.

Berliner, D. C. (1979). Tempus educare. In P. L. Peterson & H. L. Walberg (Eds.), *Conceptions of teaching.* Berkeley, CA: McCutchan.

Boekaerts, M., Pintrich, P. R., & Zeidner, M. (Eds.). (2000). *Handbook of self-regulation.* San Diego, CA: Academic Press.

Brown, A. L. (1994). The advancement of learning. *Educational Researcher, 23,* 4–12.

Butler, D. L. (2002). Qualitative approaches to investigating self-regulated learning: Contributions and challenges. *Educational Psychologist, 37*(1), 59–64.

Brunner, C., Bennett, D., & Honey, M. (1998). Girl Games and technological desire. In J. Cassell & H. Jenkins (Eds.), *From Barbie to Moral Kombat* (pp. 72–88). Cambridge, MA: MIT Press.

Chase, W. G., & Simon, H. A. (1973). Perception in chess. *Cognitive Psychology, 4,* 55–81.

Collins, A., Brown, J. S., & Newman, S. E. (1989). Cognitive apprenticeship: Teaching the craft of reading, writing, and mathematics. In L. B. Resnick (Ed.), *Knowing, learning, and instruction: Essays in honor of Robert Glaser* (pp. 453–494). Hillsdale, NJ: Erlbaum.

Cooper, H. (1989). *Homework.* White Plains, NY: Longman.

Corno, L. (1981). Cognitive organizing in classrooms. *Curriculum Inquiry, 11,* 359–377.

Corno, L. (1989). Self-regulated learning: A volitional analysis. In B. J. Zimmerman & D. H. Schunk (Eds.), *Self-regulated learning and academic achievement: Theory, research, and practice* (pp. 111–142). New York: Springer-Verlag.

Corno, L. (1993). The best-laid plans: Modern conceptions of volition and educational research. *Educational Researcher, 22,* 14–22.

Corno, L (1996). Homework is a complicated thing. *Educational Researcher, 25,* 27–30.

Corno, L (2000). Looking at homework differently. *Elementary School Journal, 100,* 529–548.

Corno, L. (2001). Volitional aspects of self-regulated learning. In B. J. Zimmerman & D. H. Schunk (Eds.), *Self-regulated learning and academic achievement: Theoretical perspectives* (2nd ed., pp. 191–226). Mahwah, NJ: Erlbaum.

Corno, L., Collins, K., & Capper, J. (1982). *Where there's a way there's a will: Self-regulating the low achieving student.* (ERIC Document Reproduction Services No. ED222499)

Corno, L., & Mandinach, E. B. (1983). The role of cognitive engagement in classroom learning and motivation. *Educational Psychologist, 18*(2), 88–108.

Csikszentmihalyi, M. (1975). *Beyond anxiety and boredom: The experience of play in work and games.* San Francisco: Jossey-Bass.

Deci, E. L. (1980). *The psychology of self-determination.* Lexington, MA: D. C. Heath.

Elawar, M. C., & Corno, L. (1985). A factorial experiment in teachers' written feedback on student homework: Changing teacher behavior a little rather than a lot. *Journal of Educational Psychology, 77,* 162–173.

Engle, R. A., & Conant, F. R. (2002). Guiding principles for fostering productive disciplinary engagement: Explaining an emergent argument in a community of learners classroom. *Cognition and Instruction, 20,* 399–483.

Furrer, C., & Skinner, E. (2003). Sense of relatedness as a factor in children's academic engagement and performance. *Journal of Educational Psychology, 95,* 148–162.

Gee, J. P. (2000). New literacy studies: From "socially situated" to the work of the school. In D. Barton, M. Hamilton, & R. Ivanic (Eds.), *Situated literacies: Reading and writing in context.* (pp. 180–196). London: Routledge.

Gibson, J. J. (1977). The concept of affordances. In R. Shaw & J. Bransford (Eds.), *Perceiving, acting, and knowing* (pp. 67–82). Hillsdale, NJ: Erlbaum.

Gill, B. P., & Schlossman, S. L. (2003). Parents and the politics of homework: Some historical perspectives. *Teachers College Record, 105,* 846–871.

Greeno, J. G. (1998). The situativity of knowing, learning, and research. *American Psychologist, 52,* 5–26.

Greeno, J. G., Collins, A. M., & Resnick, L. (1996). Cognition and learning. In D. C. Berliner & R. C. Calfee (Eds.), *Handbook of educational psychology* (pp. 15–46). New York: Macmillan.

Hadwin, A. F., & Winne, P. H. (2001). CoNoteS2: A software tool for promoting self-regulation. *Education Research and Evaluation, 7*(2-3), 313–334.

Herrnstein, R. J., & Murray, C. (1994). *The bell curve: The reshaping of American life by differences in intelligence.* New York: Free Press.

Higgins, R. (2003, February 9). The truck gene. *The Boston Globe Magazine,* pp. 6–7.

Honey, M. (1999). *Old wine in new bottles: Ethics and the Internet.* New York: EDC Center for Children and Technology.

Honey, M. (2002). New approaches to assessing students' technology-based work. In N. Dickard (Ed.), *Great expectations: Leveraging America's investment in educational technology* (pp. 24–28). New York: EDC Center for Children and Technology.

Klinger, E. (1996). Emotional influences on cognitive processing, with implications for theories of both. In P. M. Gollwitzer & J. A. Bargh (Eds.), *The psychology of action: Linking cognition and motivation to behavior* (pp. 168–189). New York: Guilford Press.

Kuhl, J. (1984). Volitional aspects of achievement motivation and learned helplessness: Toward a comprehensive theory of action control. In B. A. Maher (Ed.), *Progress in experimental personality research* (Vol. 12, pp. 99–170). New York: Academic Press.

Lajoie, S. P., & Azevedo, R. (2000). Cognitive tools for medical informatics. In S. P. Lajoie (Ed.), *Computers as cognitive tools: No more walls* (Vol. 2, pp. 247–271). Mahwah, NJ: Erlbaum.

Lenhart, A., Simon, M., & Graziano, M. (2001). *The Internet and education: Findings of the Pew Internet and American life project* [Online]. Washington, DC: Pew Internet and American Life Project. Retrieved February 14, 2003 http://www.pewinternet.org/

Leone, C. M., & Richards, M. H. (1989). Classwork and homework in early adolescence: The ecology of achievement. *Journal of Youth and Adolescence, 18,* 531–548.

Lewis, M. (2001). *Next: The future just happened.* New York: Norton.

Mandinach, E. B. (1984). *The role of strategic planning and self-regulation in learning an intellectual computer game.* Unpublished doctoral dissertation, Stanford University, Stanford, CA.

Mandinach, E. B. (1988). *Self-regulated learning substudy: Systems thinking and curriculum innovation (STACI) project* (TR88-25). Cambridge, MA: Harvard Graduate School of Education, Educational Technology Center.

Mandinach, E. B., & Cline, H. F. (1994). *Classroom dynamics: Implementing a technology-based curriculum innovation.* Hillsdale, NJ: Erlbaum.

Mandinach, E. B., & Corno, L. (1985). Cognitive engagement variations among students of different ability level and sex in a computer problem solving game. *Sex Roles, 13*(3/4), 241–251.

McCaslin Rohrkemper, M (1989). Self-regulated learning and academic achievement: A Vygotskian view. In B. J. Zimmerman & D. H. Schunk (Eds.), *Self-regulated learning and academic achievement: Theory, research, and practice* (pp. 143–168). New York: Springer-Verlag.

McCaslin, M., & Hickey, D. T. (2003). Self-regulated learning and academic achievement: A Vygotskian view. In B. J. Zimmerman & D. H. Schunk (Eds.), *Self-regulated learning and academic achievement: Theoretical perspectives* (pp. 227–252). Mahwah, NJ: Erlbaum.

McLaughlin, M. W., Irby, M. A., & Langman, J. (1994). *Urban sanctuaries: Neighborhood organizations in the lives and futures of inner-city youth.* San Francisco: Jossey-Bass.

Meyer, D. K. & Turner, J. C. (2002). Using instructional discourse analysis to study the scaffolding of student self-regulation. *Educational Psychologist, 37,* 17–26.

Michaels, C. F., & Carello, C. (1981). *Direct perception.* New York: Appleton-Century-Crofts.

Mithaug, D. E. (1994). *Self-regulation theory: How optimal adjustment maximizes gain.* Westport, CT: Praeger.

Olsen, L. (1997). *Made in America.* New York: New Press.

Pajares, F. (2002). Gender and perceived self-efficacy in self-regulated learning. *Theory into Practice, 41*(2), 116-125.

Paris, S. G., & Cross, D. R. (1983). Ordinary learning: Pragmatic connections among children's beliefs, motives, and actions. In J. Bisanz, & R. Kail (Eds.), *Learning in children* (pp. 137–169). New York: Springer-Verlag.

Paris, S. G., & Byrnes, J. P. (1989). The constructivist approach to self-regulation and learning in the classroom. In B. J.Zimmerman & D. H. Schunk (Eds.), *Self-regulated learning and academic achievement: Theory, research, and practice* (pp. 169–200). New York: Springer-Verlag.

Paris, S. G., Byrnes, J. P., & Paris, A. H. (2003). Constructing theories, identities, and actions of self-regulated learners. In B. J. Zimmerman & D. H. Schunk (Eds.), *Self-Regulated learning and academic achievement: Theoretical perspectives* (pp. 253–288). Mahwah, NJ: Erlbaum.

Patrick, H., Turner, J. C., Meyer, D. K., & Midgley, C. (2003). How teachers establish psychological environments during the first days of school: Associations with aviodance in mathematics. *Teachers College Record, 105,* 1521-1558.

Randi, J., & Corno, L. (2000). Teacher innovations in self-regulated learning. In M. Boekaerts, P. R. Pintrich, & M. Zeidner (Eds.), *Handbook of self-regulation* (pp. 651–686). San Diego, CA: Academic Press.

Reed, J. H., Schallert, D. L., & Deithloff, L. F. (2002). Investigating the interface between self regulation and involvement processes. *Educational Psychologist, 37,* 53–64.

Reigeluth, C. M. (Ed.). (1983). *Instructional design theories and models: Vol. 1. An overview of their current status.* Hillsdale, NJ: Erlbaum.

Reigeluth, C. M. (Ed.). (1999). *Instructional design theories and models: Vol. II. A new paradigm of instructional theory.* Mahwah, NJ: Erlbaum.

Rogers, D. M. (2001). *An investigation of components in Corno and Mandinach's self-regulated learning model applied to Internet navigation.* Unpublished doctoral dissertation, University of Albany, Albany, NY.

Roth, W. (2001). Gestures: Their role in teaching and learning. *Review of Educational Research, 71,* 365–392.

Salomon, G. (1979). *Media, cognition, and learning.* San Francisco: Jossey-Bass.

Sandholtz, J. H., Ringstaff, C., & Dwyer, D. C. (1994). *Student engagement revisited: Views from technology-rich classrooms* (ACOT report #21). Cupertino, CA: Apple Computer, Inc.

Sandholtz, J. H., Ringstaff, C., & Dwyer, D. C. (1997). *Teaching with technology: Creating student-centered classrooms.* New York: Teachers College Press.

Scardamalia, M., & Bereiter, C. (1985). Fostering the development of self-regulation in children's knowledge processing. In S. F. Chipman, J. W. Segal, & R.

Glaser (Eds.), *Thinking and learning skills: Research and open questions* (pp. 563–577). Hillsdale, NJ: Erlbaum.

Schofield, J. W. (1997). Computers and classroom social processes: A review of the literature. *Social Science Computer Review, 15*(1), 27–39.

Schunk, D. H. (1982). Effects of effort attributional feedback on children's perceived self-efficacy and achievement. *Journal of Educational Psychology, 74,* 548–557.

Schutz, R. (2002, September 9). *Remodeling schooling: A new architecture for preschool to precollege instruction.* Teachers College Record [Online]. Retrieved on June 9, 2003, from http://www.tcrecord.org

Shute, V., & Towle, B. (2003). Adaptive e-learning. *Educational Psychologist, 38,* 105–114.

Snow, R. E. (1974). Representative and quasi-representative designs for research on teaching. *Review of Educational Research, 44,* 265–291.

Snow, R. E. (1978). Research on aptitudes: A progress report. In L. S. Shulman (Ed.), *Review of research in education* (Vol. 4, pp. 50–105). Itasca, IL: Peacock.

Snow, R. E. (1991). The concept of aptitude. In R. E. Snow & D. F. Wiley (Eds.), *Improving inquiry in social science* (pp. 249–284). Hillsdale, NJ: Erlbaum.

Snow, R. E. (1996). Aptitude development and education. *Psychology, Public Policy, and Law, 2,* 536–560.

Snow, R. E., Corno, L., & Jackson, D., III. (1996). Individual differences in affective and conative functions. In D. C. Berliner & R. C. Calfee (Eds.), *Handbook of educational psychology* (pp. 243–310). New York: Macmillan.

Snow, R. E., & Lohman, D. F. (1984). Toward a theory of cognitive aptitude for learning from instruction. *Journal of Educational Psychology, 76,* 347–376.

Snow, R. E., & Yalow, E. (1982). Education and intelligence. In R. J. Sternberg (Ed.), *Handbook of human intelligence* (pp. 493–585). New York: Cambridge University Press.

Stanford Aptitude Seminar: Corno, L., Cronbach, L. J., Kupermintz, H., Lohman, D. F., Mandinach, E. B., Porteus, A. W., & Talbert, J. E. (2002). *Remaking the concept of aptitude: Extending the legacy of Richard E. Snow.* Mahwah, NJ: Erlbaum.

Stayrook, N. G., Corno, L., & Winne, P. H. (1978). Path analyses relating student perceptions of teacher behavior to student achievement. *Journal of Teacher Education, 29,* 51–57.

Strelau, J. (1983). *Temperament-personality-activity.* New York: Academic Press.

Tesser, A., & Campbell, J. (1982). A self-evaluation maintenance approach to school behavior. *Educational Psychologist, 17,* 1–13.

Thornburgh, D., & Lin., H. S. (Eds.). (2002). *Youth, pornography, and the Internet.* Washington, DC: National Academy Press.

Valentine, J. C., Cooper, H. B., Bettencourt, A., & Dubois, D. L. (2003). Out-of-school activities and academic achievement: The mediating role of self-beliefs. *Educational Psychologist, 37,* 245–256.

Vygotsky, L.S. (1978). *Mind in society: The development of higher psychological processes.* Cambridge, MA: Harvard University Press.

Wallace, R., Kupperman, J., Krajcik, J., & Soloway, E. (2000). Students online in a sixth-grade classroom. *Journal of the Learning Sciences, 9*(1), 75–104.

Web-based Education Commission. (2000). *The power of the Internet for learning: Moving from promise to practice* [Online]. Report of the Web-based Commission to the President and the Congress of the United States, Washington, DC.

Retrieved February 14, 2003, from http://ed.gov/offices/AC/WBEC/FinalReport.

Weiner, B. (1979). A theory of motivation for some classroom experiences. *Journal of Educational Psychology, 71*, 3–25.

Weiner, B. (1980). *Human motivation*. New York: Holt, Rinehart and Winston.

Wenger, E. (1998). *Communities of practice: Learning, meaning, and identity*. Cambridge, MA: Harvard University Press.

Wertsch, J. V. (1991). *Voices of the mind: A sociocultural approach to mediated action*. Cambridge, MA: Harvard University Press.

White, B. Y., & Frederiksen, J. R. (1998). Inquiry, modeling, and metacognition: Making science accessible to all students. *Cognition and Instruction, 16*(1), 3–118.

White, B. Y., Shimoda, T. A., & Frederiksen, J. R. (2000). Facilitating students' inquiry learning and metacognitive development through modifiable software advisers. In S. P. Lajoie (Ed.), *Computers as cognitive tools: No more walls* (Vol. 2, pp. 97–132). Mahwah, NJ: Erlbaum.

Winne, P. H. (2001). Self-regulated learning viewed from models of information processing. In B. J. Zimmerman & D. H. Schunk (Eds.), *Self-regulated learning and academic achievement* (2nd ed., pp. 153–189). Mahwah, NJ: Erlbaum.

Winne, P. H., & Fick, D. (2000). *STUDY: An environment for authoring and presenting adaptive learning tutorials* (Version 3.5) [Computer software]. Burnaby, BC: Simon Fraser University.

Winne, P. H., & Hadwin. A. F. (1998, August). *Using CoNoteS2 to study and support self-regulated learning*. Paper presented at the meeting of the International Association of Applied Psychology, San Francisco.

Winne, P. H., & Jamieson-Noel, D. (2002). Self-regulating studying by objectives for learning: Students' reports compared to a model. *Contemporary Educational Psychology*.

Winne, P. H., & Marx, R. W. (1982). Students' and teachers' views of thinking processes for classroom learning. *Elementary School Journal, 82*, 493–518.

Winne, P. H., & Marx, R. W. (1989). A cognitive processing analysis of motivation within classroom tasks. In C. Ames & R. Ames (Eds.), *Research on motivation in education* (Vol. 3, pp. 223–257). Orlando, FL: Academic Press.

Xu, J. (1994). *Doing homework: A study of possibilities*. Unpublished doctoral dissertation, Teachers College, Columbia University, New York.

Xu, J., & Corno, L. (1998). Case studies of families doing third-grade homework. *Teachers College Record, 100*, 402–436.

Xu, J., & Corno, L. (2003). Family help and homework management reported by middle school students. *Elementary School Journal, 103*, 503–516.

Zimmerman, B. J., & Schunk, D. H. (Eds.). (1989). *Self-regulated learning and academic achievement: Theory, research and practice*. New York: Springer-Verlag.

Zimmerman, B. J., & Schunk, D. H. (Eds.). (2001). *Self-regulated learning and academic achievement: Theoretical perspectives* (2nd ed). Mahwah, NJ: Erlbaum.

CHAPTER 14

HOW SCHOOLS SHAPE TEACHER EFFICACY AND COMMITMENT
Another Piece in the Achievement Puzzle

Helenrose Fives and Patricia A. Alexander

INTRODUCTION

For the last three years, Rennae Kelly* has been a sixth-grade teacher in a K–6 school situated in an affluent suburban neighborhood. Prior to assuming that position, Rennae was a highly-regarded teacher at an inner-city middle school. Here Rennae talks about her feelings of competence and satisfaction as a teacher and her beliefs about the conditions in herself and the educational system that contribute to those feelings.

Rennae's Dialogue

I have always known I was meant to be a teacher. There is nothing more satisfying to me than helping students discover they can understand or do something they once

Big Theories Revisited

Volume 4 in: Research on Sociocultural Influences on Motivation and Learning, pages 329–359.

Copyright © 2004 by Information Age Publishing, Inc.

ISBN: 1-59311-053-7 (hardcover), 1-59311-052-9 (paperback)

thought beyond their abilities. That is one reason I took a job at Porter Middle School*—an inner-city school with high poverty and low test scores—when all my classmates headed to the suburbs. I expected the going to be rough at Porter. But I felt ready for the challenge. These were kids who had been written off by the system and who really needed someone willing to invest time and energy in them and their futures. It was not easy to win their trust in that first year or to get my "sea legs." I worked endless hours preparing materials and organizing the classroom, but it felt good. Before the end of that first year, things began to fall into place for me and my students. The everyday routines became familiar, the stress lessened, and the kids were learning. There were behavior problems—some very trying students—but that was to be expected in a rough inner-city school. By the third year, I had a reputation among the students, parents, and the administration as a good and caring teacher who got results.

Three years ago, the pursuit of a graduate degree in education made it necessary for me to change schools. I took this job at Western Middle School.* The contrast to Porter could not have been greater. The majority of the kids at Western come from well-off homes and do not lack for anything financially. Moreover, these parents are actively involved and visit the school on a regular basis. Western students also get some of the highest scores on the State assessment. I figured this job would allow me to try out the new pedagogical approaches and teaching strategies that I was learning in my graduate classes. But things have not gone as expected. After the first year at Western, it became apparent to the school administration that I could "get results" with the more difficult students. Therefore, for the past two years, the principal saddled me with all the serious behavior problems in the sixth grade, as I was "most equipped to handle" them. I never imagined how many children from presumably "good" homes suffer from serious social/emotional and attention/hyperactivity problems. More of my day is spent in behavior management than in teaching.

The parents of my students have a great impact on my teaching and school policy. To strengthen the bond between the school and home, parents at Western are allowed to request specific teachers for their children. Once the parents have been allowed to choose me as a teacher, they feel comfortable calling me by my first name, making demands such as wanting to be emailed daily, and finding ways to be at school, all day. The interest and involvement of these parents are encouraging, particularly after working at Porter where parents seldom showed up for report card conferences, much less to volunteer in the classroom. I appreciate the parents, but sometimes they get too involved in the everyday teaching and leave me with that feeling one gets when someone runs her fingernails down the chalkboard.

Added to these factors—my newfound role of disciplinarian and overly involved parents—the principal is determined to keep the test scores at Western at the top of the heap. So, our curriculum does not leave much room for creativity. At least at Porter I was allowed to focus the curriculum to meet my student's needs and interests. We did not have a third of the materials and supplies I have at Western, but, at least, I was allowed to use those that we did have in the methods I felt would best serve my students. Here at Western it seems that every pedagogical decision needs to be validated by how it will serve to improve test scores.

Lately, I have dreaded walking into the school building. This is not what I envisioned when I signed on to become a teacher. I feel more like a babysitter than a teacher, and I do not feel needed, appreciated, or trusted in the way I was at Porter. Could this be the onset of teacher burnout?

Based on the extensive literature in achievement motivation, there is little doubt about the power that motivation exerts on learners, learning, and the learning environment (Pintrich & Schunk, 1996). From the research on goal orientation, interest, and self-efficacy to studies of choice/self-determination and engagement, the paths between motivational constructs and academic achievement have been strongly and consistently charted (Murphy & Alexander, 2000). For example, students who seek to master the content report more personal interest in the domains and topics, and those feel more self-efficacious manifest more positive academic outcomes than those lower in these motivational constructs (Alexander & Murphy, 1998; Bandura, 1977). Likewise, students given more choice and more determination in their own learning and who are more involved and participatory in the educational environment achieve better than others (Deci & Ryan, 2002; Guthrie, 1996). Similarly, the paths between teachers' motivations and the performance of the teachers themselves, as well as their students, have been equally well established for an array of motivational constructs, including self-efficacy, locus of control, goal orientation, and autonomy (Coldarci, 1992; Gibson & Dembo, 1984; Tschannen-Moran, Woolfolk-Hoy, & Hoy, 1998).

Yet, what is missing within this richly constructed portrait of teacher motivation and learner achievement is an understanding of the influence that schools as sociocultural contexts exert on teachers' motivations, and ultimately on learners and learning. Rennae's experiences and her reflections demonstrate a few of the ways that schools as sociocultural environments can shape teachers' motivations. In this chapter, we will explore how teachers' motivations, specifically their self-efficacy and commitment, are fostered or diminished by the contextual forces present within the school context.

The motivational constructs of efficacy and commitment were selected as the focus of this exploration for two reasons. First, within the literature on teacher motivation, these constructs repeatedly emerged in studies or parts of studies that also considered educational environmental or contextual influences. Second, each of these constructs taps into an informative and somewhat distinct area of motivation that may better help us understand teachers' actions and reactions.

Teacher Efficacy

Teacher efficacy describes teachers' beliefs in their ability to perform specific tasks in order to achieve desirable educational outcomes (Tschannen-Moran et al., 1998). Teacher efficacy was first conceptualized by RAND researchers when they included two items reflecting locus of control in a larger survey given to teachers (Berman, McLaughlin, Bass, Pauly, & Zellman, 1977). These researchers were surprised at the amount of variance in student achievement and other positive outcomes that these two items were able to explain. These two items reflected both external locus of control ("When it comes right down to it, a teacher really can't do much because most of a student's motivation and performance depends on his or her home environment," McLaughlin & Marsh, 1978, p. 85) and internal locus of control ("If I try hard, I can get through to even the most difficult or unmotivated students," Berman et al., 1977, p. 137) were named teacher efficacy.

At the same time, Bandura (1977) published his first work on the importance of self-efficacy theory. Self-efficacy, according to Bandura, is distinct from locus of control. In fact, Bandura (1997) considered self-efficacy to be the exercise of control, as the title of his most recent text suggests. From this perspective, self-efficacy is the individual's belief that he or she is able to organize and execute particular actions in order to bring about desired results (Bandura, 1997). Self-efficacy is also distinguished from locus of control theory, which focuses on whether or not the attainment of outcomes is within an individual's control. For example, it may be within Rennae's control to call the parents of her students at home every evening; that is, it is within her abilities and power. Thus, we would say she has an internal locus of control. However, Rennae may feel little or no efficacy for this task. In other words, she may not consider herself to be capable of actually making those calls on a daily basis, for whatever reason. In this way, we can think of efficacy as individuals' choice to wield the control they have.

These two lines of research (i.e., locus of control and efficacy) were merged by Gibson and Dembo (1984) when they created the Teacher Efficacy Scale. This work suggested that efficacy was comprised of two factors, general and personal teaching efficacy. The first factor, *general teaching efficacy*, refers to beliefs about what teachers' could do in general and is reflective of the external locus of control item from RAND. The second factor, *personal teaching efficacy*, assessed beliefs about what responding teachers felt they themselves could accomplish, reflecting the internal locus of control item and Bandura's self-efficacy theory. This understanding of efficacy and the Gibson and Dembo (1984) measure has dominated the teacher efficacy literature until recently. Catalysts for that shift in perspective were two studies conducted by Tschannen-Moran and colleagues. Specifically, Tschannen-Moran and colleagues (1998) conducted an extensive review of the teacher efficacy literature that offered a new understanding of teacher efficacy rooted in Bandura's self-efficacy theory. Additionally, Tschannen-Moran and Woolfolk-Hoy (2001) provided an in-depth review of the measures of teacher efficacy, concluding with a new measure they have developed that was again strongly influenced by Bandura's theoretical perspective on efficacy.

Although the Tschannen-Moran and colleagues (1998) and the Tschannen-Moran and Woolfolk-Hoy (2001) reviews afforded important insights into teacher efficacy beliefs and their measurement, the current analysis extends understanding of efficacy in several important ways. First, several recent studies of teacher efficacy have been conducted since the publication of those reviews (e.g., Goddard & Goddard, 2001; Henson, 2000). These works are incorporated in our examination. Moreover, the reviews conducted by Tschannen-Moran and colleagues sought to establish the history of teacher efficacy research in general (Tschannen-Moran et al., 1998) and later to explore the specific methods for measuring teacher efficacy (Tschannen-Moran & Woolfolk-Hoy, 2001). Additionally, both of these reviews direct the reader toward an understanding of teacher efficacy from the perspective of Bandura's theory.

Our intention is not to advocate for any one research perspective or to restrict our analysis to studies that were undertaken from that viewpoint. Consequently, our review incorporates works that reflect the two-factor model of Gibson and Dembo (1984), as well as Bandura's orientation toward efficacy. Despite our inclusion of multiple perspectives, the underlying meaning of efficacy as a reflection of teachers' beliefs about their ability to bring about desired outcomes in the classroom remains consistent across the measurement and development of teacher efficacy in the studies analyzed herein.

Finally, our analysis deviates from the work of Tschannen-Moran and colleagues (1988) in that, our primary interest is in our primary interest in the relations between teacher efficacy and sociocontextual factors. It is our contention that teacher efficacy is a changeable and developing construct that fluctuates with experience, knowledge, and interpretation of contextual factors. Thus, efficacy represents both an immediate response and ongoing process evoked throughout individuals' teaching experience. When Rennae spoke about her expectations for her first position at Porter Middle School, she said she felt up to the challenge. This comment represents Rennae's sense of efficacy, rooted to a specific time and teaching task set within a specific teaching context.

Teacher Commitment

Commitment is more readily revealed in Rennae's opening statement: "I have always known I was meant to be a teacher." Individuals' commitment to teaching is understood as their emotional or psychological attachment to the profession (Coldarci, 1992). The exploration of commitment in this chapter affords us a focused view of more deeply held and often emotionally laden beliefs teachers have about their profession and their place in it (Kushman, 1992). Furthermore, commitment can be directed toward both student learning and the school as an organization. Rennae reveals her commitment to student learning in her description of her work at Porter. She describes the long hours she put in and her firm belief in her students' abilities to learn. However, in her description of her experiences at Western Middle School, we begin to see some breakdown in her commitment to this particular school. She describes how she arrived ready to take on new challenges and work with new pedagogical strategies. Yet, the focus of the organization, embedded in the principal's goals and actions, remained on behavior management and the maintenance of high test scores, leaving little room for innovation and creativity.

Although researchers have looked at both teacher efficacy and commitment, the majority of this research has focused on simple relationships with minimal attention to contextual influences. For example, the motivation literature has explored teacher efficacy by focusing on uncovering the link between efficacy and the facilitation of student learning (Tschannen-Moran et al., 1998). In contrast, the professional development literature has investigated the importance of school contexts on teachers' affective beliefs, including their commitment to teaching, stress, and professional burnout (Coldarci, 1992; Firestone & Pennell, 1993; Parkay, Greenwood, Olejnik, & Proller 1988). Still, little attention has been given to the impact of those affective states on teaching and learning outcomes (Kushman, 1992). Here we examine the motivation and professional development research in order to develop a fuller picture of teacher motivations *in situ*. That is, we hope to understand how the context affects both teachers' efficacy and commitment, recognizing the important role each of these plays in positive educational outcomes.

REVIEW PURPOSE, PARAMETERS, AND PROCEDURES

As stated, our purpose here is to investigate the associations between the sociocultural context of schools and the motivations of the teachers who orchestrate the learning environment.

We focus on the role of motivation in individual teacher practice, and how this motivation is fostered or diminished by the contextual influences teachers experience in schools. As we saw in the opening vignette, there are multiple factors in the school context that can have an impact on teachers' motivations. It is our intention to bring these pieces of the achievement puzzle together so that their individual and combined effects can be better visualized. Of course, we recognize that this is an exploratory effort to understand how school context and teacher motivation have been defined, explained, and interrelated in the research literature.

Guiding Questions

In order to understand the efficacy and commitment of teachers like Rennae and how their motivations are influenced by the educational context, we undertook a review of the literatures in teacher education and motivation. Given the exploratory nature of the questions we were asking, we felt that a thorough review of the relevant literature would be a critical first step. This review was guided by the following question: How do contextual influences affect teachers' motivation? Specifically, how do school climate, school leadership, colleagues, opportunities for autonomy and decision making, and constant school aspects such as student characteristics, school facilities, and resources within a school influence the degree and types of motivations teachers experience? This preliminary question was supported by related queries such as: How is motivation defined in the literature and how are contextual conditions characterized? Together these questions provided the framework for a thorough search of the literature.

In our search of the literature, we sought to locate studies that had considered both teacher motivation and school context, looked for discernible patterns in the reported findings, and used those patterns to formulate hypotheses that could guide future research and educational practice. It was through this exploration that we were able to identify teacher efficacy and teacher commitment as central motivational constructs in understanding the role of context on teacher motivation.

Search Parameters

We set several parameters for our search of the literature. First, we limited our inquiry to empirical studies of a quantitative nature. We do not discount the power of qualitative research to describe, inform, and extend understanding of educational processes and constructs. However, we felt that a quantitative examination of the literature would be a useful first step to unraveling the relation between teacher efficacy and commitment and the educational context. The constructs in quantitative studies would generally be more specific, with dedicated measures or indicators for those constructs. This would allow us to make more direct comparisons across studies and to discern emerging patterns with regard to teacher motivations and the school or classroom contexts.

We conducted our searches using several academic and educational databases, specifically PsycINFO, Academic Search Elite, and ERIC. We focused our search on peer-reviewed journals that were outlets for research on motivation, teaching, and teacher education. Among the key terms used to guide this search were *teacher motivation, teacher efficacy, teacher commitment, socialization, school culture, school climate,* and *school context.* Given the scarcity of articles meeting our desired criteria we did not limit the age of the research gathered through our electronic search. Abstracts of the articles culled from these searches were then read to determine the articles' relevance to the current investigation. At this point, qualitative studies were omitted to provide a more consistent lens through which to interpret findings. Theoretical and review pieces were used as background information, to help elaborate and extend our understanding of the central constructs, and to provide greater direction in the data collection via the examination of reference lists. These theoretical and review pieces however, are not included in the summary table presented and discussed. Rather, those works were used as background to provide detail, definitions, and theoretical elaboration, when appropriate.

Once we had used the electronic databases to identify a pool of suitable articles, we extended our search in two ways. First, we physically examined issues of key teacher education and educational psychology journals for the past 5 years. The journals examined included the *Journal of Educational Psychology, Review of Educational Research, Sociology of Education,* and *Teaching and Teacher Education.* This examination targeted the title and abstracts of the published articles. Second, we scanned the reference lists of selected articles, as well as relevant literature reviews, to identify additional articles that might be included in our analysis. Through this process, we were able to locate relevant conference papers and formal reports that were incorporated in our analysis, enhancing our understanding of the constructs of interest.

Organizational Approach

As a result of our search procedure, we located a number of articles that dealt with either teacher efficacy, commitment, or both, and that provided data about the school or classroom context. Because we wanted to capture any information in these publications that could help us understand the relationship between teachers' efficacy and commitment and the school context, we examined key dimensions of each article. For instance, we considered how context was conceptualized in terms of its assessment and description. Additionally, we attended to the definitions of efficacy and commitment, in order to ensure consistency of meaning across the works reviewed. This allowed us to analyze how these researchers might interpret Rennae's comments about her experiences and feelings. What would they see as relevant to her efficacy or indicative of her commitment?

We also wanted to know about the teachers and students in these studies. It could be that patterns in teachers' self-efficacy beliefs or their commitment are tied to the grade levels, subject matter, or student populations taught. For example, does it make a difference that Rennae is a middle school teacher and did the type of school district (urban versus suburban) influence her feelings about her own abilities or about the profession? And what about the students who populate the classroom? How do the behavioral problems of her students at Porter or Western Middle School play into Rennae's positive or negative feelings?

Finally, we documented the types of contextual conditions explored in the identified articles. Do the studies provide information on the general school climate, for example, or focus more specifically on administrative practices and support? For instance, how much did the principal's decision to "saddle" Rennae with behavioral problems color her feelings of competence or commitment? Does parental involvement matter in teachers' efficacy beliefs or their investment in their chosen profession?

In the discussion that follows, we offer what we see as emergent patterns across the identified studies that shed light on the potential relationship between teacher motivations and the educational context. We refer to these patterns as emergent because we recognize that they must be subjected to direct empirical testing for confirmation. Still, we feel that these patterns serve as important hypotheses with implications not only for future research but also educational practice.

EMERGENT PATTERNS

The quantitative, empirical studies relevant to this investigation cover a broad spectrum of teacher characteristics, school characteristics, and motivation-related outcomes. Additionally, the research agenda of these studies revealed a variety of foci and interests. In order to gain a better understanding and perspective on these foci we first sought to organize the studies gathered in a meaningful way. To achieve this end, we identified seven common contextual factors that were frequently addressed across the studies of teacher efficacy and commitment. Those factors included a general assessment of what we call school climate, but also entailed specific components, such as culture, environment, community, or collective efficacy. In addition to this general assessment several specific components of school context were assessed. Those components were administrator factors (roles or relations), collaboration, teacher involvement in decision making, and teacher autonomy. The final set of factors we considered were more fixed, including demographic aspects of schools such as student background (e.g., socioeconomic status and ethnicity), student achievement levels, student–teacher ratio, teacher salary, resources available to teachers, and the extent to which a school was categorized as disadvantaged, and descriptive teacher factors (e.g., experience, grade level). Table 14.1 provides the list of articles considered in this review, their sampling

TABLE 14.1.
Research exploring context and motivational variables.

Author(s)	Sample	Significant Relations						
		Climate	Administrator Factors	Collaboration	Decision-Making	Autonomy	Fixed Factors	Teacher Factors
Bacharach, Bombery, Conley, & Bauer (1990)	1,513 NEA members				C	C		
Chester & Beaudin (1996)	173 new or novice teachers		E	E			E	E
Coladarci (1992)	252 Maine teachers		C				C	C^1
Fuller & Izu (1986)	1,305 elementary teachers						E	
Goddard & Goddard (2001)	438 urban teachers	E^2					E	
Henson (2000)	8 teachers 3 assistants in an alternative school	E^P		E^G				
Hoy & Woolfolk (1993)	179 NJ elementary teachers	E^P	E^P					
Hoy, Tartar, & Bliss (1990)	56 NJ schools		C		C			
Kushman (1992)	63 urban elementary and middle schools; 750 teachers	C	C		C			C
Lee, Dedrick, & Smith (1991)	8,488 public and Catholic school teachers	E	E			E	E	
Ma & MacMillan (1999)	2202 Canadian		C					
Midgley, Anderman, & Hicks (1995)	Teachers: 50 elementary; 108 middle school; students: 291 elementary; 678 middle school	E					E	C

Study	Sample						
Midgley, Feldlaufer, & Eccles (1988)	107 6th-grade; 64 7th-grade mathematics teachers					E	E
Miskel, McDonald, & Bloom (1983)	1,442 teachers; 890 students			E			
Morrison, Walker, Wakefield, & Solberg (1994)	Preservice: 50 elementary, 20 secondary. Practicing: 45 elementary, 40 secondary					E^P E^G	E^P E^G
Newman, Rutter, & Smith (1989)	ATS survey—built on High School and Beyond data. Data collected from 30 random teachers in each of 353 public high school.	E	E	E	E		
Parkay, Greenwood, Olejnik, & Proller (1988)	321 teachers	E				E	E
Parker (1994)	239 teachers in 19 schools	E					
Raudenbush, Rowan, & Cheong (1992)	315 teachers in 16 urban and suburban high schools in the West and Midwest			E		E	E
Riehl & Sipple (1996)	NCESS—National Center for Statistics, Schools, and Staffing (1987-1988); n = 14,844 HS teachers	C	C	C		C	
Rosenholtz & Simpson (1990)	1,213 elementary teachers	C	C	C		C	
Ross (1994)	50, 7th ,8th , and 9th grade teachers; 1,228 students	C					E
Ross, Cousins, & Gadalla (1996)	52 high school teachers						E

(continued)

TABLE 14.1.
Continued

Author(s)	Sample	Administrator Factors				Fixed Factors	Fixed Teacher Factors	Significant Relations
		Climate	Collaboration	Decision-Making	Autonomy			
Shachar & Shmuelevitz (1997)	121 Israeli junior high school teachers		E^G					
Soodak & Podell (1997)	169 preservice teachers; 457 practicing teachers					E^P E^G	E^P	
Taylor & Tashakkori (1995)	9,987 10th grade teachers from the NELS study.	E		E				
Warren & Payne (1997)	8th grade teachers form 12 schools; n = 82					E^P		
Wu & Short (1996)	612 public school teachers				C		C	

Notes: E, teacher efficacy; E^G, general teacher efficacy; E^P, personal teacher efficacy; C, commitment
1. Personal and general teaching efficacy were the two strongest predictors of commitment to teaching.
2. In the combined model only collective efficacy was a significant predictor of differences in teacher efficacy among schools

information, and significant relations found between teacher efficacy (E) or commitment (C) and the context variables.

We structured the literature to consider both the motivational factors and contextual components. Therefore, we first discuss emergent patterns under the two broad categories of teacher motivation, efficacy, and commitment. Second, under each of these headings, we specify themes relative to contextual factors emerging within the literature. In light of the goals of this study, we pay particular attention to the interplay between motivational and contextual factors. Within the discussion of each theme, we offer further exposition of the measurement of the factors and key findings relative to each theme. Following this delineation, we consider the significance of the exploration for educational research and practice.

Efficacy

Efficacy can be defined as individuals' belief in their ability to accomplish a particular task (Pintrich & Schunk, 1996). This construct serves to explain individuals' reasons for attempting and completing tasks (Bandura, 1977). Teacher efficacy, a specific form of self-efficacy, has been defined as teachers' situation-specific beliefs in their ability to perform the actions necessary to bring about desired outcomes (Tschannen-Moran et al., 1998). Levels of teacher efficacy have been related to various indicators of student achievement (see Fives, 2003, for a review). However, while many studies have demonstrated the important role that teacher efficacy has on teacher practices and student outcomes, few researchers have investigated the factors that influence teacher efficacy, including organizational factors (Lee, Dedrick, & Smith, 1991). From this limited database, we culled five emergent patterns dealing with positive school environments: administrative support, collaboration among teachers, teacher autonomy, decision making, and constant or less modifiable school and background factors.

Pattern 1: Teachers working in positive school contexts focusing on student learning tend to have higher levels of efficacy. Several studies investigated the relation between efficacy and school environmental factors that tap into the general atmosphere of the school or the attitudes and beliefs emphasized within the school community. Specific variables related to this atmosphere included school climate, community, and collective efficacy. Several studies demonstrated that a positive school atmosphere is related to teachers with higher levels of efficacy. For example, Henson (2001) found that teachers' perceptions of school climate prior to an intervention significantly predicted personal teaching efficacy at the end of the study. Similarly, Lee and colleagues (1991) found that higher efficacy and positive sense of school community co-occurred. More specifically, school climate in conjunction with teacher efficacy has been conceptualized as a schoolwide focus on learning (Hoy & Woolfolk, 1993; Midgely et al., 1995), organizational characteristics including student orderliness and sense of community (Lee et al., 1991; Newman et al., 1989), as well as in terms of the schools' sense of collective efficacy (Goddard & Goddard, 2001; Parker, 1994).

A relationship between the school environment and efficacy was found in the extent to which schools emphasize student learning. For example, Midgely and colleagues (1995) investigated the relations between school emphasis on learning versus performance goals and the impact of that preference on teachers' efficacy. Learning and performance goal orientations are one way that students' general approach to academic achievement has been described. Individuals espousing performance goals are concerned with looking smart and doing well in order to receive recognition (Meece & Holt, 1993; Nicholls, 1984). In contrast, those with learning goal orientations are interested in mastering or understanding the content matter (Dweck & Leggett, 1988). Results from Midgely and colleagues' work indicated that teachers in middle schools emphasizing learning-oriented goals for students demonstrated higher levels of teacher efficacy than those emphasizing performance goals. Thus, when the entire school community was perceived as encouraging students to achieve a mastery of the content rather then merely demonstrate high performance regardless of understanding, teachers reported higher levels of efficacy.

Rennae draws attention to this notion when she describes her principal at Western and his determination to keep the test scores up, resulting in a tightly packed curriculum. This performance orientation is not a problem in and of itself but Rennae sees this as interfering with her ability to teach more creatively and effectively. In essence, her comments suggest that student performance would come at a cost to student learning. All of this seemingly adds to Rennae's sense of discouragement with her position and may ultimately affect her sense of efficacy.

Hoy and Woolfolk (1993) found that teachers' sense of personal efficacy was significantly related to a schoolwide emphasis on academics. In the same study, the researchers found that teachers who perceived that their colleagues set high achievable goals for students and created an orderly and academically oriented environment also reported higher levels of efficacy then those working under different conditions. It is important to note that an emphasis on achievement does not preclude an emphasis on learning-oriented goals. Rather, these two perspectives may work hand in hand to both improve student learning as well as teachers' sense of efficacy. Focusing on academic achievement may afford teachers a sense of direction and allow them to identify specific goals to pursue and methods to attain them.

School environments have been considered in terms of organizational characteristics or the social organization of the school. Newman and colleagues (1989) considered the influence of a variety of organizational characteristics (e.g., orderliness, teacher influence in decision making, and support for innovation) on teacher efficacy. In their work, organizational characteristics were found to consistently account for a substantial amount of variance in efficacy beyond the influence of background variables, such as students' socioeconomic level. In similar work, Lee and colleagues (1991) found that the social organization of the school (including teachers' perception of control over classroom policies, community, orderliness and encouragement of innovations) was strongly related to efficacy. In both studies, perceived orderliness in student behavior and sense of community or consensus were related to teachers' sense of efficacy.

Two studies tapped the school environment through measures of collective efficacy (Goddard & Goddard, 2001; Parker, 1994). Collective efficacy can be defined as "a group's shared belief in its conjoint capabilities to organize and execute the courses of action required to produce given levels of attainments" (Bandura, 1997, p. 477). In theory, collective efficacy is considered to affect the goal setting, motivation, effort, and persistence with challenging tasks or situations of groups. Within school contexts, this collective belief in the schools' and its members' ability to bring about desired outcomes, serves as an environmental influence on individual members of the community.

Goddard and Goddard (2001) and Parker (1994) found collective efficacy to be related to teachers' sense of personal or self-efficacy for instruction. Parker (1994) found evidence to support the role of collective efficacy as a mediator between school background characteristics (e.g., achievement level and socioeconomic status) and teachers' and administrators' beliefs about their school's instructional efficacy (i.e., mean self-efficacy for teaching reading, language, and mathematics). This suggests that background factors may inform the collective efficacy of the school, which is then related to teachers' beliefs about instruction. In this proposition, the level of collective efficacy may be able to counteract common background characteristics known to decrease individual teachers' sense of efficacy.

Goddard and Goddard (2001) found collective efficacy to be a significant independent predictor of variation among schools in personal teaching efficacy. These authors modeled the effects of socioeconomic status, prior achievement, and collective efficacy on personal teaching efficacy. They found collective efficacy to be the only significant predictor in this model to the extent that variation in collective efficacy explains variability in personal teaching efficacy above and beyond that explained by other context variables. Again, this suggests that the sense of collective efficacy experienced in a school may serve to mediate the context variables that teachers experience.

It could be that Rennae's sense of accomplishment at Porter Middle School was tied to the schools' orientation toward student learning over their test performance. Perhaps other teachers, like Rennae, signed on to this school with the goal and expectation of investing "time and energy" in these students and "their futures."

Pattern 2: Higher levels of efficacy arise when the administration provides teachers with needed resources and serves as a buffer to forces that constrain teachers' instructional flexibility and creativity. In the opening vignette, Rennae voices frustration and aggravation about decisions made by the administration with regard to her class composition. In any school environment, the administration holds a great deal of power over teachers and can deeply affect their sense of motivation and commitment through the decisions made and the means by which the decisions are attained and communicated.

Several studies have explored the relation between specific administrative practices and teachers' efficacy. Practices that have been explored include supervisor/principal attention to instruction (Chester & Beaudin, 1996), principal leadership (Lee et al., 1991), principals' influence with their superiors (Hoy & Woolfolk, 1990), and administrative responsiveness to teacher needs (Newman et al., 1989).

In their review of the teacher efficacy literature, Tschannen-Moran and colleagues underscore the finding that higher levels of efficacy are demonstrated when the administration provides "resources and buffers of disruptive factors but allowed teachers flexibility over classroom affairs" (Tschannen-Moran et al., 1998, p. 220). Administrators must continually find a balance between attending to the needs of the individual teacher or student and the needs of the school as a whole. Rennae perceived the placement of many difficult students in her class as a punishment for doing a good job. It is doubtful that the administration intended this. Rather, they were more likely making a decision for the greater good of the school, believing that Rennae could best meet the needs of those students.

The compelling aspect for our purposes is Rennae's interpretations of those events and the respective impact of these interpretations on her motivation for teaching. Rennae saw the actions of the administration as relegating her to the role of disciplinarian rather than teacher. Thus, the administration, rather than providing a buffer against disruptive factors, actually became a disruptive force. Resolving this tension is a challenging task that requires the joint efforts of both the teacher and the administration that begins with an acknowledgment of the problem. Administrators need to attend to the needs and concerns of their teachers. In turn, teachers like Rennae need to make their needs and concerns known in a professional and honest manner.

Pattern 3: Teachers given the opportunity and encouragement to work collaboratively seem to feel more efficacious. Schools in which collaboration among all members of the school community are encouraged have been found to have more teachers with higher levels of efficacy than schools where such collaboration is less prevalent (e.g., Miskel, McDonald, & Bloom, 1983). For example, Chester and Beaudin (1996) investigated the effects of school practices, such as opportunities to collaborate with colleagues, on changes in new teachers' (novices and new hires) efficacy beliefs from September to February of the school year. Using regression analysis, the researchers found that in low collaboration schools all experienced new hires and most novices reported declines in their efficacy beliefs. No such declines were reported for new hires in high collaboration schools.

Collaboration among teachers has been related to teachers' sense of personal teaching efficacy (Raudenbush, Rowan, & Cheong, 1992) and their general teaching efficacy, or their beliefs regarding what teachers in general can accomplish (Henson, 2000; Shachar & Shmuelevitz, 1997). In fact, Taylor and Tashakkori (1995) found faculty communication to be one of the strongest correlates with teacher efficacy.

Henson (2000) found that as collaboration among teachers increased over the course of an intervention, during which teachers researched their own teaching, levels of general teaching efficacy also increased. That is, teachers' beliefs about teachers' capabilities, in general, rose. This suggests that a product of collaboration may also be higher beliefs about the potential for teachers as a professional group to make a difference in the lives of students.

In a similar vein, Shachar and Shmuelevitz (1997) found higher levels of collaboration among colleagues to be related to higher general teaching efficacy and efficacy for enhancing student social relations. It makes sense that as teachers collaborate, they gather information about their colleagues capabilities and this information may, in turn, affect their beliefs about what teachers in general are able to achieve. This notion is supported by the work of Newman and colleagues' (1989), who found teacher efficacy and sense of community to be related to teachers' knowledge of other teachers' courses and spirit of innovation. Thus, in environments where they are given both the opportunity and encouragement to combine their efforts, teachers seem to experience greater efficacy for teaching. Rennae's perspective on her teaching takes a decidedly individualistic stance. As such, she offers little insight into how she communicated with or related to her fellow teachers. Whether this was indicative of the environment in which she taught cannot be determined.

Pattern 4: There appears to be a positive relationship between teacher efficacy and both decision making and autonomy. The extent to which teachers are able to participate in decision making at both the classroom and school level has been investigated in conjunction with teacher efficacy to a limited degree. Newman and colleagues (1989) found teacher efficacy to be higher in schools where there were higher levels of shared decision making regarding instruction among teachers. Taylor and Tashakkori (1995) also found teacher efficacy to be significantly correlated to decision participation. However, when other school climate factors were included, decision participation failed to explain much of the variance in teachers' sense of efficacy. These different findings suggest that further investigation may be needed to better understand the relations between participation in decision making and teachers' sense of efficacy. Perhaps if Rennae had been involved in the decision-making processes related to the assignment of students, she may have felt a greater willingness to work with these students and, in turn, experienced less frustration with the administration.

Two studies found significant relationships between teachers' efficacy and their perception of autonomy or control over their classrooms (Lee et al., 1991) or school policy (Raudenbush et al., 1992). In both of these studies, teachers reporting higher levels of control also reported higher levels of efficacy. It is important to note that control and efficacy have long been connected in the literature. For example, according to Bandura's (1997) conceptualization, self-efficacy is the exercise or implementation of control. Therefore, it would be rare if not impossible to have high levels of efficacy in situations where teachers felt they had little control. If teachers feel overly constrained with regard to a particular task because of circumstances beyond their control, their efficacy may well be undermined. We see evidence of this in Rennae's reflections on the school's emphasis on test scores and the limited opportunity for creativity in instructional practices.

Pattern 5: Teachers' efficacy is influenced by demographic, aspects of schools such as grade level, school type, school organization, resources available, student factors of ability level and socioeconomic status, and teacher factors such as experience and preparedness. Several researchers have investigated the relation between teacher efficacy and demographic factors, such as school level (elementary, middle, high), school structure, and school type (public, Catholic). A common finding among efficacy studies is that teachers' efficacy differs by grade or school level. In general, teachers in elementary schools demonstrate higher levels of efficacy than those in middle or high school (Fuller & Izu, 1986; Midgely et al., 1995; Midgely, Feldlaufer, & Eccles, 1988; Morrison, Walker, Wakefield, & Solberg., 1994; Parkay et al., 1988; Soodak & Podell, 1997). Additionally, Lee and colleagues (1991) found that teachers in Catholic high schools were more efficacious than their counterparts in public high schools.

Chester and Beaudin (1996) explored the relation between teacher efficacy of new teachers to schools and the availability and quality of resources in their school (e.g., classroom materials, library, computers). These researchers found that resources served to mediate new teachers' efficacy beliefs over the course of their first year in the school. Specifically, they found that teachers in schools with few resources experienced only slight increases in efficacy and that older new teachers (both novice and experienced) experienced increases in efficacy if their school had high levels of resources.

The type of school organization has also been linked to teachers' sense of efficacy (Warren & Payne, 1997). Warren and Payne (1997) compared schools organized as traditional departments or as cross-disciplinary teams.

Furthermore, they looked at teams with and without scheduled planning time. In this work, teachers in schools organized in teams with planning time experienced higher levels of personal teaching efficacy than teachers in the other two organizational structures.

Student factors have also been considered in conjunction with teacher efficacy. Students' prior achievement (Goddard & Goddard, 2001), perceived ability level by the teacher (Lee et al., 1991), and track (vocational, general–noncollege, general–college, honors/mixed; Raudenbush et al., 1992) were positively related to teacher efficacy. Student background in terms of socioeconomic and minority status have also been considered with regard to teachers' sense of efficacy. Findings indicate that students' socioeconomic status is related to teachers' sense of efficacy (Goddard & Goddard, 2001; Lee et al., 1991). However, the degree of minority concentration in the school was unrelated to teachers' efficacy (Goddard & Goddard, 2001).

Rennae demonstrated unique responses to each of the school environments in which she taught. At Porter, she anticipated that the work would be challenging. Yet, she considered herself up to the task, and described putting in many late hours in order to achieve success. In contrast, she seemed to expect more from the environment at Western. She seemed to assume that the advantages of a suburban school with greater resources and less behavior issues would allow her an opportunity to be more creative and to try new teaching techniques. Instead, she found her curriculum bounded by standardized testing and her free time allocated to satisfying parents. Thus, the school structure in terms of its curricular focus may have had a greater impact on Rennae and her ability beliefs than the socioeconomic status of her students.

Teacher background factors of experience (Morrison et al., 1994; Soodak & Podell, 1997) and preparedness (Raudenbush et al., 1992) have been considered in conjunction with teacher efficacy. Morrison and colleagues (1994) reported significant difference in teacher efficacy by experience and grade level, such that preservice elementary teachers had higher levels of efficacy than practicing secondary teachers. Additionally, Soodak and Podell (1997) report changes in efficacy across experience levels. Preservice teachers report high levels of efficacy, which drop drastically in the first two years of teaching, and then gradually increase with experience, although they never returned to the preservice levels. In contrast to experience level, Raudenbush and colleagues (1992) explored teachers' feelings of preparedness in relation to teacher efficacy. They found that teachers felt greater efficacy for classes in which they felt more prepared to teach. Certainly, coming out of her preservice program, Rennae voiced confidence in her ability to meet the challenges she faced at Porter Middle School. It is also evident from her statement that she encountered certain difficulties in winning over her students, although she apparently succeeded through her persistence and hard work. In this way, Rennae mirrored the efficacy patterns of teachers in these various studies.

In summary, the relation between efficacy and school structure has been explored in the literature in various ways. This research has demonstrated a connection between school atmosphere, administration practices, collaboration support, parental involvement, and fixed environmental factors and teachers' sense of efficacy. Overall, the intention of these studies has been to identify the positive linkages between teacher efficacy and educational context.

Commitment

As noted, teachers' commitment signifies their psychological attachment to and identification with teaching as their chosen profession (Coldarci, 1992). Kushman (1992) forwarded two conceptualizations of this construct: organizational commitment and commitment to student learning. Kushman defines organizational commitment as the "degree that an individual internalizes organizational values and goals and feels a sense of loyalty to the workplace" (p. 6). In contrast, Kushman described commitment to student learning as involving three interrelated components: teacher efficacy, expectations for student success, and "the willingness to put forth the effort required for student learning to occur" (p. 9).

Conceived in these ways, commitment to the organization (i.e., schools) has been shown to be a crucial element in organizational success (Rosenholtz & Simpson, 1990). Furthermore, commitment has been related to the successful implementation of change in education reform (Darling-Hammond, 1995), and a spark for collaboration, innovation, and a positive work culture (Kushman, 1992). Specifically, organizational commitment is considered a factor in teachers' intrinsic motivation (Kushman, 1992). Katz and Kahn (1978) contend that internalized organizational values provide a stronger source of motivation than extrinsic rewards and forced rule compliance. Thus, in investigating the effects of contextual factors on teachers' motivation, commitment becomes an informative measure.

The elements of contextual characteristics were as varied in the commitment studies as they were in the studies using teacher efficacy as the motivational outcome. Across these studies, four themes emerged relative to contextual characteristics. Those themes dealt with school culture or climate (e.g., Coldarci, 1992), relationship between teachers and administration (e.g., Ma & MacMillan, 1999), teachers' sense of autonomy and involvement in decision making (e.g., Bacharach, Bamberger, Conley, & Bauer 1990) and more constant, fixed or less modifiable context factors, such as student–teacher ratio (e.g., Rosenholtz & Simpson, 1990).

Pattern 1: Aspects of school climate or culture have implications for teachers' sense of commitment. Within the educational literature, school climate or culture has been measured in terms of teacher work factors as well as by means of more traditional climate instruments. For example, Kushman (1992) and Ma and MacMillan (1999) looked at the school context in terms of teacher work factors. Specifically, Kushman (1992) investigated the components of teachers' decision-making power and extrinsic rewards. By comparison, Ma and MacMillan (1999) used the term *organizational culture* to represent a composite of several items indicative of teacher work-related factors. Those items included a positive attitude among the teachers, shared beliefs about learning, and a sense that the community of teachers work effortfully to increase student learning. School climate has also been characterized by collegiality (Coladarci, 1992; Riehl & Sipple, 1996), administrative support, teacher influence (Riehl & Sipple, 1996), and the orderliness of the environment (Rosenholtz & Simpson, 1990).

The work of Kushman (1992), Ma and MacMillan (1999) and Riehl and Sipple (1996) emphasized a strong relation between the organizational culture and teachers' sense of commitment. A positive attitude among the teachers, shared beliefs with regard to student learning, and a sense of fairness in that everyone works hard to achieve student learning were similarly associated with higher levels of teachers' commitment (Ma & MacMillan, 1999).

Two interesting points should be made based on the aforementioned findings. First, while Kushman (1992) investigated the influence of extrinsic rewards on teachers' commitment, such rewards were not found to be significant. This suggests that teachers' sense of commitment may be more deeply related to less tangible forces such as shared beliefs and decision making. Second, Ma and MacMillan (1999) found that teachers who felt everyone was working hard in the school demonstrated greater levels of commitment than those who reported otherwise. This response pattern may help us to understand the frustration that Rennae exhibits in the opening vignette. Although she does not state it openly, part of Rennae's resentment for being "saddled" with the "bad" students may come from an underlying belief that she is expected to do more than other teachers in the school.

Kushman (1992) and Coldarci (1992) employed measures of school climate in lieu of or in addition to work factors. Kushman measured school climate in terms of motivational and behavioral climate and collected data from high school students, teachers, and administrators. Motivational climate assessed whether students were motivated to and interested in learning. Behavioral climate measured whether the school was a safe, orderly place, free of behavioral disruptions to learning. Riehl and Sipple (1996) and Rosenholtz and Simpson (1990) also employed measures of school orderliness as conceptualizations of school climate. In contrast, Coldarci (1992) assessed school climate by gathering responses from elementary school teachers regarding their relationships with their principals and their fellow teachers. Principal climate items focused on the perceived activeness and openness of the principal, as well as an emphasis on instructional issues and shared decision making. Teacher climate items targeted a cooperative team spirit among the faculty, a communal quest for better methods of teaching, and a sense of accountability for student achievement among the teachers.

Similar to findings for work factors, teachers' sense of commitment was related to school climate factors. Specifically, positive motivational climates (Kushman, 1992) and increased orderliness (Kushman, 1992, Riehl & Sipple, 1996; Rosenholtz & Simpson, 1990) were related to higher levels of teacher commitment. In contrast, school climate, as assessed by Coldarci (1992), was unrelated to commitment to teaching. Rather, Coldarci found that teachers' sense of personal and general teaching efficacy were two of the strongest predictors of commitment. The impact of climate on efficacy was discussed in the previous section. These findings may add to the evidence that teacher efficacy serves as a mediator between climate factors and outcomes such as commitment to teaching.

Pattern 2: The relationship between teachers and administrators is related to teachers' feelings of commitment to teaching. The majority of studies investigating teacher commitment included variables representing principal or administrative characteristics, such as administrative control, shared beliefs (Ma & MacMillan, 1999), principal as school advocate (Coldarci, 1992), administrative support (Hoy, Tarter, & Bliss, 1990; Rosenholtz & Simpson, 1990), buffering, and instructional support (Riehl & Sipple, 1996). For example, Ma and MacMillan (1999) examined the construct of administrative control in their research. These researchers defined administrative control in terms of teacher perceptions of shared beliefs with the principal, the amount of administrative duties they were expected to complete, and fair evaluation methods. Furthermore, they determined that teachers who perceived high or positive levels of administrative control also reported higher levels of commitment to teaching.

In addition, Ma and MacMillan (1999) found that a sense of shared beliefs between teachers and administration was related to greater levels of commitment on the part of teachers. In Rennae's situation, we see several instances in which the administration's goals or purposes for schooling and her beliefs appeared at odds. This is evidenced in differences with regard to the importance of statewide testing and an emphasis on behavior management rather than on innovative teaching. A potential link to Rennae's waning commitment was captured in her statement: "This is not what I envisioned when I signed on to become a teacher."

Coldarci (1992) reported a tendency for greater commitment on the part of teachers who worked with a principal regarded positively in terms of school advocacy and instructional leadership. Furthermore, teachers in this study also reported higher commitment if their administrator maintained good relations with students and staff. This suggests that teachers' personal relationship with administrators and their impressions and evaluations of those individuals may also affect the degree of commitment they feel for the workplace.

Rosenholtz and Simpson (1990) investigated the relationship between years of experience and administrative support on teacher commitment. These researchers found that teachers' commitment is influenced differently at different stages in their careers. Novice teachers' commitment was influenced more by organizational support for classroom management and boundary-related issues in terms of the principal buffering index. The principal buffering index was a measure of the administration's effectiveness at insulating teachers from external demands and pressures. These teachers felt greater commitment when they perceived that the administration was providing structured support for behavior management concerns, as well as helping to maintain professional boundaries between the teacher and the students and parents. In contrast, mid-career teachers, who demonstrated the lowest levels of commitment, were most influenced by task autonomy. That is, these mid-career teachers felt greater commitment to their profession when the administration allowed them to pursue their own interests and teaching practices. It could be that these teachers inferred this type of support as a validation of and trust in their teaching abilities. Finally, experienced teachers were most influenced by organizational qualities that afforded them opportunities for professional development. In effect, these teachers valued inservices and other professional opportunities to improve their pedagogical craft.

According to Rosenholtz and Simpson's (1990) schema, Rennae would be classified as a mid-career teacher. Thus, her sense of commitment to teaching should be increased by greater independence for her teaching practices. However, the school environment she describes at Western is fraught with administrative expectations that directly impact the instruction she can provide. For example, the emphasis on test scores as the goal for the school contributes to an instructional emphasis on specific curriculum activities and topic choices. As such, her opportunity for task autonomy seems inhibited, perhaps explaining her waning commitment.

Riehl and Sipple (1996) gained similar findings in their exploration of administrative support and teacher commitment to both the profession and their specific organization. Commitment to the profession, to teaching in general, was associated with principal buffering, administrative support for instruction, and resources. Commitment to the goals and values of the school, organizational commitment, was related to resources, protection from intrusions on teaching, and instructional support. Thus, administrative factors seem to be an influential force on teachers' sense of commitment. As such, this may also be a point of intervention for administrators to explore.

Pattern 3: Commitment is related to teachers' sense of autonomy and involvement in decision making. As with teacher efficacy, researchers investigating commitment have also found relevant relations to teachers' sense of autonomy and involvement in decision making. Bacharach and colleagues (1990), Riehl and Sipple (1996), and Rosenholtz and Simpson (1990) found significant relations among teachers' sense of autonomy and their sense of commitment. Additionally, Bacharach and colleagues (1990), Hoy and colleagues (1990), and Kushman (1992) found commitment to be related to teacher participation in decision making. Similar to these investigations, Wu and Short (1996) found teachers' sense of empowerment to be related to their feelings of commitment to the organization.

Rosenholtz and Simpson (1990) found teachers' sense of autonomy for teaching was the best predictor of their commitment to teaching. Similarly, Bacharach and colleagues (1990) found a negative association between lack of autonomy and teachers' sense of commitment, as well as their job satisfaction.

Riehl and Sipple (1996) examined the relation of autonomy to two forms of commitment, professional and organizational. In that investigation, professional commitment reflected teachers' commitment to the profession of teaching in general. In contrast, organizational commitment was assessed as their commitment to working at a particular school. Organizational commitment was considered in terms of the extent teachers in a given school held a shared mission, the amount of effort put forth (assessed by time spent teaching), and whether teachers would choose to remain at their given school. In that study, higher levels of organizational commitment were related to having increased influence on schoolwide policies, but not to autonomy. In contrast, teachers' sense of professional commitment was positively related to measures of autonomy.

Rennae commented that at Porter she was able to base her curriculum on her students' needs, whereas at Western curricular decisions were bounded by standardized test requirements. Despite the challenges she faced at Porter, Rennae's comments seemed to reflect a greater sense of commitment in that environment than she currently experiences at Western, where she has far less autonomy.

Teachers' participation in decision making was considered in differential degrees by each of the studies presented here. However, this evidence suggests that some form of decision-making participation is related to higher levels of commitment. For example, Hoy and colleagues (1990) found higher commitment in schools where principals acted on teachers' suggestions. That is, in schools where principals' sought and acted on teachers' advice and input, the faculty reported higher levels of commitment. Kushman (1992) found that teachers reported a greater level of commitment when they perceived themselves as having greater amounts of decision-making power (Kushman, 1992). Thus, Kushman's (1992) findings extend those of Hoy and colleagues (1990) by suggesting that actual participation in the decisions, rather than just an opportunity to provide suggestions, is related to higher levels of commitment. How might Rennae's sense of commitment to her school be different had she been given the opportunity to participate in some of the decisions that affected her daily practice?

Pattern 4: Demographic school factors and student characteristics are associated with teacher commitment. School structure factors and student characteristics have also been investigated in terms of their relation to teacher commitment. Specifically, student and community background have been measured in terms of socioeconomic status, ethnicity (e.g., Rosenholtz & Simpson, 1990), stability of the student body, and prior student achievement (Kushman, 1992). School size (Kushman, 1992), student–teacher ratio (Coldarci, 1992), and the task environment, including teachers' course load and class schedules (Riehl & Sipple, 1996), have also been associated with teacher commitment.

Interestingly, schools judged to be in greater need were linked to higher levels of reported commitment by teachers (Kushman, 1992). Rennae described feeling needed, appreciated, and trusted when she was working in the urban environment of Porter Middle School. Furthermore, she spoke of working "endless hours" but feeling good. This suggests that the payoff for her effort at Porter, in terms of student learning, contributed to her emotional well-being. Perhaps achieving success in a school where success is hard won and unexpected serves to deepen teachers' sense of commitment to the students and their profession. Additionally, it could be that in these struggling schools, where there is so much room for improvement, teachers feel a sense of urgency that feeds their commitment to student learning.

Kushman (1992) sought to identify teacher, student, and school antecedent variables that would predict teachers' level of organizational commitment and student learning commitment. This study revealed that organizational commitment, internalized goals of the organization, and felt sense of loyalty were predicted by student characteristics, school structure, school climate, and teacher decision making. Furthermore, commitment to student learning was related to teaching experience and student characteristics of race, stability, and perceived need. Finally, teacher ratings of climate accounted for a significant percent (34%) of the variance in commitment scores when school and student background variables were controlled (i.e., SES, stability, and academic achievement). Principal ratings of climate accounted for 14%, and teacher decision making accounted for 13% of the variance. Thus, both demographic factors of the school environment and student characteristics influence teacher commitment.

Coladarci (1992) found a tendency for greater commitment among women and in schools with lower student–teacher ratios. However, salary and years experience were unrelated to commitment. Riehl and Sipple

(1996) looked at specific features of teachers' task environment, considering the number of class preparations, number of total students, class schedule, and the achievement level of students taught. They found that higher commitment was associated with teaching students with higher achievement levels on average. Furthermore, liking one's class schedule was associated with greater commitment to the goals or mission of the school context. This suggests that specific contextual practices may have differential effects on unique components of commitment.

FINAL THOUGHTS AND FUTURE DIRECTIONS

From the research we reviewed, one can conclude that contextual influences do relate to the degree and form of teachers' motivation. Specifically, school climate and teacher decision making are related to organizational commitment (Kushman, 1992). Teacher control, student ability, and school organization are associated with teacher efficacy (Lee et al., 1991). Furthermore, we have seen that stress on the mastery of content over performance within the learning environment is tied to increases in teacher efficacy (Midgely et al., 1995).

Embedded in these findings is the underlying premise that teacher efficacy and teacher commitment are related to other positive educational outcomes and, as such, should be fostered and developed. This review of the literature suggests certain key and tangible factors within the educational context that may be manipulated in order to enhance teacher motivation. Furthermore, this body of research, and Rennae's reflection on her own motivations, emphasized that efficacy and commitment may have different contextual influences. Specifically, commitment related significantly to both teacher characteristics (Coldarci, 1992; Ma & MacMillan, 1999) and contextual characteristics (Coldarci, 1992; Kushman, 1992; Ma & MacMillan, 1999; Rosenholtz & Simpson, 1990), whereas the primary influence on teacher efficacy seemed to be contextual factors alone (e.g., Hoy & Woolfolk, 1990).

Moreover, a highly efficacious teacher like Rennae may begin to lose her sense of commitment to teaching as the result of a variety of context-related factors. This combination of high efficacy and declining commitment we see in Rennae may help us understand the fear of burnout she voices. These differential feelings expressed in this review, as well as in the research findings described, highlight the need to look at teachers' motivations from multiple vantage points. As demonstrated in this chapter, the dual focus on teachers' very specific task-related efficacy beliefs and their broader commitment to student learning and their profession afford a unique vista on teachers and teaching.

Next Steps for Inquiry

In light of the differential patterns reported for teacher efficacy and teacher commitment, the distinct precursors to each of these beliefs should be investigated. Investigation into the nature of the antecedents for teacher efficacy and commitment can inform school organizations and teacher educators on the means by which positive efficacy and commitment can be developed, enhanced, and maintained. Additionally, the interrelations between context, efficacy, and commitment should be explored. Coldarci (1992) found efficacy to be the strongest predictor of commitment, and contextual factors as significant predictors of efficacy. Therefore, the potential path from context to efficacy to commitment warrants exploration. In this hypothesized model, efficacy may prove to be the process through which one develops a sense of commitment to a school and to the field of education.

Related to the latter issue, we noted that much of the relevant research we identified in this review was of a correlational nature. This suggests that more direct empirical tests of the relation between teacher motivations and the educational context are needed. At best, we were able to identify emergent patterns within the existing literature. However, those emergent patterns can only hint at the true nature of these critical constructs and cannot begin to establish causality. Moreover, while we focused on empirical, quantitative studies in this exploration, we acknowledge that rich qualitative investigations may illuminate the bonds between teachers' motivations and the educational context that cannot be captured solely through quantitative research.

Finally, investigations of processes by which teachers become socialized into the school environment and enculturated into the profession are desirable. The research presented in this chapter looked at slices of the teaching experience but did not address the development of teacher efficacy, commitment, or the construction of positive school climates. How teachers come to feel committed and part of a positive collaborative school culture need to be researched. Qualitative research and longitudinal studies may be particularly valuable in portraying the character of these socialization and enculturation processes.

Next Steps for Instruction

While we recognize the exploratory nature of this review, we feel that tentative recommendations for educational practices can be offered based on the emergent patterns. Those emergent patterns suggest the importance of collaboration among teachers, shared beliefs throughout the school, a focus on academics, shared decision making, and an overall sense of community. One factor that we believe underlies those intangibles is communication. Communication between and among teachers, administrators, and policymakers, as educational stakeholders, is necessary to achieve these desirable outcomes. Additionally, the practices and decisions of administrators exert great influence on the educational and social aspects of the school. Here we forward two broad educational guidelines dealing with communication and administrative support followed by specific steps teachers can take to realize those outcomes.

- Teachers should work together to open and maintain lines of communication.
  - Teachers should recognize their power to improve collaboration with and among their colleagues by seeking out others, engaging in professional discussions about student learning, and offering assistance and support when appropriate (Chester & Beaudin, 1996).
  - Teachers should strive to maintain a strong focus on academics for their students and in their interactions with colleagues and other educational stakeholders. They should be vigilant in projecting a learning focus in their instruction and other professional communications. For example, teachers should stress the intrinsic value of the educational content and the pleasure of knowing during instruction over the completion of external mandates (Alexander, 1997).
  - A positive community, like any relationship, needs to be nurtured by its members in order for it to be sustained. Thus, teachers should be active and positive members of the school community. They should work to share their successes and highlight the positive aspects of their school in conversations with others.
- Administrators should provide leadership and support for teachers with regard to creating a positive school environment.
  - Administrators should support collaboration among their teachers. This support needs to be conveyed in verbal encouragement and evidenced in tangible actions such as providing time for collaboration. Teachers often take their cues from the administration (Firestone & Pennell, 1993). If collaboration is seen as a valued activity by the school administration, teachers may be more likely to collaborate.
  - Administrators should provide opportunities for teachers to feel a sense of autonomy and control in the school environment. One method for achieving this objective is by including teachers in decision making. By involving teachers meaningfully in decision making, administrators should contribute to teachers' perception that their knowledge and skills are valued (Senge, 1990). In turn,

such actions may foster a greater sense of community by allowing school members to have power over their own experiences (Firestone & Bader, 1992).

– Shared beliefs provide a foundation for community and success in a school. In order for beliefs to be shared, they must first be voiced. Thus, administrators should make a concerted effort to share their educational and pedagogical beliefs with their faculty and other invested parties. Furthermore, because teachers, administrators, parents, and policy makers are more successful when their beliefs are aligned with one another (Ma & MacMillan, 1999), efforts to achieve consensus on key issues are worthwhile (Senge, 1990).

REFERENCES

Alexander, P. A. (1997). Knowledge seeking and self-schema: A case for the motivational dimensions of exposition. *Educational Psychologist, 32,* 84–94.

Alexander, P. A., & Murphy, P. K. (1998). Profiling the differences in students' knowledge, interest, and strategic processing. *Journal of Educational Psychology, 90,* 435–447.

Bacharach, S.B., Bamberger, P., Conley, S.C., & Bauer, S., (1990). The dimensionality of decision participation in educational organizations: The value of a multi-domain evaluative approach. *Educational Administration Quarterly, 26,* 126–167.

Bandura, A. (1977). Self-efficacy: Toward a unifying theory of behavioral change. *Psychological Review, 84,* 191–215.

Bandura, A. (1997). *Self-efficacy: The exercise of control.* New York: W.H. Freeman.

Berman, P., McLaughlin, M., Bass, G., Pauly, E., & Zellman, G. (1977). Federal programs supporting educational change (Vol. 3): Factors affecting implementation and continuation (Report No. R-1589/8-Hew). Santa Monica, CA: Rand. (ERIC Document Reproduction Service No. ED 140 432)

Chester, M.D., & Beaudin, B.Q. (1996). Efficacy beliefs of newly hired teachers in urban schools. *American Educational Research Journal, 33,* 233–257.

Coldarci, T. (1992). Teachers sense of efficacy and commitment to teaching. *Journal of Experimental Education. 60,* 323–334.

Darling-Hammond, L. (1995). Policy for restructuring. In A. Lieberman (Ed.), *The work of restructuring schools: Building from the ground up* (pp. 157–175). New York: Teachers College Press.

Deci, E. L., & Ryan, R. M. (2002). *Handbook of self-determination research.* Rochester, NY: University of Rochester Press.

Dweck, C. S., & Leggett, E. L. (1988). A social-cognitive approach to motivation and achievement. *Psychology Review, 95,* 256–273.

Firestone, W. A., & Bader, B. D. (1992). *Redesigning teaching: Professionalism or bureaucracy?* Albany: State University of New York Press.

Firestone, W. A., & Pennell, J. R. (1993). Teacher commitment, working conditions, and differential incentive policies. *Review of Educational Research, 63,* 489–523.

Fives, H. (2003, April). *What is teacher efficacy and how does it relate to teachers' knowledge? A theoretical review.* Paper presented at the annual meeting of the American Educational Research Association, Chicago.

Fuller. B., & Izu, J. A. (1986). What shapes the organizational beliefs of teachers? *American Journal of Education 94,* 501–535

Gibson, S. & Dembo, M. H. (1984). Teacher efficacy: a construct validation. *Journal of Educational Psychology. 76,* 569–582.

Goddard, R. D., & Goddard, Y. L. (2001). A multilevel analysis of the relationship between teacher and collective efficacy in urban schools. *Teaching and Teacher Education, 17,* 807–818.

Guthrie, J. T. (1996). Educational contexts for engagement in literacy. *The Reading Teacher, 49,* 432–445.

Henson, R.K. (2001). The effects of participation in teacher research on teacher efficacy. *Teaching and Teacher Education, 17,* 819–836.

Hoy, W. K., & Woolfolk, A. E. (1993). Teachers' sense of efficacy and the organizational health of schools. *Elementary School Journal, 93,* 355–372.

Hoy, W. K., Tarter, C. J., & Bliss, J. (1990). Organizational climate, school health, and effectiveness. *Educational Administration Quarterly, 26,* 260–279.

Hoy, W. K., & Woolfolk, A. E. (1990). Socialization of student teachers. *American Educational Research Journal, 27,* 279–300.

Katz, D., & Kahn, R. L. (1978). *The social psychology of organizations.* New York: Wiley.

Kushman, J. W. (1992). The organizational dynamics of teacher workplace commitment: A study of urban elementary and middle schools. *Educational Administration Quarterly, 28,* 5–42.

Lee, V. E., Dedrick, R. F., & Smith, J. B. (1991). The effect of the social organization of schools on teachers' efficacy and satisfaction. *Sociology of Education, 64,* 190–208.

Ma, X., & MacMillan, R. B. (1999). Influences of workplace conditions on teachers' job satisfaction. *Journal of Educational Research, 93,* 39–47.

McLaughlin, M. W., & Marsh, D. D. (1978). Staff development and school change. *Teachers College Record, 80,* 70–94.

Meece, J. L., & Holt, K. (1993). A pattern analysis of students' achievement goals. *Journal of Educational Psychology, 85,* 582–590.

Midgley, C., Anderman, E., & Hicks, L. (1995). Differences between elementary and middle school teachers and students: A goal theory approach. *Journal of Early Adolescence, 15,* 90–114.

Midgley, C., Feldlaufer, H., & Eccles, J. S., (1989). Change in teacher efficacy and student self- and task-related beliefs in mathematics during the transition to junior high school. *Journal of Educational Psychology, 81,* 247–258.

Miskel, C., McDonald, D., & Bloom, S. (1983). Structural and expectancy linkages within schools and organizational effectiveness. *Educational Administration Quarterly, 19*(1), 49–82.

Morrison, G. M., Walker, D., Wakefield, P., & Solberg, S. (1994). Teacher preferences for collaborative relationships: Relationship to efficacy for teaching in prevention-related domains. *Psychology in Schools, 31,* 221–231.

Murphy, P. K., & Alexander, P. A. (2000). A motivated look at motivational terminology. [Special issue]. *Contemporary Educational Psychology, 25,* 3–53.

Newmann, F. M., Rutter, R. A., & Smith, M. S. (1989). Organizational factors that affect school sense of efficacy, community and expectations. *Sociology of Education, 62,* 221–238.

Nicholls, J. G. (1984). Achievement motivation: Conceptions of ability, subjective experience, task choice, and performance. *Psychological Review, 91,* 328–346.

Parkay, F. W., Greenwood, G., Olejnik, S., & Proller, N. (1988). A study of the relationships among teacher efficacy, locus of control and stress. *Journal of Research and Development in Education, 21,* 13–21.

Parker, L. E. (1994). Working together: Perceived self- and collective-efficacy at the workplace. *Journal of Applied Social Psychology, 24,* 43–59.

Pintrich, P. R., & Schunk, D. H. (1996). *Motivation in education: Theory, research, and applications.* Englewood Cliffs, NJ: Prentice-Hall.

Raudenbush, S. W., Rowan, B., & Cheong, Y. F. (1992). Contextual effects on the self-perceived efficacy of high school teachers. *Sociology of Education, 65,* 150–167.

Riehl, C., & Sipple, J. W. (1996). Making the most of time and talent: Secondary school organizational climates, teaching task environments, and teacher commitment. *American Educational Research Journal, 33,* 873–901.

Rosenholtz, S. J., & Simpson, C. (1990). Work place conditions and the rise and fall of teacher commitment. *Sociology of Education, 63,* 241–257.

Ross, J. A. (1994). The impact of an inservice to promote cooperative learning on the stability of teacher efficacy. *Teaching and Teacher Education, 10,* 382–394.

Ross, J. A., Cousins, J. B., & Gadalla, T. (1996). Within-teacher predictors of teacher efficacy. *Teaching and Teacher Education, 12,* 385–400.

Senge, P. (1990). *In the fifth discipline: The art and practice of the learning organization.* New York: Currency/Doubleday.

Shachar, H. & Shmuelevitz, H. (1997). Implementing cooperative learning, teacher collaboration and teachers' sense of efficacy in heterogeneous junior high schools. *Contemporary Educational Psychology, 22,* 53–72.

Soodak, L., & Podell, D. (1997). Efficacy and experience: Perceptions of efficacy among preservice and practicing teachers. *Journal of Research and Development in Education, 30,* 214–221.

Taylor, D. L., & Tashakkori, A. (1995). Decision participation and school climate as predictors of job satisfaction and teachers' sense of efficacy. *Journal of Experimental Education, 63,* 217–230.

Tschannen-Moran, M., & Woolfolk-Hoy, A. (2001). Teacher efficacy: capturing an elusive construct. *Teaching and Teacher Education, 17,* 783–805.

Tschannen-Moran, M., Woolfolk-Hoy, A., & Hoy, W. K. (1998). Teacher efficacy: Its meaning and measure. *Review of Educational Research, 68,* 202–248.

Warren, L. L., & Payne, B. D. (1997). Impact of middle grades' organization on teacher efficacy and environmental perceptions. *Journal of Educational Research, 90,* 301–308.

Wu, V., & Short, P. M. (1996). The relationship of empowerment to teacher job commitment and job satisfaction.

SUBJECT INDEX

Academic self-regulation, 139-159
    definition of, 141
    phases of, 142-146
    and self-reflection, 141
    and sociocultural influence, 142-146
Achievement choices, 170
Achievement gap, 123
Achievement motivation, 61
    and attributional style model, 64-68
    and cognitive style model, 64-68
Adaptive inferences, 146
Affect, 303
African Americans, 24
    dropout rates, 24-26
Amotivation, 38
Attainment value, 189
Attribution theory, 14-19
    exam outcome, 15
    intrapersonal motivation in, 15-19
Attributional feedback, 130-131

Attributional theory model, 64-68
    and achievement motivation, 64
    definition of, 65
    positions in 67-68
    research, 65-68
Autonomy, 44-45
Autonomy
    environments, 46-47
    and lack of structure, 50
    and structure and control, 51
    support and structure, 50-52
    support in the classroom, 46-52
    supportive motivating style, 47-49
    and teachers' motivating style, 47
Autonomy-support, 52-53
    developmental gains from, 52-53
Autonomy-supportive teachers, 47
    aspects of, 47-48
    learning to be, 49-50
    malleability assumption, 49
    points of, 50

Big Theories Revisited
Volume 4 in: Research on Sociocultural Influences on Motivation and Learning, pages 361–367.
Copyright © 2004 by Information Age Publishing, Inc.
All rights of reproduction in any form reserved.
ISBN: 1-59311-053-7 (hardcover), 1-59311-052-9 (paperback)

Basic needs theory, 34-35
  and autonomy, 34
  and cognitive evaluation theory,
    37
  and competence, 34
  definition of, 34
  and organismic integration
    theory, 40
  and relatedness, 35
Big theories revisited
  the challenge, 1-11
  chapter preview, 2-11
  setting the stage, 1

Causal attribution, 145
Causal properties, 18
Causal space, 17
Causality orientation theory, 40-41
  definition of, 40
Children's emergent identity, 262-
  267
Children's identity, 262-267
Citizenship, 259-262
Classroom management, 259-262
Cognition, 284-291
  foundations of, 285
  social influences on, 285-286
Cognitive evaluation theory, 35-37
  and basic needs theory, 37
  definition, 35
  and external events, 36
  and motivation, 36
  research in, 36-37
Cognitive modeling, 150
Cognitive processing, 156
Cognitive style model, 64-68
Collective efficacy, 237
Computer games, 315
CoNoteS2, 319
Context, 303-304
Control, costs of, 52-53
Controllability, 18
Coping skills, 133
Cross-complaints, 96-102
  and faculty dynamics, 97-98

grades, 99
  and motivation, 100
  role of students, 99
  and self-worth theory, 96
  and student dynamics, 96-97
  solutions for, 98-102
  strategies for, 100-102
  student expectations, 99
Cross-cultural research, 79-82, 179-
  180
  attainment value, 189
  and conceptions of ability, 186-
    188
  and conceptions of task value,
    188-190
  and development of expectations,
    180-190
  and development of values, 180-
    190
  differences in beliefs, 182-183
  differences in meanings, 185-186
  differences in values, 182-184
  and expectancies, 184-185
Cross-situational generality. 17
Cultural challenge, 22-28
  African Americans, 24
  constructs of, 23
  dropout rates, 24-27
  obesity, 27-28
  self esteem, 24
Cultural plurality, 13-29

Decision theory, 62-76
  cultural considerations, 63
  definition of, 62
Deep learning strategies, 80
Developmental differences, 261-262
Dialectical framework, 41-46
  and affordances and external
    events, 44
  and autonomy, 44-45
  diagram, 42
  in the classroom, 43-44
  and interpersonal motivating
    styles, 45-46

and relationships and communities, 44
and self-determination theory, 41
and sociocultural influences, 43-44
Dropout rates, 24-27
   African Americans, 24-26
   ethnic differences, 24-27

Ecological mode, 70-72
   and acculturative stress, 71
   definition of, 70
   effects in, 71
   levels of, 70
   Piagetian, 71
Education, self-efficacy in, 115-135; see also Self-efficacy in education.
Emulative level, 154
Engaged participation, 232, 237
Engagement, 102-110
Etic-emic model, 68-70
   measures for, 70
   steps for, 69
Expectancy value theory, 165
   and achievement, 201
   background, 167-174
   and beliefs, 174-175
   changes in, 175-176
   and changes in level, 181-182
   and children's conceptions, 177
   considerations, 172-174
   and cross-cultural research, 179-180, 182
   diagram of, 170
   in western culture, 174-178
   and gender-role socialization, 172
   models of, 167, 168
   modern models, 167
   and motivation, 200-203
   and subjective task values, 178-179
   relationship to choice, 176
   relationship to performance, 176-177

Facilitating Conditions Questionnaire, (FCQ), 76
Failure-avoiding tactics, 95
FCQ (see Facilitating Conditions Questionnaire)
Forethought phase, 142-144
Frustration, 258

General teacher efficacy, 332
Goal theory, 72-73
   orientations for, 72

Homework, background, 312-314

Identity, 233-234
Individual differences, 262
Inner motivational resources, 41-43
   aspects of, 41
Interpersonal motivation, 19-22
   attributional perspective of, 19-22
   diagram, 20
   metaphor, 20
Interpersonal theory of motivation, 15
Intrapersonal and interpersonal motivation, 21
   cultural challenges, 22-28
   interrelationships, 21-22
Intrapersonal attributional theory of motivation, 16
Intrapersonal motivation, 15
Inventory of school motivation (ISM), 79
ISM (see Inventory of school motivation)

Judgement, 288-290

Learner beliefs, 257-258
Learning responsibility, 259-262
Legitimate peripheral participation, 234
Lemony Snicket, 275
Locus, 18
   effects of, 18

Malleability assumption, 49
Metacognition, 284-291
  and judgement, 288-290
  social influences on, 286-287
  and social variables, 284-291
Metacognitive theory, 275-293
  background, 275-277
  and cognition, 284-291
  definition of, 277-278
  implications for research and
    practice, 291-292
  and metacognition, 284-291
  and metamemorial belief systems,
    283-284
  and private self, 279-282
  and public self, 279-282
  and self-monitoring, 282-283
  and social variables, 284-291
  and social-cognitive components,
    279-284
  uses, 277
  what's missing?, 278-279
Metamemorial belief systems, 283-
  284
Motivation, 18, 61-85, 200-206, 231-
  237
  and expectancy value theory, 200-
    203
  as personal investment, 61-85
  research, 200-203
Motivational messages, 199-219
  and learning, 199-219
Motivational variables, 338-340

Obesity, ethnic differences in
    reaction to, 27-28
  Hispanic reaction 27-28
Organismic integration theory, 37-
  40
  and amotivation, 38
  and basic needs theory, 40
  definition, 37
  and self-determinism, 38
Organizational culture, 82-83
  conceptualization of, 82-83

Outcome expectancies, 143
Overstrivers, 95

Parental inducement of self-
    regulation, 149
Parenting styles, 262-267
Participation, studies, 239-242
Paying for engagement, 102-110
  description of experiment, 103
  experimental findings, 105
  and intrinsic interest, 112
  principles behind, 102
  role playing, 104
  student evaluation, 109
  student reactions, 105-110
  student responses, 108
PCS (see Perceived Competence
  Scale)
Perceived Competence Scale
  (PCS), 180-181
Performance and self-efficacy,
  calibration between, 127-130.
  See also Self-efficacy and
  performance, calibration
  between,
Performance phase, 144-145
  and self-observation, 144
Personal commitments, 262-267
Personal Investment Theory, 73-76
  analysis of, 77
  components of,74
  deep learning strategies in, 80
  enriching, 76-79
  essential elements of, 74
  extending, 76-79
  findings, 78
  historical, 74
  interview results, 78
  inventory of school motivation,
    79
  justification of, 83-85
  and learning strategies, 79-82
  and organizational culture, 82-83
  perspectives in, 74
  phases of, 73-74

practicality of, 83-85
predictors in, 78
research in, 77, 79, 81
scales for, 80
usefulness of, 83-85
variations in, 78
332
Proactive learnings, 143
Problem-based learning, 152-153
classes of, 153
Problem-solving activities, 256-257

Reconciliation
individual activity, 237-239
social activity, 237-239
studies, 239-242

SCA (*see* Self-concept of ability)
Schools, organization of, 140
SDQ (*see* Self-Description
Questionnaire)
SDT (*see* Self-determination theory)
Self-concept of ability (SCA), 184
Self-Description Questionnaire
(SDQ), 180
in China, 180
in Taiwan, 181
Self-determination continuum, 39
Self-determination theory (SDT),
31-53
definition of, 33
Self-efficacy and performance
and accuracy, 129
and attributional feedback, 130-
131
calibration between, 127-130
clinical studies in, 127-128
and coping skills, 133
cultural issues, 132
and education, 128
and environmental conditions,
130
and school culture, 130
in schools, 131
and sociocultural factors, 128

Self-efficacy for learning, 124-127
as a predictor of motivation and
performance, 125-126
background, 124-125
clinical studies, 125
studies in, 127
Self-efficacy for performance, 126
Self-efficacy
general, 132-134
general versus specific, 132-134
Self-efficacy in education, 115-135
as a construct, 118
background, 116-120
conceptual framework for, 116-
118
and confidence, 120
definition of, 116-117
distinctions with other constructs,
119-12
and environmental events, 118
and information dynamics, 117
and outcome expectations, 119
and persuasion, 117
range of, 119
and self-concept, 119
and student behavior, 118
and students' abilities, 119
and triadic reciprocality, 118
Self-efficacy in educational settings,
120-134
and achievement differences, 123
and achievement gap, 123
background, 120-121
effects of, 121-124
and effort, 121
and medium, 122-123
and performance, 124
and persistence, 121
Triadic reciprocality, 118
Self-efficacy, specific, 132-134
Self-monitoring, 282-283
Self-motivational beliefs, 144
Self-reflection, 141
Self-reflection stage, 145
Self-regulated learning (SRL), 300

Self-regulatory competence, 153-157
  and cognitive processing, 156
  development of, 153
  emulative level, 154
  features of, 154
  self-controlled level of, 155
Self-regulatory development, 157-158
Self-satisfaction, 146
Self-worth theory
  background, 94-96
  and college, 91-113
  and cross-complaints, 96-102
  definition of, 94-96
  and failure-avoiding tactics, 95
  final points, 113
  and motivation theories, 91-113
  research in, 92-93
Situational affordances, 309-311
Social collaboration, 152-153
  definition of, 152
Social feedback, 151-152
Social identity, 232
Social modeling, 150-151
  and cognitive modeling, 150
  subprocesses in, 150
Social practices, 232
Social support structures, 230
Social-cognitive components, 279-284
Socialization processes, and students' academic learning, 150-153
Sociocultural dimensions, in self-regulatory development, 157-158
Sociocultural factors, 128
Sociocultural influence, 139-159
  and academic self-regulation, 146-149
  Chinese study, 148
  on students, 146-149
  research in, 147
  and student motivation, 31-53

Sociocultural models of learning, 203-206
  case studies, 206-213
  families in, 213-317
  homes in, 213-217
  and motivation, 203-204
  research, 204-206
Sociocultural theory
  acknowledged nonparticipation, 236
  and collected efficacy, 237
  and engaged participation, 232
  engagement, 233-234
  identity, 233-234
  influence on in engagement and motivation theories, 223-243
  interpretations of, 227-228
  knowing, 226-228
  learning, 226-228
  legitimate peripheral participation, 234
  motivation in, 230-231
  and nonparticipation, 234-235
  and reconciliation between individual and social activity, 237-239
  of engagement, 231-237
  philosophical roots, 228-237
  political roots, 228-237
  research on, 224
  social support structures, 230
  trajectories, 234
SRL (see Self-regulated learning)
Strategic planning, 143
Student background, 263-264, 299-323
  and affect, 303
  and apprenticeship, 306
  and aptitude, 308
  and computer games, 315
  and computer-based tools, 317
  and context, 303-304
  current methods, 305
  and homework, 312-321
  ecological perspective, 307-311

emergence of, 312-321
implementation studies, 316-317
and Internet, 319
and motivation, 303
past analyses of, 300-304
past research methods, 302-303
self-regulated learning, 300
and situational affordances, 309-311
and sociocultural theory, 305-307
and technology-based environments, 314-321
Student motivation
case studies, 265-267
and children's identity, 262-267
and citizenship, 259-262
and classroom management, 259-262
coregulation of opportunity, activity, and identity in, 249-272
and curriculum expertise, 269-271
and curriculum tasks, 267-271
and developmental differences, 261-262
and frustration, 258
and individual differences, 262
and learner beliefs, 257-258
and learning motivation, 267-271
and learning responsibility, 259-262
and mutual validation, 267-271
and parenting styles, 262-267
and personal commitments, 262-267
and problem-solving activity, 256-257
research illustrations for, 255-271
and self-directed inner speech, 255-256
and student background, 263-264
and task difficulty, 256-258
and tedium, 258
Vygotskian themes in, 249-272

Students' academic learning, and socialization processes, 150-153
STUDY, 318
Styles of parenting, 148

Teacher commitment, 329-357
educational guidelines, 356-357
guiding questions, 335
patterns of, 337-341, 349-354
search parameters, 335-336
story, 329-331
Teacher efficacy, 329-357
definition of, 331-332, 341
educational guidelines, 356-357
emergent patterns, 337-341
general, 332
guiding questions, 335
patterns of, 341-348
personal, 332, 342
research, 332
search parameters, 335-336
story, 329-331
Tedium, 258
Theoretical unity, 13-29
ThinkerTools, 318
Trajectories, 234

Vygotskian theory, 250-253
affective, 253
coregulated activity, 254
developmental focus, 251
elaborations on, 253-254
intellectual, 253
and internalization, 252
tenets in, 250
and language, 251-252
and social mediation, 250

WUMPUS, 315

Zone of proximal development (ZPD), 227, 229, 252
ZPD (*see* Zone of proximal development)

Printed in the United States
R3177100001B/R31771PG76776LVX7B/4-18